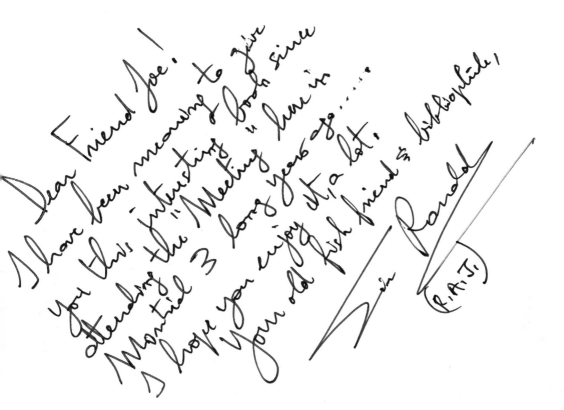

Dear Friend Joe!

I have been meaning to give you this interesting book since attending the "Meeting" here in Montréal 3 long years ago.......

I hope you enjoy it, a lot!

Your old fish friend & bibliophile,

Sincerely Ronald

(R.A.J.)

Annual Meeting of the
Toxicology Society
Of America
November 2006

Chemically Induced Alterations in Functional Development and Reproduction of Fishes

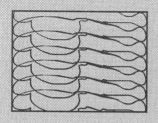

Chemically Induced Alterations in Functional Development and Reproduction of Fishes

edited by

Rosalind M. Rolland
World Wildlife Fund
Washington, D.C.

Michael Gilbertson
Work Group on Ecosystem Health
Great Lakes Science Advisory Board
International Joint Commission
Detroit, Michigan

Richard E. Peterson
University of Wisconsin School of Pharmacy
Madison, Wisconsin

Proceedings from a session at
the Wingspread Conference Center
21–23 July 1995
Racine, Wisconsin

Publication sponsored by the
Society of Environmental Toxicology
and Chemistry (SETAC)

SETAC Technical Publications Series

Cover by Michael Kenney Graphic Design and Advertising
Typesetting by Wordsmiths Unlimited

Library of Congress Cataloging-in-Publication Data

Chemically induced alterations in functional development and reproduction of fishes : proceedings from a session at the Wingspread Conference Center, 21–23 July 1995, Racine, Wisconsin / edited by Rosalind M. Rolland, Michael Gilbertson, Richard E. Peterson.
        p.   cm. -- (SETAC technical publications series)
    "Publication sponsored by the Society of Environmental Toxicology and Chemistry (SETAC) and the SETAC Foundation for Environmental Education. '
    Includes bibliographical references.
    ISBN 1-880611-19-8 (hardcover)
    1. Fishes--Effect of chemicals on--Congresses. 2. Endocrine toxicology--Congresses. 3. Fishes--Development--Congresses. 4. Fishes--Reproduction--Congresses.   I. Rolland, Rosalind. II. Gilbertson, Michael. III. Peterson, Richard E. (Richard Eugene), 1945– . IV. SETAC (Society) V. SETAC Foundation for Environmental Education. VI. Series.
SH174.C48   1997
571.9'5171--dc21
                                                                                97-28652
                                                                                 CIP

International Standard Book Number 1-880611-19-8
Printed in the United States of America
04 03 02 01 00 99 98 97   10 9 8 7 6 5 4 3 2 1

⊚ The paper used in this publication meets the minimum requirements of the American National Standard for Information Sciences—Permanence of Paper for Printed Library Materials, ANSI Z39.48-1984.

Reference Listing: Rolland RM, Gilbertson M, Peterson RE, editors. Chemically induced alterations in functional development and reproduction of fishes. Proceedings from a session at the Wingspread Conference Center; 21–23 July 1995; Racine WI. Published by the Society of Environmental Toxicology and Chemistry (SETAC), Pensacola, Florida, USA. 224 p.

The SETAC Technical Publications Series

The SETAC Technical Publications Series was established by the Society of Environmental Toxicology and Chemistry (SETAC) to provide in-depth reviews and critical appraisals on scientific subjects relevant to understanding the impacts of chemicals and technology on the environment. The series consists of single- and multiple-authored or edited books on topics reviewed and recommended by the SETAC Board of Directors and approved by the Publications Advisory Council for their importance, timeliness, and contribution to multidisciplinary approaches to solving environmental problems. The diversity and breadth of subjects covered in the series reflects the wide range of disciplines encompassed by environmental toxicology, environmental chemistry, and hazard and risk assessment. Despite this diversity, the goals of these volumes are similar; they are to present the reader with authoritative coverage of the literature, as well as paradigms, methodologies and controversies, research needs, and new developments specific to the featured topics.

The SETAC Technical Publications are useful to environmental scientists in research, research management, chemical manufacturing, regulation, and education, as well as to students considering or preparing for careers in these areas. The series provides information for keeping abreast of recent developments in familiar subject areas and for rapid introduction to principles and approaches in new subject areas.

Chemically Induced Alterations in Functional Development and Reproduction of Fishes presents the collected papers stemming from a session at a Wingspread Conference, Racine, Wisconsin, 21–23 July 1995. The session focused on unresolved scientific issues and needed significant research in the area of current and possible future approaches to synthetic chemical exposure and disruption of the development and/or function of the reproductive, endocrine, immune, or nervous systems of fishes. This book represents the views of the authors and the participants in attendance. Each chapter was peer reviewed by leading scientists and revised before the compiled book was scrutinized for technical and editorial accuracy and consistency by the editors and by SETAC editorial staff.

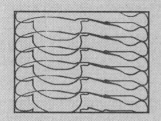

Consensus Statement:
Chapter 1

Risk Assessment:
Chapter 2

Mechanisms and
Biomarkers:
Chapters 3, 4, 5, 6, 7, 8

Ecoepidemiology
and Causality:
Chapters 9, 10, 11, 12, 13

Contents

List of Figures xv
List of Tables xvi
Foreword xvii
Preface xxv
Acknowledgments xxvi
Abbreviations xxvii

1

Statement from the work session on chemically induced alterations in functional development and reproduction of fishes   3

Consensus Statement 4
Work Session Participants 6

2

The TCDD toxicity equivalence approach for characterizing risks for early life-stage mortality in trout   9

Philip M. Cook, Erik W. Zabel,
Richard E. Peterson

Methods 12
   Lake trout eggs 12
   Determination of chemical
   concentrations in feral
   lake trout eggs 12
Results and Discussion 13

Fish-specific TEFs 13
Toxicity of PCDD, PCDF, and PCB congener pairs 16
Toxicity of a PCDD, PCDF, and PCB mixture 17
Retrospective assessment of lake trout early life-stage
survival in Lake Ontario and Lake Michigan 18
Comparison of lake trout sac-fry mortality predictions
using different TEFs 20
Conclusions 22

3

Mechanisms of chemical interference with reproductive endocrine function in sciaenid fishes 29

Peter Thomas, Izhar A. Khan

Materials and Methods 32
    Estrogenic actions of chlordecone (Kepone) 32
        Estrogen receptor competition studies 32
        In vitro vitellogenesis bioassay 33
    Cadmium interference with signal transduction systems at
    pituitary and gonads 33
        Pituitary gonadotropin secretion 33
        Ovarian steroidogenesis 33
    Alteration of neuroendocrine function by lead 33
        Experimental animals 33
        Experimental protocols 33
        Determination of biogenic amines and their metabolites 34
        Pituitary GtH release in vitro 34
        Plasma steroid levels 34
        Statistical analyses 35
Results and Discussion 33
    Estrogenic effects of Kepone 35
    Cadmium interference with signal transduction systems
    at the gonad and pituitary 37
    Alterations of neuroendocrine function by lead 40
Concluding Remarks 46

4

Environmental antiandrogens: potential effects
on fish reproduction and development   53
Emily Monosson, William R. Kelce,
Michael Mac, L. Earl Gray
Environmental Antiandrogens...53
Wildlife...54
Fish...55
Sex Differentiation 56
Maturation..56
Environmental Contaminants...56
Conclusion...58

5

Evidence for developmental and skeletal responses
as potential signals of endocrine-disrupting
compounds in fishes   61
William P. Davis
Benefits of Fishes as Study Organisms......................................62
Overview of the Skeletal System as a Generic Indicator...................63
Kepone 64
Trifluralin 65
Dibutylphthalate 66
Effects upon Sex-linked Morphology 67
Summary...68

6

Development of biomarkers for environmental contaminants affecting fish   73
Nancy D. Denslow, Marjorie Chow, Ming M. Chow, Sherman Bonomelli, Leroy C. Folmar, Scott A. Heppell, Craig V. Sullivan
Materials and Methods 74
    Collection of samples 74
        Preparation of antibodies 74
        Western blots 75
        Two-dimensional gel electrophoresis 75
        N-terminal sequencing 76
Results and Discussion 76
    Identification of possible biomarkers associated with contamination 76
    Development of monoclonal antibodies against vitellogenin 77
    Conservation of epitopes in VTG as measured by monoclonal antibodies 79
    Usefulness of antibodies in detecting estrogen or estrogen-mimicking contaminants in the environment 83
Summary 83

7

Assessment of estrogenic activity in fish   87
Alison C. Nimrod, William H. Benson
Vitellogenesis 88
Sexual Differentiation in Fish 88
Identifying Estrogenic Chemicals in Fish 88
Experimental Methods and Results 89
    Catfish model 89
        Exposure 90

Validation of vitellogenesis as an estrogenic screen 90
Screening xenobiotics for estrogenic activity 91
Alterations of vitellogenesis by xenoestrogens 93
Detection of vitellogenin in small fish species 94
Utility of Japanese medaka as a reproductive
toxicity model 94
Exposure and detection of vitellogenin in serum and
cytosolic fraction 96
Conclusions 97

8

**Effect of pulp and paper mill contaminants on
competence of rainbow trout macrophages** 101

*Isabelle Voccia, Jaime Sanchez-Dardon, Muriel Dunier,
Stefan Chilmonczyk, Michel Fournier*

Material and Methods 102
Experimental animals 102
Collection of samples 102
Chemicals 103
Cytotoxicity tests 103
Phagocytosis 103
Respiratory burst 103
Statistics 104
Results 104
Effect of DHAA on phagocytosis and the respiratory
burst of head kidney macrophages 104
Effects of TCP on phagocytosis and respiratory burst
of head kidney macrophages 104
Effects of TeCC on phagocytosis and respiratory burst
of head kidney macrophages 107
Effects of TeCG on phagocytosis and respiratory burst
of head kidney macrophages 107
Discussion 107

9

Reproductive and endocrine status of female kelp bass
from a contaminated site in the Southern California
Bight and estrogen receptor binding of DDTs   113
                              Robert B. Spies, Peter Thomas
Methods 115
    Field studies.. 115
        Measurement of reproductive indices, gonad histology,
        and age.. 115
        Endocrinological methods 117
        Chemical methods 118
    Binding of xenobiotic compounds to the estrogen receptor . 119
    Statistical methods 119
Results 119
    Field-exposed kelp bass 119
        Morphometrics and age 119
        Tissue contaminant concentrations 119
        Gonad size, presence of yolky oocytes, and
        oocyte atresia 120
        Endocrine status 121
        Competition for the estrogen receptor by chlorinated
        hydrocarbons 127
Discussion 127

10

Early mortality syndrome in salmonid fishes from
the Great Lakes   135
                              Susan V. Marcquenski, Scott B. Brown
    Definition of Terms 136
    Historic Occurrences of Early Life-stage Mortality in the
    Great Lakes 136

Clinical Signs of EMS 138
Early Mortality Syndrome versus Premature Hatch versus
Blue-sac Disease versus Swim-up Syndrome versus
Drop-out Syndrome versus Feeding-fry Syndrome 140
Possible Causes of Early Mortality Syndrome 142
    Fish culture 142
    Broodstock management and genetics 142
    Pathogens 142
    Ecosystem change 143
    Contaminants 143
    Nutrition 143
Definition of Early Mortality Syndrome 143
Related Syndromes 144
Cayuga Syndrome 144
M74 145
Focus of Current EMS Research 146
    Relationship between EMS and thiamine 146
    Relationship between EMS and diet 147
    Relationship between EMS, thiamine, and contaminants 147
    Relationship between EMS and oxidative stress 148
Conclusions 149

11

M74 syndrome: a review of potential etiological factors   153

Hans Börjeson, Leif Norrgren

M74 Syndrome 153
    General characteristics of M74 153
    Historical review 154
    Biochemical changes 155
        Carotenoids 155
        α-Tocopherol and ubiquinone levels 158
        Cytochrome P450 induction 159
        Thiamine levels 160
    Reconditioning of broodfish 161

Ecological Factors 161
    The Baltic Sea 161
        Water inflow events 162
        Influence of cod stocks 163
    M74 versus Early Mortality Syndrome: a Comparison 163
    Conclusions 164

12

Laboratory and field observations of sublethal damage
in marine fish larvae: lessons from the
Exxon Valdez oil spill   167

Richard M. Kocan, Jo Ellen Hose

    Methods 168
    Results 169
    Discussion 171

13

Reproductive and developmental effects of contaminants
in fish populations: establishing cause and effect   177

Emily Monosson

    Methods 178
        Table 13-1 178
            Summary of Table 13-1 180
        Table 13-2 181
            Summary of Table 13-2 183
        Table 13-3 184
            Table 13-3 summary 184
    Discussion 187
    Conclusion 190

List of Figures

Figure 2-1   Representative lake trout sac fry exposed as a fertilized egg to water/acetone vehicle or to TCDD in vehicle 11

Figure 2-2   TCDD TEs and TECs in 1991 Lake Ontario lake trout eggs and 1993 Lake Michigan lake trout eggs 21

Figure 3-1   Potential sites of chemical interference with reproductive endocrine function in female teleosts 30

Figure 3-2   Competition of Kepone for seatrout estrogen receptor and effects of Kepone on basal and estrogen-stimulated production of VTG from seatrout liver slices in vitro 36

Figure 3-3   Effects of increasing concentrations of cadmium on in vitro production of testosterone, estradiol, and cAMP accumulation by vitellogenic ovaries of spotted seatrout ... 38

Figure 3-4   Representative profile of gonadotropin secretion from Atlantic croaker pituitaries perifused with DMEM with or without cadmium or LHRHa 39

Figure 3-5   Lead-induced alterations in serotonin (5-HT) metabolism in the POAH and MPH of croaker brain 41

Figure 3-6   Lead-induced alterations in DA, 3,4-DOPAC and 3-MT concentrations in the POAH and MPH of croaker brain 42

Figure 3-7   Lead-induced alterations in the DOPAC/DA and 3-MT/DA ratios in the POAH and MPH of croaker brain 43

Figure 3-8   In vitro GtH release in response to an LHRH analog (LHRHa) from the pituitaries of the control and lead-exposed fish 44

Figure 3-9   Lead-induced alterations in GSI and plasma testosterone (T) and 11-KT levels in Atlantic croaker 44

Figure 3-10   Schematic diagram of the enzymatic conversion of biogenic amines (5-HT and DA) into their major metabolites within the individual neurons 45

Figure 4-1   Tissue concentrations (whole fish/wet weight) of p,p'-DDE in Lake Michigan bloater versus sex ratio in fish collected from Lake Michigan 59

Figure 6-1   Characterization of serum proteins from female bullhead fish by 2D-PAGE 77

Figure 6-2   Western blot showing the cross-reactivity of mAb 1C8 79

Figure 6-3   Phylogenetic tree showing the species recognized by 3 of the better characterized antibodies: mAbs 1C8[1], 3H1[2] and 2D3[3] 81

Figure 6-4   Preliminary analysis for epitopes recognized by monoclonal antibodies to VTG 82

Figure 6-5   Western blot analysis of serum collected from bluegill sunfish in a privately owned pond and nearby creek 84

Figure 7-1   Induction of vitellogenesis in catfish by xenoestrogens 91

Figure 7-2   Alteration of vitellogenesis by xenoestrogens following co-administration of xenobiotic with E2 95

Figure 7-3   Alteration of vitellogenesis by methoxychlor (MXC) and p-nonylphenol (NP) following co-administration of xenobiotic with E2 96

Figure 8-1   Phagocytosis of rainbow trout head kidney macrophages exposed for 18 hours to various concentrations of DHAA, TCP, TeCC, and TeCG 105

Figure 8-2   Respiratory burst response of RBT head kidney macrophages exposed for 18 hours to various concentrations of DHAA, TCP, TeCC, and TeCG 106

Figure 9-1   Location of fish collection sites in the Southern California Bight 116

Figure 9-2   Concentrations of contaminants in livers of kelp bass 121

Figure 9-3   Plasma gonadotropin (II) concentrations in fish from Palos Verdes and Dana Point 123

Figure 9-4   Vitellogenic growth measures in fish from Palos Verdes and Dana Point female kelp bass 124

Figure 9-5   In vitro steroid production (pg steroid/mg tissue) by ovaries of female kelp bass 125

Figure 9-6   Cytosolic equilibrium dissociation constant of the hepatic estrogen receptor in fish 127

Figure 9-7   Competition by estrogen and DDT compounds for the estrogen receptor in kelp bass liver 128

Figure 10-1 A comparison of EMS mortality between 1986-87 and 1993-94 141

Figure 11-1 The Baltic Sea drainage area 155
Figure 11-2 M74 mortality rate in Baltic salmon by year (1974–1995) 156
Figure 11-3 Mortality rate from M74 by river population 156
Figure 11-4 Percentage of families from the River Luleälven salmon population that died
           from M74, grouped according to roe color 157

Figure 12-1 Anatomical malformations in herring larvae exposed to increasing concentrations of
           an oil–water dispersion of Prudhoe Bay crude oil in the laboratory and in herring
           larvae exposed in situ at oiled and unoiled sites in Prince William Sound in 1989 170
Figure 12-2 Chromosome damage in herring larvae exposed to increasing concentrations of an
           OWD of Prudhoe Bay crude oil in the laboratory and in herring larvae exposed in
           situ at oiled and unoiled sites in PWS in 1989 172
Figure 12-3 Dry weights of herring larvae exposed to an OWD of Prudhoe Bay crude oil
           in the laboratory and weights of larvae exposed in situ at oiled and unoiled
           sites in PWS in 1991 173

List of Tables

Table 2-1 PCDD, PCDF, and PCB congener concentrations in lake trout eggs,
           early life-stage mortality TEFs, and TEs for Lake Ontario in 1991 and
           Lake Michigan in 1993 14
Table 2-2 Toxicity equivalency factors for PCDD, PCDF, and PCB congeners 15
Table 2-3 Summary of types of responses observed for pairs of PCDD, PCDF, and PCB
           congeners in causing RBT early life-stage mortality 17

Table 6-1 Cross-reactivity of 4 IgG-type monoclonal antibodies against vitellogenins from
           a number of different fish species tested by Western Blots 80

Table 7-1 Mammalian xenoestrogens that did not induce vitellogenesis in immature channel
           catfish following a single i.p. injection 93
Table 7-2 Vitellogenin induction following i.p. injection of p-nonylphenol and methoxychlor 94
Table 7-3 Comparison of VTG detection in serum and cytosolic fraction 98

Table 9-1 Summary of field-collected kelp bass in June 1992 117
Table 9-2 Percentages of fish from each collection site with ovaries in various stages of atresia 122

Table 10-1 A comparison of clinical signs among salmonids exhibiting mortality at an
           early life stage 139
Table 10-2 Changes in the onset and duration of EMS in coho and chinook salmon and
           steelhead trout based on temperature units 140
Table 10-3 Mean total thiamine concentrations (nmol/g) in salmonid eggs that develop EMS
           versus concentrations in eggs from reference sites 146

Table 11-1 The coloration of Baltic salmon roe and the measured levels of total carotenoids,
           astaxanthin, and the astaxanthin/carotenoid ratio 158
Table 11-2 Concentrations of vitamin E and ubiquinone (Q) in livers from alevins with
           M74 and from viable alevins 159
Table 11-3 Reconditioning of ascending spawners of the River Dalälven stock caught
           and stripped of roe and M74 mortality in their progeny 162

Table 13-1 Reproductive and developmental effects in wild populations of fish that are
           probably caused by contaminants 179
Table 13-2 Selected studies in which reproductive and developmental effects in fish have
           been associated with contaminant exposure in the field 182
Table 13-3 Selected studies reporting effects in wild populations of fish in which some
           component may involve contaminant exposure 185

Foreword

Wingspread Conferences and Endocrine Disruptors

The term "endocrine disruptor" (ED) has entered the mainstream of both scientific literature and the popular press over the last six years. It was coined in 1991 at the first of a series of six work sessions that have focused upon the effects of exposure to synthetic chemicals in the environment on the development and function of the endocrine, reproductive, nervous, and immune systems of wildlife, fish, and humans. These work sessions are colloquially known as Wingspread Conferences, taking the name of the Wingspread Conference Center in Racine, Wisconsin (owned by The Johnson Foundation), where five of the six sessions have been held. The name "Wingspread" refers to a place but also describes the style of these meetings, all of which are variations on the theme of endocrine disruptors. Table 1 lists the 6 Wingspread Conferences held to date, including the references for the proceedings from each work session. The material in this volume is the result of the fourth Wingspread Conference, which focused on chemically induced alterations in development and reproduction in fishes.

The first Wingspread meeting examined chemically induced alterations in sexual development, emphasizing the human/wildlife connection. This meeting was prompted by findings in wildlife in North America (particularly in the Great Lakes region) and in Europe, which indicated that the offspring of several wildlife species were experiencing developmental problems resulting in declines in some populations. Similar effects were being seen in different species in both the same and different geographic regions. The problem stemmed from adult exposure to xenobiotics, which resulted in effects seen in the offspring: these have been called "transgenerational effects." The underlying mechanism of many of the described effects was disruption of the endocrine system, hence the term "endocrine disruptor."

At this first conference, the participants recognized that human, wildlife, and fish populations are exposed to chemicals that have been released in the environment and that have the potential to disrupt the endocrine system. In fact, past damage to wildlife populations was already well documented in the scientific literature, these effects had been demonstrated in laboratory studies, and compelling parallels with the experience with diethylstilbestrol in humans were recognized. Because the endocrine system has been highly conserved evolutionarily, it was acknowledged that environmental exposures that result in effects in wildlife and fish populations present a potential threat to the health of human populations as well. This group of scientists decided at the meeting to voice their concern by summarizing the group's conclusions in the form of a consensus statement.

Subsequent work sessions have expanded the initial focus on reproductive effects of xenobiotic exposure to include effects on wildlife development, effects on the developing immune system, neural and behavioral effects, impacts on reproduction and development in fishes, and health risks posed by current-use pesticides. A consensus statement has resulted from all 6 meetings, and the proceedings have been, or are being, published in the peer reviewed scientific literature.

Wingspread work sessions are distinguished from most meetings or conferences by the multidisciplinary expertise of the participating scientists and the highly interactive environment. Three lines of evidence have been pursued, covering field studies of fish and wildlife populations, laboratory studies, and epidemiological studies of human populations. Participants have ranged from physicians and anthropologists working in human health-related issues to toxicologists and chemists carrying out controlled laboratory experimentation to biologists studying wildlife populations in the field. These work sessions cross disciplinary barriers within the sciences, taking a comparative approach to the basic sciences, epidemiology, ecotoxicology, and traditional toxicology, resulting in a holistic integration of the body of scientific evidence. This approach has brought together scientists who most likely would never have interacted but whose research is complementary or related, considerably broadening everyone's perspective on the issue and resulting in numerous collaborative efforts. The outcome of these meetings has been influential both in the development of policy and in stimulating new scientific research and fora. There are currently many initiatives underway in government agencies and in private and public institutions in North America and abroad dealing with the topic of endocrine disruptors.

It is the body of evidence taken as a whole across species, geographic regions, and scientific disciplines that has proved cause for concern. Individual research results are limited in their implications if considered alone, but when similar effects or responses are being seen from diverse sources, great strength is given to the existing evidence. In the case of field wildlife research and human epidemiological studies, while a study may be compelling in its results, it is rarely conclusive in and of itself. In these instances, one can never absolutely prove a cause–effect relationship between exposure to a xenobiotic and alterations in development and function of major physiological systems at chronic low dose exposure levels such as in the environment. Exposure to environmental mixtures of chemicals further complicates the picture. Field and epidemiological research can never be reliably replicated in the laboratory with all the inherent variables that such research entails. Because of these factors, it is the weight of the entire body of scientific evidence that must be brought to bear in cases of challenging environmental problems such as defining the threat posed by exposure to endocrine-disrupting chemicals.

A number of conclusions have been reached which span the work being done in all of these disciplines. These include the crucial importance of the timing of the exposure to an endocrine-disrupting chemical in determining the effect. It was recognized at all 6 sessions that there are critical periods during the life cycle of all organisms during which there is a greatly heightened sensitivity to exposure to endocrine disruptors. It is not just the dose that makes the poison, as scientists have traditionally believed, but the dose in combination with the timing of the exposure that determines the outcome. The period of early development when body systems are differentiating and being programmed for function throughout life is the most sensitive stage. This can be before or after birth or hatching and during lactation for mammals. Often the effects produced by early exposures during this organizational period of development are not visible at birth, and depending upon the timing of exposure, they may be irreversible. Other periods of increased sensitivity to endocrine disruptors and sensitive subpopulations probably exist.

Low dose exposure (acute, chronic, and pulsatile) can produce unique effects that may not be seen when using high dose testing protocols in the laboratory. In fact, the dose-response to at least some endocrine disruptors has been shown to be non-monotonic or nonlinear, making it impossible to extrapolate from high doses to predict responses at lower exposure levels. It is an inherent attribute of the endocrine system to down regulate at higher exposure levels when receptors become saturated and negative feedback loops kick in. As a result, traditional high dose testing protocols have failed to identify the unique threats posed by endocrine-disrupting chemicals.

It has become increasingly apparent that there are a multitude of mechanisms through which xenobiotics can interfere with the endocrine system. Initially, the focus was on synthetic chemicals that have the ability to bind to the cellular receptor for the female sex steroid hormone estrogen, either mimicking or blocking the hormone. Numerous substances can bind to the receptor in addition to the natural hormone, and the ability to bind to the receptor has been difficult to predict from the chemical structure of the compound. It turns out that the issue is much broader than this, involving other hormones and other non-receptor mediated methods of interference with hormones on a molecular and biochemical level. For example, scientists only recently recognized that p,p'-DDE, the persistent breakdown product of DDT, binds with high affinity to the androgen receptor, acting as an antagonist or hormone blocker. Additionally, xenobiotics can interfere with metabolism or excretion of hormones, alter levels and sensitivity of cellular receptors, and interfere with hormone transport proteins in the blood. The concern goes well beyond the hormone estrogen and receptor binding.

An important realization was that exposure to endocrine-disrupting chemicals in the environment is widespread. Some exposures may be local and transitory in nature. For example, below sewage treatment plants that discharge estrogenic compounds, fish have been found to synthesize abnormal amounts of an estrogen-responsive glycophospho lipoprotein called vitellogenin. Other endocrine disruptors are persistent in the environment and lipophilic, allowing them to bioaccumulate in tissues and biomagnify up the food web. These include chemicals such as DDT and its metabolites, the polychlorinated biphenyls, dioxins, furans, chlordane, toxaphene and others. Many of these chemicals are now distributed globally, moving through ocean currents and atmospheric transportation in a process known as "global distillation." Depending on physical characteristics such as volatility and water solubility, these chemicals vaporize at warmer temperatures and condense at cooler temperatures, resulting in net movement toward the Northern Hemisphere. Thus, chemicals that have been banned or restricted can pose a continuing threat because of long persistence and global transport: exposure is no longer just a local or regional problem.

Chemically Induced Alterations in Functional Development and Reproduction of Fishes

The Wingspread work session that led to this collection of papers was prompted by growing concern for the effects that synthetic chemicals are having on fish populations inhabiting both freshwater and saltwater ecosystems. The recent crash of many of the world's commercial marine fisheries, the depletion of freshwater fish species in several locations, and the recognition of the global distribution of many endocrine disruptors have led to concern about the possible role that xenobiotics could have played and are playing in the demise of fish populations. In the past, the focus has been on the visible acute effects of high-level exposure of fish to pollution such as fish kills and neoplasia. However, exposure to EDs can lead to more difficult to detect insidious effects, such as a decline in reproductive success or delayed sexual maturation potentially undermining the long-term survival of fish populations and compromising their ability to compensate for other stressors such as overfishing, habitat alterations, introduction of exotic species, and potentially the effects of global warming.

The group of scientists at this work session was assembled to examine the available scientific evidence on the link between exposure to xenobiotics and reproductive and developmental effects in fishes. This evidence was examined along several tiers of biological organization including the molecular, organismal, population, and ecosystem levels. The research presented at the work session and represented in the chapters of this book includes field studies, laboratory studies, and ecoepidemiological research. The field studies cover several geographic areas including papers from the Great Lakes Region, coastal Southern California, Prince William Sound, Alaska, and the Baltic Sea.

The overall objectives of the work session were to discuss 1) what is known about the effects of synthetic chemicals on reproduction and development in fishes, 2) what are the major gaps in this knowledge, and 3) what is the impact of these effects at the population level? During the first segment of the meeting, participants presented their research findings relevant to the topic of the work session. They were then divided into 4 work groups and were asked to come to some conclusions about these 3 questions based on their professional knowledge and on the information that had been presented. Each group presented their conclusions in a plenary session followed by an open discussion. Chapter 1 of this book is a synthesis of the conclusions that these scientists reached in answer to the 3 questions posed. The result is a Consensus Statement signed by all the participating scientists, which was prepared by repeatedly sending updated drafts to each scientist in an iterative process. The opinions in this statement represent the professional wisdom of these scientists; however, the statement should not be construed to reflect the policies or opinions of the agencies or institutions in which the workshop participants are employed.

After assessing the scientific evidence, this group of scientists concluded that there is a high degree of certainty that some wild fish populations have been affected by exposure to synthetic chemicals in the environment but that the extent of the risk to fish populations is difficult to determine because of the lack of data needed to make a valid assessment of the magnitude of the problem. The research needs and data gaps required to better assess the effects and ongoing risk to fishes of exposure to xenobiotics are outlined in the Consensus Statement in Chapter 1.

The remaining chapters are a combination of reviews and original research. They have been broadly organized into 3 categories: risk assessment, mechanisms and biomarkers, and ecoepidemiology and causality.

Risk Assessment

In the environment, fish are exposed to complex mixtures of chemicals that may act through a common mode of toxicity complicating risk assessment. In Chapter 2, Cook, Zabel, and Peterson discuss the 2,3,7,8,-tetrachlorodibenzo-p-dioxin (TCDD) toxicity equivalence approach for evaluating the toxicity of mixtures of chemicals all acting through the aryl hydrocarbon receptor. Using the case of early mortality in lake trout in the Great Lakes as a model for ecological risk assessment, the authors discuss the use of toxicity equivalence factors (TEFs). Based upon the toxicity of TCDD, the toxicity of complex mixtures of polychlorinated dioxins, furans, and biphenyls is evaluated using a toxicity equivalence approach. They illustrate the importance of using fish-specific TEFs for early life stage mortality risk assessment. Based on historical data on population demographics and TCDD concentrations, they suggest that 5 pg TCDD toxicity equivalents/egg is the threshold level for survival of lake trout to recruitment in Lakes Michigan and Ontario.

Mechanisms and Biomarkers

In Chapter 3, Thomas and Kahn emphasize the complexity of the reproductive endocrine system in teleosts. This chapter includes an in-depth review of the control of reproduction in teleosts by hormones secreted by the hypothalamic-pituitary-gonadal axis and stresses how disruption at one point of this neuroendo-crine axis can have widespread effects on reproductive fitness. Using the examples of kepone, cadmium, and lead in the Atlantic croaker (*Micropogonias undulatus*), they illustrate the wide variety of mechanisms through which chemicals can inter-fere with reproductive endocrine function in teleosts.

After 50 years of research on the toxicity of DDT and its metabolites, scientists have only recently revealed that p,p'-DDE acts as an androgen antagonist in mammalian cells by binding and blocking the androgen receptor. Because p,p'-DDE is the primary DDT metabolite present in the tissues of fishes globally, this finding could have great relevance for the health of fish. In Chapter 4, Monosson and co-authors examine the new research on antiandrogenic chemicals, including p,p'-DDE and the fungicide vinclozolin. They review the potential effects of environ-mental antiandrogens on fishes and the physiological basis for 2 hormone sensitive developmental stages in fish: sexual differentiation and maturation. The potential mechanisms through which kraft mill effluent and p,p'-DDE can interfere with these processes is reviewed, stressing the need for more research in teleosts.

Use of developmental, morphological, and skeletal biomarkers for evidence of life history disruption by synthetic chemicals are reviewed by Davis in Chapter 5. Because of the complex integration of the physiological processes controlling development, Davis stresses that the effects of disruption can be ultimately mani-fested as skeletal or morphological changes. Using the examples of kepone and trifluralin, the interrelationship of chemicals causing skeletal effects and endocrine disruption is explored.

The use of protein biomarkers to indicate exposure to synthetic chemicals is dis-cussed in Chapter 6. Denslow and co-authors describe the development of a vitellogenin assay using monoclonal antibodies. They explore the phylogenetically diverse structure of vitellogenin between different orders of fishes and the use of cross-reactive antibodies to vitellogenin. They provide examples of the use of vitellogenin as a biomarker in fish caught in the wild. They also discuss the use of another protein, apolipoprotein A1, as a biomarker for hepatic neoplasia in brown bullheads (*Ameiurus nebulosus*) exposed to contaminants.

In Chapter 7, Nimrod and Benson describe the use of vitellogenin in laboratory studies as a biomarker to assess estrogenic activity of chemicals in fish. Using a channel catfish (*Ictalarus punctatus*) model, they describe the validation of vitellogenin induction as a biomarker for acute exposure to environmental estrogens. The model was used to screen several xenobiotics that are known to be estrogenic in mammals. A technique for assessing vitellogenesis in Japanese medaka (*Oryzias latipes*) is also described.

Fish residing in polluted waters have been shown to suffer from increases in infectious diseases coinciding with suppression of immune system function. In Chapter 8, Voccia and co-authors describe the effects of 4 of the predominant chemicals in pulp and paper mill effluent on 2 parameters of the immune response of rainbow trout (*Onchorhynchus mykiss*): macrophage phagocytosis and respiratory burst. Although environmental chemicals may act on numerous biological systems, such as the endocrine and immune systems, little is known about how they interact.

Ecoepidemiology and Causality

In Chapter 9, Spies and Thomas compare measures of reproductive endocrine function in sexually mature female kelp bass (*Paralabrax clathratus*) from a site near Los Angeles that is heavily contaminated with PCBs and DDT to a less contaminated site off the California coast. Their research reveals significant differences in plasma estradiol, maturational gonadotropin, in vitro production of testosterone, and binding affinity of estradiol to its receptor in kelp bass from the contaminated and reference sites. Using an in vitro competitive binding assay, they also show that o,p'-DDE and o,p'-DDT have the ability to bind kelp bass estrogen receptors and therefore have the potential to exert estrogenic effects in this fish species.

Chapters 10 and 11 describe early mortality syndromes seen in salmonids in the Great Lakes of North America and in the Baltic Sea respectively. In Chapter 10, Marcquenski and Brown describe the early mortality syndrome seen in the Great Lakes salmonids, thoroughly reviewing the history, clinical signs, and probable causes including the existing evidence for the role of xenobiotics in the etiology of this syndrome. The early mortality syndrome in the Baltic salmon, called M74, has caused devastating losses of salmon fry in some years. Börjeson and Norrgren review the etiology of this syndrome in Chapter 11. Recent research has revealed that in both cases eggs contain low levels of thiamine and that thiamine can be used to successfully treat affected roe and fry. Changes in food web dynamics and the presence of thiaminase in salmonid prey, as well as environmental contaminants, are being investigated as factors contributing to this nutritional deficiency. Both chapters discuss the striking similarities and the differences between these 2 syndromes that cause early mortality of salmonids in different geographic regions.

Sublethal damage to Pacific herring (*Clupea pallasi*) exposed to oil from the *Exxon Valdez* spill in Prince William Sound, Alaska, is described by Kocan and Hose in Chapter 12. This oil spill coincided with the annual migration of herring to spawning sites resulting in exposure of about half of the 1989 year class during embryonic development. Laboratory and field investigations by these researchers revealed identical adverse effects in newly hatched larvae. These findings are especially intriguing because of the unusually high mortality seen in 1993 when the 1989 year class returned to spawn, presumably caused by a viral epizootic. Current research is exploring the possible link between early embryonic oil exposure in these herring and initiation of this viral disease outbreak 4 years after the exposure occurred.

The difficulty in translating effects in individuals to population-level effects is addressed by Monosson in Chapter 13. The tables in this chapter were developed by participants at the work session in response to the question "To what extent are environmental contaminants contributing to fish population declines or impeding recovery of depleted stocks?" Monosson has added the descriptive text and summarized the major points and conclusions. This chapter points to the need for better integration of laboratory and field studies in order to establish cause–effect linkages between exposure to contaminants in the environment and reproductive and developmental effects in fishes and to determine the consequences at the population level.

As the chapters in this book demonstrate, there is ample research showing that environmental contaminants can adversely affect reproduction and development in fishes. However, the magnitude of the problem and the significance of these effects for wild fish populations is difficult to evaluate based upon existing information. Population-level effects of xenobiotics have been conclusively demonstrated for wildlife species such as colonial nesting water birds. Often these effects were not recognized until a drastic change in population numbers was seen, and retrospective assessments have demonstrated the link with exposure to environmental contaminants. Because of the multitude of anthropogenic and ecological stressors currently affecting wild fish populations, delineating the role that xenobiotics are playing, or may play in the future, in population attrition in fishes is a problem that can only be addressed through multidisciplinary collaborative research. Clearly, the causes of these changes in fish populations must be understood if fisheries researchers are to continue to contribute to the protection and restoration of freshwater and marine fisheries.

R.M. Rolland
M. Gilbertson
R.E. Peterson

Table 1   Wingspread Conferences and resulting publications

Wingspread I	Chemically-Induced Alterations in Sexual Development: The Wildlife/Human Connection. 26-28 July 1991. Wingspread Conference Center, Racine, Wisconsin
	Published in Colborn T, Clements C, editors. 1992. Chemically-Induced Alterations in Sexual and Functional Development: The Wildlife/Human Connection. Advances in Modern Toxicology, Princeton Scientific Publishing, Princeton NJ, USA.
Wingspread II	Environmentally-Induced Alterations in Development: A Focus on Wildlife. 10-12 December 1993. Wingspread Conference Center, Racine, Wisconsin
	Published in Rolland R, Gilbertson M, Colborn T, editors. *Environmental Health Perspectives Supplement* 103(4) May 1995.
Wingspread III	Chemically-Induced Alterations in the Developing Immune System: The Wildlife/Human Connection. 10-12 February 1995. Wingspread Conference Center, Racine, Wisconsin
	Published in *Environmental Health Perspectives Supplement* 104(4) August 1996.
Wingspread IV	Chemically-Induced Alterations in the Functional Development and Reproduction of Fishes. 21-23 July 1995. Wingspread Conference Center, Racine, Wisconsin
	Published in this volume.
Wingspread V	Environmental Endocrine Disrupting Chemicals: Neural, Endocrine, and Behavioral Effects. 5-10 November 1995. Erice, Sicily, Italy
	In preparation in *Toxicology and Industrial Health.*
Wingspread VI	Health Effects of Contemporary-Use Pesticides: The Wildlife/ Human Connection. 27-29 September 1996. Wingspread conference Center, Racine, Wisconsin
	Publication under development.

Preface

This book contains the proceedings from a work session with the same title that was held at the Wingspread Conference Center in Racine, Wisconsin from 21–23 July 1995. A multidisciplinary group of 21 research scientists from the United States, Canada, and Europe were chosen to attend based upon their published research about exposure to synthetic chemicals and disruption of the development and/or function of the reproductive, endocrine, immune, or nervous systems of fishes. A particular emphasis was placed on exposure to chemicals during early developmental stages, both pre- and post-hatching. The research encompassed both laboratory and field studies on a wide variety of freshwater and marine fish species. Most of the research was from North America with a particular emphasis on the Great Lakes region, which was discussed at the work session as a model for the study of the effects of xenobiotics on reproduction and development of fishes. The case of M74 in Baltic salmon was included because of the apparent similarities between this syndrome and the early mortality syndrome seen in salmonid species in the Great Lakes of North America. Other good research is ongoing in Europe and elsewhere, which this volume does not cover.

Much of the information and data that were presented at the work session are encompassed in the chapters of this book. The first chapter is a consensus statement that was developed from discussions that took place at the work session, and all of the participants contributed their opinions and expertise to the development of this statement. The remaining chapters are the contributions of individual authors and their co-authors, and each chapter is meant to stand alone. Except for the consensus statement from the work session in Chapter 1, all of the chapters in this book have been peer reviewed externally in accordance with the requirements of the Society of Environmental Toxicology and Chemistry (SETAC). In addition, each chapter has been through internal review by the volume editors, by other participants at the work session, and by other colleagues.

This work session led to a productive interchange of information and ideas and new research directions and collaborations among the participating scientists. Through publishing these proceedings, we hope to share these results with the larger scientific community.

Acknowledgments

We are indebted to the numerous individuals who generously contributed their time and expertise to critically review the manuscripts in this book. Their comments and suggestions substantially improved the scientific quality of this publication. Special thanks go to the authors of these manuscripts and to all of the participants in the work session from which this publication was developed. In addition to contributing papers, many of these scientists internally reviewed each other's papers and provided invaluable guidance in the development of this publication.

We are especially grateful to the organizations and foundations who took an interest in this project and provided the funding to see it realized. This project was supported by the Dodge Foundation, the Joyce Foundation, the Keland Endowment Fund of the Johnson Foundation, The Pew Charitable Trusts, the Society of Environmental Toxicology and Chemistry (SETAC), and World Wildlife Fund-U.S. Finally, our heartfelt thanks to Mr. Charles Bray of the Johnson Foundation and his staff at the Wingspread Conference Center who hosted the work session from which these papers were developed.

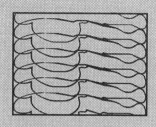

Abbreviations

2D-PAGE	2-dimensional polyacrylamide gel electrophoresis
11-KT	11-ketotestosterone
3-MT	3-methoxytyramine
5-HIAA	5-hydroxyindolacetic acid
5-HT	serotonin
5-HTP	5-hydroxytryptophan
ACR	astaxanthin/carotenoids ratio
AGD	anogenital distance
Ah	aryl hydrocarbon
AHH	aryl hydrocarbon hydroxylase
ANCOVA	analysis of covariance
ANOVA	analysis of variance
AR	androgen receptor
ARE	androgen response element
AROM	Aromatase
ATP	adenosine triphosphate
BKME	bleached kraft mill effluent
BLAST	Basic Local Alignment Search Tool
BRL	Bethesda Research Laboratory
BSA	bovine serum albumin
BSAF	biota-sediment accumulation factor
COMT	catechol-O-methyltransferase
Cr^{51}	chromium 51
cAMP	cyclic 3',5'-adenosine monophosphate
DA	dopamine
DBP	di-n-butylphthalate
DCFDA	dichloro-fluorescein diacetate
DDD	dichlorodiphenylethane
DDE	dichlorodiphenyldichloroethylene
DDMU	dichlorodiphenylchloroethane
DDT	dichlorodiphenyltrichloroethane

DEHP	di-2-ethylhexyphthalate
DES	diethylstilbestrol
DHAA	dehydroabietic acid
DHT	dihydrotestosterone
DMEM	Dulbecco's modified Eagle's medium
DOPAC	dihydroxyphenylacetic acid
DWSE	Duwamish Waterway sediment extracts
E	epinephrine
EE2	ethinylestradiol
E2	estradiol
ED50	effective dose for 50% of test organisms
EDCs	endocrine disrupting chemicals
ELISA	enzyme-linked immunosorbent assay
EMS	Early Mortality Syndrome
EROD	ethoxyresorufin-O-deethylase
EVO	*Exxon Valdez* oil
EVOS	*Exxon Valdez* oil spill
GABA	γ-aminobutyric acid
GC/ECD	gas chromatography/electron capture detection
GnRH	gonadotropin-releasing hormone
GRIFs	gonadotropin release-inhibiting factors
GSI	gonadosomatic index
GTH	gonadotropin
HBSS	Hank's Balanced Salt Solution
HMW	high molecular weight
HPG	hypothalamus-pituitary-gonadal
HPLC	high pressure liquid chromatography
HRGC/HRMS	high resolution gas chromatography/high resolution mass spectrometry
HVA	homovanillic acid
IgG	immunoglobulin G
IgM	immunoglobulin M
i.p.	intraperitoneal
kDa	kilodalton
KME	kraft mill effluent
LD50	lethal dose for 50% of test organisms
LH	luteinizing hormone
LHRHa	luteinizing hormone-releasing hormone

M1	primary degradation product of Vinclozolin (fungicide)
M2	primary degradation product of Vinclozolin (fungicide)
M74	alevin mortality syndrome seen in Baltic salmon
mAb	monoclonal antibody
MAO	monoamine oxidase
ME2	mestranol
MES	morpholinoethane sulphonic acid
MIS	maturation-inducing steroids
MPH	medial and posterior hypothalamus
mRNA	messenger ribonucleic acid
MW	molecular weight
NCBI	National Center for Biotechnology Information
NE	norepinephrine
NOAEL	no-observed-adverse-effect level
NOEL	no-observed-effect level
NRDA	Natural Resource Damage Assessment
OWD	oil-water dispersion
PAH	polycyclic aromatic hydrocarbon
PCB	polychlorinated biphenyl
PCP	pentachlorophenol
PCDD	polychlorinated dibenzo-*p*-dioxin
PCDF	dibenzofuran
PI	propidium iodide
PLHC	Poeciliopsis-Lucida hepatocellular carcinoma cell line
PMA	phorbol myristate acetate
PMSF	phenylmethylsulfonylfluoride
POAH	preoptic-anterior hypothalamic area
PVDF	polyvinyledene difluoride
PWS	Prince William Sound
Q	ubiquinone
RIA	radio immunoassay
RPMI	Roswell Park Memorial Institute
SD	standard deviation
SDS-PAGE	sodium dodecyl sulfate polyacrylamide gel electrophoresis
SEM	standard error of the mean
SL	standard length

T	testosterone
TBST	buffer solution (10mM Tris, pH7, 150mM NaCl, 0.5% Tween)
TCB	tetrachlorobiphenyl
TCDD	tetrachlorodibenzo-p-dioxin
TCP	trichlorophenol
TE	toxicity equivalents
TeCG	tetrachlorogaiacol
TEC	toxicity equivalence concentration
TeCC	tetrachlorocatechol
TEF	toxicity equivalence factor
TIE	toxicity identification evaluation
TMX	tamoxifen
UK	United Kingdom
U.S.	United States
USEPA	U.S. Environmental Protection Agency
VHSV	viral hemorrhagic septicemia virus
VIMS	Virginia Institute of Marine Sciences
VTG	vitellogenin
WSF	water soluble fraction
WHO	World Health Organization

Chemically Induced Alterations in Functional Development and Reproduction of Fishes

Statement from the work session on chemically induced alterations in functional development and reproduction of fishes

During the past several years, there has been growing acknowledgment that synthetic chemicals released into the environment have disrupted the development and/or function of the reproductive, endocrine, immune, and nervous systems of vertebrates. Effects of this nature have been documented for many wildlife species in the field and have also been demonstrated in laboratory studies. In several instances, exposure to endocrine-disrupting chemicals (EDCs) has led to instability or declines in wildlife populations. To address the relevance of these findings to freshwater and saltwater fishes, a group of scientists gathered in retreat at a work session at Wingspread, in Racine, Wisconsin, on 21–23 July 1995, to examine the scientific evidence and to come to some conclusions about the magnitude and scope of these effects. A multidisciplinary group of 22 scientists participated in the work session, including experts in the fields of aquatic sciences, biochemistry, biometrics, chemistry, ecology, endocrinology, fisheries biology, immunology, marine sciences, pathology, pharmacology, physiology, toxicology, veterinary medicine, wildlife biology, and zoology. Participants were asked to address the following questions:

1) What is the present state-of-knowledge concerning the effects of chemical exposure on fish development and reproduction?

2) What are the major gaps in this knowledge? What research is needed to answer the major questions?

3) To what extent are environmental contaminants contributing to fish population declines or impeding recovery of depleted stocks?

Consensus Statement

1) We are confident of the following points:

- Several classes of synthetic chemicals present in the aquatic environment disrupt reproduction, endocrine, immune and nervous system functions, growth, and development in fishes (e.g., polychlorinated biphenyls [PCBs], dibenzo-*p*-dioxins [PCDDs], and dibenzofurans [PCDFs], dichlorodiphenyl-trichloroethane [DDT]-group chemicals, alkylphenols, and their metabolites). Some naturally occurring compounds used in industrial and agricultural processes also have this capability (e.g., heavy metals). Laboratory studies have shown that these chemicals can act directly as hormone mimics or blockers. They can also act indirectly through effects on neuroendocrine homeostasis, and they can affect immune system function.

- A wide range of effects may result from exposure to these chemicals, including anatomical malformations, functional alterations, and biochemical or molecular changes. Developing embryos and larvae are particularly sensitive to chemical exposure; however, adult fish are also affected. Depending upon the timing of exposure, irreversible effects can occur in the offspring of exposed fish which may not be immediately apparent. Because many of these chemicals eventually reach aquatic ecosystems, fish may serve as reliable sentinels of effects of chemicals in other vertebrates, including humans.

- Many fish populations in both saltwater and freshwater are presently threatened by chemicals introduced into the environment through human activities. There is a high degree of certainty that some wild fish populations have already been affected.

- The well-characterized toxic effects of PCDDs, PCDFs, and PCBs on lake trout sac larvae, the past exposure conditions, and the effects found in Lake Ontario provide compelling evidence that these chemicals probably caused reproductive or developmental damage to entire stocks of fish. In most other cases, the specific agents responsible for injury have not been definitively identified, nor has damage to reproduction and development been adequately assessed.

- Of great concern is the global distribution of many known reproductive and developmental toxicants. These deleterious agents can move through the environment, expose fishes distant from their points of release, and accumulate to high levels in some locations.

- Steps need to be taken to safeguard fish stocks from the effects of synthetic chemical exposures. The general public and many scientists are not aware of the extent to which fish species, including economically important fisheries, are presently at risk or have already been injured.

2) There are many uncertainties in our predictions for the following reasons:

- Few multigenerational studies of wild fish populations have looked in detail at the sublethal effects caused by synthetic chemical exposure which lead to long-term functional impairment (e.g., developmental, endocrine, reproductive, neurologic, immunologic) or long-term consequences (e.g., endocrine disruption leading to reproductive failure and population decline). Because few chemicals have been tested for these effects in fishes, only a limited number of compounds have been analyzed in field studies. Furthermore, only in rare cases have field and laboratory research been coordinated to establish causality in a given situation.

- Environmental variables complicate field research linking exposure to chemicals with effects on wild fish populations. Epidemiological studies are complicated by the influence of changing climatic and geophysical forces on fish population dynamics. Additional confounding factors include impacts of human activities, such as overfishing, release of hatchery-reared fishes, habitat alterations, and the introduction of exotic species.

- Inherent characteristics of fish biology further complicate field research. For example, year class recruitment is affected by variables that are difficult to quantify; reproductive strategies vary greatly among different fish species, making interspecies comparisons difficult; little is known about normal physiological parameters for most fish species; and routine sampling and observation of specific fish populations is logistically difficult.

3) To improve our predictive capability, we must accomplish the following:

- More knowledge is needed of fundamental physiological processes and developmental mechanisms in fish at levels of organization from molecular and cellular to the whole organism. In particular, basic research is needed for a variety of species on sexual differentiation, ontogeny of the neuroendocrine system, hormone receptor structure and function, normal levels of circulating hormones at various life stages, and normal developmental processes.

- Better assessments of the present threat to fish stocks are needed, requiring a) detailed information on the demographics and reproductive health of fish populations where developmental or reproductive dysfunction is occurring; b) knowledge of the extent and patterns of discharge and accumulation of potential and known toxicants in aquatic ecosystems; c) ecoepidemiological studies to identify chemicals involved; d) realistic replication in the laboratory of environmental chemical exposures to demonstrate cause and effect and delineate the mechanisms of action; and e) consideration of the effects of other stressors, either alone or in combination, on the toxicological action of chemicals present in the environment.

- Field and laboratory research strategies should include identification of critical times within specific life stages when organisms are most sensitive to the toxic actions of chemicals: this will require long-term multigenerational studies. The effects of chemical exposure during development must be linked to later life history characteristics (e.g., behavioral, reproductive, nutritional, immunological, and neurological), which subtly alter the organism's ability to survive and reproduce. Field studies should also address the long-term effects of chemical exposures on fish population and community structure.

- Field studies should quantify the tissue burdens of chemicals associated with injury in standardized units of measure to facilitate coordinated laboratory research. This information will guide laboratory studies by calibrating the exposure required to produce the effects observed in the field. However, there is a particular concern for non-bioaccumulative agents which are not detectable in the organism when the damage is expressed, making it difficult to establish causal relationships. Toxicological studies of these chemicals must include exposures of ova, embryos, and early life stages followed by detailed observations for effects in the mature adults and their offspring (i.e., second generation effects). It is very important that these studies incorporate the impact of maternal transfer of contaminants to the ova before spawning, mimicking the conditions in the environment.

- More basic research into the mechanisms and sites of action of known toxicants is needed. This research should include both direct and indirect effects of chemicals on specific reproductive and developmental processes, and it should identify the most sensitive endpoints and the most sensitive fish species. From this information, reliable biomarkers of the effects of specific chemicals should be developed.

- In vivo and in vitro screening methods are needed to assess the potential reproductive and developmental toxicity of compounds to fishes before these chemicals are released into the environment.

- The possibility of multiple impacts of several chemicals or chemical classes should be considered, because the net effects of complex mixtures of chemicals cannot always be explained on the basis of the individual actions of known components of the mixture. Models are needed for utilizing information a) about single chemical effects to predict effects from exposures to mixtures of chemicals with a common mode of action and b) to predict effects from exposures to mixtures of chemicals with different modes of action.

- The difficulties in assessing the causes of fish population declines need to be addressed through cooperative, multidisciplinary research. Field observations of dysfunction at individual, population, community, and ecosystem levels should direct the course of coordinated experimental and analytical laboratory studies. The results from these coordinated field and laboratory studies on chemical exposures, effects, and dose-response can then be used to characterize risk and to address the causes of fish population declines.

- These activities will require long-term multidisciplinary studies by an international consortium of scientists from academia, the private sector, governmental, and nongovernmental organizations. These efforts should be supported by governments, the private sector, and an informed citizenry.

Work Session Participants

William H. Benson, Professor and
 Coordinator, Environmental and
 Community Health Research
School of Pharmacy
The University of Mississippi
University MS

Howard A. Bern, Professor
Department of Integrative Biology and
 Cancer Research Laboratory
University of California
Berkeley CA

Brian Bue, Biometrician
Alaska Department of Fish and Game
Anchorage AK

Theo Colborn, Senior Scientist
World Wildlife Fund
Washington DC

Philip Cook, Research Chemist
Office of Research and Development
United States (U.S.) Environmental
Protection Agency
Duluth MN

William P. Davis, Research Ecologist
Gulf Ecology Division
U.S. Environmental Protection Agency
Gulf Breeze FL

Nancy Denslow, Director
BEECS Molecular Biomarkers Core Facility
Department of Biochemistry and
  Molecular Biology
University of Florida
Gainesville FL

Edward M. Donaldson, Section Head
Biotechnology Genetics and Nutrition
Department of Fisheries and Oceans
West Vancouver Laboratory
West Vancouver, Canada

Carol Cotant Edsall, Fishery Biologist
NBS Great Lakes Science Center
Ann Arbor MI

Michel Fournier, Professor
Toxicologie de L'environnement (TOXEN)
University of Quebec at Montreal
Montreal, Canada

Michael Gilbertson
Work Group on Ecosytem Health
International Joint Commission
Great Lakes Science Advisory Board
Detroit MI

Rodney Johnson, Research Biologist
U.S. Environmental Protection Agency
Duluth MN

Richard Kocan, Professor, Aquatic
  Toxicology
School of Fisheries
University of Washington
Seattle WA

Emily Monosson, Research Assistant
  Professor
Department of Forestry and Wildlife
University of Massachusetts
Amherst MA

Leif Norrgren, Associate Professor
Department of Pathology
Swedish University of Agricultural
  Sciences
Uppsala, Sweden

Richard E. Peterson, Professor of
  Toxicology
School of Pharmacy
University of Wisconsin
Madison WI

Rosalind Rolland, Conservation Scientist
World Wildlife Fund
Washington DC

Michael Smolen, Conservation Scientist
World Wildlife Fund
Washington DC

Robert Spies, President
Applied Marine Sciences
Livermore CA

Craig Sullivan, Associate Professor
Department of Zoology
North Carolina State University
Raleigh NC

Peter Thomas, Professor
Marine Sciences Institute
University of Texas at Austin
Port Aransas TX

Glen Van Der Kraak, Associate Professor
Department of Zoology
University of Guelph
Guelph, Canada

This consensus statement reflects the professional wisdom of the scientists at the work session and not necessarily the institutions or agencies in which they are employed.

Acknowledgments

Funding for this work session was provided by the International Joint Commission, The Joyce Foundation, The Keland Endowment Fund of the Johnson Foundation, The Dodge Foundation, and World Wildlife Fund-US.

The TCDD toxicity equivalence approach for characterizing risks for early life-stage mortality in trout

Philip M. Cook, Erik W. Zabel,
Richard E. Peterson

Polychlorinated dibenzo-p-dioxin (PCDD), dibenzofuran (PCDF), and biphenyl (PCB) congeners — toxic via the same aryl hydrocarbon (Ah) receptor-mediated mechanism as 2,3,7,8 tetrachlorodibenzo-p-dioxin (TCDD) — contaminate fish in many aquatic ecosystems, including the Great Lakes. The toxicity equivalence factor (TEF) method is proposed for use in aquatic ecological risk assessments to describe individual congener potency relative to the prototype congener, TCDD, and to calculate a mixture's total TCDD toxicity equivalence concentration (TEC) based on concentrations in fish eggs or tissue. The TEF method assumes that congeners produce toxicity by the same mechanism and by acting additively. Our laboratories sought to validate the TEF method for fish early life-stage mortality risk assessment by determining 1) early life-stage mortality-specific TEFs for PCDD, PCDF, and PCB congeners in rainbow trout (RBT); 2) whether congeners act additively, both in binary and complex mixtures, to produce this response; and (3) whether TEFs based on early life-stage mortality in different fish species (RBT and lake trout) are similar.

The results support using an additive TCDD toxicity equivalence model (with fish early life-stage mortality-specific TEFs) to assess risks from fish embryos' exposure to TCDD and related compounds. Alternative TEFs, which are based on biochemical responses in RBT and mammals, tend to predict greater toxicity to lake trout in the Great Lakes than RBT early life-stage mortality TEFs — but all are within a factor of 10, even when TCDD contributes only a small fraction of the TEC.

Although robust sports fisheries have been established with stocked lake trout in the Great Lakes, attempts since the 1960s to reestablish and maintain naturally reproducing populations of lake trout (*Salvelinus namaycush*) have met with limited success. In the 1940s, lake trout populations declined and by the mid 1950s were deemed extinct throughout the Great Lakes, except for isolated populations in Lake Superior (Eshenroder et al. 1984). Subsequent stocking of the Great Lakes with fin-clipped, yearling lake trout resulted in stocked fish reaching sexual maturity and producing fertilized eggs but there was no recruitment of young into the population. Many ecological factors may contribute to this problem including toxicity associated with the presence of chemical contaminants. Two distinctly different syndromes observed in lake trout sac fry have been investigated for chemical etiologies: 1) blue-sac disease which occurs in sac fry prior to swim-up and onset of exogenous feeding (Symula et al. 1990) and 2) swim-up syndrome (Mac et al. 1985). While the exposure of trout embryos to tetrachlorodibenzo-p-dioxin (TCDD) and related chemicals has been shown to cause the blue-sac disease signs and mortality (Spitsbergen et al. 1991; Walker et al. 1991), there is presently no established association between exposure to TCDD and polychlorinated biphenyl (PCB) and incidence of swim-up syndrome (Mac et al. 1993; Fitzsimons et al. 1996).

Fish in many aquatic ecosystems, including the Great Lakes, contain detectable concentrations of polychlorinated dibenzo-p-dioxin (PCDD), dibenzo-furan (PCDF), and PCB congeners (Zacharewski et al. 1989; Carey et al. 1990; USEPA 1992; Kuehl et al. 1994). Mixtures of PCDDs, PCDFs, and PCBs that act via an aryl hydrocarbon (Ah) receptor mechanism may contribute to recruitment failure of lake trout by causing early life-stage mortality or sublethal toxicity which reduce survival. Most fishes, including salmonids, express the *Ah* receptor (Hahn et al. 1992) and therefore potentially have the capacity to respond to 2,3,7,8-TCDD and related chemicals (Walker and Peterson 1994a). Also PCDD, PCDF, and PCB congeners that act by an *Ah* receptor-mediated mechanism have been detected in eggs of Lake Ontario and Lake Michigan lake trout (Cook et al. 1994). Such congeners are approximate isostereomers of TCDD and cause signs of toxicity in fish identical to those caused by TCDD. Early life stages of fish are particularly vulnerable to toxic effects caused by these chemicals (Walker and Peterson 1994a). Developmental toxicity manifested by these congeners in trout sac fry (Figure 2-1) results in mortality and includes symptoms such as yolk sac and pericardial edema, subcutaneous hemorrhages, regional ischemia, and craniofacial malformations, which morphologically resemble blue-sac disease (Spitsbergen et al. 1991; Walker et al. 1991; Walker and Peterson 1994b). Furthermore, among salmonid fish species that have been evaluated, lake trout were discovered to be the most sensitive to TCDD-induced early life-stage mortality. The lethal dose for 50% of test organisms (LD50) for sac-fry mortality was determined to be 47 to 65 pg TCDD/g egg (Walker et al. 1991, 1994). Brook trout, another char species, are also very sensitive with a sac-fry LD50 of approximately 200 pg TCDD/g egg (Walker and Peterson 1994b).

Efforts to evaluate the toxicity of complex mixtures of PCDDs, PCDFs, and PCBs to lake trout in the Great Lakes illustrate the state of data and models for dioxin toxicity risk assessment. Procedures for assessing exposure, bioaccumulation, and risks for toxic effects to fish have been reported for TCDD (Cook et al. 1993). Because PCDDs, PCDFs, and PCBs are found in aquatic environments as complex mixtures, a method is needed to simplify the characterization of their risk to lake trout early life stages and other fish species. The TCDD toxicity equivalence factor (TEF) method, which has been proposed for human health risk assessments (Safe 1990), may be used for aquatic ecological risk assessments (Cook et al. 1991). Toxicity equivalence factors describe the potencies of individual congeners that are *Ah* receptor agonists relative to the most potent congener, TCDD, and are generally defined as the effective dose for 50% of test organisms (ED50) or LD50 for TCDD divided by the ED50 or LD50 for the individual congener. Toxicity equivalence factors may be multiplied by concentrations of congeners in an organism, or preferably, vulnerable tissues to determine the TCDD toxicity equivalents (TEs) contributed by that congener. Toxicity equivalents for all the individual congeners in the sample may then be added to calculate the total TCDD toxicity equivalence concentration (TEC). Toxicity equivalence concentrations are compared to the laboratory-determined concentrations of TCDD associated with toxicity in order to estimate the risk to exposed organisms. Early life-stage mortality in fish can be evaluated effectively on the basis of TECs in eggs. TEC_{egg} for a mixture of n congeners equals the sum of each congener's TE_{egg} (pg TCDD TE/g wet egg), which is the product of the concentration of the congener in the eggs, C_{egg}, (pg congener/ g wet egg) times the TEF (pg TCDD TE/pg congener):

$$TEC_{egg} = \sum_{i=1}^{n} \left[(C_{egg})_i \cdot (TEF)_i \right]$$ (2-1).

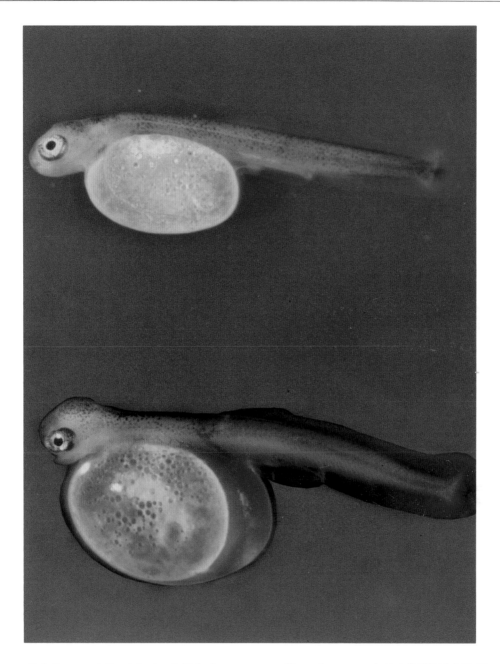

Figure 2-1 Representative lake trout (*Salvelinus namaycush*) sac fry exposed as a fertilized egg to water/acetone vehicle (top) or to TCDD in vehicle (bottom). Signs of TCDD toxicity resemble those of blue-sac disease which include yolk sac and pericardial edema, subcutaneous hemorrhages, and craniofacial malformations. (Adapted with permission from National Research Council of Canada.)

Toxicity equivalence factors have been determined in many mammalian systems (Safe 1990; Tillitt et al. 1991; DeVito et al. 1993; Ahlborg et al. 1994). Most mammalian TEFs are based on biochemical responses, primarily related to cytochrome P4501A induction. Important distinctions may be whether the biochemical indicator measurements are made in vivo or in vitro and whether the biochemical response is a reliable indicator of relative potencies for the toxic effect of concern. Also, exposure conditions, including time to response measurement and other pharmacokinetic considerations can influence toxic potency estimates (DeVito and Birnbaum 1995). Preference should be given for dosimetry and TEFs based on steady-state concentrations of TCDD and related chemicals in tissues associated with the effects to be evaluated. If large differences exist in TEFs based on mammals versus fish or in vivo versus in vitro responses, use of nonspecific TEFs for assessing early life-stage mortality in fish could be inaccurate. Since fish toxicity problems, such as the evaluation of halogenated aromatic chemical effects on Great Lakes lake trout recruitment, can require extreme accuracy for useful risk predictions, fish-specific TEFs were needed. In this report we will review the development of TEFs based on trout early life-stage mortality and demonstrate their application, in comparison to other TEFs, for assessment of early life-stage survival of lake trout in the Great Lakes in relation to TEC_{egg}.

Methods

Sources of trout eggs and methods used for sampling, toxicity testing, analysis of PCDD, PCDF, and PCB congener doses, and statistical analysis of data in TEF and congener mixture toxicity studies are as described in the references cited for each study reviewed here. The procedures used to obtain TEC_{egg}s for Lake Ontario and Lake Michigan lake trout eggs are described here since the Lake Michigan egg data have not been reported elsewhere.

Lake trout eggs

Eggs for assessment of recent concentrations of PCDDs, PCDFs, and PCBs in Great Lakes lake trout embryos and sac fry were obtained from 18 females from 2 locations in Lake Ontario in 1991 (Guiney et al. 1996) and 3 females from Lake Michigan near Sturgeon Bay in 1993 (kindly provided by Michael Toneys, Wisconsin Department of Natural Resources). The Lake Ontario eggs were analyzed by high resolution gas chromatography/high resolution mass spectrometry (HRGC/HRMS) as composite samples from the 2 sites, and the Lake Michigan eggs were analyzed as individual samples.

Determination of chemical concentrations in feral lake trout eggs

Egg samples (10.1 ± 0.1g wet weight) were ground, homogenized, and blended with anhydrous sodium sulfate (50g). After addition of $^{13}C_{12}$-labeled surrogate standards for PCDDs and PCDFs (Marquis et al. 1994) and PCBs (Kuehl et al. 1991), the samples were Soxhlet extracted with hexane/methylene chloride (v:v, 1:1) for 12 hours. Lipids, cholesterol, fatty acids, and other interferences were removed through gel permeation chromatography followed by 1% deactivated silica gel column chromatography. Polychlorinated dibenzo-p-dioxins, PCDFs, and PCBs in the purified extracts were isolated from more polar chemicals through high pressure liquid chromatography (HPLC) using a cyanopropyl (Phase-Sep, United Kingdom) semi-preparative column in normal phase with a hexane/methylene chloride solvent gradient. Further HPLC treatment of the nonpolar fraction containing the analytes of interest was accomplished with a pyrenyl column (Nacalai Tesque, Japan) in normal phase with a hexane/toluene gradient which resulted in 3 fractions for HRGC/HRMS analysis: PCDDs and PCDFs, non-orthochlorinated biphenyls, and orthochlorinated biphenyls. Concentrations of individual PCDD, PCDF, and PCB congeners in lake trout eggs were analyzed with a Finnigan-Mat 8230 double-focusing HRGC/HRMS instrument using a 30m DB-5 gas chromatography column. Polychlorinated biphenyls 28, 52, 128, 138, 156, and 170 were measured by gas chromatography/electron capture detection (GC/ECD) with co-eluting congeners listed in Table 2-1. The HRGC/HRMS conditions, quantification procedures, and quality assurance criteria have been described previously (Marquis et al. 1994) with the exception that minimum levels of detection for this study were calculated on the basis of a 3:1 signal to noise criteria for each analyte in each sample.

Trout-specific TCDD TEFs for each congener, based on the concentration of each congener in the egg (nmole congener/g wet egg) that causes 50% mortality in rainbow trout (RBT) sac fry (Walker and Peterson 1991; Zabel et al. 1995a), were used to calculate TCDD TEs due to PCDDs, PCDFs, and PCBs in lake trout eggs (TE_{egg}s) as the product of each congener's TEF and its concentration in the eggs (pg congener/g wet egg). (Because the TEFs were originally determined with LD50s based on nmole congener/g wet egg, they must be adjusted to account for differences in congener molecular weights when used with mass concentrations.) The sum of the individual congener TE_{egg}s in an egg equals the TEC_{egg} (pg TCDD toxicity equivalents/g wet egg). Concentrations measured in individual or composite egg samples were averaged to calculate mean TE_{egg}s and TEC_{egg}s (Table 2-1) for Lake Ontario and Lake Michigan.

Results and Discussion

Fish-specific TEFs

Toxicity equivalence factors for several PCDD, PCDF, and PCB congeners in RBT and associated cell lines have been determined (Table 2-2). Toxicity equivalence factors determined by Bol et al. (1989) for mortality following waterborne exposure of sac fry are nearly identical to those determined from RBT sac-fry mortality after egg injection (Walker and Peterson 1991; Zabel et al. 1995a). Egg injection has been shown for lake trout to produce the same TCDD dose-response as maternal or waterborne routes of embryo exposure (Walker et al. 1994). Toxicity equivalence factors based on hepatic 7-ethoxyresorufin-O-deethylase activity (EROD) in RBT cell culture (Clemons et al. 1993, 1994) and aryl hydrocarbon hydroxylase (AHH) activity in juvenile RBT liver (Janz and Metcalfe 1991a; Harris et al. 1994) are larger than RBT early life-stage TEFs. In addition to RBT TEFs listed in Table 2-2, Wisk and Cooper (1990) and Janz and Metcalfe (1991a) calculated TEFs using embryo mortality in Japanese medaka, and Tillitt et al. (1992) determined TEFs in Poeciliopsis-Lucida hepatocellular carcinoma (PLHC) (top minnow) cell cultures. Hahn et al. (1996), using PLHC-1 fish hepatoma cells grown in multiwell plates, demonstrated that immunodetectable CYP1A protein measurements are less likely to overestimate

Table 2-1 PCDD, PCDF, and PCB congener concentrations in lake trout eggs (pg/g egg), early life-stage mortality TEFs, and TEs (TE_{egg} in pg TCDD eq/g egg) for Lake Ontario in 1991 and Lake Michigan in 1993

Chemical	Lake Ontario (pg/g egg)	Lake Michigan (pg/g egg)	RBT ELS TEF pg chemical/pg TCDD equivalent	Lake Ontario lake trout egg TCDD TE_{egg}	Lake Michigan lake trout egg TCDD TE_{egg}
2,3,7,8-TCDD	6.03	0.7	1	6.03	0.7
2,3,7,8-TCDF	5.83	11	0.030	0.175	0.330
1,2,3,7,8-PeCDD	0.7	1.6	0.659	0.461	1.054
1,2,3,7,8-PeCDF	2.61	1.4	0.032	0.084	0.045
2,3,4,7,8-PeCDF	4.6	3.5	0.340	1.564	1.190
1,2,3,4,7,8-HxCDD	<.8	<.8	0.263	<.210	<.210
1,2,3,6,7,8-HxCDD	<.8	<.8	0.020	<.016	<.016
1,2,3,4,7,8-HxCDF	1.6	<1	0.240	0.384	<.24
1,2,3,4,6,7,8-HpCDD	<.8	<1	0.0015	<.001	<.002
PCB 28+31	9800	11000	<.000009	<.088	<.099
PCB 52	14900	9000	<.000007	<.104	<.063
PCB 77	997	1813	0.00018	0.179	0.326
PCB 81	46	133	0.00062	0.028	0.082
PCB 105	9760	27000	<.000002	<.020	<.054
PCB 118	39000	49000	≤.000003	<.117	<.147
PCB 126	356	350	0.0049	1.744	1.715
PCB 128	9200	8000	<.000001	<.009	<.008
PCB 138+163	94000	53000	<.000001	<.094	<.053
PCB 153		61000	0	0	0
PCB 156+171+202	8700	3900	<.000001	<.009	<.004
PCB 169	17	9	0.00003	0.0005	0.0003
PCB 170+190	20000	12000	<.000004	<.08	<.048
MIN –MAX TEC_{egg}				10.47–11.21	5.44–6.38

Maximum TECs (MAX TEC_{egg}) are based on inclusion of TE_{egg} detection limits associated with nondetection of either congener concentrations in eggs or mortality in RBT early life stage (ELS) exposures.

congener potency than EROD activity which tends to have attenuation of response as congener concentration is increased.

Rank order of PCDD, PCDF, and PCB congener potencies are generally similar between test systems. Toxicity equivalence factors for PCB congeners are much lower in fish than those originally proposed for human health risk assessment (Safe 1990); however, DeVito et al. (1993) suggested that TEFs for PCBs that are appropriate for human health risk assessment may actually be similar to fish-specific TEFs shown in Table 2-2. Although mono-orthochlorinated PCBs such as #105 and #118 did not produce detectable TCDD-like toxicity in trout sac fry (Zabel et al. 1995a), they did induce detectable P4501A activity in vitro in RBT liver cell cultures (Clemons et al. 1996) as found in vivo in mouse livers (Birnbaum and DeVito 1995) and in vitro in rat H4IIE cell cultures (Tillitt et al. 1991). Since inducible P4501A

Table 2-2 Toxicity equivalence factors for PCDD, PCDF, and PCB congeners based on early life-stage mortality in RBT, induction of monooxygenase activity in vivo or in liver cell cultures, mRNA expression in RBT gonad cell cultures,[a] and expert opinion for human health risk assessment

	Early life-stage (ELS) mortality		P4501A activity in vivo		P4501A activity/expression in vitro			Human health risk assessment	
Congener	RBT egg exposure	RBT sac-fry[c] exposure	RBT liver EROD	Mouse liver[g] EROD	RBT liver EROD	RBT gonad[k] mRNA	Rat H4IIE EROD	Safe[m]	WHO[n]
PCDDs									
2,3,7,8-TCDD	1.0[a]	1.0	1.0[d,e,f]	1.0	1.0[h,i,j]	1.0	1.0[h,j]	1.0	1.0
1,2,3,7,8-PeCDD	0.659[a]	0.77	1.8[d]	0.5	2.6[h]	1.56	1.1[h]	0.5	0.5
1,2,3,4,7,8-HxCDD	0.263[a]		0.4[d]		1.1[h]	0.1	0.5[h]	0.1	0.1
1,2,3,6,7,8-HxCDD	0.020[b]		0.4[d]		0.2[h]	0.058	0.2[h]	0.1	0.1
1,2,3,4,6,7,8-HpCDD	0.0015[b]		0.05[d]		0.2[h]	0.031	0.1[h]	0.01	0.01
PCDFs									
2,3,4,7,8-PeCDF	0.339[a]	0.35	2.0[d]	0.1	1.9[h]	0.5	0.4[h]	0.5	0.5
1,2,3,4,7,8-HxCDF	0.240[a]		0.4[d]		1.1[h]	0.36	0.3[h]	0.1	0.1
1,2,3,7,8-PeCDF	0.032[a]		0.4[d]	0.01	0.2[h]	0.093	0.2[h]	0.05	0.05
2,3,7,8-TCDF	0.030[a]		0.5[d]	0.01	0.2[h]	0.5	0.03[h]	0.1	0.1
Non-Ortho-Cl PCBs									
3,3',4,4',5-PeCB (#126)	0.0049[a]		0.002[e]	0.02	0.2[i]	0.056	0.022[l]	0.1	0.1
3,4,4',5-TCB (#81)	0.00062[b]		0.004[f]			0.0084			
3,3',4,4'-TCB (#77)	0.00018[a]		0.005[e]	0.00001	0.003[i]	0.0094	0.000018[l]	0.01	0.0005
3,3',4,4',5,5'-HxCB (#169)	0.00004[b]			0.001	0.003[i]	0.00074	0.00047[m]	0.05	0.01
Ortho-Cl PCBs									
2,4,4'-TriCB (#28)	<0.000009[b]								
2,3',4,4',5-PeCB (#118)	<0.000003[b]			0.00001	0.00002[j]	<0.00001	0.000001[l]	0.0001	0.0001
2,3,3',4,4'-PeCB (#105)	<0.000002[b]			0.000001	0.00005[j]	<0.00001	0.000008[l]	0.001	0.0001
2,3,3',4,4',5-HxCB (#156)	<0.000001[b]			0.000001	0.00003[j]	0.000008		0.001	0.0005

[a] Walker and Peterson 1991. Exposure using egg injection. TEFs here are adjusted to mass equivalence ratios from molar equivalence ratios reported
[b] Zabel et al. 1995a. Exposure using egg injection. TEFs here are adjusted to mass equivalence ratios from molar equivalence ratios reported.
[c] Bol et al. 1989. Based on waterborne exposure of sac fry.
[d] Parrott et al. 1995.
[e] Janz and Metcalfe 1991a.
[f] Harris et al. 1994.
[g] Birnbaum and DeVito 1995
[h] Clemons et al. 1994
[i] Clemons et al. 1993
[j] Clemons et al. 1996
[k] Zabel et al. 1996.
[l] Tillitt et al. 1991.
[m] Safe 1990.
[n] Ahlborg et al. 1994.

activity from exposure to mono-orthochlorinated PCBs occurs at doses equal to or greater than those attained in the RBT sac-fry tests (Zabel et al. 1995a), these congeners may be toxic to trout sac fry at greater doses.

Zabel et al. (1995a) sought to determine if the lower potency of coplanar (non-orthochlorinated) PCBs and the inability to detect mortality in fish from mono-orthochlorinated PCBs is due to faster elimination of these congeners during early life-stage development. Two PCDD, two PCDF, and four PCB congeners (#77, 126, 105, and 118) were injected into RBT eggs, and congener concentrations were measured 3 times during development using congener-specific HRGC/HRMS. Poly-chlorinated biphenyl congeners were eliminated from RBT early life stages to a similar extent as PCDD and PCDF congeners. Congener retention at the middle of the sac-fry stage was 78 to 88% for PCBs versus 62 to 91% for PCDDs and PCDFs. Thus, increased elimination of PCBs relative to PCDDs and PCDFs is not responsible for the lower potency of the non-orthochlorinated biphenyl congeners for causing RBT early life-stage mortality and the failure of the mono-orthochlorinated biphenyl congeners to elicit this response.

Even though lake trout is the primary fish species thought to be at risk in the Great Lakes, most fish-specific TEFs have been determined in RBT. Zabel et al. (1995b) sought to compare the relative potency for one important congener (PCB 126) between RBT and lake trout for causing early life-stage mortality. They deter-mined a TEF of 0.003 for PCB 126 in causing lake trout sac-fry mortality, which is similar to the RBT early life-stage TEF of 0.005 (Walker and Peterson 1991). This suggests that the relative potencies of congeners are similar between RBT and lake trout despite the fact that lake trout are more sensitive to toxicity caused by this class of congeners.

Toxicity of PCDD, PCDF, and PCB congener pairs

A major assumption of the TEF method is that congeners act additively to produce toxicity. If congeners do not act additively as assumed, more complex models may be necessary for the use of TEFs in risk assessments. In order to determine whether congeners act additively to produce toxicity, researchers have studied the toxicity of pairs of PCDD, PCDF, and PCB congeners in RBT. Janz and Metcalfe (1991b) found evidence of synergism between PCB 77 and TCDD at a ratio of 53:1 for causing AHH induction in RBT liver after an intraperitoneal (i.p.) injection. Bol et al. (1989) also found synergism between these 2 congeners at ratios from 1,200:1 to 40,000:1 for causing sac-fry toxicity using waterborne exposure. In this same study, several pairs of PCDDs and PCDFs acted additively. Newsted et al. (1995) saw synergism between PCB 77 and TCDD at several ratios and antagonism between PCB 126 and TCDD at a ratio of 200:1 for causing EROD and CYP1A protein induction in RBT liver after i.p. injection. Zabel et al. (1996) observed that PCDD and PCDF pairs acted additively for causing RBT sac-fry mortality after egg injection (Table 2-3), while PCB 77 and TCDD showed synergism at ratios of 3,500:1 and 4,500:1, and PCB 126 and TCDD showed synergism at a ratio of 400:1. Differences from additivity were less than risk assessment safety factors of 10-fold. The non-TCDD-like congener 2,2',4,4',5,5'-hexachlorobiphenyl (PCB 153) and TCDD showed a trend, although not statistically significant, toward antagonism at the highest injected dose of 5,000:1. This ratio is much lower than the ratio found in Great Lakes lake trout of approximately 100,000:1.

Table 2-3 Summary of types of responses observed for pairs of PCDD, PCDF, and PCB congeners in causing RBT early life-stage mortality at various congener dose ratios injected into eggs[a]

Congener pair[b]		Statistical analysis of full dose response data[c]		Isobolographic analysis of LD50s[d]	
		Type of action	P value	Dose ratio deviating from additivity	Type of action
1,2,3,7,8-PCDD	TCDD	Additive	$p = 0.012$	None	Additive
2,3,4,7,8-PCDF	1,2,3,7,8-PCDD	Additive	$p = 0.022$	None	Additive
2,3,7,8-TCDF	2,3,4,7,8-PCDF	Additive	$p = 0.016$	None	Additive
2,3,4,7,8-PCDF	TCDD	Additive	$p = 0.023$	None	Additive
PCB 77	PCB 126	Additive	$p = 0.059$	None	Additive
PCB 105	TCDD	Additive	$p = 0.014$	None	Additive
PCB 153	TCDD	Additive	$p = 0.82$	None	Additive
PCB 105	PCB 126	Additive	$p = 0.56$	None	Additive
PCB 118	PCB 126	Additive	$p = 0.34$	None	Additive
PCB 126	TCDD	Nonadditive	$p < 0.001$	400:1	Synergistic
PCB 77	TCDD	Nonadditive	$p < 0.001$	1,250:1 3,500:1 4,500:1	Antagonistic Synergistic Synergistic

[a] Adapted from Zabel et al. (1995c).
[b] Congener abbreviations: PCB 77 (3,3′,4,4′-tetrachlorobiphenyl), PCB 118 (2,3′,4,4′,5-pentachlorobiphenyl), PCB 126 (3,3′,4,4′,5-pentachlorobiphenyl), PCB 105 (2,3,3′,4,4′-pentachlorobiphenyl), PCB 153 (2,2′,4,4′,5,5′-hexachlorobiphenyl), 1,2,3,7,8-PCDD (1,2,3,7,8-pentachlorodibenzo-p-dioxin), 2,3,7,8-TCDF (2,3,7,8-tetrachlorodibenzofuran), 2,3,4,7,8-PCDF (2,3,4,7,8-pentachlorodibenzofuran), TCDD (2,3,7,8-tetrachlorodibenzo-p-dioxin)
[c] P-values were derived using an SAS program which determines the importance of the interaction between congeners when modelling the dose response data for congeners alone and congener pair mixtures in a probit model (Gennings et al. 1990). A test of the model's interaction terms as a group was performed and $p < 0.01$ was considered to be sufficiently strong evidence of a deviation from additivity (Zabel et al. 1995b).
[d] Ratios deviating from additivity were determined using isobolographic analysis (Gessner 1974). Ratios were considered to deviate from additivity if the 95% fiducial limits of the ratio's LD50 overlap the expected "additivity" line.

From the studies described above, a tendency for PCB 77 and TCDD to act synergistically is apparent. Other congener pairs appear to act additively or show no consistent pattern of synergism or antagonism. These differences, although slight and equivocal, may have to be taken into account in ecological risk assessments for fish exposed to PCDDs, PCDFs, and PCBs, especially when PCBs are the predominant fraction of the TEC.

Toxicity of a PCDD, PCDF, and PCB mixture
Walker et al. (1996) investigated the toxicity to trout sac fry of a complex mixture of TCDD-like PCDD, PCDF, and PCB congeners at ratios found in feral lake trout eggs from Lake Michigan. Trout early life-stage mortality was used as the assessment endpoint to determine how accurately the toxicity of the mixture could be

predicted with TEFs based on potency for causing RBT early life-stage mortality (Walker and Peterson 1991; Zabel et al. 1995a) and the additive TCDD toxicity equivalence model. Fertilized lake trout eggs were exposed via water either to [^{3}H]-TCDD or a complex mixture of 4 PCDD, 4 PCDF, and 3 non-ortho PCB congeners, 2 mono-ortho PCB congeners (#105 and 118), and 1 di-ortho PCB congener (#153) at ratios similar to those in Lake Michigan lake trout (Table 2-1). The resulting concentration of [^{3}H]-TCDD was determined using liquid scintillation counting and concentrations of all chemicals in the complex mixture were determined by HRGC/HRMS for lake trout eggs. Rainbow trout eggs were exposed to graded doses of TCDD or the congener mixture by injection (Walker et al. 1992). Because the injected doses were known, concentrations of TCDD or the mixture chemicals in the RBT eggs were not measured.

The TCDD TEC$_{egg}$ associated with each graded dose of the mixture of 14 congeners was calculated according to Equation 2-1. In RBT and lake trout early life stages, the complex congener mixture caused the same signs of toxicity as TCDD with the same time-course of development. The egg dose-sac fry mortality response curves for TCDD and the congener mixture, with egg dose expressed as TEC$_{egg}$, were parallel, suggesting that the mixture acts via the same mechanism as TCDD alone (Walker et al. 1996). For both species, however, the LD50 for the mixture with dose expressed as TEC$_{egg}$ was reported to be significantly greater ($p <$ 0.05) than that for TCDD alone. Rainbow trout LD50s were 200 pg TCDD/g egg and 362 pg TCDD TE/g egg, and lake trout LD50s were 74 pg TCDD/g egg and 97 pg TCDD TE/g egg for TCDD alone and the congener mixture, respectively, suggesting a slightly less than additive response for the combination of congeners. The slight deviation from additivity observed for lake trout is not significant if the lake trout-specific TEF for PCB 126 of 0.003 (Zabel et al. 1995b) is used to calculate TEC$_{egg}$ for the mixture.

If the relatively small degree of less than additive toxicity to RBT from the mixture is not due to experimental variability, it may be due to the presence of large concentrations of non-TCDD-like PCB congeners #105, 118, and 153 relative to the TCDD-like congeners. Antagonism between TCDD and PCB 153 has been reported in mammalian studies (Biegel et al. 1989; Morrissey et al. 1992), but significant differences from additivity were not seen in a RBT early life-stage mortality study of pairs of these congeners when injected together in varying dose ratios into eggs (Zabel et al. 1995). Walker et al. (1996) observed that PCB 153, which was at much greater concentrations in the complex mixture relative to TCDD, may have acted as a competitive antagonist for *Ah* receptor binding and thereby slightly reduced toxic potency of TCDD and other congeners in the mixture at each dose level.

Retrospective assessment of lake trout early life-stage survival in Lake Ontario and Lake Michigan

Validation of the toxicity equivalence approach can be facilitated by examination of the accuracy of retrospective predictions of effects on fish populations from exposures to complex mixtures of TCDD and related chemicals. Bioaccumulation factors are needed in order to relate past environmental concentrations of TCDD and related chemicals to concentrations in fish eggs which are the dosimetric for prediction of early life-stage mortality. Sediment-based bioaccumulation factors, such as the biota-sediment accumulation factor (BSAF), allow measured concentrations of TCDD and related chemicals in the environment to be used to predict concentrations in eggs when direct analysis is not possible (Cook et al. 1993). A BSAF is the ratio of the lipid-normalized concentration of a chemical in tissue (C_ℓ) to the organic carbon-normalized concentration in sediment (C_{soc}). Since trout early life-stage mortality has been evaluated on a whole egg, rather than lipid-normalized basis, and trout eggs do not vary significantly in fraction of lipid (f_ℓ), a TEC based on whole egg (TEC_{egg}) may be calculated with congener-specific BSAFs for eggs $(BSAF_{egg}s)$:

$$TEC_{egg} = \sum_{i=1}^{n} \left[(C_{soc})_i \ (BSAF_{egg})_i \ (f_\ell) \ (TEF)_i \right]$$ (2-2).

In such calculations of TEC_{egg} from sediment data, BSAFs account for differences in metabolism and bioavailability, and TEFs account for differences in toxic potency of each congener. The TEC_{egg} may be directly compared to the TCDD dose-mortality response data for the species in order to estimate toxicity risks from environmental exposures.

When reliable historical data for concentrations of TCDD and related chemicals in fish eggs are not available, $TEC_{egg}s$ can be predicted from radionuclide-dated sediment core sections from reference sites in the ecosystem. Retrospective risk assessment with trout early life-stage mortality TEFs and site, species, and lake trout egg-specific BSAFs indicates that prior to 1960 in Lake Ontario, lake trout exposures to TCDD and related chemicals probably contributed to the decline and virtual extinction of lake trout populations in Lake Ontario (Cook et al. 1994; Cook et al. 1997). Similar predictions of lake trout sac-fry mortality in Lake Ontario during the period of 1978-1984 from $TEC_{egg}s$ agree well with measured rates of blue-sac mortality (Symula et al. 1990).

Since 1990, continued gradual decrease in exposures to lake trout in both Lake Ontario and Lake Michigan have resulted in $TEC_{egg}s$ of known *Ah* receptor agonists well below the lake trout sac-fry mortality no-observed-effect level (NOEL) of 30 pg TCDD/g egg. Table 2-1 summarizes the chemical concentrations measured in eggs and TEFs used to calculate $TEC_{egg}s$. Polychlorinated dibenzo-*p*-dioxins, PCDFs, and PCBs 77, 81, 105, 118, 126, 153, and 169 were measured by HRGC/HRMS (Guiney et al. 1996). Polychlorinated biphenyls 28, 52, 128, 138, 156, and 170 were measured by GC/ECD with co-eluting congeners listed in Table 2-1. Detection limits for chemical concentrations in eggs and sac-fry mortality in TEF determinations were used to calculate maximum (assuming untested *Ah* receptor agonists are present at concentrations too small to be significantly toxic) $TEC_{egg}s$. Despite below detection $TE_{egg}s$ for more than half of the congeners, the inclusion of TE_{egg} detection limits in the TEC_{egg} calculation resulted in only slight increase in the $TEC_{egg}s$.

The primary difference between Lake Michigan and Lake Ontario lake trout eggs is the 9-fold greater exposure to TCDD in Lake Ontario. The detectable TEC_{egg} without TCDD is 4.9 pg TCDD equivalent/g egg in both lakes. Both Lake Ontario and Lake Michigan lake trout eggs have $TEC_{egg}s$ less than the 30 pg TCDD/g egg

NOEL for early life-stage mortality from blue-sac syndrome. The estimated TEC_{egg} of 10.5 pg TCDD toxicity equivalent/g in the 1991 Lake Ontario lake trout eggs did not produce a detectable incidence of blue-sac disease mortality (Guiney et al. 1996). However, when eggs from these same fish were exposed to graded doses of TCDD, blue sac syndrome-associated mortality was observed at the same doses as for lake trout eggs from Lake Superior or a hatchery which has much smaller TEC_{egg}s. The similar TCDD dose-related responsiveness of the Lake Ontario lake trout sac fry to TCDD exposure indicated that chronic sublethal exposure of Great Lakes lake trout to TCDD and related chemicals does not provide resistance to toxicity from subsequent exposure to TCDD as was reported for *Fundulus heroclitus* collected from a TCDD contaminated bay (Prince and Cooper 1995).

Specific sublethal effects of TCDD and related chemicals that could reduce feral lake trout survival and reproduction have not been investigated. Lake Ontario lake trout reproduction and population monitoring studies in the past 10 years have noted a progression of improvements in survival of sac fry (Marsden and Krueger 1991) and juvenile lake trout (Schneider et al. 1995) which suggests that recruitment through survival of lake trout from natural reproduction may soon return after more than a 50-year absence. The capability for natural lake trout reproduction does not appear to have been lost in Lake Superior during the same period despite problems with lamprey predation. TEC_{egg}s in Lake Superior lake trout eggs presently are less than 0.5 pg TCDD TE/g egg (Guiney et al. 1996) and probably did not exceed 5 pg TCDD TE/g egg in the past. The Lake Superior history and observations of increased lake trout early life-stage survival in Lake Ontario indicate that reduction of TEC_{egg}s in lake trout eggs to less than 5 pg TCDD TE/g egg will probably insure future survival of young lake trout from natural reproduction in the Lake Ontario and Lake Michigan ecosystems if other developmental problems encountered by salmonid species in the Great Lakes, such as swim-up syndrome, are not critical.

Comparison of lake trout sac-fry mortality predictions using different TEFs

The extent to which TEFs are similar across species and across endpoints within a species is uncertain. At this time, use of trout early life-stage TEFs for assessment of possible chemical etiologies for lack of trout early life-stage survival is a uniquely direct and rigorous application of the toxicity equivalence approach. Since much uncertainty remains for application of TEFs to other species and effects, it is informative to examine alternative predictions of trout early life-stage mortality obtained from application of TEFs which are less specifically based on the organism and toxic effect. Eggs of lake trout in Lake Michigan contain a mixture of PCDDs, PCDFs, and PCBs which is typical of many contaminated aquatic ecosystems in contrast to the TCDD-rich mixture in Lake Ontario (Cook et al. 1994). Toxicity equivalence factor sets which include dioxin-like PCB congener potencies are required for a meaningful comparison of total TCDD TE predictions. TEC_{egg}s calculated from alternative sets of TEFs presented in Table 2-2 and PCDD, PCDF, and PCB concentrations (Table 2-1) in eggs collected from feral lake trout from Lake Ontario in 1991 and from Lake Michigan in 1993, are compared in Figure 2-2. All of the alternative TEFs are based on biochemical responses. There does not appear to be a significant difference between TEC_{egg}s predicted from in vivo versus in

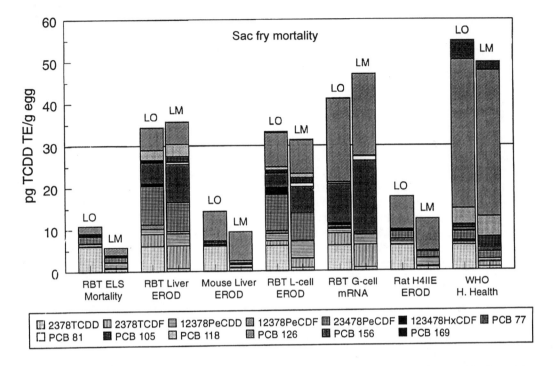

Figure 2-2 TCDD TEs and TECs in 1991 Lake Ontario lake trout eggs and 1993 Lake Michigan lake trout eggs as determined with TEFs based on RBT early life-stage mortality, EROD activity in RBT livers, EROD activity in mouse livers, EROD activity in RBT liver cell cultures, CYP1A mRNA expression in RBT gonad cell cultures, EROD activity in rat H4IIE cell cultures, and WHO expert opinion values. TECs less than 30 pg TCDD toxicity equivalents/g egg indicate low risk of lake trout sac-fry mortality due to blue-sac syndrome.

vitro EROD TEFs, either for RBT liver or rodent liver. The 3 sets of RBT biochemical response-based TEFs, which predict $TEC_{egg} > 30$ pg TCDD toxicity equivalents/g egg in either Lake Ontario or Lake Michigan lake trout eggs, probably provide a false positive prediction of mortality in 1991 to lake trout sac fry prior to swim-up. However, each of the 6 predictions of TEC_{egg} in lake trout eggs from independent sets of TEFs differ by less than a factor of 10 despite the disparate species and effects used to measure the TEFs.

The RBT early life-stage mortality TEFs predict a Lake Michigan lake trout TEC_{egg} of 6 pg TCDD toxicity equivalents/g egg of which TCDD accounts for only 12%. In contrast, the Lake Ontario lake trout eggs have a TEC_{egg} of 11 pg TCDD toxicity equivalents/g egg of which TCDD contributes 55%. The 2-fold difference between Lake Michigan and Lake Ontario trout early life-stage TEC_{egg}s is not predicted by any of the alternative TEFs which are all based on biochemical effects. The differences between TEC_{egg}s calculated from chemical concentrations in Great Lakes' lake trout eggs and each TEF set seem to be attributable to TEF differences for a few key chemicals. Polychlorinated biphenyl 126 (3,3',4,4',5-pentachlorobiphenyl) and 2,3,4,7,8-pentachlorodibenzofuran are most notable. The TEC_{egg}s are very sensitive to the TEF used for PCB 126. None of the experimentally derived PCB 126 TEFs reviewed here support the World Health Organization (WHO) estimate of the PCB 126 TEF which is 20 times the RBT early life-stage TEF. The WHO TEFs thus predict a TEC_{egg} in both lakes which is nearly equal to the TCDD LD50 for lake trout sac-fry mortality.

Conclusions

Application of TEFs with an additive toxicity equivalence model is an important component of both human health and ecological risk assessments of PCDD, PCDF, and PCB congeners that act via an *Ah* receptor mediated mechanism. Initially, mammalian TEFs, which were based on in vitro biochemical responses (Safe 1994), appeared to be up to 3 orders of magnitude different from TEFs determined for fish early life-stage mortality. For this reason, fish-specific TEFs such as those determined in RBT early life stages (Walker and Peterson 1991; Zabel et al. 1995a) were developed for accurate ecological risk assessments involving fish exposed to complex mixtures of TCDD-like PCB, PCDD, and PCDF congeners. Although the use of early life-stage mortality specific TEFs and the TE_{egg} additivity model predicts that PCDDs, PCDFs, and PCBs in Great Lakes lake trout are currently below levels that cause early life-stage mortality (Cook et al. 1994), in agreement with recent observations of juvenile lake trout survival, uncertainties for general use of TEFs remain. Some of the uncertainties are 1) whether all toxic congeners are accounted for, 2) whether all congeners act additively to produce TCDD-like effects in fish, 3) whether TEFs are species-specific or endpoint-specific, and 4) the basis for perceived differences in relative congener potencies between in vivo and in vitro assays (e.g., the lack of detectable toxicity from mono-ortho PCBs in trout sac fry in contrast to P4501A activity in mammalian tests).

Most pairs of TCDD-like congeners or TCDD-like congeners paired with non-TCDD-like congeners cause additive toxicity. Small differences from additivity have been seen for the congener pair PCB 77 and TCDD for causing various responses in RBT, and a complex congener mixture acted slightly less than additively in causing early life-stage toxicity in RBT (Walker et al. 1996). The greatest deviations from additivity in these studies (less than 2-fold for LD50s) were less than safety factors that may be applied in risk assessments.

Zabel, Walker et al. (1995) showed that the TEF for PCB 126 in producing lake trout early life-stage mortality is similar to the TEF for the same response in RBT. These results are significant because they suggest that TCDD-like congeners show similar relative potencies in RBT and lake trout and support both the use of RBT TEFs in assessments of risks to lake trout and, perhaps, other fish species. While the agreement in TEFs for PCB 126 between trout species is encouraging, further comparisons of TEFs for other potent congeners and more disparate fish species are needed.

A comparison of TEC_{egg}s determined for lake trout eggs in Lakes Michigan and Ontario using different sets of TEFs indicates that all TEFs, regardless of species or endpoints used, would provide protection if used for screening risks for trout early life-stage mortality. It is not clear why TEFs based on enzyme induction tend to be greater than trout early life-stage TEFs for some key chemicals such as PCB 126.

This may be due to artifacts in the methods used to calculate the TEFs (e.g., variation in a chemical's potency relative to TCDD associated with nonparallel dose-response curves) or, most likely, intrinsic differences in potency associated with differences in mechanism of action between biochemical and organismal levels of effects. When considering these possibilities, it is remarkable that TEFs based on widely different species, dosimetry, effects, and measurements are so similar.

Tetrachlorodibenzo-*p*-dioxin and related compounds, at concentrations below those that produce mortality, may affect various organ systems (immune, reproductive, nervous) to cause functional alterations that seriously compromise fish survival. Thus, impacts on survival or reproductive potential from post-swim-up effects induced by embryo and/or chronic early life-stage exposures to TCDD and related chemicals should be investigated. Ecological factors and chemical, physical, and biological stressors could interact with sublethal exposures to *Ah* receptor agonists to influence fish physiology and survival. The extent to which sublethal effects of TCDD and related chemicals have contributed to lack of recruitment by reintro-duced Great Lakes lake trout populations during the past 2 decades is still un-known, yet sublethal developmental, neurobehavioral, reproductive, and immune system effects in mammals are known to occur at TCDD doses which are orders of magnitude less than lethal doses. Should sublethal effects that impact survival of fish be identified, TEFs will have to be selected for use in ecological risk assess-ments on the basis of potencies of congeners for the sublethal effects, as previ-ously demonstrated for trout early life-stage mortality.

Other polychlorinated, polybrominated, and brominated/chlorinated congeners of dibenzo-*p*-dioxins, dibenzofurans, diphenyl ethers, biphenyls, etc. that act through the same *Ah* receptor mechanism as TCDD may be present in Great Lakes fish or could be inadvertently introduced in the future. Chemical formulations used to control sea lamprey predation on lake trout in the Great Lakes were recently found through a toxicity identification evaluation (TIE) approach to contain TCDD-like impurities, which induce P450IA activity in fish (Hewitt et al. 1996). Also, there may be interactions of PCDDs, PCDFs, and PCBs with other chemicals that bioaccu-mulate in feral fish and act through different mechanisms, such as mercury and dichlorodiphenyldichlorethylene (DDE). For these reasons, the risk posed by PCDDs, PCDFs, and PCBs to lake trout early life stages remains a concern.

It is important that future research address the remaining uncertainties for risk assessments which involve exposure of fish to TCDD and related chemicals. The extent and basis for species and life stage differences in sensitivity to TCDD and related compounds, including whether structure-activity relationships are similar across species and life stages, are poorly understood. Toxicity equivalence factors could be significantly response-specific in some cases if the TE model does not accommodate differences in bioavailability to tissue sites of action. The *Ah* receptor has been cloned from fish (Hahn and Karchner 1995) and, specifically, RBT (Abnet et al. 1996) and is homologous with birds and mammals. However, it is unknown whether all ecologically relevant effects of TCDD and related compounds in fish are mediated through the *Ah* receptor. It is presumed that effects of these com-pounds are associated with this receptor, as they are in mammals, but definitive proof is not available for fish. The background *Ah* receptor activity should be assessed by identifying the endogenous ligand for this receptor and the normal range of responses mediated by it.

Acknowledgments

We would like to thank Brian Butterworth and Marta Lukasewycz of the USEPA and John Libal of Integrated Laboratory Systems for HRGC/HRMS analyses of feral lake trout egg samples. We would also like to recognize the work of Dr. Mary Walker, University of Wisconsin, who provided a strong foundation for the use of TEFs in aquatic ecological risk assessment. Portions of this research were funded by U.S. Environmental Protection Agency Cooperative Agreement CR819065-02-0. The views of the authors do not necessarily reflect the views of the USEPA, and no official endorsement should be inferred.

References

Abnet C, Markwardt D, Heideman W, Hahn M, Pollenz R, Peterson R. 1996. Cloning of the rainbow trout AhR and Arnt: mechanistic examination of interspecies differences in sensitivity to AhR agonists. *Soc Environ Toxicol Chem Abstracts* 17:425.

Ahlborg UG, Becking GC, Birnbaum LS, Brouwer A, Derks HJGM, Feeley M, Golor G, Hanberg A, Larsen JC, Liem D, Safe SH, Schlatter C, Younes M, Yrjänheikki E. 1994. Toxic equivalency factors for dioxin-like PCBs. *Chemosphere* 28:1049–1067.

Biegel L, Harris M, Davis D, Rosengren R, Safe L, Safe S. 1989. 2,2′,4,4′,5,5′-hexachlorobiphenyl as a 2,3,7,8-tetrachlorodibenzo-*p*-dioxin antagonist in C57BL/65J mice. *Toxicol Appl Pharmacol* 97:561–571.

Birnbaum LS, DeVito MS. 1995. Use of toxic equivalency factors for risk assessment for dioxins and related compounds. *Toxicol* 105:391–402.

Bol J, van den Berg M, Seinen W. 1989. Interactive effects of PCDD's, PCDF's and PCB's as assessed by the E.L.S.-bioassay. *Chemosphere* 19:899–906.

Carey AE, Shifrin NS, Cook PM. 1990. Derivation of a Lake Ontario bioaccumulation factor for 2,3,7,8-TCDD. New York NY: U.S. Environmental Protection Agency (USEPA) Region II. Chapter 9, Lake Ontario TCDD bioaccumulation study: final report.

Clemons JH, van den Heuvel MR, Dixon DG, Bols NC. 1993. Comparison of toxic equivalent factors derived with rainbow trout, RTL-W1 and rat, H4IIE cell lines for polychlorinated biphenyls (PCBs). *Soc Environ Toxicol Chem Abstracts* 14:280.

Clemons JH, van den Heuvel MR, Stegeman JJ, Dixon DG, Bols NC. 1994. A comparison of toxic equivalent factors for selected dioxin and furan congeners derived using fish and mammalian liver cell lines. *Can J Fish Aquat Sci* 51:1577–1584.

Clemons JH, Lee LEJ, Myers CR, Dixon DG, Bols NC. 1996. Cytochrome P4501A1 induction by poly-chlorinated biphenyls (PCBs) in liver cell lines from rat and trout and the derivation of toxic equivalency factors (TEFs). *Can J Fish Aquat Sci* 53:1177–1185.

Cook PM, Kuehl DW, Walker MK, Peterson RE. 1991. Bioaccumulation and toxicity of TCDD and related compounds in aquatic ecosystems. Plainview NY: Cold Spring Harbor Pr. Banbury Report 35: Biological basis for risk assessment of dioxins and related compounds. p 143–167.

Cook PM, Erickson RJ, Spehar RL, Bradbury SP, Ankley GT. 1993. Interim report on data and methods for assessment of 2,3,7,8-tetrachlorodibenzo-p-dioxin risks to aquatic life and associated wildlife. Duluth MN: U.S. Environmental Protection Agency (USEPA). EPA/600/R-93/055.

Cook PM, Butterworth BC, Walker MK, Hornung MW, Zabel EW, Peterson RE. 1994. Lake trout recruit-ment in the Great Lakes: relative risks for chemical-induced early life stage mortality. *Soc Environ Toxicol Chem Abstracts* 15:58.

Cook PM, Endicott DD, Robbins JA, Marquis PJ, Berini C, Libal JJ, Kizlauskis A, Guiney PD, Walker MK, Zabel EW, Peterson RE. 1997. Effects of polychlorinated aromatic chemicals with an Ah receptor mediated mode of early life stage toxicity on lake trout reproduction in Lake Ontario: retrospective and prospective risk assessments. In preparation.

DeVito MJ, Maier WE, Diliberto JJ, Birnbaum LS. 1993. Comparative ability of various PCBs, PCDFs and TCDD to induce cytochrome P-450 1A1 and 1A2 activity following 4 weeks of treatment. *Fund Appl Toxicol* 20: 125–130.

DeVito MJ, Birnbaum LS. 1995. The importance of pharmacokinetics in determining the relative potency of 2,3,7,8-tetrachlorodibenzo-p-dioxin and 2,3,7,8-tetrachlorodibenzofuran. *Fund Appl Toxicol* 24: 145–148.

Eshenroder RL, Poe TP, Olver CH. 1984. Strategies for rehabilitation of lake trout in the Great Lakes: Proceedings of a conference on lake trout research; 1983 Aug. Ann Arbor MI: Great Lakes Fish Comm Tech Rep 40. p 1–63.

Fitzsimons JD, Huestis S, Williston B. 1996. Occurrence of a swim-up syndrome in Lake Ontario lake trout in relation to contaminants and cultural practices. *J Great Lakes Res* 21 (Supplement 1):277–285.

Gennings C, Carter Jr WH, Campbell ED, Staniswalis JG, Martin TJ, Martin BR, White Jr KL. 1990. Isobolographic characterization of drug interactions incorporating biological variability. *J Pharmacol Exp Therap* 252:208–217.

Gessner PK. 1974. The isobolographic method applied to drug interactions. In: Morselli PL, Garattini S, Cohen SN, editors. Drug interactions. New York NY: Raven Pr. p 349–362.

Guiney PD, Cook PM, Casselman JM, Fitzsimons JD, Simonin HA, Zabel EW, Peterson RE. 1996. Assessment of 2,3,7,8-tetrachlorodibenzo-p-dioxin (TCDD)-induced sac fry mortality in lake trout (*Salvelinus namaycush*) from different regions of the Great Lakes. *Can J Fish Aquat Sci* 53:2080–2092.

Hahn ME, Poland A, Glover E, Stegeman JJ. 1992. The Ah receptor in marine animals: phylogenetic distribution and relationship to cytochrome P450IA inducibility. *Mar Environ Res* 34:87–92.

Hahn ME, Karchner SI. 1995. Evolutionary conservation of the vertebrate Ah (dioxin) receptor: amplification and sequencing of the PAS domain of a teleost Ah receptor cDNA. *J Biochem* 310: 383–387.

Hahn ME, Woodward BL, Stegeman JJ, Kennedy SW. 1996. Rapid assessment of induced cytochrome P450IA protein and catalytic activity in fish hepatoma cells grown in multiwell plates: response to TCDD, TCDF, and two PCBs. *Environ Toxicol Chem* 15:582–591.

Harris GE, Kiparissis Y, Metcalfe CD. 1994. Assessment of the toxic potential of PCB congener 81 (3,4,4,5-tetrachlorobiphenyl) to fish in relation to other non-ortho-substituted PCB congeners. *Environ Toxicol Chem* 13:1405–1413.

Hewitt LM, Servos MR, Scott IM, Carey JH, Munkittrick KR. 1996. Use of a MFO-directed toxicity identification evaluation to isolate and characterize bioactive contaminants from a lampricide formulation. *Environ Toxicol Chem* 15:894–905.

Janz DM, Metcalfe CD. 1991a. Relative induction of aryl hydrocarbon hydroxylase by 2,3,7,8-TCDD and two coplanar PCBs in rainbow trout (*Onchorhynchus mykiss*). *Environ Toxicol Chem* 10:917–923.

Janz DM, Metcalfe CD. 1991b. Nonadditive interactions of mixture of 2,3,7,8-TCDD and 3,3,4,4 - tetrachlorobiphenyl on aryl hydrocarbon hydroxylase induction in rainbow trout (*Onchorhynchus mykiss*). *Chemosphere* 23:467–472.

Kuehl DW, Butterworth BC, Libal JJ, Marquis PJ. 1991. An isotope dilution high resolution gas chromatographic-high resolution mass spectrometric method for the determination of coplanar polychlorinated biphenyls: applications to fish and marine mammals. *Chemosphere* 22:849–858.

Kuehl DW, Butterworth BC, Marquis PJ. 1994. A national study of chemical residues in fish. III: Study results. *Chemosphere* 29:523–535.

Mac MJ, Edsall CC, Seelye JG. 1985. Survival of lake trout eggs and fry reared in water from the upper Great Lakes. *J Great Lakes Res* 11:520–529.

Mac MJ, Schwartz TR, Edsall CC, Frank AM. 1993. Polychlorinated biphenyls in Great Lakes lake trout and their eggs: relations to survival and congener composition 1979–1988. *J Great Lakes Res* 19:752–765.

Marsden JE, Kreuger CC. 1991. Spawning by hatchery-origin lake trout (*Salvelinus namaycush*) in lake Ontario: data from egg collections, substrate analysis, and diver observations. *Can J Fish Aquatic Sci* 48:2377–2384.

Marquis PJ, Hackett M, Holland LG, Larsen ML, Butterworth B, Kuehl DW. 1994. Analytical methods for a national study of chemical residues in fish. I. Polychlorinated dibenzo-p-dioxins/dibenzofurans. *Chemosphere* 29:495–508.

Morrissey RE, Harris MW, Diliberto JJ, Birnbaum LS. 1992. Limited PCB antagonism of TCDD-induced malformations in mice. *Tox Lett* 60:19–25.

Newsted JL, Giesy JP, Ankley GT, Tillitt DE, Crawford RA, Gooch JW, Jones PD, Denison MS. 1995. Development of toxic equivalency factors for PCB congeners and the assessment of TCDD and PCB mixtures in rainbow trout. *Environ Toxicol Chem* 14:861–871.

Parrott JL, Hodson PV, Servos MR, Huestis SL, Dixon DG. 1995. Relative potency of polychlorinated dibenzo-*p*-dioxins and dibenzofurans for inducing mixed-function oxidase activity in rainbow trout. *Environ Toxicol Chem* 14:1041–1050.

Prince R, Cooper KR. 1995. Comparisons of the effects of 2,3,7,8-tetrachlorodibenzo-p-dioxin on chemically impacted and nonimpacted subpopulations of *Fundulus heteroclitus*: I. TCDD toxicity. *Environ Toxicol Chem* 14:579–587.

Safe S. 1990. Polychlorinated biphenyls (PCBs), dibenzo-*p*-dioxins (PCDDs), dibenzofurans (PCDFs), and related compounds: environmental and mechanistic considerations which support the development of toxic equivalency factors (TEFs). *Crit Rev Toxicol* 21:51–88.

Safe S. 1994. Polychlorinated biphenyls (PCBs): environmental impact, biochemical and toxic responses, and implications for risk assessment. *Crit Rev Toxicol* 24:87–149.

SAS Institute Inc. 1988. Additional SAS/STAT™ procedures, Release 6.03. Cary NC: SAS Institute. SAS[R] Technical Report P-179.

Schneider CP, Eckert TH, Elrod JH, O'Gorman R, Owens RW, Schaner T. 1995. Lake trout rehabilitation in Lake Ontario, 1994. Albany NY: New York Department of Environmental Conservation (NY DEC). Section 7, NY DEC annual report to the Lake Ontario Committee and the Great Lakes Fishery Commission.

Spitsbergen JM, Walker MK, Olson JR, Peterson RE. 1991. Pathological alterations in early life stages of lake trout, *Salvelinus namaycush*, exposed to 2,3,7,8-tetrachlorodibenzo-p-dioxin as fertilized eggs. *Aquat Toxicol* 19:41–72.

Stahl UB, Kettrup A, Rozman K. 1992. Comparative toxicity of four chlorinated dibenzo-p-dioxins (CDDs) and their mixture. Part I: acute toxicity and toxic equivalency factors (TEFs). *Arch Toxicol* 66:471–477.

Symula J, Meade J, Skea JC, Cummings L, Colquhoun JR, Dean HJ, Miccoli J. 1990. Blue-sac disease in Lake Ontario lake trout. *J Great Lakes Res* 16:41–52.

Tillitt DE, Giesy JP, Ankley GT. 1991. Characterization of the H4IIE rat hepatoma cell bioassay as a tool for assessing toxic potency of planar halogenated hydrocarbons in environmental samples. *Environ Sci Technol* 25:87–92.

Tillitt DE, Cantrell SE. 1992. Planar halogenated hydrocarbon (PHH) structure-activity relationship in a teleost (PLHC) cell line. *Soc Environ Toxicol Chem Abstracts* 13:45.

Tysklind M, Tillitt D, Erikson L, Lundgren K, Rappe C. 1994. A toxic equivalency factor scale for poly-chlorinated dibenzofurans. *Fund Appl Toxicol* 22:277–285.

[USEPA] U.S. Environmental Protection Agency. 1992. National study of chemical residues in fish. Washington DC: USEPA. EPA 823-R-92-008a.

Walker MK, Peterson RE. 1991. Potencies of polychlorinated dibenzo-*p*-dioxin, dibenzofuran and biphenyl congeners, relative to 2,3,7,8-tetrachlorodibenzo-*p*-dioxin for producing early life stage mortality in rainbow trout (*Onchorhynchus mykiss*). *Aquat Toxicol* 21:219–238.

Walker MK, Spitsbergen JM, Olson JR, Peterson RE. 1991. 2,3,7,8-Tetrachlorodibenzo-*p*-dioxin (TCDD) toxicity during early life stage development of lake trout (*Salvelinus namaycush*). *Can J Fish Aquat Sci* 48:875–883.

Walker MK, Hufnagle LC, Clayton MK, Peterson RE. 1992. An egg injection method for assessing early life stage mortality of polychlorinated dibenzo-p-dioxins, dibenzofurans, and biphenyls in rainbow trout (*Onchorhynchus mykiss*). *Aquat Toxicol* 22:15–38.

Walker MK, Cook PM, Batterman AR, Butterworth BC, Berini C, Libal JJ, Hufnagle LC, Peterson RE. 1994. Translocation of 2,3,7,8-tetrachlorodibenzo-*p*-dioxin from adult female lake trout (*Salvelinus namaycush*) to oocytes: effects on early life stage development and sac fry survival. *Can J Fish Aquat Sci* 51:1410–1419.

Walker MK, Peterson RE. 1994a. Aquatic toxicity of dioxins and related chemicals. In: Schecter A, editor. Dioxins and health. New York NY: Plenum Pr.

Walker MK, Peterson RE. 1994b. Toxicity of 2,3,7,8-tetrachlorodibenzo-p-dioxin to brook trout (*Salvelinus fontinalis*) during early life stage development. *Environ Toxicol Chem* 13:817–820.

Walker MK, Cook PM, Butterworth BC, Zabel EW, Peterson RE. 1996. Potency of a complex mixture of polychlorinated dibenzo-*p*-dioxin, dibenzofuran and biphenyl congeners compared to 2,3,7,8-tetrachlorodibenzo-*p*-dioxin in causing fish early life stage mortality. *Fund Appl Toxicol* 30:178–186.

Wisk JD, Cooper KR. 1990. Comparison of the toxicity of several polychlorinated dibenzo-*p*-dioxins and 2,3,7,8-tetrachlorodibenzofuran in embryos of the Japanese medaka (*Oryzias latipes*). *Chemosphere* 20:361–377.

Zabel EW, Cook PM, Peterson RE. 1995a. Toxic equivalency factors of polychlorinated dibenzo-*p*-dioxin, dibenzofuran and biphenyl congeners based on early life stage mortality in rainbow trout (*Onchorhynchus mykiss*) *Aquat. Toxicol* 31:315–328.

Zabel EW, Cook PM, Peterson RE. 1995b. Potency of 3,3,4,4,5-Pentachlorobiphenyl (PCB 126), alone and in combination with 2,3,7,8-tetrachlorodibenzo-*p*-dioxin (TCDD), to produce lake trout early life stage mortality. *Environ Toxicol Chem* 14:2175–2179.

Zabel EW, Walker MK, Hornung MW, Clayton MK, Peterson RE. 1995. Interactions of polychlorinated dibenzo-*p*-dioxin, dibenzofuran and biphenyl congeners for producing rainbow trout early life stage mortality. *Toxicol Appl Pharmacol* 134:204–213.

Zabel EW, Pollenz R, Peterson RE. 1996. Relative potencies of individual polychlorinated dibenzo-p-dioxin, dibenzofuran, and biphenyl congeners and congener mixtures based on induction of cytochrome P450IA mRNA in a rainbow trout gonadal cell line (RTG-2L). *Environ Toxicol Chem* 12:2310–2318.

Zacharewski TL, Safe S, Chittim B, DeVault D, Wiberg K, Bergquist PA, Rappe C. 1989. Comparative analysis of polychlorinated dibenzo-p-dioxin and dibenzofuran congeners in Great Lakes fish extracts by gas chromatography: mass spectrometry and in vitro enzyme induction activities. *Environ Sci Technol* 23:730–735.

Mechanisms of chemical interference with reproductive endocrine function in sciaenid fishes

Peter Thomas, Izhar A. Khan

Teleost reproduction is controlled primarily by hormones secreted by the hypothalamus–pituitary–gonadal (HPG) axis. Chemicals potentially can act at numerous sites on the HPG axis and by a variety of mechanisms to alter hormone secretion, action, or metabolism and disrupt reproductive function. Some mechanisms of endocrine disruption that have been identified in Atlantic croaker (*Micropogonias undulatus*) are discussed. Evidence is presented that Kepone (chlordecone) can exert estrogenic effects at the liver to stimulate vitellogenesis in vitro by binding to the hepatic estrogen receptor. Other in vitro studies show that cadmium can act directly at the pituitary and at the ovary to stimulate hormone secretion. These results indicate that the stimulatory effect of cadmium on gonadal steroidogenesis is mediated by activation of the adenylate cyclase second messenger system. Finally, we show that impairment of reproductive function in male croaker after chronic exposure to lead in vivo is associated with a lack of pituitary response to stimulation by luteinizing-hormone releasing hormone (LHRH). Interestingly, the decline in gonadotropin secretion was accompanied by decreases in the hypothalamic content of serotonin, a neurotransmitter that has been shown to augment the gonadotropic response to LHRH in this species. Taken together, these results suggest that lead impairs reproductive function by disrupting the serotonergic system in the hypothalamus that regulates gonadotropin secretion. We conclude that chemicals can act via a variety of mechanisms to disrupt reproductive endocrine function in teleosts.

Teleost reproduction is a complex process involving extensive physiological coordination which is primarily controlled by the hormones secreted by the hypothalamus–pituitary–gonadal (HPG) axis. Environmental stimuli (e.g., photoperiod and temperature) are detected by sense organs (Figure 3-1, Site 1) which relay this information to the hypothalamus, a major integration center in the brain, resulting in alterations in the release of neurotransmitters such as serotonin (Khan and Thomas 1992) and γ-aminobutyric acid (GABA) (Trudeau and Peter 1995) in specific hypothalamic nuclei (Figure 3-1, Site 2). The neurotransmitters modulate the synthesis and secretion of a decapeptide, gonadotropin-releasing hormone (GnRH) from neurosecretory hypothalamic neurons which in turn regulate the secretion of 2 glycoprotein hormones, gonadotropins I and II (GtH I and GtH II) from the pituitary (Figure 3-1, Site 3). Other forms of GnRH have been identified in other brain regions in teleosts and probably have different functions (Gothilf et al. 1995). Inhibitory pathways (gonadotropin release-inhibiting factors [GRIFs] e.g., dopaminergic) are also present in some teleost species (Trudeau and Peter 1995). Both the stimulatory and inhibitory pathways have nerve endings directly on the pituitary gonadotrops to regulate gonadotropin secretion. Binding of GnRH to specific receptors on the gonadotrops activates the phosphoinositol calcium-dependent second messenger pathway and possibly other signal transduction systems to stimulate gonadotropin release (Chang and Jobin 1994). The 2 gonadotropins are released into the circulation in response to GnRH stimulation and act via specific receptors at the gonads (Figure 3-1, site 4) to stimulate the production of steroid hormones and to induce gametogenesis, follicular development, ovulation or spermiation, and ultimately gamete release.

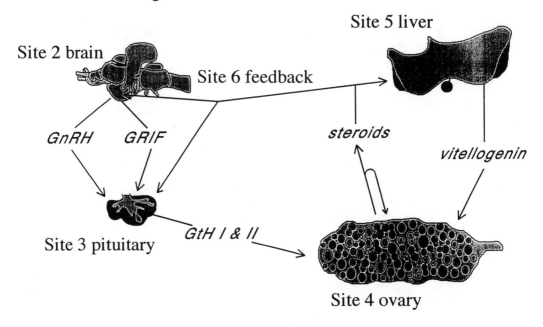

Site 1 sense organs

Site 5 liver

Site 2 brain

Site 6 feedback

GnRH   GRIF

steroids

vitellogenin

Site 3 pituitary

GtH I & II

Site 4 ovary

Figure 3-1 Potential sites of chemical interference with reproductive endocrine function in female teleosts (redrawn from Thomas 1990, with permission).
Site 1. Sense organs: Eyes, pineal, olfactory organs, etc.
Site 2. Brain: Hypothalamic areas - neurotransmitters and neuropeptides
Site 3. Pituitary: Gonadotrops - GtH I and GtH II
Site 4. Ovary: Oocytes, ovarian follicles , steroidogenic cells
Site 5. Liver: Hepatocytes - estrogen receptors, VTG (yolk precursor protein)
Site 6. Feedback by gonadal steroids at hypothalamus and pituitary. GnRH-gonadotropin-releasing hormone. GRIF - gonadotropin release-inhibiting factor. Steroids: estradiol (E2) and testosterone (T) in either sex; 11-KT, a male specific androgen in fish; 17α,20b-dihydroxy-4-pregnen-3-one and 17α,20β-21—trihydroxy-4-pregnen-3-one, maturation-inducing steroids (MIS) in fish. E2 binds to estrogen receptors in the liver to induce VTG production. Vitellogenin is sequestered by the growing oocytes to form yolk. The MIS acts on oocytes to induce final oocyte maturation. E2, T, and 11-KT feedback at the hypothalamus and pituitary to influence GtH release.

Several lines of evidence suggest that GtH I controls earlier stages of the reproductive cycle in salmonid fishes whereas GtH II controls the final maturational and events prior to spawning. It has been shown that plasma GtH I levels in several salmonid species are elevated during oocyte growth and spermatogenesis whereas GtH II levels are very low at this time (Swanson 1991). Plasma GtH II levels increase dramatically during final oocyte maturation and spermiation at the same time as plasma GtH I levels decline. Gonadotropins activate several second messenger pathways upon binding to specific receptors on steroidogenic cells in teleost gonads, although the adenylate cyclase system and calcium appear to be of primary importance in mediating the steroidogenic actions of gonadotropin (Van Der Kraak and Wade 1994). During early stages of the reproductive cycle when the gonads are growing rapidly, gonadotropin (presumably GtH I in most teleost species) stimulates the synthesis and release of estradiol and testosterone from follicle cells in females and 11-ketotestosterone (11-KT) and testosterone in males (Fostier et al. 1983). These steroid hormones exert their reproductive effects by binding to specific nuclear receptors in target tissues (Smith and Thomas 1990).

A major function of estradiol is regulation of vitellogenin (VTG) (yolk precursor protein) and lipoprotein production in the liver (Figure 3-1, Site 5). In addition, estradiol exerts both negative and positive feedback effects on gonadotropin secretion at the brain and pituitary (Figure 3-1, Sites 2 and 3). Testosterone through aromatization to estradiol also enhances pituitary responsiveness to GnRH (Figure 3-1, Site 3). Other ovarian factors such as inhibin also influence gonadotropin secretion. The steroid feedback modulation of GnRH function may involve specific neurotransmitter neurons (interneurons) which contain steroid receptors to influence GnRH synthesis and/or release because GnRH neurons themselves lack steroid receptors. Gonadal steroids also have paracrine actions (act on nearby cells) in the gonads (Figure 3-1, Site 4), and high receptor concentrations have been detected in these tissues (e.g., Smith and Thomas 1990). For example, the androgens testosterone and 11-KT have important functions in the hormonal regulation of spermatogenesis. Plasma estrogen levels decline in many teleost species after ovarian and oocyte growth is complete. When the conditions are suitable for spawning, a surge in maturational gonadotropin secretion causes a switch in the steroidogenic pathway from estrogen and androgen synthesis to the ovarian production of a maturation-inducing steroid (17,20β-dihydroxy-4-pregnen-3-one or 17,20β,21-trihydroxy-4-pregnen-3-one in most species), which by binding to its receptor on GtH II-primed oocytes (Figure 3-1, Site 4) leads to final oocyte maturation. These steroids also are produced in males immediately prior to spawning and stimulate milt production and sperm motility.

Chemicals can possibly exert their effects at multiple sites on the HPG axis and by several mechanisms to interfere with reproductive endocrine function (Figure 3-1; Mattison et al. 1983; Thomas 1990; Van Der Kraak et al. 1992). Chemicals may be detected as noxious by peripheral sense organs (Figure 3-1, Site 1) or directly interfere with neural activity by altering neurotransmitter function (Figure 3-1, Site 2; Seegal et al. 1986; Khan and Thomas 1996). Alterations in hypothalamic neurotransmitter activity could influence GnRH secretion. Changes in the secretion of GnRH would secondarily affect secretion of gonadotropin from the pituitary (Figure 3-1, Site 3; Cicero et al. 1977). Alternatively certain chemicals can act directly at the pituitary to influence signal transduction systems and gonadotropin secretion (Cooper et al. 1987; Thomas 1993). Chemically induced changes in gonadotropin secretion result in altered gonadal steroid secretion and gonadal function (Figure 3-1, Site 4; Thomas 1989). Certain chemicals have also been shown to act directly on the gonads to disrupt second messenger systems and steroidogenic enzymes (Singhal et al. 1985; Phelps and Laskey 1989; Sangalang and O'Halloran 1973; Van Der Kraak et al. 1992). Increased metabolic clearance of steroids due to induction of hepatic P-450 enzymes (Figure 3-1, Site 5) would also alter plasma steroid levels and steroid function (Sivarajah et al. 1978; Yano and Matsayama 1986). Alterations in steroid levels in the blood will have profound effects on reproductive function, e.g., hepatic estrogen receptor levels and VTG production in fish. Changes in the circulating levels of gonadal steroids can secondarily influence neuroendocrine function by steroid feedback mechanisms in the hypothalamus and pituitary (Figure 3-1, Site 6). Steroid function can also be altered directly by chemicals which act as steroid agonists or antagonists by binding to steroid receptors (Bulger and Kupfer 1985; Huang and Nelson 1986; Thomas and Smith 1993). Thus, chemically induced changes in endocrine function at one level of the HPG axis will ultimately result in alterations in the activity of other levels of the axis. The overall complexity of the reproductive endocrine system, the integrated nature of its response to environmental stimuli, and the wide variety of potential chemical effects have complicated investigations of the primary sites and mechanisms of chemical interference with reproductive endocrine function and its detection in fish populations.

In this paper some sites and mechanisms of xenobiotic interference with the HPG axis identified in the Atlantic croaker (*Micropogonias undulatus*) and spotted seatrout (*Cynoscion nebulosus*), marine perciform fishes belonging to the same family (Sciaenidae), are discussed. Estrogenic and antiestrogenic actions of an organochlorine, Kepone, on VTG production by liver slices (Figure 3-1, Site 5) are described. Kepone is estrogenic in mammals (Bulger and Kupfer 1985) and binds to the estrogen receptor in spotted seatrout (Thomas and Smith 1993). Cadmium and lead, representatives of another major class of reproductive toxicants (Mattison et al. 1983), disrupt endocrine function in Atlantic croaker at environmentally realistic concentrations (Thomas 1988; Thomas 1989). Results of in vitro studies demonstrate that cadmium can exert direct actions both at the pituitary and gonads to alter signal transduction systems and hormone secretion (Figure 3-1, Sites 3 and 4). Finally, evidence is provided that lead, which is neurotoxic, can disrupt neuroendocrine function and gonadotropin secretion in croaker by altering neurotransmitter function (Figure 3-1, Site 2).

Materials and Methods

Estrogenic actions of chlordecone (Kepone)
Livers were collected from adult female spotted seatrout at a midpoint of ovarian recrudescence when vitellogenesis is maximal (Smith and Thomas 1990) for both the estrogen receptor competition assays and the in vitro liver slice vitellogenesis bioassay.

Estrogen receptor competition studies
Hepatic tissues for the competition studies were stored at −80°C for up to 3 months prior to assay. The competition assays with Kepone were conducted by the same method as that used to establish steroid hormone specificity in seatrout liver tissues (Thomas and Smith 1993) using assay protocols developed and previously validated for estrogen receptor measurement in this species (Smith and Thomas 1990). Chlordecone (Kepone) was dissolved in ethanol and added to the liver cytosolic preparations (ethanol: <0.1% final assay volume) over a range of concentrations (10^{-9} to 10^{-4} M) at the same time as the radiolabelled steroid (4 nM per tube) and incubated for 24 hours before separation of bound from free with dextran-coated charcoal. The amount of ethanol added to the assay buffer did not interfere with the measurement of [^{3}H] estradiol binding.

In vitro vitellogenesis bioassay

Livers were sliced (1- to 2-mm thick) and the slices (approx. 50 mg) were incubated for 2 hours in 1 mL Dulbecco's modified Eagles medium (DMEM) in 48-well microtiter plates (Copeland and Thomas 1988). At the end of the preincubation period, the medium was replaced with 1 mL DMEM alone or in the presence of 0.07, 0.35, and 1.75 nM estradiol, and 0.1 mM Kepone or combinations of the two for 24 hours at 24°C under an atmosphere of oxygen. The incubation was stopped by placing the microtiter plates in an ice-bath, and the media was removed and frozen for subsequent direct VTG measurement in a homologous seatrout radioimmunoassay (RIA) (Copeland and Thomas 1988).

Cadmium interference with signal transduction systems at pituitary and gonads

Pituitary gonadotropin secretion

Direct actions of cadmium at the pituitary level of the HPG axis were investigated in an in vitro pituitary tissue perifusion system (Thomas 1993). Croaker hemipituitaries were placed in a perifusion chamber and perifused with DMEM at a flow rate of 1 mL/minute for 6 hours. The pituitaries were exposed to pulses of cadmium (0.1M, equivalent to 11.2 ppt) or luteinizing hormone-releasing hormone (LHRHa 100 ng/mL). Fractions (5 to 10 mL) were collected for GtH II measurement by a homologous RIA (Copeland and Thomas 1989a).

Ovarian steroidogenesis

Direct effects of cadmium on steroidogenesis and cyclic 3',5'-adenosine monophosphate (cAMP) content in spotted seatrout ovaries were examined in an in vitro incubation system (Singh and Thomas 1993). Ovarian fragments from vitellogenic females were incubated in culture media (DMEM) containing a wide range of cadmium concentrations (0.01 to 1000 ppm; equivalent to 0.09 μM to 9 mM). Media were collected after 9 hours and 18 hours of incubation for measurement of testosterone and estradiol, respectively, by direct RIAs (Singh and Thomas 1993). In a parallel experiment, ovarian tissue was removed after 1 hours incubation with cadmium for measurement of cAMP by the protein binding method of Gilman (1970).

Alteration of neuroendocrine function by lead

Experimental animals

Atlantic croaker were collected at the beginning of the reproductive season in August–September and acclimated to laboratory conditions in large recirculating seawater tanks under simulated natural photoperiod and constant temperature (24 $\pm$ 1°C) for at least one month prior to the experiments. All the fish were in the early stages of their gonadal recrudescence when the exposure was started, and the control fish had fully developed (spermiating) testes when the experiment was terminated.

Experimental protocols

Two groups of 25 male fish, each weighing 50 to 60 g, were fed a diet containing lead chloride (0.5 or 1.5 mg Pb/100 g body weight/day) for 30 days, and a third group of 25 control fish was fed an uncontaminated diet for 30 days. Lead chloride was mixed with a diet of ground shrimp and commercial fish pellets. Croaker thrive on this diet, and no decline in food intake was observed during the course of this experiment. Fish were fed 3% of their body weight of contaminated food followed by another 2% of the control food in the treatment group (a total of 5% of the body weight/day). Intestinal uptake of lead from the diet is probably the major site of accumulation in this benthic estuarine species (Somero et al. 1977). Lead concentrations in croaker livers are approximately 2 ppm, after 30 days feeding 1.2 mg Pb/100g body weight/day (Thomas and Juedes 1992). Lead concentrations are frequently greater than 2 ppm in the tissues of environmentally exposed fish (Sorensen 1991). The doses were selected based on an earlier study in croaker where the higher dose of lead significantly impaired gonadal recrudescence in female fish (Thomas 1988). At the end of the exposure period, 10 to 12 fish from each experimental group were sacrificed within 15 seconds of capture to minimize handling stress, and their brains were rapidly excised and frozen on dry ice before storage in a −80° freezer. The remaining fish were anesthetized, and blood was collected from the caudal vein with heparinized syringes. The sampling was completed between 9:00 and 11:00 hours to avoid diurnal variations in the selected parameters. Gonadal tissues were weighed, and gonadosomatic indices (GSIs) were calculated as gonad weight × 100 / (body weight − gonad weight). Pituitaries were removed and transferred to the incubation medium on ice for subsequent determination of in vitro GtH release.

Determination of biogenic amines and their metabolites

The frozen brain samples were dissected on ice with the aid of a croaker brain atlas (Khan and Thomas 1993) to remove the hypothalamic regions including the preoptic-anterior hypothalamic area (POAH) and the medial and posterior hypothalamus (MPH). The concentrations of biogenic amines (epinephrine [E], norepinephrine [NE], dopamine [DA], and serotonin [5-HT]) and their major metabolites (3,4-dihydroxyphenylacetic acid [DOPAC], 3-methoxytyramine [3-MT], homovanillic acid [HVA], 5-hydroxytryptophan [5-HTP], and 5-hydroxyindolacetic acid [5-HIAA]) were determined by the method of Saligaut et al. (1986) and validated for croaker brain tissues (Khan and Thomas 1996).

Pituitary GtH release in vitro

Pituitary fragments of the control and exposed fish were pre-incubated for one hour and then incubated for 12 hours in 1 mL DMEM (pH 7.6) at 20° in the presence or absence of LHRHa (20 ng/mL media) as described previously (Copeland and Thomas 1989a). The GtH II concentration in the incubation media was measured with a homologous RIA (Copeland and Thomas 1989a).

Plasma steroid levels

Plasma was obtained by centrifugation and stored at −80° until analyzed for testosterone (T) and 11-KT by RIA procedures described previously (Singh et al. 1988).

Statistical analyses
Data were analyzed by analysis of variance (ANOVA) followed by Tukey's HSD for comparison of group means. Significance was tested at the 0.05 level.

Results and Discussion

Estrogenic effects of Kepone

Kepone effectively competed with [^{3}H]-estradiol for binding to the estrogen receptor in spotted seatrout and caused a concentration-dependent displacement of [^{3}H]-estradiol at the higher concentrations tested (10^{-3} M; Figure 3-2a). The relative binding affinity of Kepone was approximately 0.01% that of estradiol and diethylstilbestrol (DES) (10,000 × less affinity for the receptor).

The accumulation of VTG in the incubation media from liver slices incubated for 24 hours with 1.75 nM estradiol was 4-fold greater than that of controls ($P < 0.05$; Figure 3-2b), whereas lower estradiol concentration did not significantly stimulate vitellogenesis. Kepone alone at a concentration of 10^{-4} M also significantly stimulated vitellogenesis. However, Kepone significantly decreased the vitellogenic response to estradiol (1.75 mM) when added together with the estrogen (Figure 3-2b).

The finding that Kepone binds to the seatrout liver cytosolic estrogen receptor with an affinity approximately 0.01% that of estradiol confirms our earlier results using a different solvent carrier system (Thomas and Smith 1993). A similar relative binding affinity of Kepone has been reported for the chicken oviduct estrogen receptor (0.02% that of estradiol, Eroschenko and Palmiter 1980), however, binding is 10 times higher to the rat estrogen receptor (Bulger and Kupfer 1985).

The vitellogenesis bioassay results show that Kepone can mimic the actions of estrogen and stimulate VTG production in vitro. Extensive investigations in birds and mammals have shown that Kepone clearly exerts estrogenic activities in these species (Eroschenko and Palmiter 1980; Bulger and Kupfer 1985; Reel and Lamb 1985). However, only weak estrogenic effects of Kepone have been reported in some target tissues (Reel and Lamb 1985), and the pesticide has been shown to have an antagonistic action on estrogen-induced augmentation of the gonadotropin response to GnRH in rat pituitary cells in in vitro culture (Huang and Nelson 1986). Our preliminary results indicate that Kepone can also antagonize the actions of estradiol in the in vitro vitellogenesis bioassay, suggesting a possible antiestrogenic action in this teleost model. Eroschenko and Palmiter have shown previously that although Kepone induces ovalbumin ribonucleic acid (mRNA) synthesis in chicken oviduct cultures, it antagonizes the action of estradiol on mRNA induction which these authors suggested was related to nonestrogenic toxic actions of the pesticide (Eroschenko and Palmiter 1980). Additional experiments with different doses of Kepone will be required to confirm its antagonistic actions on estrogen stimulation of vitellogenesis in seatrout and whether this is due to an antiestrogenic or a nonspecific toxic action of the organochlorine. A re-examination of the effects of Kepone on female sexual behavior in rats indicated that the inhibitory effect of the insecticide was unlikely to be mediated by binding to the estrogen receptor as earlier proposed but was due to alterations in neurotransmitter function

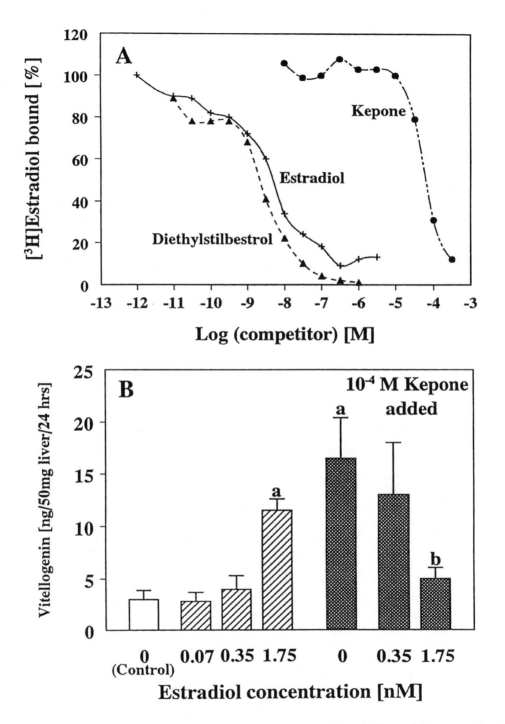

Figure 3-2 Competition of Kepone for seatrout estrogen receptor (A) and effects of Kepone on basal and estrogen-stimulated production of VTG from seatrout liver slices in vitro (B). a: Significantly different from controls. b: Significantly different from the group treated with the same dose of estradiol alone (P < 0.05).

(Brown et al. 1991). These studies suggest that nonestrogenic actions of weakly estrogenic xenobiotics should also be considered during investigations of the reproductive toxicity of these compounds.

Cadmium interference with signal transduction systems at the gonad and pituitary

At the ovarian level, cadmium caused a concentration-dependent stimulation of ovarian estradiol secretion and cyclic AMP accumulation and also enhanced testosterone secretion in vitro (Figures 3-3a, 3-3b, 3-3c). The lowest cadmium concentration tested, 0.01 ppm, significantly increased ovarian production of estradiol and testosterone but not cyclic AMP content. All 3 biochemical indices were significantly elevated over the range of cadmium exposures from 0.1 to 100 ppm. However, the stimulation of steroidogenesis and cyclic AMP content by cadmium was attenuated at the highest concentration (1000 ppm).

Secretion of gonadotropin from hemi-pituitaries perifused with DMEM alone was low (1 to 2 ng/mL) but increased dramatically by 10 to 25 ng/mL within 20 minutes of cadmium infusion (Figure 3-4). The pituitary fragments maintained their responsiveness to LHRHa stimulation after cadmium treatment and released large amounts of gonadotropin after infusion of the peptide (Figure 3-4).

The results of these in vitro experiments demonstrate that cadmium can exert direct effects both at the pituitary and gonad of sciaenid fishes to stimulate hormone secretion. An earlier study had shown that exposure of Atlantic croaker to 1 ppm cadmium in the water for 40 days at the beginning of ovarian recrudescence significantly accelerated ovarian growth and increased plasma estradiol concentrations (Thomas 1989). The increase in circulating estradiol levels was accompanied by approximately a 3-fold increase in the total ovarian production of estradiol in vitro. Spontaneous gonadotropin secretion from pituitary fragments of these cadmium-treated fish was also increased several-fold compared to controls (Thomas 1989). On the basis of these results, it was suggested that the stimulation of ovarian growth and steroidogenesis was due to increased gonadotropin secretion in the cadmium-treated fish. However, the present results suggest that cadmium may also act at the gonadal level to alter ovarian function.

Extrapolation of the concentration-response relationships established in these acute in vitro experiments to gonads and pituitaries chronically exposed to cadmium in vivo is complicated by a number of factors. For example, cadmium readily binds to lipoproteins in plasma, especially VTG (Ghosh and Thomas 1995a), thereby decreasing the concentration of free cadmium in the circulation. Pituitary exposure to the metal is likely to be reduced, whereas ovarian exposure will increase due to sequestration of the VTG-cadmium complex by the growing oocytes (Ghosh and Thomas 1995a). Despite these reservations, we propose that our findings have environmental relevance because steroidogenesis was altered by cadmium concentrations as low as 0.01 ppm and tissue burdens in the 0.1 to 10.0 ppm range have been reported in estuarine fish collected from contaminated environments (Shackley et al. 1981; Evans et al. 1993).

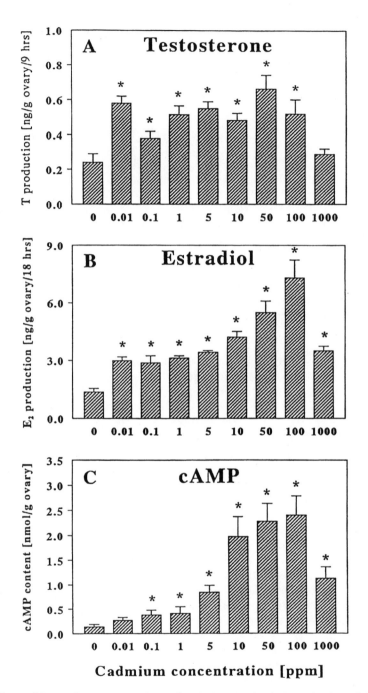

Figure 3-3 Effects of increasing concentrations of cadmium on in vitro production of (A) testosterone (B) estradiol and (C) cAMP accumulation by vitellogenic ovaries of spotted seatrout. Each bar represents the mean ± S.E. of 6 observations. Asterisks denote means significantly different from controls (P < 0.05, Newman Keul's multiple range 't' test).

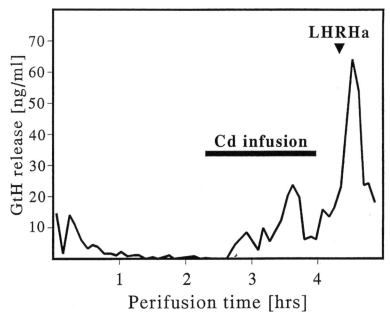

Figure 3-4 Representative profile of gonadotropin secretion from Atlantic croaker pituitaries perifused with DMEM with or without cadmium (50μM) or LHRHa (100 ng/mL). Reprinted from *Marine Environmental Research,* 35, P. Thomas, "Effects of cadmium on gonadotropin secretion from Atlantic croaker pituitaries incubated in vitro," p. 143, copyright 1993, with kind permission from Elsevier Science Ltd., The Boulevard, Langford Lane, Kidlington OX5 1GB, UK.

Stimulation of gonadal steroid production by cadmium was associated with elevations in the cyclic AMP content of seatrout ovarian tissues. Similar elevations of ovarian cyclic AMP concentrations were also observed after chronic exposure of croaker to cadmium in vivo (Thomas, unpublished). Thus both the in vitro and in vivo studies implicate the cyclic AMP second messenger system in mediating the disruptive effects of cadmium on ovarian function.

The involvement of cyclic AMP in the regulation of gonadal steroidogenesis has been clearly demonstrated in teleosts and other vertebrate species (e.g., Singh and Thomas 1993; Adashi and Resnick 1986). Overall there is a remarkable degree of conservation among vertebrates in the transduction systems that mediate the actions of gonadotropins on gonadal tissues (Van Der Kraak and Wade 1994). Calcium from both intracellular and extracellular pools is also intimately involved in gonadotropin actions in vertebrate gonadal tissues. Therefore, xenobiotics can potentially interfere with a variety of signal transduction systems to modulate the actions of gonadotropin. The elevation of cyclic AMP levels in seatrout ovaries may be due to increased biosynthesis of the cyclic nucleotide by adenylate cyclase, because cadmium has been shown to stimulate the activity of this enzyme in rat testes (Singhal 1981). Cadmium could also increase cyclic AMP levels and steroidogenesis by its well-known effects on calcium homeostasis and calmodulin activation (Singhal et al. 1985; Viarengo and Nicotera 1991). The attenuation of the cAMP increase with the highest cadmium concentration may be due to stimulation of phosphodiesterase activity as has been shown in rat testes (Singhal 1981) or possibly by inhibition of adenylate cyclase activity by high cadmium concentrations, as proposed for certain enzymes by Vallee and Ulmer (1972). Interestingly, stimulation of steroidogenesis by low concentrations of cadmium, zinc, cobalt, and nickel and inhibition at higher metal concentrations have also been shown with rat Leydig cells in vitro (Laskey and Phelps 1991). However a dose-dependent depression in both gonadotropin- and dibutyl-cyclic AMP-stimulated testosterone production was also observed in this in vitro system. Moreover, cadmium has been shown to depress reproductive function and steroidogenesis in a broad range of male vertebrate species including teleosts (Phelps and Laskey 1989; Sangalang and O'Halloran 1973). Therefore cadmium and some other metals stimulate or inhibit gonadal steroidogenesis in vertebrates depending on the dose and possibly sex of individuals.

The croaker pituitary perifusion results corroborate earlier findings with rat pituitaries that cadmium treatment significantly increases gonadotropin secretion in vitro (Cooper et al. 1987). Earlier in vivo studies had shown that cadmium treatment increases gonadotropin secretion from croaker pituitaries (Thomas 1989) and had caused superovulation in mammals (Mattison et al. 1983).

The signal transduction systems involved in stimulation of gonadotropin secretion by GnRH are broadly similar amongst the vertebrate groups (Chang and Jobin 1994). Binding of GnRH to its receptor activates phospholipase C producing inositol phosphates and diaglycerol and subsequently stimulating protein kinase C and possibly calmodulin. Calcium is also an ubiquitous mediator of gonadotropin secretion. Calcium is released from intracellular stores and enters the gonadotrops via voltage-sensitive calcium channels in both mammals and fish in response to GnRH (Naor 1990; Chang et al. 1993). Interestingly, we have found that the calcium channel blocker, verapamil, not only blocks the stimulatory effect of GnRH on gonadotropin secretion from croaker pituitaries, but also blocks the stimulatory effects of cadmium (Thomas, unpublished). In addition, the loss of the stimulatory effect of GnRH on gonadotropin secretion in calcium-free media is restored in the presence of cadmium. These results suggest that cadmium acts via calcium channels on gonadotrops to stimulate gonadotropin secretion and that it acts through the calcium-dependent component of the signal transduction system.

In conclusion, certain metals such as cadmium can interfere with hormone signaling pathways at multiple sites on the HPG axis to disrupt endocrine function. Likely sites of cadmium action include binding to cysteine and histidine residues of enzymes, replacement of zinc in metalloenzymes, and alterations of calcium homeostasis.

Alterations of neuroendocrine function by lead

No significant difference in the concentrations of the biogenic amines and their metabolites in the hypothalamic areas of croaker was observed except for a decline in 3-MT concentration with the higher dose of lead (Figure 3-5 and Figure 3-6). However, the 5-HIAA to 5-HT ratio was significantly higher (Figure 3-5), whereas that of 3-MT/DA was lower (Figure 3-7) in both the POAH and MPH of the exposed fish. The increase in the 5-HIAA/5-HT ratio was dose-related. The in vivo lead exposure significantly inhibited both basal and LHRHa-induced GtH II release from pituitary fragments in vitro (Figure 3-8). In addition, lead exposure resulted in

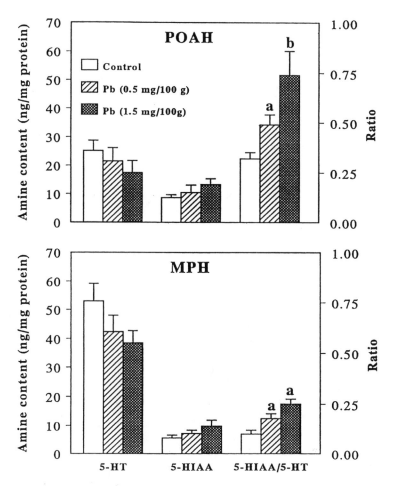

Figure 3-5 Lead-induced alterations in 5-HT metabolism in the POAH and MPH of croaker brain. Bars represent means ± standard error of the mean (SEM) of 10 to 12 observations. a: Significantly different from the respective control group. b: Significantly different from the low dose group.

a dose-related inhibition of gonadal recrudescence as evidenced by lower GSIs, and lower circulating T and 11-KT concentrations in the exposed fish (Figure 3-9).

The present study provides indirect evidence to support the hypothesis that the effects of lead on gonadotropin secretion may be partially mediated by altered hypothalamic serotonergic activity. Lead exposure in croaker blocks gonadal recrudescence of both sexes (Thomas 1988; present study). In addition, both basal and LHRHa-induced GtH release in vitro is impaired by prior exposure of the fish to lead in vivo. The impairment of GtH secretion is associated with a significant change in the metabolism of a key neurotransmitter, 5-HT, which is involved in the control of GtH secretion in fish (Somoza et al. 1988; Khan and Thomas 1992) and mammals (Vitale et al. 1986). These results point to a possible correlation between altered hypothalamic 5-HT metabolism and pituitary GtH secretion.

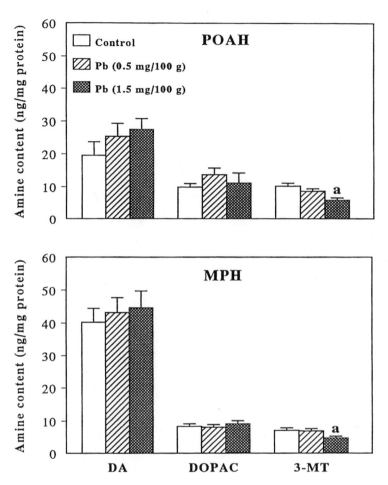

Figure 3-6 Lead-induced alterations in DA, 3,4-DOPAC and 3-MT concentrations in the POAH and MPH of croaker brain. Bars represent means ± SEM of 10 to 12 observations. a: Mean values significantly different from control group.

The levels of monoamine neurotransmitters and their metabolites are influenced by alterations in the key enzymes that control synthesis and metabolism of these neurotransmitters within the individual neurons. A schematic diagram showing the enzymatic conversion of 5-HT and DA to their major metabolites is presented in Figure 3-10. Although 5-HT or 5-HIAA concentrations were not significantly altered by lead exposure in the present study, they showed consistent dose-related trends with lower average 5-HT and higher 5-HIAA levels. Consequently, the 5-HIAA/5-HT ratio showed a significant increase in both the POAH and MPH in croaker exposed to lead which would indicate enhanced catabolism by monoamine oxidase (MAO) and/or reduced 5-HT synthesis. However, the fact that the DOPAC/DA ratio was not higher in the hypothalamic areas of the lead-exposed fish argues against increased MAO activity because a differential effect of lead on the same enzyme in 2 different neuronal populations in hypothalamic areas appears highly unlikely. Therefore, tryptophan hydroxylase, the rate limiting enzyme in 5-HT biosynthesis,

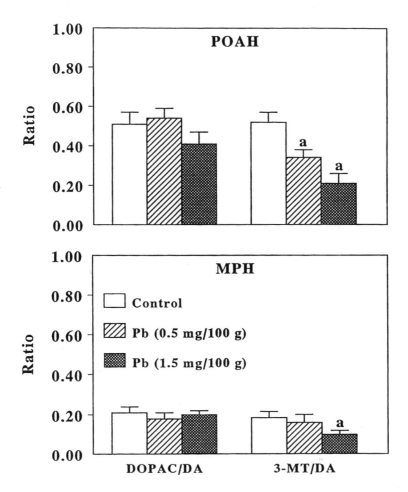

Figure 3-7 Lead-induced alterations in the DOPAC/DA and 3-MT/DA ratios in the POAH and MPH of croaker brain. Bars represent means ± SEM of 10 to 12 observations. a: Mean values significantly different from control group.

could be the principal target of lead-induced impairment of hypothalamic 5-HT metabolism. A previous study with croaker exposed to Aroclor 1254 showed a marked increase in the 5-HIAA/5-HT and DOPAC/DA ratios and a decrease in 5-HT and DA concentrations in the hypothalamic areas of polychlorinated biphenyl (PCB)-exposed fish (Khan and Thomas 1996). Therefore, the change in 5-HT metabolism in the case of Aroclor 1254 could be due to both enhanced oxidative deamination by MAO and reduced 5-HT synthesis. These studies suggest that different classes of xenobiotics can alter neurotransmitter metabolism by a variety of mechanisms and thereby disrupt neuroendocrine function.

The lead-induced increase in the 5-HIAA/5-HT ratio was more pronounced in the POAH, which contains predominantly the 5-HT nerve terminals, than in the MPH where most of the cell bodies are located (Khan and Thomas 1993). We have previously shown that 5-HT potentiates the stimulatory effect of LHRHa on GtH

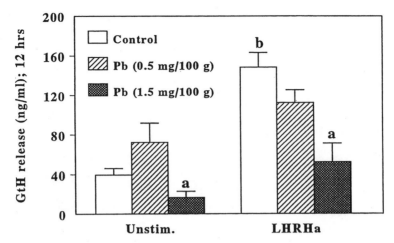

Figure 3-8 In vitro GtH release in response to an LHRH analog (LHRHa) from the pituitaries of the control and lead-exposed fish. Bars represent means ± SEM of 10 to 12 observations. a: Mean values significantly different from the respective control groups. b: Significantly different from the unstimulated control group.

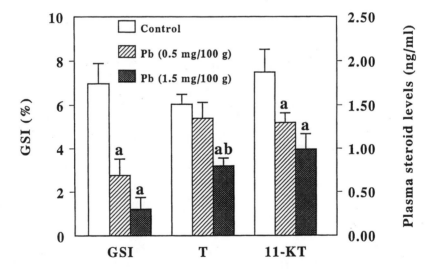

Figure 3-9 Lead-induced alterations in GSI and plasma testosterone (T) and 11-KT levels in Atlantic croaker. Bars represent means ± SEM of 10 to 12 observations. a: Mean values significantly different from respective control groups. b: Significantly different from low-dose group.

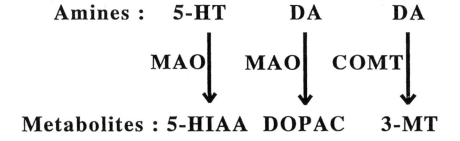

Figure 3-10 Schematic diagram of the enzymatic conversion of biogenic amines (5-HT and DA) into their major metabolites within the individual neurons. Increased metabolite to the parent amine ratios represent increased catabolism (by MAO in the nerve terminal and by catechol-O-methyltransferase [COMT] in the synaptic cleft) and/or reduced availability of the parent amine for a neurophysiological function.

release in croaker (Khan and Thomas 1992 1994). In addition, 5-HT can influence GnRH function at the level of POAH as well as act directly at the pituitary to stimulate GtH release in teleosts (Yu et al. 1991; Khan and Thomas 1992). The changes in 5-HT metabolism in the POAH are likely to be reflected in the pituitary because the 5-HT and GnRH neurons originating in the POAH directly innervate the pituitary gland in teleosts (Kah et al. 1993; Khan and Thomas 1993). Thus, the impairment of 5-HT metabolism in the POAH, and possibly in the pituitary, may influence GnRH function at the level of the pituitary gland. The decline in GnRH release may prevent the up-regulation of GnRH receptors in the pituitary which would account for the decline in the gonadotropic response to stimulation by LHRHa in lead-exposed versus control fish. A direct effect of lead on GnRH synthesis (Klein et al. 1994) and/or release could also be partially responsible for the lower GtH release from pituitaries of croaker exposed to the higher dose of lead.

The impairment of GtH secretion most likely results in lower circulating T and 11-KT levels in lead-exposed fish. Similar to our observation in male croaker, lead exposure suppresses blood and intra-testicular T levels in rats (Sokol et al. 1985; Klein et al. 1994). It is also possible that lower circulating steroids may prevent up-regulation of GnRH receptors in the pituitary and reduce gonadotropic response to LHRHa because the number of GnRH receptors increases with gonadal growth in fish (Habibi et al. 1989).

The decline in 3-MT concentrations and 3-MT/DA ratio with the higher dose of lead suggests a possible decline in catechol-O-methyltransferase (COMT) activity. However, these changes in hypothalamic DA metabolism are unlikely to be associated with reproductive neuroendocrine disruption because DA is not involved in the control of GtH release in croaker (Copeland and Thomas 1989b) which is similar to recent observations in rats (Mohankumar et al. 1994).

A variety of xenobiotics, including lead, can alter monoamine neurotransmitter metabolism in both mammals (Uphouse 1985; Seegal et al. 1986; Singh and Ashraf 1989) and fish (Katti and Sathyanesan 1986; Spieler et al. 1995; Khan and Thomas, in press). These xenobiotics have also been shown to influence pituitary GtH release (Uphouse 1985; Thomas 1989; Foster 1992). In addition, the regulation of

GnRH and GtH by hypothalamic monoaminergic systems has been extensively characterized in both mammals and fish (Vitale et al. 1986; Yu et al. 1991; Kah et al. 1993; Khan and Thomas 1992, 1994). However, only a few studies have tried to correlate altered hypothalamic monoaminergic activity with GtH secretion (Uphouse 1985; Goldman et al. 1990). Chlordecone (Kepone) administration in female rats suppresses 5-HT and DA concentrations in the preoptic area and results in reduced circulating luteinizing hormone (LH) levels (Uphouse 1985). In addition, Goldman et al. (1990) have demonstrated a significant decline in circulating LH levels associated with an impairment of in vitro GnRH release in response to stimulation by NE from mediobasal hypothalamic explants of rats exposed to chlordimeform, a systemic acaricide belonging to the formamidine class of pesticides. This pesticide also suppresses brain NE and 5-HT concentrations in rats (Johnson and Knowles 1983). Therefore, the reduction in 5-HT may additionally lower circulating LH levels in chlordimeform-treated rats. Further studies with other classes of xenobiotics are needed to establish a direct link between altered hypothalamic neurotransmission and pituitary GtH release. Interpretation of alterations in neurotransmitter function induced by xenobiotics is often complicated by the discrepancies in experimental protocols such as 1) changes in whole brain versus those changes in discrete brain areas, 2) measurement of the biogenic amine concentrations versus their metabolism, and 3) lack of information about sampling time and reproductive stage. Moreover, possible sources of variation due to external environmental conditions, reproductive stage, and time of sampling (Khan and Joy 1990; Spieler et al. 1995) should be taken into account while designing these experiments.

The results of the present study together with those of our previous study with Aroclor 1254 (Khan and Thomas 1996) suggest that the impairment of hypothalamic 5-HT activity may be one of the important mechanisms by which xenobiotics could influence reproductive neuroendocrine function in vertebrates.

Concluding Remarks

Several mechanisms of reproductive endocrine disruption in sciaenid fishes by toxic chemicals have been identified in this study. The results show that Kepone exerts an estrogenic action on VTG production by binding to the spotted seatrout hepatic estrogen receptor. A rapidly growing list of organic chemicals appear to possess estrogenic activity in fish. Sumpter and coworkers have identified alkylphenols and phthalates (Jobling and Sumpter 1993; Jobling et al. 1995), and Van Der Kraak's group have evidence that the phytoestrogen, β-sitosterol, has an estrogenic action in the goldfish (MacLatchy and Van Der Kraak 1995). We have found that *ortho, para* derivatives of dichlorodiphenyltrichloroethane (DDT) and hydroxylated PCBs as well as a broad range of phytoestrogens bind to the seatrout estrogen receptors with similar binding affinities to those reported in mammalian tissues (Thomas unpublished). In addition, recent evidence from McLachlan's group suggests possible synergistic effects of environmental chemicals on estrogen receptor activation (Arnold et al. 1996).

Most studies to date have examined the estrogenic effects of these chemicals on vitellogenesis (Figure 3-1, Site 5). Attention should be given to possible estrogenic actions of these compounds at other sites on the HPG axis. Currently, there is a lack of direct evidence that xenoestrogens influence the positive and negative steroid feedback system controlling gonadotropin secretion in teleosts (Figure 3-1, Site 6). In addition, it has not been demonstrated that the adverse effects of xenoestrogens on testicular function in fish (Figure 3-1, Site 4) are mediated via a testicular estrogen receptor. Estrogen receptors have been identified in mammalian and amphibian testes (Dickson and Clarke 1981; Mak et al. 1983) but not in fish, although specific binding for estradiol has been found in croaker testis (Thomas unpublished). Estrogens are present in low concentrations in male teleosts (Fostier et al. 1983) and alter testicular function (Billard et al. 1980), which suggest that estrogens may play an important role in regulating testicular function in teleosts. The minute amounts of estradiol produced by the mammalian testis are sufficient to inhibit the steroidogenic enzymes, 17-hydroxylase and 17,20-lyase, leading to a decline in androgen production (Nozu et al. 1981). Interestingly, we have observed dramatic declines in androgen production from testes of adult croaker exposed to o,p'-DDT. It is likely, though, that the testis is most sensitive to estrogenic chemicals during differentiation (Twonbly 1995).

Estrogens also have important functions in the mammalian ovary and are major inducers of follicular atresia (Dierschke et al. 1994). Follicular atresia is a frequent response to chemical exposure in teleost ovaries. It may be difficult, however, to establish whether the inhibitory actions of xenoestrogens on ovarian follicles in teleosts are related to their estrogenicity and estrogen receptor binding or are due to other toxic actions of these compounds. The interpretation of experimental results with xenoestrogens is further complicated by their potential to exert inhibitory or antagonistic actions under certain conditions, as shown in the present study.

Finally, certain xenoestrogens may disrupt endocrine function by nonestrogenic mechanisms. We have shown that Kepone is an effective competitor for binding of a progestin, 17,20β,21-trihydroxy-4-pregnen-3-one (20β-S), to its membrane receptor on croaker oocytes and antagonizes the action of 20β-S on maturation of croaker oocytes in vitro (Ghosh and Thomas 1995b). Thus, certain xenoestrogens can also disrupt endocrine function by binding to an entirely different class of steroid receptors, membrane receptors. Other xenoestrogens such as DDT and chlordane have been shown to stimulate the adenylate cyclase system in mammalian tissues (Kacew and Singhal 1974) and therefore, could potentially exert similar effects on ovarian steroidogenesis as those shown with cadmium in the present study.

Evidence is also presented that cadmium can disrupt endocrine function by interfering with signal transduction systems involved in gonadotropin and gonadal steroid secretion (Figure 3-1, Sites 3 and 4). Moreover, we have preliminary evidence that the effect of cadmium on gonadotropin secretion involves alterations of calcium homeostasis. The calcium-dependent phosphoinositol system and the adenylate cyclase systems are ubiquitous intracellular transducers of biochemical signals, including hormones. Therefore, in addition to reproductive endocrine dysfunction, it is likely that a wide range of other physiological functions are disrupted by chemicals which interfere with signal transduction systems.

A large body of evidence suggests that many chemicals, including lead, mercury, organochlorine and organophosphorous pesticides, PCB mixtures, central nervous system drugs, and synthetic steroids impair reproductive endocrine function at the hypothalamic level in mammals, fish, and other vertebrates (Mattison et al. 1983; Katti and Sathyansan 1986; Wilson and Leigh 1992). The neuroendocrine control of the teleost reproductive endocrine system is highly complex involving a suite of neurotransmitters, neural pathways, and steroid feedback sites and the GnRH system (Trudeau and Peter 1995), thereby complicating investigations of the mechanisms of neuroendocrine toxicity. However, there is a strong likelihood that many of these chemicals interfere with neuroendocrine activity and GnRH secretion by altering neurotransmitter function in the hypothalamus.

We have demonstrated that lead and Aroclor 1254 alter serotonin metabolism in croaker brain hypothalamic areas and also impair gonadotropin secretion. The xenoestrogen Kepone has also been shown to alter serotonin metabolism and gonadotropin secretion in mammals. It will be necessary, though, to establish a causal relationship between chemical-induced alterations in neurotransmitter levels and neuroendocrine disruption. It is possible that some of the chemicals may additionally influence GnRH gene expression and/or steroid receptor function in the hypothalamic areas of the brain to impair neuroendocrine function. The recent availability of molecular probes to study GnRH and estrogen receptor mRNA expression in teleost brains should greatly facilitate studies on the mechanisms of neuroendocrine toxicity in fishes.

Acknowledgments

This research was supported by Public Health Service grant ES04214 to P.T. The contributions of J.S. Smith and H. Singh to the research presented in this paper are gratefully acknowledged.

References

Adashi EY, Resnick CE. 1986. 3',5'-Cyclic monophosphate as an intracellular second messenger of luteinizing hormone: application of the forskolin criteria. *J Cell Biochem* 31:217–228.

Arnold SF, Kotz DM, Collins BM, Vonier PM, Guillette LJ, McLachlan JA. 1996. Synergistic activation of estrogen receptor with combinations of environmental chemicals. *Science* 272:1189–1192.

Billard R, Breton B, Richard M. 1980. On the inhibitory effect of some steroids on spermatogenesis in adult rainbow trout (*Salmo gairdneri*). *Can J Zool* 59:1479–1487.

Brown HE, Salamanca S, Stewart G, Uphouse L. 1991. Chlordecone (Kepone) on the night of proestrus inhibits female sexual behavior in CDF-344 rats. *Toxicol Appl Pharmacol* 110:97–106.

Bulger WH, Kupfer D. 1985. Estrogenic activity of pesticides and other xenobiotics on the uterus and male reproductive tract. In: Thomas JA, Korach KS, McLachlan JA, editors. Endocrine toxicity. New York NY: Raven Pr, p 1–24.

Chang JP, Jobin RM. 1994. Regulation of gonadotropin release in vertebrates: a comparison of GnRH mechanisms of action. In: Davey KG, Peter RE, Tobe SS, editors, Perspectives in comparative endocrinology. Ottawa, Canada: National Research Council of Canada. p 41–51.

Chang JP, Jobin RM, Wong AOL. 1993. Intracellular mechanisms mediating gonadotropin and growth hormone release in goldfish, *Carassius auratus*. *Fish Physiol Biochem* 11:25–33.

Cicero TJ, Badger TM, Wilcox CE, Bell RD, Meyer ER. 1977. Morphine decreases luteinizing hormone by an action on the hypothalamic-pituitary axis. *J Pharmacol Exp Therap* 203:548–555.

Cooper RL, Goldman JM, Rehnberg GL, McElroy WK, Hein JF. 1987. Effects of metal cations on pituitary hormone secretion in vitro. *J Biochem Toxicol* 2:241–249.

Copeland PA, Thomas P. 1988. The measurement of plasma vitellogenin levels in a marine teleost, the spotted seatrout (*Cynoscion nebulosus*) by homologous radioimmunoassay. *Comp Biochem Physiol* B91:17–23.

Copeland PA, Thomas P. 1989a. Purification of maturational gonadotropin from Atlantic croaker (*Micropogonias undulatus*) and development of a homologous radioimmunoassay. *Gen Comp Endocrinol* 73:425–441.

Copeland PA, Thomas P. 1989b. Control of gonadotropin release in the Atlantic croaker (*Micropogonias undulatus*): evidence for a lack of dopaminergic inhibition. *Gen Comp Endocrinol* 74:474–483.

Dickson RB, Clarke CR. 1981. Estrogen receptors in male. *Arch Androl* 7:205–217.

Dierschke DJ, Chaffin CL, Jutz RJ. 1994. Role and site of estrogen action on follicular atresia. *Trends Endocrinol Metab* 5:215–219.

Eroschenko VP, Palmiter RD. 1980. Estrogenicity of Kepone in birds and mammals. In: McLachlan JA, editor. Estrogens in the environment. New York NY: Elsevier. p 305–325.

Evans DW, Dodoo DK, Hanson PJ. 1993. Trace element concentrations in fish livers: implications of variations with fish size in pollution monitoring. *Mar Poll Bull* 26:329–334.

Foster WG. 1992. Reproductive toxicity of chronic lead exposure in the female cynomolgus monkey. *Reprod Toxicol* 6:123–131.

Fostier A, Jalabert B, Billard R, Breton B, Zohar Y. 1983. The gonadal steroids. In: Hoar WS, Randall BJ, Donaldson EM, editors. Volume IX, Fish physiology. New York NY: Academic Pr. p 277–372.

Ghosh S, Thomas P. 1995a. Binding of metals to red drum vitellogenin and incorporation into oocytes. *Mar Environ Res* 39:165–168.

Ghosh S, Thomas P. 1995b. Antagonistic effects of xenobiotics on steroid-induced final maturation of Atlantic croaker oocytes in vitro. *Mar Environ Res* 39:159–163.

Gilman AG. 1970. A protein binding assay for adenosinc 3',5'-cyclic monophosphate. *Proc Nat Acad Sci USA* 67:305–312.

Goldman JM, Cooper RL, Laws SL, Rehnberg GL, Edwards TL, McElroy WK, Hein JF. 1990. Chlordimeform-induced alterations in endocrine regulation within the male rat reproductive system. *Toxicol Appl Pharmacol* 104:25–35.

Gothilf Y, Elizur A, Zohar Y. 1995. Three forms of gonadotropin-releasing hormone in gilthead seabream and striped bass: Physiological and molecular studies. In: Goetz FW, Thomas P, editors. Reproductive physiology of fish; Fish Symposium 95; Austin TX. p 52–54.

Habibi HR, DeLeeuw R, Nahorniak CS, Goos HJTh Goos, Peter RE. 1989. Pituitary GnRH receptor activity in goldfish and catfish: seasonal and gonadal effects. *Fish Physiol Biochem* 7:109–118.

Huang ES-R, Nelson FR. 1986. Anti-estrogenic action of chlordecone in rat pituitary gonadotrophs in vitro. *Toxicol Appl Pharmacol* 82:62–69.

Jobling S, Reynolds T, White R, Porter MG, Sumpter JP. 1995. A variety of environmentally persistent chemicals, including some phthalate plasticizers are weakly estrogenic. *Environ Health Perspect* 103:582–588.

Jobling S, Sumpter JP. 1993. Detergent components in sewage effluent are weakly oestrogenic to fish: an in vitro study using rainbow trout (*Onchorhynchus mykiss*) hepatocytes. *Aquat Toxicol* 27:361–372.

Johnson TL, Knowles CO. 1983. Influence of formamidines on biogenic amine levels in the rat brain and plasma. *Gen Pharmacol* 14:591–596.

Kacew S, Singhal RL. 1974. Effect of certain halogenated hydrocarbon insecticides on cyclic adenosine 3',5'-monophosphate-^{3}H formation by rat kidney cortex. *J Pharmacol Exp Therap* 188:265–276.

Kah O, Anglade I, Leperte E, Dubourg P, de Monbrison D. 1993. The reproductive brain in fish. *Fish Physiol Biochem* 11:85–98.

Katti SR, Sathyanesan AG. 1986. Lead nitrate induced changes in the brain constituents of the freshwater fish *Clarias batrachus* (L). *Neurotoxicology* 7:47–52.

Khan IA, Joy KP. 1990. Differential effects of photoperiod and temperature on hypothalamic monoaminergic activity in the teleost *Channa punctatus* (Bloch). *Fish Physiol Biochem* 8:291–297.

Khan IA, Thomas P. 1992. Stimulatory effects of serotonin on maturational gonadotropin release in the Atlantic croaker, *Micropogonias undulatus*. *Gen Comp Endocrinol* 88:388–396.

Khan IA, Thomas P. 1993. Immunocytochemical localization of serotonin and gonadotropin-releasing hormone in the brain and pituitary gland of the Atlantic croaker, *Micropogonias undulatus*. *Gen Comp Endocrinol* 91:167–180.

Khan IA, Thomas P. 1994. Seasonal and daily variations in the plasma gonadotropin II response to a LHRH analog and serotonin in Atlantic croaker (*Micropogonias undulatus*): evidence for mediation by 5-HT$_2$ receptors. *J Exp Zool* 269:531–537.

Khan IA, Thomas P. 1996. Disruption of neuroendocrine function in Atlantic croaker exposed to Aroclor 1254. *Mar Environ Res* 42:145–149.

Klein D, Wan YY, Kamyab S, Okuda H, Sokol RZ. 1994. Effects of toxic levels of lead on gene regulation in the male axis: increase in messenger ribonucleic acid and intracellular stores of gonadotrophs within the central nervous system. *Biol Reprod* 50:802–811.

Laskey JW, Phelps PV. 1991. Effect of cadmium and other metal cations on in vitro Leydig cell testosterone production. *Toxicol Appl Pharmacol* 108:296–306.

MacLatchy DL, Van Der Kraak GJ. 1995. The phytoestrogen β-sitosterol alters reproductive endocrine status of goldfish (*Carassius auratus*). *Toxicol Appl Pharmacol* 134:305–312.

Mak P, Callard IP, Callard GV. 1983. Characterization of an estrogen receptor in the testis of the urodele amphibian *Necturus maculosus*. *Biol Reprod* 28:261–270.

Mattison DR, Gates AH, Leonards A, Wide M, Hemminki K, Copius Peereboom-Stegeman JHH. 1983. Reproductive and developmental toxicity of metals: female reproductive system. In: Clarkon TW, Norberg GN, Sager PR, editors. Reproductive and developmental toxicity of metals. New York NY: Plenum Pr. p 41–92.

Mohankumar PS, Thyagarajan S, Quadri SK. 1994. Correlations of catecholamine release in the medial preoptic area with proestrous surges of luteinizing hormone and prolactin: effects of aging. *Endocrinology* 135:119–126.

Naor Z. 1990. Signal transduction mechanisms of Ca^{2+} mobilization hormones: the case of gonadotropin releasing hormone. *Endocr Rev* 11:326–353.

Nozu K, Dufau ML, Catt KJ. 1981. Estradiol-receptor-mediated regulation of steroidogenesis in gonadotropin-sensitized Leydig cells. *J Biol Chem* 256:1915–1922.

Phelps PV, Laskey JW. 1989. Comparison of age-related changes in in vivo and in vitro measures of testicular steroidogenesis after acute cadmium exposure in the Sprague-Dawley rat. *J Toxicol Environ Health* 27:95–105.

Reel JR, Lamb IV JC. 1985. Reproductive toxicology of chlordecone (Kepone). In: Thomas JA, Korach KS, McLachlan JA, editors. Endocrine toxicology. New York NY: Raven Pr. p 357–391.

Saligaut C, Chretien P, Daoust M, Moore N, Boismare F. 1986. Dynamic characteristics of dopamine, NE and serotonin metabolism in axonal endings of the rat hypothalamus and striatum during hypoxia: a study using HPLC with electrochemical detection. *Meth Find Exp Clin Pharmacol* 8:343–349.

Sangalang, GB, O'Halloran MJ. 1973. Adverse effects of cadmium on brook trout testis and on in vitro testicular androgen synthesis. *Biol Reprod* 9:394–403.

Seegal RF, Brosch KO, Bush B. 1986. Regional alterations in serotonin metabolism induced by oral exposure of rats to polychlorinated biphenyls. *Neurotoxicology* 7:155–166.

Shackley SE, King PE, Gordon SM. 1981. Vitellogenesis and trace metals in a marine teleost. *J Fish Biol* 18:349–352.

Singh AK, Ashraf M. 1989. Neurotoxicity in rats sub-chronically exposed to low levels of lead. *Vet Hum Toxicol* 31:21–25.

Singh H, Griffith RW, Thomas P, Takahashi A, Kawauchi H, Stegeman JJ. 1988. Regulation of gonadal steroidogenesis in *Fundulus heteroclitus* by recombinant salmon growth hormone and purified salmon prolactin. *Gen Comp Endocrinol* 72:144–153.

Singh H, Thomas P. 1993. Mechanism of stimulatory action of growth hormone on ovarian steroidogenesis in spotted seatrout *Cynoscion nebulosus*. *Gen Comp Endocrinol* 89:341–353.

Singhal RL. 1981. Testicular cyclic nucleotide and adrenal catecholamine metabolism following chronic exposure to cadmium. *Environ Health Perspectives* 38:111–117.

Singhal RL, Vijayvargia R, Shukla GS. 1985. Toxic effects of cadmium and lead on reproductive functions. In: Thomas JA, Korach KS, MaLachlan JA, editors. Endocrine toxicology. New York NY: Raven Pr. p 149–180.

Sivarajah K, Franklin CS, Williams WP. 1978. The effects of polychlorinated biphenyls on plasma steroid levels and hepatic microsomal enzymes in fish. *J Fish Biol* 13:401–409.

Smith JS, Thomas P. 1990. Binding characteristics of the hepatic estrogen receptor of the spotted seatrout, *Cynoscion nebulosus*. *Gen Comp Endocrinol* 77:29–42.

Sokol RZ, Madding CE, Swerdloff RS. 1985. Lead toxicity and hypothalamic-pituitary-testicular axis. *Biol Reprod* 33:722–788.

Somero GN, Chow TJ, Yancey PH, Snyder CB. 1977. Lead accumulation in the tissues of an estuarine fish, *Gillichthys mirabilis*: salinity and temperature effects. *Arch Environ Contam Toxicol* 6:337–341.

Somoza GM, Yu KL, Peter RE. 1988. Serotonin stimulates gonadotropin release in female and male goldfish, *Carassius auratus* L. *Gen Comp Endocrinol* 72:374–382.

Sorensen EMB. 1991. Metal poisoning in fish. Boca Raton FL: CRC Pr. 374 p.

Spieler RE, Russo AC, Weber DN. 1995. Waterborne lead affects circadian variations of brain neurotransmitters in fathead minnows. *Bull Environ Contam Toxicol* 55:412–418.

Swanson P. 1991. Salmon gonadotropins: reconciling new and old ideas. In: Scott AP, Sumpter JP, Kime D, Rolfe MS, editors. Reproductive physiology of fish; Fish Symposium 91; Sheffield UK. p 2–7.

Thomas P. 1988. Reproductive endocrine function in female Atlantic croaker exposed to pollutants. *Mar Environ Res* 24:179–183.

Thomas P. 1989. Effects of Aroclor 1254 and cadmium on reproductive endocrine function and ovarian growth in Atlantic croaker. *Mar Environ Res* 28:499–507.

Thomas P. 1990. Teleost model for studying the effects of chemicals on female reproductive endocrine function. *J Exp Zool* (Suppl.) 4:126–128.

Thomas P. 1993. Effects of cadmium on gonadotropin secretion from Atlantic croaker pituitaries incubated in vitro. *Mar Environ Res* 35:141–145.

Thomas P, Smith JS. 1993. Binding of xenobiotics to the estrogen receptor of spotted seatrout: a screening assay for potential estrogenic effects. *Mar Environ Res* 35:147–151.

Trudeau VL, Peter RE. 1995. Functional interactions between neuroendocrine systems regulating GtH II release. In: Goetz FW, Thomas P, editors. Reproductive physiology of fish; Fish Symposium 95; Austin TX. p 44–48.

Twonbly R. 1995. Assault on the male. *Environ Health Perspect* 103:802–805.

Uphouse L. 1985. Effects of chlordecone on neuroendocrine function of female rats. *Neurotoxicology* 6:191–210.

Vallee BL, Ulmer DD. 1972. Biochemical effects of mercury, cadmium and lead. *Annu Rev Biochem* 41:91–128.

Van Der Kraak GJ, Munkittrick KR, McMaster ME, Portt CB, Chang JP. 1992. Exposure to bleached kraft pulp mill effluent disrupt the pituitary-gonadal axis of white sucker at multiple sites. *Toxicol Appl Pharmacol* 115:224–233.

Van Der Kraak G, Wade MG. 1994. A comparison of signal transduction pathways mediating gonadotropin actions in vertebrates. In: Davey KG, Peter RE, Tobe SS, editors. Perspectives in comparative endocrinology. Ottawa, Canada: National Research Council of Canada. p 59–63.

Viarengo A, Nicotera R. 1991. Possible role of Ca^{++} in heavy metal cytotoxicity. *Comp Biochem Physiol* 100E:81–84.

Vitale ML, Parisi MN, Chiocchio SR, Tramezzani JH. 1986. Serotonin induces gonadotrophin release through stimulation of LHRH release from the median eminence. *J Endocrinol* 111:309–315.

Wilson CA, Leigh AJ. 1992. Endocrine toxicology of the female reproductive system. In: Atterwill CK, Flack JD, editors. Endocrine toxicology. Cambridge MD: Cambridge Univ Pr. p 313–398.

Yano T, Matsuyama H. 1986. Stimulatory effect of PCB on the metabolism of sex hormones in carp hepatopancreas. *Bull Japan Soc Scient Fish* 52(10):1847–1852.

Yu KL, Rosenblum PM, Peter RE. 1991. In vitro release of gonadotropin-releasing hormone from the brain preoptic-anterior hypothalamic region and pituitary of female goldfish. *Gen Comp Endocrinol* 81:256–267.

Environmental antiandrogens: potential effects on fish reproduction and development

Emily Monosson, William R. Kelce, Michael Mac, L. Earl Gray

Steroid hormones and their receptors control fundamental events in embryonic development, sex differentiation, and maturation. Environmental chemicals with hormonal and/or antihormonal activity can disrupt the action of functional steroid hormone receptors in fish, wildlife, and humans. Field and laboratory studies identify adverse effects of many of these chemicals on the developing reproductive tracts of wildlife and laboratory species; however, little information exists regarding the effects of these chemicals, particularly antiandrogens, in fish. As with mammals, the fish life cycle includes critical periods where adverse organizational and/or activational effects can occur via the absence of endogenous hormones or the presence of endocrine-disrupting chemicals (EDCs). In addition, different species of fish have different reproductive strategies such that the critical period is embryonic in some species while others do not differentiate until later in life. While the timing of these critical periods varies greatly, all appear to be sex steroid hormone-dependent and therefore susceptible to disruption by EDCs. Here, we review the physiological basis for 2 different hormone-dependent critical periods in fish: sex-differentiation and maturation. We also discuss potential mechanisms by which several environmentally relevant contaminants (i.e., kraft mill effluent (KME) and p,p'-DDE) may affect these developmental processes in fish.

Steroid hormones and hormone receptors control fundamental events in embryonic development, sex differentiation, and maturation through their function as ligand-inducible transcription factors that either activate or repress transcription of target genes. The consequences of disrupting these processes can be especially profound during development due to the crucial role hormones play in controlling transient and irreversible developmental processes. As the function of steroid hormone receptors is highly conserved across species, it is not surprising that environmental chemicals are capable of disrupting the action of functional steroid hormone receptors in fish, wildlife, and humans. While laboratory studies have confirmed many abnormalities of reproductive development observed in the field and have, in some cases, provided mechanisms to explain the effects in wildlife and humans, we are only beginning to understand these processes in fish. Recognizing this deficit of information and the fact that the field of environmental endocrine disrupters recently has been expanded to include antiandrogenic chemicals (Gray et al. 1994; Kelce et al. 1994; Kelce et al. 1995), our objective here is to briefly review what we know regarding antiandrogenic chemicals in the environment and then discuss 2 life-cycle stages in which fish may be most susceptible to the effects of antiandrogens (e.g., sexual differentiation and maturation). Finally we will attempt to combine this information and speculate on how antiandrogens may affect fish populations.

Environmental Antiandrogens

Vinclozolin (V) is a dicarboximide fungicide commonly used on grapes, ornamental plants, and turfgrasses (Kelce et al. 1994). Detailed developmental studies by Gray et al. (1994, 1997 in preparation) identified vinclozolin as a potent antiandrogen in developing rats. Maternal exposure to 50 to 200 mg V/kg/day during the critical developmental period for sexual differentiation resulted in reduced anogenital distance (AGD), retained nipples, reduced sex accessory gland weights, urogenital malformations (e.g., hypospadias and vaginal pouches), and reduced fertility as adults (Gray et al. 1994). Concentrations of V as low as 3mg/kg/day induced transient effects in AGD and sex accessory gland weight, while the effects induced with concentrations greater than or equal to 6mg/kg/day were permanent (Gray et al. 1997 in preparation). To date, a no-observed-adverse-effect level (NOAEL) for V has not been established.

The biochemical and molecular mechanism responsible for the antiandrogenic effects of vinclozolin has been elucidated. While the parent chemical vinclozolin is not an effective inhibitor of androgen receptor (AR) binding, 2 primary metabolites, M1 and M2, do compete effectively with endogenous ligand for binding to the AR (Kelce et al. 1994). Once bound to the receptor, both active metabolites target the AR to the nucleus but fail to initiate transcription primarily by inhibiting the ability of AR to bind androgen response element (ARE) DNA and thereby preventing transcription of androgen-dependent genes (Wong et al. 1995). Together these data demonstrate that metabolites of V behave as classical antiandrogens (i.e., similar to hydroxyflutamide). The importance of V (or other fungicides with similar activity such as procymidone) in aquatic systems is unknown, although it is possible that aquatic systems (and resident wildlife populations) in close vicinity to the crops upon which V is used could be affected by exposure to V or its metabolites.

More recently, Kelce et al. (1995) identified 1,1-dichloro-2,2-bis(p-chlorophenyl)ethylene (p,p'-DDE), the persistent metabolite of DDT, as an environmental antiandrogen. In vivo, when p,p'-DDE was administered to pregnant rats (100 mg/kg/day) from gestational day 14 to 18, the male progeny displayed significantly reduced AGD and retained thoracic nipples. Both characteristics are indicative of prenatal antiandrogen activity (Imperato-McGinley et al. 1992). In vitro, p,p'-DDE binds to the AR, is efficiently imported into the nucleus, but fails to initiate transcription with about the same potency as the antiandrogenic drug hydroxyflutamide. Thus, like vinclozolin, p,p'-DDE acts as an antiandrogen by inhibiting the transcription of androgen-dependent genes. The effects of this ubiquitous pesticide have implications for many different wildlife species, including fish, because it persists in the environment and it bioaccumulates.

Wildlife

Although the use of DDT has been banned in the United States (U.S.), Canada, and Western Europe, it is still exported in large quantities from the U.S. (300 tons from 1992 to 1994) and used in large quantities in many other countries (FASE 1996). "Hot-spots" of DDT contamination also remain in the U.S. from past usage and/or spills (LaRoe et al. 1995), including a DDT and dicofol spill that occurred in Lake Apopka, Florida in 1980. Following this spill, persistent reproductive problems were observed in resident alligators (Guillette et al. 1995). Further investigation revealed smaller penises in young male alligators together with altered ratios of sex steroid hormones that were typically characteristic of females rather than males (Guillette et al. 1995). The authors speculated that the alligators may have been feminized following exposure to o,p'-DDT, which is a minor estrogenic metabolite of DDT. After the publication by Kelce et al. (1995), the antiandrogenic effects of the major DDT metabolite, p,p'-DDE, were considered. Concentrations of p,p'-DDE within developing alligator eggs were approximately 5.8 ppm (Guillette et al. 1995) or about 80 times the concentration of p,p'-DDE required to inhibit androgen action in vitro (Kelce et al. 1995). The specific role of p,p'-DDE in the demasculinization of the Lake Apopka alligators is currently under investigation.

In raptors, p,p'-DDE levels of about 2 to 14 ppm are associated with reproductive failure due to eggshell thinning (Spitzer et al. 1978). This effect on natural populations has been reproduced in the laboratory where p,p'-DDT and p,p'-DDE exposures are found to inhibit Ca^{++}-ATPase dependent activities and carbonic anhydrase and to reduce calcium concentrations in the oviduct of susceptible avian species (Spitzer et al. 1978). Ring doves given 10 ppm p,p'-DDT exhibit increased hepatic activity and decreased serum estradiol concentrations leading to a delay in egg laying, a decrease in bone calcium deposition, and a reduced eggshell weight. Fry and Toone (1981) observed feminization of male chicks following in ovo exposure to o,p'-DDT and p,p'-DDE. It seems likely that the actions of o,p'-DDT can be attributed to the estrogenic activity of this DDT congener; however, recent studies with p,p'-DDE indicate that this metabolite acts as an antiandrogen with little or no estrogenic activity, at least in the mammalian system (Kelce et al. 1995). Although estrogen controls sexual differentiation in birds, these latter data suggest that demasculinization of wild birds may be attributed, in part, to exposure to environmental antiandrogens.

Fish

Similar to mammals, there are critical periods during the fish life cycle where adverse organizational and/or activational effects (Adkins-Regan 1987) can occur via the absence of necessary hormones, or the presence of disrupting hormones. Organizational effects are typically permanent effects that most likely occur during a critical period for development (e.g., during sex differentiation), whereas activational effects may occur during maturation. Thus, inappropriate alterations of sex steroid hormone levels may cause permanent or transient effects depending on the timing of exposure. The earliest stages of development are highly conserved across vertebrates so that there is a great degree of morphologic similarity during embryogenesis. Dickoff et al. (1990) suggest the possibility that there may be extensive commonalties in the endocrine control of early development among vertebrates as well. Unlike mammals, however, fish display a wide range of reproductive strategies, and critical periods for proper steroid hormone exposure can vary dramatically among species. There are several reviews on the timing and factors involved in maturation and on sex differentiation (Yamamoto 1969; Bye 1983; Hunter and Donaldson 1983). In this paper we will only discuss what is known in general about the role of androgens during both of these life-history stages.

Sex Differentiation

While genetics may be important for sex determination in some species (a relatively small percentage of fishes even have heteromorphic sex chromosomes), it does not appear to be the determining factor in all species (Adkins-Regan 1987; Chan and Yeung 1983), as fish have a wide variety of species-specific factors that control sex determination and differentiation. In fish species that have critical periods for sex determination, this period varies based on genetics, environment, and even geographical components (Conover and Fleisher 1986). The role of sex steroid hormones as "inducers" of sex differentiation versus "products of sex differentiation" is still unclear (Yamamoto 1969; Feist et al. 1990; Fitzpatrick et al. 1993). Sex differentiation can, however, be altered by administration of sex steroids around the time of hatching (Hunter and Donaldson 1983; Piferrer et al. 1993, 1994) such that functional males can be produced from genetic females. The critical period for sex differentiation usually occurs when the gonads begin to develop into either testes or ovaries, the timing of which can vary dramatically between species. The ability of steroid hormones to direct or alter sexual differentiation in fish exposed during critical periods is well documented (Yamamoto 1969; Hunter and Donaldson 1983; Piferrer et al. 1993; Piferrer et al. 1994). If steroid hormones directly affect sex differentiation, then it is likely that environmental contaminants that mimic or block steroid hormone action or otherwise alter steroid hormone concentrations could have dramatic effects on these processes in fish.

Maturation

Another critical period where steroid hormones must be in the "proper ratio" is during recrudescence or maturation. There exist a wide variety of spawning strategies in fish; some spawn once in a lifetime, while others spawn once every few years, once a year, or several times a year (Bye 1983). In general, all fish species undergo a hormonal cycle associated with proper maturation. In fish, 11-ketotestosterone (11-KT) is the male specific androgen, while testosterone (T) is found in both males and females. Many studies have demonstrated that 11-KT is more effective than T for experimental masculinization during sex differentiation (Piferrer et al. 1993). These androgens are also important during maturation and for proper development of secondary sex characteristics and behavior (Miura et al. 1991; Fostier et al. 1983). Therefore, the action of these androgens appears to be necessary for proper sexual maturation in male fish; consequently, it is not difficult to hypothesize that exposure to antiandrogens during maturation may result in adverse effects ranging from delayed maturation to reduced spermiation.

Environmental Contaminants

The discovery of apparently all-male populations of mosquito fish (*Gambusia affinis*) in Eleven Mile Creek, Florida, was one of the first indications that anthropogenic activity could affect sexual development in fish (Howell et al. 1980; Davis and Bortone 1992; Bortone and Davis 1994). Upon closer inspection, it was noted that there were females present (as determined by the presence of a female pigment spot, and some were even gravid), even though they were clearly masculinized.

Subsequent studies indicated that phytohormones apparently released in kraft mill effluent (KME) were active androgens. The effects of KME seemed to be permanent, as fish removed from the creek and held in the laboratory remained masculinized. Whether these effects were the result of exposure during a critical period of sex differentiation or exposure later in life is unclear.

Our knowledge of antiandrogens is derived mainly from studies in mammalian systems (Gray et al. 1994; Kelce et al. 1994; Gray et al. 1996). Do chemicals known to be antiandrogenic in mammals act similarly in fish? Unfortunately, the relationship between the AR in fish and the endogenous androgens, T and 11-KT, is not as well understood as the relationship between the active mammalian androgens (T and dihydrotestosterone [DHT]) and the mammalian AR. As discussed above, 11-KT, a metabolite of T, is considered to be the active and more important androgen (Fostier et al. 1983). However, finding a nuclear receptor that binds 11-KT has proven to be difficult (Pasmanik and Callard 1985; Callard and Callard 1987). At least 2 groups (Pasmanik and Callard 1985; Pottinger 1988) have isolated a nuclear AR in fish that binds both T and DHT, although this receptor has little to no affinity for 11-KT; a cytosolic receptor that binds 11-KT, however, has been isolated from coho salmon ovaries (Fitzpatrick et al. 1994). Taken together, these studies illustrate the difficulties in extrapolating from observations made in mammalian systems where the AR binds T to observations in fish where the relationship between the presumably more important androgen (11-KT) and the AR is unclear. There is limited and conflicting information on the antiandrogenic effects of cyproterone acetate, a mammalian nonsteroidal antiandrogen, in fish (Hunter and Donaldson 1983). Cyproterone acetate can partially block development of some secondary sexual characteristics in several species (reviewed in Hunter and Donaldson (1983)). In contrast Rastogi and Chieffi (1975) reported no effect of cyproterone acetate on development of secondary sex characters of swordtails (*Xiphophorus helleri*).

Currently, studies with V, M1, M2, and p,p'-DDE are being conducted in fish (Peter Thomas, personal communication). The results of these studies will help reduce the uncertainty associated with predicting the effects of mammalian antiandrogens in fish. Understanding the interaction between contaminants and the AR, both in vitro and in vivo, was critical to the mammalian work and likely will be critical to our understanding of the effects of these chemicals in fish as well. We now provide the following example as an interesting case that, following a better understanding of the AR in fish, may deserve further attention.

The bloater (*Coregonus hoyi*) is a freshwater coregonid that inhabits large lakes. In Lake Michigan, bloater support a commercial fishery, but their abundance has varied dramatically with the expansion of exotic species. Although little is known about the physiological changes bloater undergo during reproduction, they are known to spawn annually in deep waters. As with the majority of fish species, very little is known about sex differentiation (e.g., critical period, importance of genetics versus environmental factors). However, based on many of the studies on maturation and sex differentiation included in the reviews cited previously, we can speculate that exposure to antiandrogens or lack of exposure to native androgens during either maturation or sex differentiation could have dramatic effects on this species.

Chemistry data collected from Lake Michigan bloater, ranging from the early 1970s though the late 1980s, show a decline in p,p'- DDE and o,p'-DDT tissue concentrations (Hesselberg et al. 1990). In 1969, the first year for which tissue concentrations of p,p'-DDE were available, tissue concentrations were as high as 3.8 ppm. In the mid 1980s after DDT was banned, tissue concentrations were reduced to lower, yet sustained levels around 0.5 ppm. Concomitant with the very high levels of p,p'-DDE and o,p'-DDT was the very odd observation of an almost completely female population of bloater (up to 97% in 1967), which has yet to be explained (Brown et al. 1987). As p,p'-DDE and o,p'- DDT concentrations decreased with time following the ban of DDT, the ratio of female to male bloaters also decreased, until ratios were approximately 1:1 in the late 1980s (Figure 4-1; r^2=96). With the current knowledge that p,p'-DDE is antiandrogenic and o,p'-DDT is estrogenic in mammalian systems (and maybe in reptiles as well) it is possible that high concentrations of these chemicals passed from female bloaters to their offspring during oocyte development and may have affected sex differentiation, resulting in population sex ratios skewed toward females. There are, however, many uncertainties in this example, such as the following?

1) Is p,p'-DDE antiandrogenic in fish (o,p'-DDT does appear to be estrogenic [Sumpter 1995])?

2) Are there two different receptors for androgens in fish (so that perhaps only the activity of T might be blocked, while 11-KT is not)?

3) What is the critical period for sex differentiation in bloater (one might expect the larval phase to be the most susceptible period, since yolk as the sole food source was likely highly contaminated with p,p'-DDE and o,p'-DDT inherited from the mother)?

4) Could any of the other chlorinated chemicals that were present together with p,p-DDE and o,p'-DDT affect sex differentiation? Clearly there are many unknowns.

Conclusion

There is increasing evidence that environmental contaminants such as p,p'-DDE can affect wildlife populations. However, many of the questions listed above for bloater can be applied to fish in general. Until we know more about the structure and function of ARs in fish and the effects of contaminants (e.g., antiandrogens) during critical periods (e.g., sex differentiation), we can only speculate about the effects on fish populations of contaminants that interfere with steroid hormone activity. This will require an increased effort towards this end, both in the laboratory and in the field. Laboratory studies should include mechanistic studies with the AR, T, and 11-KT; studies designed to better understand critical periods for sex differentiation in different species; and studies that will clarify the role of the AR and androgens during this period. Field studies that provide information on population structure in combination with morphological and biochemical studies of species residing in sites contaminated with potential antiandrogens will also contribute to our understanding of the effects of these chemicals on fish populations.

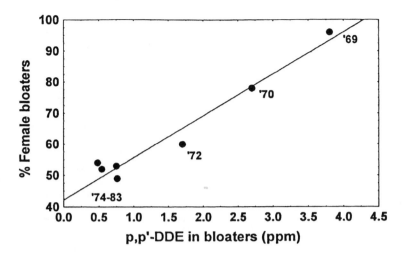

Figure 4-1 Tissue concentrations (whole fish/wet weight) of p,p'-DDE in Lake Michigan bloater versus sex ratio (female/male) in fish collected from Lake Michigan (r^2=96). Sources: Brown et al. 1987; Hesselberg et al. 1990.

References

Adkins-Regan E. 1987. Hormones and sex differentiation. In: Norris DO, Jones RE, editors. Hormones and reproduction in fishes, amphibians, and reptiles. New York NY: Plenum. p 1–30.

Bortone SA, Davis WP. 1994. Fish intersexuality as indicator of environmental stress. Bioscience. 44:165–172.

Brown EH, Argyl RL, Payne NR, Holey ME. 1987. Yield and dynamics of destabilized chub (*Coregonus spp.*) populations in Lakes Michigan and Huron, 1950–1984. *Can J Fish Aquat Sci* 44, supplement 2:371–383.

Bye V. 1983. The role of environmental factors in the timing of reproductive cycles . In: Fish reproduction. London UK: Academic Pr. p 187–205.

Callard IP, Callard GV. 1987. Sex steroid receptors and non-receptor binding proteins. In: Norris DO, Jones RE, editors. Hormones and reproduction in fishes, amphibians, and reptiles. New York NY: Plenum Pr. p 355–384.

Chan STH, Yeung WSB. 1983. Sex control and sex reversal in fish under natural conditions. In: Hoar WS, Randall DJ, Donaldson EM, editors. Volume 9B, Fish physiology. New York NY: Academic Pr. p 171–222.

Conover DO, Fleisher MH. 1986. Temperature-sensitive period of sex determination in the Atlantic silverside, *Menidia menidia. Can J Fish Aquat Sci* 43:514–520.

Davis WP, Bortone SA. 1992. Effects of kraft mill effluent on the sexuality of fishes: An environmental early warning? In: Colborn TC, Clement C, editors. Chemically-induced alterations in sexual and functional development: the wildlife/human connection. Princeton NJ: Princeton Sci.

Dickoff W, Brown C, Sullivan C, Bern H. 1990. Fish and amphibian models for developmental endocrinology. *J Exp Zoo* supplement 4:90–97.

[FASE] Foundation for Advancements in Science Education. 1996. Research report, Spring 1996. Los Angeles CA: FASE.

Feist G, Schreck CB, Fitzpatrick MS, Redding JM. 1990. Sex steroid profiles of coho salmon (*Onchorhynchus kisutch*) during early development and sexual differentiation. *Gen Comp Endocrinol* 80:299–313.

Fitzpatrick MS, Pereira CB, Schreck CB. 1993. In vitro steroid secretion during early development of mono-sex rainbow trout: Sex differences, onset of pituitary control, and effects of dietary steroid treatment. *Gen Comp Endocrinol* 91:199–215.

Fitzpatrick MS, Gale WL, Schreck CB. 1994. Binding characteristics of an androgen receptor in the ovaries of coho salmon, *Onchorhynchus kisutch. Gen Comp Endocrinol* 94:399–408.

Fostier A, Jalabert B, Billard R, Breton B, Zohar Y. 1983. The gonadal steroids. In: Hoar WS, Randall DJ, editors. Volume 9A, Fish physiology. New York NY: Academic Pr. p 277–372.

Fry DM, Toone CK. 1981. DDT-induced feminization of gull embryos. Science 213:922–924.

Gray LE, Ostby JS, Kelce WR. 1994. Developmental effects of an environmental antiandrogen: the fungicide vinclozolin alters sex differentiation of the male rats. Tox Appl Pharm 129:46–52.

Gray Jr. LE, Monosson E, Kelce WR. 1996. Emerging issues: the effects of endocrine disrupters on reproductive development. In: DiGiulio RT, Monosson E, editors. Interconnections between human and ecosystem health. London UK: Chapman and Hall. p 46–74.

Gray LE, Otsby J, Kelce WR, Monosson E. 1997. Low dose effects of vinclozolin on sex differentiation in rats. In preparation.

Guillette LJ, Gross TS, Gross DA, Rooney AA, Percival HF. 1995. Gonadal steroidogenesis in vitro from juvenile alligators obtained from contaminated or control lakes. Env Health Perspec 103, supplement 4:31–36.

Hesselberg RJ, Hickey JP, Nortrup DA, Willford WA. 1990. Contaminant residues in the bloater (Coregonus hoyi) of Lake Michigan (1969–1986). J Great Lakes Res 16:121–129.

Howell WM, Black DA, Bortone SA. 1980. Abnormal expression of secondary sex characters in a population of mosquitofish: evidence for environmentally induced masculinization. Copeia 1980:676–681.

Hunter GA, Donaldson EM. 1983. Hormonal sex control and its application to fish culture. In: Hoar WS, Randall DJ, Donaldson EM, editors. Volume 9B, Fish physiology. New York NY: Academic Press. p 223–303.

Imperato-McGinley J, Sanchez RS, Spencer JR, Yee B, Vaugan ED. 1992. Comparison of the effects of the 5α-reductase inhibitor finisteride and the antiandrogen flutamide on prostate and genital differentiation: Dose response studies. Endo 131:1149–1156.

Kelce WR, Monosson E, Gamsik MP, Laws SC, Gray LE. 1994. Environmental hormone disrupters: evidence that vinclozolin developmental toxicity is mediated by antiandrogenic metabolites. Tox Appl Pharm 126:276–285.

Kelce WR, Stone CR, Laws SC, Gray LE, Kemppainen JA, Wilson EM. 1995. Persistent DDT metabolite p,p'-DDE is a potent androgen receptor antagonist. Nature 375:581–585.

LaRoe ET, Farris GS, Puckett CE, Doran PD, Mac JM. 1995. Our living resources. Washington DC: U.S. Department of the Interior-National Biological Service.

Miura T, Yamauchi K, Takahashi H, Nagahama Y. 1991. Hormonal induction of all stages of spermatogenesis in vitro in male Japanese eel (Anguilla japonica). Proc Nat Acad Sci, USA 88:5774–5778.

Pasmanik M, Callard G. 1985. Identification and characterization of an androgen receptor in the brain of goldfish (Carassius auratus). Am Zoo 25:115A.

Piferrer F, Baker IJ, Donaldson EM. 1993. Effects of natural, synthetic, aromatizable, and nonaromatizable androgens in inducing male sex differentiation in genotypic female chinook salmon (Onchorhynchus tshawytscha). Gen Comp Endocrinol 91:59–65.

Piferrer F, Zanuy S, Carrillo M, Solar II, Devlin RH, Donaldson EM. 1994. Brief treatment with an aromatase inhibitor during sex differentiation causes chromosomally female salmon to develop as normal, functional males. J Exp Zoo 270:255–262.

Pottinger TG. 1988. Seasonal variation in specific plasma- and target-tissue binding of androgens, relative to plasma steroid levels, in the brown trout, Salmo trutta L. Gen Comp Endocrinol 70:334–344.

Rastogi RK, Chieffi G. 1975. The effects of antiandrogens and antiestrogens in nonmammalian vertebrates. Gen Comp Endocrinol 26:79–91.

Spitzer PR, Risebrough R, Walker W, Hernandez R, Poole A, Puleston D, Nisbet IC. 1978. Productivity of ospreys in Connecticut-Long Island increases as DDE residues decline. Science 202:333–335.

Wong CI, Kelce WR, Wilson EM. 1995. Androgen receptor antagonist verses agonist activities of the fungicide vinclozolin relative to hydroxyflutamide. J Biol Chem 270:19998–20003.

Evidence for developmental and skeletal responses as potential signals of endocrine-disrupting compounds in fishes

William P. Davis

Integrated sets of bioindicators and ecological signals would be desirable for rapid detection and assessment of endocrine disruptor syndrome in wild populations of fish and wildlife. Early warning signals would be especially desirable to enable identification before the onset of major reproductive dysfunction or population consequences. Comparison of various research reports in the literature reveals that many of the same compounds that induce developmental, morphological, and/or skeletal anomalies are later identified as endocrine disruptors. Kepone, mirex, polychlorinated biphenyls (PCBs), trifluralin, dibutylphthalate (DBP), kraft-mill effluents (KMEs), and others induce skeletal, developmental, and/or sex-linked morphological abnormalities that become manifest biomarkers among surviving mature fishes. This report examines several specific cases of skeletal and external morphological responses and suggests their relevance as markers signaling the probability of disruption of an endocrine modulated function.

The conceptual framework for wildlife responses on a global scale to exposure to xenobiotic endocrine disrupting chemicals (EDCs) emerged from the deliberations during the 1991 conference at Wingspread Conference Center, Racine WI (Colborn and Clement 1992). As participants presented and evaluated datasets addressing the wide variety of biological responses observed, common patterns were recognized, and the concept of endocrine disruption as an environmental impact emerged. Responses among many organisms to stress are manifested as serious dysfunctions to completion of their normal life-history pattern (Colborn et al. 1993). The specific relationship of less serious effects, e.g., developmental or growth anomalies, to endocrine disruption is not always as clear a manifestation.

During subsequent debate about these emerging concepts, as should be the case with any unifying hypothesis in science, there have been challenges and critics (Stone 1994). It is, after all, quite sobering and disturbing to realize the potential significance of xenobiotic impacts that could include distortion of the outcomes of innumerable organisms' life histories, influencing population successes and potentially affecting evolutionary processes as well (Fox 1995).

The concept of EDC-induced chronic dysfunctional response bridges many research disciplines and qualifies as a syndrome (Couch 1993). Furthermore, as a syndrome, it demands coordinated thinking to simultaneously consider different scales of biological organization from molecular, biochemical, and cellular processes during development and growth, to physiological functions affecting the success of complete life history cycles, to the dynamics of ecological interactions and the dynamics of global ecosystems (Colborn et al. 1996).

The concept of an EDC response syndrome involves a broad spectrum of compounds, impacting organisms under a variety of ecological situations, affecting various functional processes, and inducing a myriad of possible effects and outcomes to each life history success. It is important to identify organisms which serve as sensitive indicators for detection of EDC effects at different functional scales and ecological levels, always being aware of the natural diversity that is involved. Furthermore, there is an inherent need for identification of the scale of significance of the effect, which would reflect responses from the level of mere perturbation, to loss of function, to serious disease, to population impact. This stratified scheme of measurements must incorporate consideration of the timing of the exposure to indicate whether the resulting perturbation represents stress to homeostasis or induces a condition impacting the successful life patterns of exposed organisms.

Benefits of Fishes as Study Organisms

Fishes provide diverse opportunities to test effects, investigate responses, and model mechanisms resulting from exposures to xenobiotics and potential EDCs (Powers 1989; Bunton 1996). Experimental approaches using fish models to assess potential risks of endocrine disruptors to wildlife and humans provide both scientific and economic advantages. Precedence for the advantages of fish models has been amply demonstrated in identification of carcinogenic responses to chemicals (Hoover 1984; Bunton 1996; Couch 1996). The advantages of fishes as test organisms noted by these authors are relevant and applicable to assessment of EDC response syndrome as well:

1) Fishes occupy a pivotal role as environmental sentinels providing comparative response data for exposure, bioaccumulation, transport, foodweb transfer, and deposition of persistent xenobiotic chemicals.

2) Fish experimental models provide good predictive and comparative data at different scales or levels of investigation.

3) Fish offer "whole body" contact exposure in the aquatic milieu and model foodweb and transgenerational transfer of xenobiotic agents.

4) The endocrine, cellular, developmental, and behavioral responses of fishes provide fundamentally predictive models of risks to other vertebrates.

5) Many fish species have rapid reproductive and life history cycles in time frames that allow multiple tests and exposures contributing to economical experimental design applications.

Fishes play critical ecological roles among the principal environmental indicators of freshwater and marine living conditions or ecosystem "health". This is relevant especially in the context that currently emphasizes environmental assessment and sustainable management. As one begins to conceive of the number and varieties of ways endocrine disruptor effects are manifested, one then appreciates the degree and complexity of the research challenge. Therefore, fishes represent the most biologically relevant, and probably the most economical, vertebrate models for aquatic exposure testing and environmental monitoring.

Overview of the Skeletal System as a Generic Indicator

Abnormal bone morphology is not necessarily the first effect that comes to mind when discussing endocrine disruption responses. One reason is that bone formation and structure are typically topics treated as developmental, with anatomical, histological, or structural descriptions. Abnormalities have been presented as examples of nutritional or metabolic causation (Mayer et al. 1978; Bengtsson 1979; Hinton 1993). Since reports of bone abnormalities have appeared in the scientific literature for decades, it may appear old-fashioned to declare that bone deformities represent potential indications of endocrine disruption when compared to recent discoveries in biochemistry, protein detection, or hormone receptors. The occurrence of bone anomalies among vertebrates often represents the first dramatic evidence of environmental xenobiotic exposure. Since we may not initially know when or how these clues are related to endocrine disruption, we should carefully examine the historical evidence and consider it in present contexts of assessment. It is notable that, as one develops lists of demonstrable or suspected xenobiotic endocrine disruptors, many of the same compounds induce skeletal or morphological anomalies among some developing fish.

Balment and Henderson (1987) state that 3 hormones, in general terms, maintain plasma calcium concentration, but emphasize that exact interrelationships are far from being comprehensively understood. Growth hormones, in addition and/or related to parathyroid, calcitonin, and Vitamin D3, as well as the activity of the corpuscles of Stannius, can all impinge on calcium homeostasis. Therefore, there are multiple ways that EDC may affect calcium dynamics and potentially, skeletal development. It follows that different EDCs may induce general or specific types of system stress. Pesticides, specific metals, phytosterols, plasticizers and vitamins, have been variously reported as teratogens inducing morphological modifications at sublethal exposures. The function of all systems in an organism is the maintenance of homeostasis. Response to any "perturbation" stimulates internal adjustments to return to the homeostatic state, and failure to succeed induces susceptibility to disease, whether classified as developmental, neoplastic, immunological, etc. In this general paradigm, the skeleton provides a record of a vertebrate's life history. Therefore, morphological effects can serve generically as alerts or signals of potential endocrine disruption.

Protochordate and vertebrate organisms are phylogenetically defined by a unique tissue, the notochord. The presence of the notochord at the axis of the body, sometime during the life history, defines chordate classification and is used to identify the time of the first appearance of the organism's fossil relatives. It is characterized as a tissue with large turgescent cells in which the vacuole often displaces the cell contents. Among so-called "advanced" or ossified vertebrates, notochord tissue is located in the center of each vertebra, much more active and prominent during embryonic through early juvenile life stages than later in adult stages. As the vertebral column develops, the notochord becomes compressed by each vertebra, expanding near the juncture of adjacent vertebrae. Histologically, the intracellular matrix structure of the notochord distinguishes it from bone or cartilage. The notochord is surrounded by a thin sheath which, in turn, is surrounded by the vertebral centra (Grizzle and Rogers 1976). The notochord probably modulates processes involved in the formation of adjacent bone and cartilage tissue. The notochord has been shown to produce proteoglycans which control chondrogenesis or cartilage and somite growth (Kosher and Lash 1975) and regulate morphogenesis of sclerotome and neural crest cells in developing avian embryos (Newgreen et al. 1986). The notochord may also function in the regulation of the production of bone by osteoblasts, or in destruction and remodeling of bone structure by osteoclasts. The notochord tissue, located in the middle of the vertebral column, reduces in relative size as ossification of the vertebrae proceeds. The notochord has remained as the axis of every vertebrate; as such, it is virtually the fundamental definer of each organism's morphology and symmetry

Among egg-laying fishes, virtually all of the embryological and juvenile developmental stages occur external to the parent. Therefore, it follows that there may be greater chance of interference with embryonic cellular processes by direct environmental exposure to endocrine disrupting xenobiotics. Toxaphene, polychlorinated biphenyls (PCBs), chlordecone (Kepone), trifluralin, dibutylphalate, or other plasticizers are among a few of the compounds reported in the literature to be involved with induction of skeletal, especially vertebral, anomalies.

Kepone

Chlordecone, registered as Kepone, and chemically similar Mirex, were manufactured from 1957 to 1976. In different formulations these products have been used in roach traps, ant baits and as an insecticide dusted on bananas, potatoes, and citrus. In addition to the wide spread application of Mirex to poison fire ants, it was also used as a fire retardant (Faroon and Kueberuwa 1995; Faroon et al. 1995). Both compounds have low solubility and do not evaporate to any extent. Within the ecosystem, outside of specific foodwebs (Bahner et al. 1977), the compounds are sediment related (Rubinstein et al. 1980) and capable of long-distance transport when they are bound to particles.

During the early 1970s, fish biologists at the Virginia Institute of Marine Sciences (VIMS) were puzzled that examples of the same fish species, members of the drum family (Sciaenidae), sampled in the James River were readily distinguishable from those sampled in the York River. Species trawled from the James River including spot (*Leiostomus xanthurus*), croaker (*Micropogonias undulatus*), and Black drum (*Pogonias cromis*) were all characterized by distinctive body proportions caused by shortened vertebral columns (Chao, personal communication). Independently, Couch et al. (1977) noticed diagnostic vertebral changes and neurological pathologic effects among sheepshead minnows (*Cyprinodon variegatus*) in experimental laboratory exposures to Kepone. As the fishery biologists and laboratory toxicologists corroborated observations and data, further environmental details emerged. So too, the public eventually learned that a major release of Kepone had occurred over several years from a manufacturing facility on the James River, located in Hopewell

VA. Data from laboratory exposures were already available as fish, including juvenile spot from the James River analyzed for chemical contaminant body burdens, revealed high Kepone levels (Stehlik and Merriner 1983). This step established the most probable cause for the observed skeletal anomalies. James River fish populations probably had been exposed to Kepone associated both with sediments and food as young and juvenile fish migrated into the estuary and river from the offshore spawning area. Although mirex, manufactured in the Great Lakes, was released during the same general time period, there have been no comparable reports of response data among wild fishes. Perhaps exposure to the xenobiotic agent at Great Lakes sites did not occur at maximal concentrations at a critical life history stage of surviving fish, explaining the difference from the Kepone case; alternatively, perhaps the data were never collected. There is another hypothesis that was never investigated: do juvenile sciaenids return to the river of their parents, and do exposures of parents affect the resistance of embryos and developing young to further EDC exposure?

During the initial months of discovery of the James River "stumpy" fishes, before realization of the Kepone problem, there was debate among researchers about the cause of a previously observed "broken back" syndrome. High levels of residual chlorine (>3ppm) were detected in the effluent discharged from a municipal treatment plant at the mouth of the James River, and this was suggested as a causal explanation for fish observed with the broken backs. However, in laboratory exposures to chlorinated water the broken-back response was not induced (Couch, personal communication). Exposure to Kepone affected ossification and produced lesions that weakened the vertebral column. Such lesions, coupled with neuromuscular effects (e.g., tetanus), could result either in a traumatic fracture (often fatal), or scoliosis in the vertebral column among surviving fishes (Couch et al. 1997). Stehlik and Merriner 1983). Shortened or compressed vertebrae resulting in the stumpy condition (which affects the fishes' morphometrics) perhaps represent exposure to lower xenobiotic concentrations, or occurrence at different developmental stages, or additive responses to other xenobiotic compounds in the habitat. Many of these significant fish observations preceded awareness of the extent of the Kepone contaminating the James River. As the extent of the Kepone contamination was realized, assessment research emphasis shifted to human health risks and both the original fishery field data and follow-up studies received little or no attention. Chao's (personal communication) radiographic data demonstrate that over 60% of the yearling (>90 mm standard length [SL]) spot of one James River sample (n=270) were clearly scoliotic or stumpy. After 1976, the frequency of the vertebral dysplasia decreased so that it is unlikely that potential confounding effects from other xenobiotics in the James River were comparable to those caused by exposure to Kepone, whose manufacture had ceased.

Trifluralin

Trifluralin, (2,6 dinitro-N, N-dipropyl-4-[trifluoromethyl] benzamine) is a halogenated (fluorine) preemergent herbicide used widely abroad and in the United States (U.S.) (17 million pounds applied in 1972 [Murphy 1986]). Couch et al. (1979) described induction of vertebral dysplasia in the form of hyperostosis, primarily involving acellular bone of anterior vertebrae. The proliferation of bone was accompanied by persistence of osteoblasts, the presence of cellular notochord tissue in the vertebral central canal, as well as outgrowth of the vertebrae into the neural canal, impingement of mesonephric ducts from the kidneys, abnormal vertebral processes, fusion of vertebrae, and loss of flexibility of associated muscular functions. Serum calcium concentrations increased to twice the levels of controls in adult fish exposed for 4 days to trifluralin. Among reports of bone response in fishes to a xenobiotic to date, none match the level of histopathological detail reported by Couch et al. (1979). Persistence of notochord tissue beyond early developmental stages has not been reported in other studies. Additionally, the rapid rise of serum calcium in response to trifluralin exposure infers either direct or indirect endocrine interference, perhaps affecting the corpuscles of Stannius which are functionally associated with regulation of calcium levels in blood (Flik et al. 1989).

Wells and Cowan (1982) report dysplasia in salmon parr exposed to a short (<1 day) exposure to trifluralin designed to simulate an environmental spill in the Eden River in Scotland. Their test exposures induced scoliotic vertebral abnormalities, considered to simulate the stumpy adults captured from the affected stream (Wells and Cowan 1982). In addition to the vertebral responses, Couch (1984) reports that trifluralin exposure induced fluid-filled pseudocysts associated with pituitary enlargement in laboratory exposure of sheepshead minnows. Wells and Cowan (1982) further noted that salmon parr in laboratory exposures were more vulnerable to fatal fungal infection, suggesting compromised immune function. These observations suggest responses to perturbation that are related to endocrine disruption.

Dibutylphthalate

Hundreds of million pounds of phthalate esters are produced annually and used among a wide variety of products. Two of the most abundant are di-2-ethylhexyphthalate (DEHP) and di-n-butylphthalate (DBP). Di-n-butylphthalate was reported to produce teratogenic effects in fish (Davis 1988) and mammals (Shiota and Nishimura 1982). Davis (1988) described and compared vertebral anomalies among the offspring of exposed fish during treatment periods. Certain distinctive anomalies virtually disappeared from offspring produced after cessation of DBP treatment of adults. No skeletal anomalies were detected among the exposed parental fish. These observations may represent one of the closest experimental approximations to a "transgenerational" response to xenobiotic exposure reported among fish. The choice to use DPB experimentally was partly based upon its "relative" ease of handling. However, this plasticizer adheres rapidly to surfaces, was very difficult to maintain in solution above specific concentrations, and presented difficult challenges to achieve controllable experimental exposures. Phthalates are ubiquitous xenobiotics in aquatic environments and might be expected to enter fishes via food rather than uptake through water exposure pathways. The "mildest" skeletal anomaly expression that Davis (1988) observed, fusion of the last 2 vertebrae before the urostyle, was reported to occur at a rate of 30% among all young mummichog killifish (*Fundulus heteroclitus*) (Gabriel 1944). Although Gabriel did not find correlation of this response with temperature, he reiterated the suggestion of others that the fusion might be influenced by the "timing of ossification". Bern (personal communication) suggests that the urophysis "gland", which may be involved in osmoregulation (Bone et al. 1995), be reinvestigated with an eye to potential interrelationship with caudal vertebral development.

The foregoing examples represent effects upon the vertebral column from xenobiotics not as a review, but illustrating how stress or perturbation biomarkers may be imprinted in an organism for life. Other investigators have reviewed (Weis and Weis 1989) and reported approaches using fishes as environmental sentinels or monitors to register skeletal anomalies (Bengtsson 1979; Bengtsson et al. 1983, 1985), especially emphasizing fish responses to metal exposures.

Ossification in fish is associated with growth, and in fish is recorded by the daily incremental growth rings of otolith structure. Fish otolith analyses are used extensively in fish aging and population assessments. Although the idea has been proposed and discussed, data have not been reported linking xenobiotic exposures, perhaps reflecting stress, to effects in otolith structure.

The only extensive histological data among examples of EDC impacts upon fish skeletal structure are reported in Couch et al. (1977, 1979) and Couch (1984). These observations and data best support the potential linkage of EDC disruption of endocrine processes that mold the morphology of the vertebral column. When challenged by perturbation, one or more elements of the endocrine system should respond to maintain homeostasis of various organism functions. Failure to reestablish homeostasis increases the organism's susceptibility to disease and, in this context, the vertebral lesions represent "tick marks" in the organism's life history record.

Effects upon Sex-linked Morphology

Other categories of EDC-induced morphological response include the masculinization of female live-bearing fishes exposed to microbially degraded phytosterols and papermill effluents (Davis and Bortone 1992; Bortone and Davis 1994). These responses demonstrate direct linkage to reproductive functional morphology and potential survival of the organism. Field responses have been duplicated in the laboratory with the pharmaceutical, spironolactone (Howell et al. 1994). The morphological responses include modifications of anal fin rays, resulting in the characteristic male gonopodium. The gonopodium is a modified anal fin that functions as an intromittent organ to internally fertilize females and that characterizes the fishes of the family Poecillidae which give birth to living young. This example differs somewhat from the preceding examples of developmental disruption. Masculinization is a response that rarely occurs in nature among vertebrates. When masculinization is observed, questions arise regarding underlying causal mechanisms and how one can distinguish between blockage of estrogen receptors, stimulation of androgenic receptors, or something else. Caruso et al. (1988) reported precocious development of migratory morphology changes and male testes among early juvenile eels (*Anguilla rostrata*) sampled from the same paper mill effluent stream that affected female live-bearing fish (*Gambusia*). These observations have been argued as representing examples and evidence of androgenic stimulation (Davis and Bortone 1992; Bortone and Davis 1994).

However, there are additional hypotheses to investigate. Piferrer et al. (1994) describe causing functional male salmonids to develop from genetically female fish after a brief early life history exposure to aromatase inhibitors. Aromatase (P450-AROM) enzyme converts the C-19 structure of androstenedione and/or testosterone to C-18 estrogens (Kime 1987). This process is particularly active in the vertebrate brain (Naftolin et al. 1975; Callard 1982, 1983; Callard et al. 1978). Some of the highest activity levels of aromatase have been measured in teleost fishes (Callard 1982, 1984). Inhibition of aromatase function could result in excess androgen levels, potentially inducing masculinization. Pharmaceutical inhibition of aromatase function induced complete change of functional sex as demonstrated by Piferrer et al. (1994). The single example that relates this response to potential xenobiotic exposure is reported by Monod et al. (1993), who observed inhibition of ovarian microsomal aromatase by imidazole fungicides in experiments with rainbow trout (RBT).

Other scientists have speculated, outside of published reports, that the "imposex" response of marine gastropods affected by tributyl tin exposure might represent another example of aromatase inhibition. However, there has been no aromatase activity or function reported among invertebrates (Callard 1984; Simpson et al. 1994). Further investigation of aromatase and its roles in sex determination among reptiles (Jeyasuria 1994; Crews et al. 1995) and sexual behavior in fishes (Bornestaf et al. 1996) and birds (Wade et al. 1994) is an active and rapidly advancing area of research.

Summary

The significance of endocrine disruptor syndrome as a concept may be diminished if it is constrained to represent only events where specific endocrines or receptors are challenged or adversely affected. Because of the complex integration of processes and functions in an organism's life history ecology, endocrine disruption syndrome may have many manifestations, potentially representing exposures to numerous agents affecting the integrated output of biochemical pathways classified as having different functions. For example, the acquisition of salinity tolerance required for salmonid migration modulated by thyroid secretion, can be affected by exposure to PCBs and petroleum (Folmar et al. 1982). Other impacts upon neuro-sensory and behavioral functions may be induced by benzopyrene exposure (Ostrander et al. 1988, 1989), while yet some other xenobiotic may affect immune competence (Wells and Cowan 1982). It is striking to consider the variety of challenges to organism survival.

Reports of abnormal development or teratogenesis among fishes and other vertebrates have been so common in the experimental and contamination literature that they may not immediately register as relevant signals of, or responses to, EDCs. The concept that Bern (1990) refers to as "New" endocrinology represents the foundation upon which we must build our future examinations and syntheses. However, although we may think we understand the integrated processes which guide the development of organisms, still we often are not able to distinguish where endocrine processes control or to a lesser degree influence, the integration involved in the exquisite genesis of each organism's life history. Obviously, any interruption of specific steps, timing, or modification of components in the integrated developmental process can induce changes consequential to structure and function that affect entire life histories of organisms. Developmental "instructions" are transmitted to the embryos via the yolk (Bern and Nishioka 1993), which provides an avenue for EDCs to induce interferences in early embryonic stages with potential consequences throughout the life histories of either the exposed organisms or their offspring.

Biochemical signals can alert us to specific stages or levels, but only after they are scientifically linked to cause and effect, demonstrating measurable displacement from a definable standard representing normal life history outcome. The correlation of such markers as hyperostosis, increases of serum calcium, marked persistence of cellular notochord, and modified histology of the pituitary as exposure responses to trifluralin (Couch et al. 1979; Couch 1984) represents a very useful model for assessment of endocrine disruption effects upon developmental and growth processes. Perhaps the scarcity of such studies helps to explain the superficiality and preliminary nature of our present understanding of the extent of endocrine disruption among organisms and consequently the implied effects in communities and populations. Similarly, these studies illustrate advantages of using fishes as study organisms, as well as the need for coordination among tests and diagnostic tools.

Should one think that some of the EDC examples cited (e.g., Kepone) are environmental problems representing only bygone eras, be aware that the environmental "half-lives" of these xenobiotics may be extensively longer than previously projected. Original calculations of degradation rates were based upon data obtained in aerobic chambers which yielded estimates of half-lives of a few decades. When and where these compounds are deposited or sequestered in anaerobic conditions however, degradation rates are considerably delayed, adding several more decades to "half-life estimates" (Summers, personal communication). Globally, we are presently witnessing a so-called "reappearance" of nondegraded DDT, and other compounds as well, in ecosystems. Many EDCs, formerly considered as contaminants of years past, in fact, remain very much with us now and will likely continue to be around in the future. This fact, coupled with the increased probability of exposures to mixtures of xenobiotics, underscores the ecological significance of EDCs, both old and new. Soto et al. (1994) have demonstrated responses at significantly lower thresholds with endocrine sensitive cells exposed to two or more chemicals, i.e., there are cumulatively induced effects. There is probably no site on the surface of the globe where one could scientifically, at least at some low concentration, demonstrate occurrence of fewer than two EDCs. This represents a new addition to selection pressures to species survival driven by human produced xenobiotics (Fox, 1995). The current state of affairs demands that we identify all response signals that can assist in the ecological assessment task that now challenges us.

The skeleton is generally presented as probably the most "conservative" tissue of a vertebrate. This tissue has been utilized in many ways as a reference record of diverse events affecting growth during an organism's life history. The multiple factors that may influence skeletal structure include, but are not exclusively, endocrine modulated processes. The vertebrate skeleton represents an important reminder of how much remains to be learned, despite what we think we know.

Acknowledgments

I wish to acknowledge Professor C. Richard Robins, who has consistently empha-
sized integration and synthesis of diverse ideas in studying and observing life. Dr.
Leroy Folmar has provided important references and guidance towards improving
my impaired understanding of fish endocrinology. Drs. J. A. Couch, A. J. McErlean,
Rosalind Rolland, and four other patient, anonymous reviewers offered objective
critiques and suggestions which significantly improved this report. The World
Wildlife Fund provided travel support to attend this conference. Contribution No.
992, Gulf Ecology Division, USEPA, NHEERL.

References

Bahner LH, Wilson Jr. AJ, Sheppard JM, Patrick Jr. JM, Goodman LR, Walsh GE. 1977. Kepone
    bioconcentration, accumulation, loss, and transfer through estuarine food chains. *Ches Sci*
    18(3):299–308.

Balment RJ, Henderson IW. 1987. Secretion of endocrine glands and their relationship to osmoregula-
    tion. In: Chester-Jones I, Ingleton PM, Phillips JG, editors. Fundamentals of comparative vertebrate
    endocrinology. New York NY: Plenum Pr. p 413–508.

Bengtsson BE. 1979. Biological variables, especially skeletal deformities in fish, for monitoring marine
    pollution. *Phil Trans R Soc Lond* B 286:457–464.

Bengtsson BE, Bengtsson A. 1983. A method to registrate spinal and vertebral anomalies in fourhorn
    sculpin, *Myoxocephalus quadricornis* L. (Pisces). *Aquilo Ser Zool* 22:61–64.

Bengtsson BE, Bengtsson A, Himberg M. 1985. Fish deformities and pollution in some Swedish waters.
    Ambio 14:32–35.

Bern HA. 1990. The "New" endocrinology: Its scope and its impact. *Amer Zool* 30:877–885.

Bern HA, Nishioka RS. 1993. Aspects of salmonid endocrinology: the known and the unknown. *Bull
    Fac Hokkaido Univ* 44(2):55–67.

Bone Q, Marshall NB, Blaxter JHS. 1995. Biology of fishes. London UK: Blackie Academic and Profes-
    sional. 332 p.

Bornestaf C, Antonopoulou E, Mayer I, Borg B. 1996. Effects of aromatase inhibitors on sexual matura-
    tion in three-spined stickleback, *Gasterosteus aculeatus*. In: Goetz FW, Thomas P, editors. Proceed-
    ings of the Fifth International Symposium on the Reproductive Physiology of Fish. Austin TX: Univ
    of Texas. p 179.

Bortone SA, Davis WP. 1994. Fish intersexuality as indicator of environmental stress. *BioScience*
    44(3):165–172.

Bunton TE. 1996. Experimental chemical carcinogenesis in fish. *Toxicologic Pathology* 24(5):603–618.

Callard GV. 1982. Aromatase in the teleost brain and pituitary: Role in hormone action. In: Richter CJJ,
    Goos HJTh, editors. Reproductive physiology of fish. The Nederlands: Pudoc, Wageningen. p 40–
    43.

Callard GV. 1983. Androgen and estrogen actions in the vertebrate brain. *Amer Zool* 23:607–620.

Callard GV. 1984. Aromatization in brain and pituitary: an evolutionary perspective. In: Celotti F, Naftolin
    F, Martini L, editors. Metabolism of hormonal steroids in the neuroendocrine structures. New York
    NY: Raven Pr p 79–102.

Callard GV, Petro Z, Ryan KJ. 1978. Phylogenetic distribution of aromatase and other androgen-
    converting enzymes in the central nervous system. *Endocrinology* 103:2283–2290.

Caruso JH, Suttkus RD, Gunning GE. 1988. Abnormal expression of secondary sex characteristics in a
    population of *Anguilla rostrata* (Pisces: Anguillidae) from a dark colored Florida stream. *Copeia*
    1988:1077–1079.

Chao LN. (personal communication) from: Chao LN, Merriner JV, Stehlik LL (unpublished manuscript).
    Description, incidence and possible mechanism for the stumpy spot syndrome in the James River
    and lower Chesapeake Bay, Virginia. Virginia Institute of Marine Science, Gloucester Point, VA.

Colborn T, Clement C. 1992. Chemically-induced alterations in sexual and functional development: the
    wildlife/human connection. In: Volume XXI, Advances in modern environmental toxicology.
    Princeton NJ: Princeton Sci.

Colborn T, Dumanoski D, Myers JP. 1996. Our stolen future. New York NY: Dutton.

Colborn T, vom Saal FS, Soto AM. 1993. Developmental effects of endocrine-disrupting chemicals in wildlife and humans. *Environ Health Perspect* 101:(5)378–384.

Couch JA. 1984. Histopathology and enlargement of the pituitary of a teleost exposed to the herbicide trifluralin. *J Fish Diseases* 7:157–163.

Couch JA. 1993. Observations on the state of marine disease studies. In: Couch JA, Fournie JW, editors. Advances in fisheries science: pathobiology of marine and estuarine organisms. Boca Raton FL: CRC Pr. p 511–530.

Couch JA. 1996. Commentary: continuing development of fish species as additional experimental models in cancer research. *Toxicologic Pathology* 24(5):602.

Couch JA, Winstead JT, Goodman LR. 1977. Kepone-induced scoliosis and its histological consequences in fish. *Science* 197:585–587.

Couch JA, Winstead JT, Hanson DJ, Goodman LR. 1979. Vertebral dysplasia in young fish exposed to the herbicide trifluralin. *J Fish Diseases* 2:35–42.

Crews D, Cantu AR, Bergeron JM, Rhen T. 1995. The relative effectiveness of androstenedione, testosterone, and estrone, precursors to estradiol, in sex reversal in the red-eared slider (*Trachemys scripta*), a turtle with temperature-dependent sex determination. *General Comp Endrocrinol* 100:119–127.

Davis WP. 1988. Reproductive and developmental responses in the self-fertilizing fish, *Rivulus marmoratus*, induced by the plasticizer, di-n-butylphthalate. *Environ Biol Fishes* 21(2):81–90.

Davis WP, Bortone SA. 1992. Effects of kraft mill effluent on the sexuality of fishes: an environmental early warning? In: Colborn T, Clement C, editors. Chemically-induced alterations in sexual and functional development: the wildlife/human connection. Princeton NJ: Princeton Sci. p 113–127.

Faroon O, Kueberuwa S. 1995. Toxicological profile for Mirex and Chlordecone. Atlanta GA: Division of Toxicology/Toxicology Information Branch, Agency for Toxic Substances and Disease Registry (ATSDR). U.S. Department of Health and Human Services, 1600 Clifton Road, Atlanta GA 30333. 333 p.

Faroon O, Kueberuwa S, Smith L, DeRosa C. 1995. ATSDR evaluation of health effects of chemicals II. Mirex and chlordecone: Health effects, toxicokinetics, human exposure and environmental fate. *Toxicol Industrial Health* 11(6):1–214.

Flik G, Labedz T, Lafeber FPJG, Bonga SEW, Pang PKT. 1989. Studies on teleost corpuscles of Stannius: physiological and biochemical aspects of synthesis and release of hypocalcin in trout, goldfish and eel. *Fish Physiol Biochem* 7(1–4):343–349.

Folmar LC, Dickhoff WW, Zaugg WS, Hodgins HO. 1982. The effects of Arochlor 1254 and no. 2 fuel oil on smoltification and sea-water adaptation of coho salmon (*Onchorhynchus kisutch*). *Aquatic Toxicol* 2:291–299.

Fox GA. 1995. Tinkering with the tinkerer: pollution versus evolution. *Environ Health Perspect* 103 (Suppl.4):93–100.

Gabriel ML. 1944. Factors affecting the number and form of vertebrae in *Fundulus heteroclitus*. *J Exp Zool* 95:105–147.

Grizzle J, Rogers WA. 1976. Anatomy and histology of the channel catfish. Auburn AL: Auburn Univ Agriculture Experiment Station.

Hinton DE. 1993. Toxicologic histopathology of fishes: A systemic approach and overview. In: Couch JA, Fournie JW, editors. Advances in fisheries science: pathobiology of marine and estuarine organisms. Boca Raton FL: CRC Pr. p 177–215.

Hoover KL. 1984. Use of small fish species in carcinogenicity testing. Washington DC: National Institute of Health Publication No. 84-2653. National Cancer Institute Monograph 65. Available from: Superintendent of Documents.

Howell WM, Hunsinger RN, Blanchard PD. 1994. Paradoxical masculinization of western mosquitofish during exposure to spironolactone. *Prog Fish Culturalist* 56:51–55.

Jeyasuria P, Jagus R, Lance VA, Place AR. 1994. Role of P-450 aromatase in sex determination of the diamondback terrapin, *Malaclemys terrapin*. *J Experimental Zool* 270(1):95–111.

Kime DE. 1987. The steroids. In: Chester-Jones I, Ingleton PM, Phillips JG, editors. Fundamentals of comparative vertebrate endocrinology. New York NY: Plenum Pr. p 3–56.

Kosher RA, Lash JW. 1975. Notochord stimulation of in-vitro somite chondrogenesis before and after enzymatic removal of perinotochordal materials. *Dev Biol* 42:362–378.

Mayer FL, Mehrle PM, Crutcher PL. 1978. Interactions of toxaphene and vitamin C in channel catfish. *Trans Am Fish Soc* 107(2):326–333.

Monod G, DeMones A, Fostier A. 1993. Inhibition of ovarian microsomal aromatase and follicular oestradiol secretion by imidazole fungicides in rainbow trout. *Mar Environ Res* 35:153–157.

Murphy SD. 1986. Toxic effects of pesticides. In: Klaassen CD, Amdur MO, Doull J, editors. Casarett and Doull's toxicology, the basic science of poisons, 3rd ed. New York NY: Macmillan. p 519–581.

Naftolin F, Ryan KJ, Davies IJ, Reddy VV, Flores F, Petro Z, White RJ, Takaoka Y, Wolin L. 1975. The formation of estrogens by central neuroendocrine tissues. *Rec Progr Horm Res* 31:295–319.

Newgreen DF, Scheel M, Kastner V. 1986. Morphogenesis of sclerotome and neural crest in avian embryos: in-vivo and in-vitro studies on the role of notochordal extracellular material. *Cell Tissue Res* 244:299–313.

Ostrander GK, Landolt ML, Kocan RM. 1988. The ontogeny of coho salmon (*Onchorhynchus kisutch*) behavior following embryonic exposure to benzo[a]pyrene. *Aquatic Toxicol* 13:325–346.

Ostrander GK, Landolt ML, Kocan RM. 1989. Whole life history studies of coho salmon (*Onchorhynchus kisutch*) following embryonic exposure to benzo[a]pyrene. *Aquatic Toxicol* 15:109–126.

Piferrer F, Zanuy S, Carrillo M, Solar II, Devlin RH, Donaldson EM. 1994. Brief treatment with an aromatase inhibitor during sex differentiation causes chromosomally female salmon to develop as normal, functional males. *J Experimental Zool* 270:255–262.

Powers DA. 1989. Fish as model systems. *Science* 246:352–358.

Rubinstein NI, D'Asaro CN, Sommers C, Wilkes FG. 1980. The effects of contaminated sediments on representative estuarine species and developing benthic communities. In: Baker RA, editor. Volume 1, Contaminants and sediments. Ann Arbor MI: Ann Arbor Sci. p 445–461.

Shiota K, Nishimura H. 1982. Teratogenicity of di-2-ethylhexy-phthalate (DEHP) and di-n-butylphthalate (DBP) in mice. *Environ Health Perspect* 45:65–70.

Simpson ER, Mahendroo MS, Means GD, Kilgore MW, Hinselwood MM, Graham-Lorence S, Amarneh B, Ito Y, Fisher R, Michael MD, Mendelson C, Bulun SE. 1994. Aromatase cytochrome P450, the enzyme responsible for estrogen biosynthesis. *Endocrine Rev* 15(3):342–355.

Soto AM, Chung KL, Sonnenschein C. 1994. The pesticides endosulfan, toxaphene and dieldrin have estrogenic effects on human estrogen-sensitive cells. *Environ Health Perspect* 102:380–383.

Stehlik LL, Merriner JV. 1983. Effects of accumulated dietary Kepone on spot (*Leiostomus xanthurus*). *Aquatic Toxicol* 3:345–358.

Stone R. 1994. Environmental estrogens stir debate. *Science* 265:308–310.

Wade J, Schlinger BA, Hodges L, Arnold AP. 1994. Fadrozole: A potent and specific inhibitor of aromatase in the zebra finch brain. *General Comp Endrochrinol* 94:53–61.

Weis JS, Weis P. 1989. Effects of environmental pollutants on early fish development. *Reviews in Aquatic Sciences* 1(1):45–72.

Wells DE, Cowan AA. 1982. Vertebral dysplasia in salmonids caused by the herbicide trifluralin. *Environ Pollut* 29:249–260.

6

Development of biomarkers for environmental contaminants affecting fish

Nancy D. Denslow, Marjorie Chow, Ming M. Chow, Sherman Bonomelli, Leroy C. Folmar, Scott A. Heppell, Craig V. Sullivan

A number of anthropogenic chemicals that have been introduced into the environment may compromise normal endocrine function and sexual development or lead to neoplastic lesions. It is therefore important to determine wildlife exposure to these chemicals and to begin to establish exposure–effect relationships. We used 2-dimensional polyacrylamide gel electrophoresis (2D-PAGE) to identify biomarkers associated with exposure of fish to contaminants. Two proteins, an acidic isoform of apolipoprotein A1 and vitellogenin (VTG), were more highly expressed in brown bullhead fish exposed to highly contaminated waters. We concentrated on VTG, the estrogen-inducible egg yolk precursor protein, as an ideal biomarker for estrogen-mimicking chemicals, and we developed a panel of high-affinity, vitellogenin-specific monoclonal antibodies (mAbs) (immunoglobulin G [IgG] type). In this report, we partially characterize 4 of the panels' most cross-reactive antibodies, which bind VTG from fish in a wide phylogenetic spectrum (including orders Perciformes, Atheriniformes, Batrachoidiformes, Salmoniformes, Cypriniformes, and Anguilliformes). While none of these antibodies cross-reacts with VTG in the order Siluriformes, another mAb 2D8 (immunoglobulin M [IgM] type) does bind to VTG from fishes in this group as well as to VTGs from chickens and snakes, but with lower affinity. The panel of high-affinity IgG-type antibodies can be used in Western blots and enzyme-linked immunosorbent assays (ELISAs) to measure the expression of VTG in plasma from oviparous wildlife exposed to estrogen or estrogen-like contaminants.

Many anthropogenic chemicals have been associated with reproductive failure or dysfunction in fish, reptiles, and birds (Colborn and Clement 1992). Special interest has centered on agricultural and industrial chemicals which disrupt the endocrine system, especially those which mimic effects of steroid hormones (Safe et al. 1991; McLachlan et al. 1992; Soto et al. 1992, 1994; McLachlan 1993; Peterson et al. 1993) or interfere with the normal biochemical processing of endogenous hormones and their receptors (DeVito et al. 1992; Safe 1994). While there are mimics and antagonists for many hormones, environmental estrogens have been of particular concern because of their possible impacts on reproduction. These xenobiotics can increase synthesis of estrogen, may mimic estrogen action and directly interact with the estrogen receptor, or may be antagonists of estrogen, inhibiting the normal interaction of estrogen with its receptor. In addition to agonist or antagonist activities, xenobiotics may also potentiate the activity of estradiol in target tissues.

To determine the potential effects of anthropogenic chemicals, it is necessary to quantify departures from normal conditions at all levels of biological organization, ranging from suborganismal to population-level phenomena. This quantification is aided by biomarkers, a term that has evolved to include all biological responses, including physiological, biochemical, and behavioral responses to chemical exposure (Mayer et al. 1992). Some biomarkers indicate exposure to contaminants (e.g., cholinesterase, aryl hydrocarbon hydroxylase (AHH), DNA adducts, aryl hydrocarbon (*Ah*) receptor, vitellogenin [VTG]) while others indicate biological effects (e.g., tumors in fish, reduced penis size in alligators, eggshell thinning in birds).

We started our investigations looking for biomarkers that might correlate with neoplastic lesions in fish exposed to high levels of polyaromatic hydrocarbons in their environment. We obtained serum from brown bullhead diagnosed with hepatocellular or cholangiocellular carcinomas that were collected from an area heavily contaminated with pyrogenic, polynuclear aromatic hydrocarbons (PAHs). Screening of the serum using 2-dimensional polyacrylamide gel electrophoresis (2D-PAGE) revealed 2 proteins that varied significantly between the fish exposed to the contaminants and a control group from a reference area. The first protein is an acidic isoform of apolipoprotein A-1 (Denslow et al. 1994). Its expression was increased in serum samples of affected fish. These results confirmed laboratory studies showing the induction of an acidic isoform of apolipoprotein-AI in cultured hepatocytes from aflatoxin-treated rainbow trout (RBT) (Delcuve et al. 1992). In the present study we illustrate the detection of increased expression of apolipoprotein A-1 in field-caught brown bullhead catfish with hepatocellular and cholangio-cellular carcinomas.

The second protein was identified as VTG, the egg yolk protein precursor (Wallace 1985), which is induced by exposure to estrogen or estrogen mimics. This protein was expressed at very high levels both in males and in females collected at a time when they should not have been vitellogenic. Based on these results, we have directed our attention to VTG and developed a panel of monoclonal antibodies that cross-react with the protein from across a large phylogenetic spectrum of fish species. These antibodies, when incorporated into detection systems such as en-zyme-linked immunosorbent assays (ELISAs) or radioimmunoassays (RIAs), are par-ticularly useful for screening chemicals for potential estrogenic or estrogen-mimicking effects in fish.

In this study we report partial characterization of our panel of IgG-type antibodies raised against VTG. We show cross-reactivity with VTGs from fish in 6 different orders: Perciformes, Atheriniformes, Batrachoidiformes, Salmoniformes, Cypriniformes, and Anguilliformes. We used these antibodies to measure exposure to estrogen-like environmental contaminants in fish (carp and bluegill sunfish) caught in the field.

Materials and Methods

Collection of samples
Brown bullheads (*Ameiurus nebulosus*) (>250 mm total length, age 3+ years) were collected from the Black River at Lorraine OH and from Old Woman Creek at Huron OH. Bluegill sunfish (*Lepomis macrochirus*) were collected from a control site and a fish farm near Pensacola FL. Their serum was collected into tubes containing aprotinin and phenylmethylsulfonylfluoride (PMSF) to inhibit proteolytic degradation of VTG (Denslow et al. 1994; Folmar et al. 1995). All other serum samples were from fish grown under laboratory conditions and used to validate the antibodies.

Preparation of antibodies
Monoclonal antibody mAb 2D8 was raised against RBT (*Onchorhynchus mykiss*) VTG in Balb/C mice and screened for reactivity to striped bass VTG as described previously (Heppell et al. 1995). Following the same protocol (Denslow et al. 1997),

3 other immunizations have been carried out in Balb/C mice. Monoclonal antibodies HL1081-1C8 and HL1082-3H1 were raised against purified striped bass VTG (Tao et al. 1993) (fusion A), mAb HL1244-3G2 against slightly degraded striped bass VTG (fusion B), and mAb HL1147-2D3 against carp VTG (fusion C). Colonies were screened by direct ELISA and Western blotting using the appropriate VTGs. Colonies which showed immunoreactivity with VTGs from multiple species were selected for cloning. Monoclonal antibodies in hybridoma culture supernatants were used directly for Western blots as described below.

Western blots

Sodium dodecyl sulfate polyacrylamide gel electrophoresis (SDS-PAGE) and Western blot analyses were done as previously described (Denslow et al. 1997). Briefly, serum samples were obtained from both vitellogenic females or estradiol (E2)-induced males and male control fish from several different species, diluted as indicated in the figure legend, and separated by electrophoresis in 7 1/2% Tris-tricine gels (Schagger and von Jagow 1987). Species sampled for analysis on the Western blot included eel (*Anguilla rostrata*), carp (*Cyprinus carpio*), brown bullhead (*Ameiurus nebulosus*), hardhead catfish (*Arius felis*), rainbow trout (*Onchorhynchus mykiss*), striped bass (*Morone saxatilis*), largemouth bass (*Micropterus salmonides*), bluegill sunfish (*Lepomis macrochirus*), pinfish (*Lagodon rhomboides*), and white mullet (*Mugil curema*). In addition to these samples, we tested brook trout (*Salvelinus fontinalis*), goldfish (*Carassius auratus*), sheepshead minnow (*Cyprinodon variegatus*), white crappie (*Pomoxis annularis*), medaka (*Oryzias latipes*), walleye pike (*Stizostedion vitreum*), toad fish (*Opsanus tau*), killifish (*Fundulus heteroclitus*), fathead minnow (*Pimephales promelas*), northern pike (*Esox lucius*), and smallmouth bass (*Micropterus dolomieui*).

The gels were electro-transferred to polyvinyledene difluoride (PVDF) membranes (Millipore Corp, Immobilon P) for immunological probing by the Western blot technique as described previously (Denslow et al. 1997). Briefly, membranes were blocked with 5% milk in TBST buffer (10 mM Tris, pH 7, 150 mM NaCl, 0.5% Tween) prior to an overnight incubation with monoclonal antibodies in tissue culture supernatant. The membranes were washed with TBST and then probed with goat anti-mouse alkaline-phosphatase conjugated secondary antibody (dilution 1:5,000) for 1 hour. The blots were developed by incubating with bromochloroindolyl phosphate/nitro blue tetrazolium substrate.

Two-dimensional polyacrylamide gel electrophoresis

Serum proteins were separated by 2D-PAGE as described previously (Denslow et al. 1994; Folmar et al. 1995). Briefly, the first dimension was a 5% acrylamide isoelectric focusing gel extending between pH 6 and 8.5. Samples were incorporated into the gel mixture before polymerization as described by Semple-Rowland et al. (1991). Electrophoresis of the first dimension gel was carried out at 750 V for 16 hours at room temperature and finally at 1000 V for 1 hour. The pH was measured using a surface electrode. Electrophoresis of the second dimension, a 7 1/2% acrylamide SDS slab gel, 1 mM thick, was carried out at constant current (20 mA/gel) until the bromophenol blue dye marker reached the bottom of the gel. Gels were either stained with Coomassie blue or electro-transferred to Problott membranes (Applied Biosystems) as described below for N-terminal sequencing. Molecular weight standards (200, 97, 69, 46, 30, and 21.5 kilodaltons [kDa], Amersham Rainbow markers) were used to calibrate the gels in the second dimension.

N-terminal sequencing

For N-terminal sequencing, proteins in 2D gels were electrophoretically transferred to Problott membranes in 10 mM morpholinoethane sulphonic acid (MES) with a pH of 6 and containing 20% methanol in a cold box for 16 hours at 20V (Denslow et al. 1992). Following transfer, the membranes were stained with 0.02% Coomassie blue in 40% methanol/5% acetic acid for 30 seconds. Spots corresponding to unique proteins, present only in the serum of the affected animals, were cut and inserted into the sequencing cartridge of an Applied Biosystems Model 473A Sequencer in the Protein Chemistry Core Facility of the University of Florida. N-terminal sequences were analyzed and compared to the databases at the National Center for Biotechnology Information (NCBI) using the Basic Local Alignment Search Tool (BLAST) network service (Altschul et al. 1990).

Results and Discussion

Identification of possible biomarkers associated with contamination

The Black River near Lorraine OH has a long history of PAH contamination from a coking facility. Brown bullhead collected from this area have shown a high incidence of neoplastic lesions (mixed hepatocellular and cholangiocellular carcinomas) for over a decade (Baumann 1992; Baumann et al. 1982). Using 2D-PAGE, we compared blood serum protein profiles of these fish with brown bullhead collected from a nearby reference area, Old Woman Creek. In general, the polypeptide patterns were similar, with both groups of fish showing approximately the same protein content. There were, however, 2 striking differences involving 2 sets of proteins that distinguished the serum of fish collected on the Black River from fish collected at the reference site (Figure 6-1). One set of proteins had high mass (~180 and ~155 kDa) and the other set had a much lower mass, ~28 kDa.

The lower mass protein, present in fish from both locations, was expressed as 2 distinct isoforms. In fish from the Black River, the more acidic isoform (pI 4.9) was expressed at a higher level than in reference fish. The more basic isoform (pI 5.2) was expressed to about the same level in all fish. Both proteins had identical N-terminal sequences over the first 20 residues and were identified as isoforms of Apolipoprotein A1 (Denslow et al. 1994). These findings substantiated a previous study (Delcuve et al. 1992) that showed a similar expression pattern for Apo A-1 isoforms in aflatoxin-fed RBT with hepatocellular- carcinomas versus control trout. All fish collected from the Black River had numerous hepatocellular and cholangiocellular carcinomas, suggesting that higher expression of the acidic isoform of apolipoprotein A1 may serve as a biomarker for these types of cancers.

The higher mass proteins were present only in serum from fish collected in the Black River, in both males and females. N-terminal sequence analysis identified the proteins as VTG, the dominant egg-protein precursor normally synthesized in the liver of female fish in response to estrogen (Folmar et al. 1995). Concurrently,

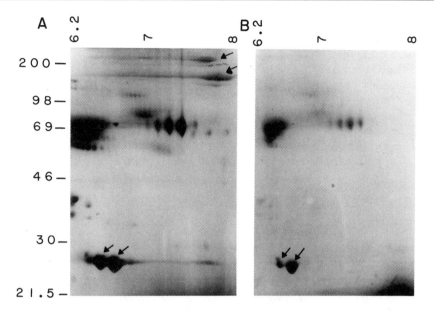

Figure 6-1 Characterization of serum proteins from female bullhead fish by 2D-PAGE. 10 µl serum
was used in each analysis. The first dimension was a 5% acrylamide isoelectric focusing
gel extending between pH 6.0 and 8.5, indicated by the numbers horizontally displayed
along the top of the gel. The second dimension was a 7.5% acrylamide SDS-PAGE gel. (A)
Fish with mixed hepatocellular and cholangiocellular carcinoma, (B) Fish without tumors.
The arrows point to the 2 vitellogenin proteins and the 2 apolipoprotein A-I isoforms.

researchers in the UK (Sumpter and Jobling 1995) detected increases in serum VTG
in male fish maintained in cages near sewage treatment plants. Using an in vitro
hepatocyte assay, those same investigators found that a wide variety of chemicals
can act as estrogen-mimics, inducing the production of VTG (Jobling and Sumpter
1993). Our results suggested that the increased levels of VTG and apolipoprotein
A1 were due either directly or indirectly to contaminants present in the water or
sediments of the Black River at Lorraine.

Our studies clearly illustrate the utility of 2D-PAGE combined with amino acid
sequencing as a means of identifying potential new biomarkers. Although Apo A-1
has good potential to become a biomarker for neoplastic disease, we decided to
focus our attention on VTG as a biomarker for estrogen-mimicking chemicals in the
environment. While some progress has been made using specific probes for VTG
mRNA (Lim et al. 1991; Pakdel et al. 1991), we decided to focus our attention
directly at the protein level by developing monoclonal antibodies against VTG.

Development of monoclonal antibodies against vitellogenin

The amino acid sequence of only a few vertebrate VTGs are reported in available
databases. Comparison of the primary sequences of the 4 frog (*Xenopus laevis*), 3
chicken (*Gallus domestica*), 2 killifish (*Fundulus heteroclitus*), 1 sturgeon (*Acipenser
transmontanus*), and 1 lamprey (*Icthyomyzon unicuspis*) VTGs shows the highly
divergent nature of this protein. Except for a few highly conserved regions, these
VTGs differ remarkably in their sequences. This lack of conservation implies that the

primary sequence can tolerate a high variability of amino acids, and thus mutations through evolution. It is thought that the main function of VTG is as a protein source for the developing embryo. Because of this wide divergence in sequence, antibodies against one specific VTG do not normally strongly cross-react with VTGs from other species. Of course, if an antibody recognizes a conserved sequence, or a conserved epitope in the 3-dimensional structure of VTG, then it would cross-react with several different species which contained the same sequence or structure. In an effort to study these conserved domains, we have prepared a panel of monoclonal antibodies against different VTGs, each antibody with its own distinct specificity.

The first monoclonal antibody, mAb 2D8, prepared against RBT VTG (Heppell et al. 1995) must recognize a highly conserved epitope since it cross-reacts with all VTGs tested to date, including several families of fishes and species from other classes of oviparous vertebrates (Heppell et al. 1995; Denslow et al. 1997). This antibody is in the immunoglobulin M (IgM) class and has been useful for detecting VTGs in both Western blots and ELISAs. However, because of its class, a high background sometimes develops in ELISA, requiring very strict assay conditions.

Repeating our earlier approach, we have developed additional mAbs using different VTGs as antigens. First, we used purified, intact striped bass VTG as antigen and obtained 25 IgG-class mAbs, of which 12 were of high affinity and disclosed striped bass VTG on Western blots. Of these, 7 cross-reacted with largemouth bass and 2 with rainbow trout. We have extensively characterized these last 2 antibodies, HL1081-1C8 and HL1082-3H1, for their cross-reactivity with a large variety of species (Denslow et al. 1997). We then repeated the experiment with slightly degraded striped bass VTG with the hope of obtaining additional antibodies to epitopes which might be less immunogenic in intact VTG as used in the first experiment. This approach generated 8 additional antibodies that cross-react with VTGs from both striped bass and rainbow trout. MAb 3G2 is a product of this fusion. We are in the process of characterizing this set of mAbs. In our third experiment, we used purified carp VTG (Folmar et al. 1996) to immunize mice and obtained 17 mAbs that recognize carp VTG, of which mAb HL1147-2D3 is the only one we have partially characterized to date.

Aside from mAb 2D8, which we have reported on in detail (Heppell et al. 1995; Denslow et al. 1997), our best characterized antibodies are 1C8 and 3H1. An example of Western blot data obtained with antibody 1C8 is presented in Figure 6-2. It is clear that mAb 1C8 recognizes striped bass, bluegill sunfish, largemouth bass, pinfish, white mullet, and rainbow trout. It does not cross-react with VTGs from eel, carp, hardhead catfish, or brown bullhead. We have also shown cross-reactivity of mAb 1C8 with VTGs from brook trout, sheepshead minnow, white crappie, medaka, walleye pike, and killifish (Table 6-1). MAb 3H1 recognizes VTGs from all of these fish and, in addition, it cross-reacts strongly with VTG from eel and toadfish and moderately with VTG from carp. However, mAb 3H1 does not cross-react with VTG from hardhead catfish or brown bullhead. What is clear from these investigations is that none of the IgG-class antibodies appear to have the widespread cross-reactivity reported for the IgM-class mAb 2D8 (Heppell et al. 1995). The immunoglobulin G (IgG) antibodies are of very high affinity with low nonspecific binding in immuno-assays and do cross-react with VTGs from a num-

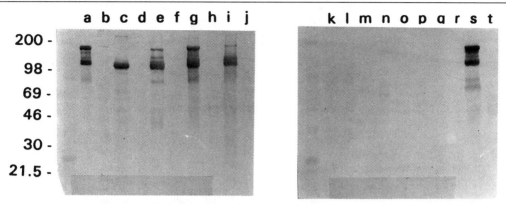

Figure 6-2 Western blot showing the cross-reactivity of mAb 1C8. Serum or plasma samples from vitellogenic females or E-2 induced male fish and control, non-induced males were placed in adjacent lanes. Fish tested included (lanes a and b) striped bass; (lanes c and d) bluegill sunfish; (lanes e and f) largemouth bass; (lanes g and h) pinfish; (lanes i and j) silver mullet; (lanes k and l) American eel; (lanes m and n) carp; (lanes o and p) hardhead catfish; (lanes q and r) brown bullhead; and (lanes s and t) rainbow trout. Molecular weight standards are 200, 97, 69, 46, 30 and 21.5 kDa.

ber of different fishes making them highly useful for our studies. Characterization of these antibodies is a continuing process. Our results to date are summarized in Table 6-1.

To summarize the cross-reactivity data of the IgG-class antibodies, we have constructed a phylogenetic tree (Figure 6-3). MAb 3H1 recognizes an epitope that is conserved in the species we have tested in the Perciformes, Atheriniformes, Batrachoidiformes, Salmoniformes (excluding northern pike), Cypriniformes (excluding goldfish), and Anguilliformes (American eel). The epitope recognized by mAb 1C8 is also highly conserved, extending through all the families tested in 3 teleost orders (Perciformes, Atheriniformes, and Salmoniformes) and in the family Oryzias latipes (medaka) in the order Cypriniformes. However, it does not recognize VTGs from fishes in the family Cyprinidae, in this same order. The 1C8 epitope, however, is less conserved than the one recognized by mAb 3H1. These 2 epitopes are in contrast to the scattered pattern of conservation observed for the epitope of mAb 2D3. For example, mAb 2D3 recognizes VTG from several species scattered over 4 of the 5 families tested in the order Perciformes. Other species in the same families are not recognized. This distribution of immunoreactivity suggests that this particular epitope is free to change, with little evolutionary pressure to remain constant. We have an additional 8 antibodies (from fusion B) that cross-react with VTG from both striped bass and rainbow trout that remain to be tested with this library of species. Our goal is to define the most conserved epitopes in VTGs that are recognized by our panel of antibodies.

Note that none of these antibodies cross-reacted with fish in the order Siluriformes.

Conservation of epitopes in VTG as measured by monoclonal antibodies

Each mAb is by definition directed against a single epitope. In order to determine whether any of the antibodies recognized the same or overlapping epitopes, we

Table 6-1 Cross-reactivity of 4 IgG-type monoclonal antibodies against vitellogenins from a number of different fish species tested by Western Blots

Species tested	mAb 1C8[1]	mAb 3H1[1]	mAb 2D3[3]	mAb 3G2[2]
Striped bass	+++	+++	+	+++
Largemouth bass	+++	+++	−	+++
Smallmouth bass	+++	+++	−	NT
Bluegill sunfish	+++	+++	−	+++
Pinfish	+++	+++	+++	+++
White mullet	+++	+++	+++	+/−
Walleyed pike	+++	+++	−	+++
White crappie	+/−	+/−	−	++
Sheepshead minnow	++	+++	−	+++
Rainbow trout	+++	+++	++	+++
Brook trout	+++	+++	NT	NT
Northern pike	+++	NT	+	NT
Medaka	+++	+++	−	NT
Carp	−	+	+++	NT
Eel	−	+++	−	NT
Toad fish	+/−	+++	−	++
Goldfish	−	−	+++	++
Fundulus	+++	+++	−	+++

(NT) not tested, (+) positive reaction, (−) no interaction. Number of +'s defines relative intensity of reaction.
[1] Fusion A (intact striped bass VTG)
[2] Fusion B (slightly degraded striped bass VTG)
[3] Fusion C (carp VTG)

partially digested several purified VTGs and separated the fragments by high resolution gel electrophoresis. The gels were run in curtain format, that is, the digested VTG was spread in a horizontal well across the width of the gel. After separation, the gel was electroblotted to a PVDF membrane and probed with mAbs known to cross-react with the intact molecules. Partial digestion results in a number of overlapping fragments, ranging from a very small size to 46 kDa in size. In the gels we are only able to discern fragments ranging from about 6 kDa to 46 kDa. An example of a typical digest stained by Coomassie blue is shown for carp VTG in Figure 6-4a. The large diffuse band appearing around 14 kDa represents a large number of fragments of approximately the same size.

Western blotting shows several different banding patterns for the antibodies in our collection (Figures 6-4b, c, and d). Each pattern implies recognition of a different epitope. In the case of the carp VTG digest, we tested 22 mAbs from fusion C

CL. Osteichthyes

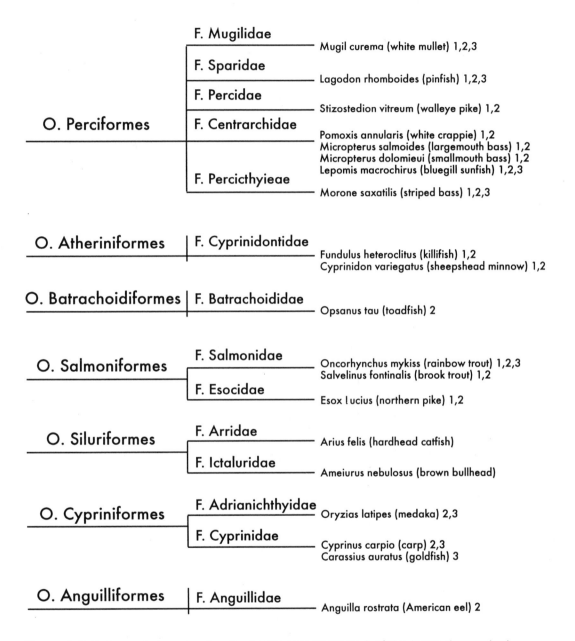

Figure 6-3 Phylogenetic tree showing the species recognized by 3 of the better characterized antibodies: mAbs 1C8[1], 3H1[2] and 2D3[3]. Note that none of these antibodies cross-reacted with fish in the Order Siluriformes.

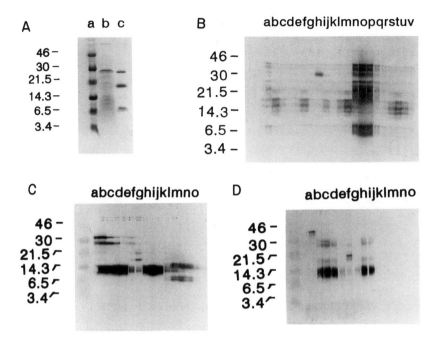

Figure 6-4 Preliminary analysis for epitopes recognized by monoclonal antibodies to VTG. VTGs were purified by DEAE chromatography and then digested with Endoproteinase LysC. (A) Coomassie blue stained gel of (lane a) MW markers, (lane b) digested carp VTG, and (lane c) Endoproteinase LysC control. (B) Western blot analysis of Endoproteinase LysC digested carp VTG probed with (lane a) mouse polyclonal antibody and antibodies from fusion C, mAbs 1G9 (lane b), 1H9 (lane c), 1A5 (lane d), 1A8 (lane e), 1B1 (lane f), 1C8 (lane g), 1C11 (lane h), 1G10 (lane i), 2A6 (lane j), 2B2 (lane k), 2C2 (lane l), 2C3 (lane m), 2D3 (lane n), 2D6 (lane o), 2F12 (lane p), 3B3 (lane q), 2C10 (lane r), 3F2 (lane s), 3H4 (lane t), 4H6 (lane u), and 5C11 (lane v); (C) Western blot analysis of Endoproteinase LysC digested stripped bass VTG with antibodies from fusion A: 1C8 (lane a), 3H1 (lane b), 1D11 (lane c), 2A3 (lane d), 2B10 (lane e), 2C5 (lane f), 2D6 (lane g), 2E5 (lane h), 2F1 (lane i), 3C4 (lane j), 3H1 (lane k), 3H6 (lane l), 4B11 (lane m), 5B2 (lane n), and 1G9 (lane o); (D) Western blot analysis of Endoproteinase LysC digested largemouth bass with the same antibodies described in C.

(Figure 6-4b). Analysis of this blot reveals 4 different patterns and thus at least 4 different epitopes. MAb 2D3 (Figure 6-4b, lane n) cross-reacts with a number of different bands, suggesting that this epitope may appear multiple times in VTG and may be the basis for the spotty cross-reactivity of this mAb with VTGs from different species.

We also digested striped bass VTG (Figure 6-4c) and largemouth bass VTG (Figure 6-4d) with endoproteinase LysC and tested 14 additional mAbs from fusion A to disclose bands containing their specific epitopes. Careful study of the blots indicates at least 5 different patterns for the antibodies reacting with the striped bass digest, suggesting at least 5 different epitopes. MAb 1C8 (Figure 6-4c, lane a) reacts with a couple of fragments around 30 kDa, while mAb 3H1 (Figure 6-4c, lane b), reacts with 2 sets, the set at 30 kDa and another set around 14 kDa. The different pattern of recognition distinguishes the epitopes for these 2 antibodies. Other antibodies on the blot correspond to other mAbs obtained from fusion A. They show 3 other patterns of recognition, suggesting at least 3 different epitopes. Only

9 of these mAbs cross-react with digested largemouth bass VTG, giving 3 distinct patterns of recognition (Figure 6-4d). The pattern for mAb 1C8 again is clearly distinguishable from the pattern of 3H1 indicating that they must be to different epitopes. We are in the process of further characterizing the epitopes of the most promising antibodies.

Usefulness of antibodies in detecting estrogen or estrogen-mimicking contaminants in the environment

We have begun to examine fish caught in the wild, especially males, for the presence of VTG in their serum. Although we examined both sexes, females show naturally cycling serum concentrations of this protein associated with the yolking component of oogenesis (Wallace 1985; Specker and Sullivan 1994). Males also possess the gene to produce VTG, but under normal circumstances where little estradiol is produced, that gene remains inactive. However, in the presence of estrogen-mimicking chemicals, serum VTG levels can increase substantially in males, and without a ready outlet for that VTG (developing oocytes), the levels will remain elevated until proteolytic degradation and excretion occur. We have reported that male carp collected in a sewage effluent channel were producing quantifiable amounts of VTG (Folmar et al. 1996), suggesting that they were exposed to significant levels of estrogenic substances or estrogen mimics.

The most pronounced vitellogenic response observed to date, however, was in bluegill sunfish obtained from a commercial rearing operation (Figure 6-5) compared to fish collected at the same time from a nearby creek. There was no readily apparent source of chemical application or runoff at the commercial fish farm, and the food tested negative both by chemical analysis for pesticides and by bioassay, feeding the same diet to another group of fish. Our data, however, clearly indicate that the bluegill sunfish have been exposed to high levels of an estrogenic substance. We are looking for the possible source of this exposure.

Summary

We have demonstrated the power of identifying aberrant proteins by 2D-PAGE and N-terminal amino acid sequence analysis. Once these proteins have been identified, polyclonal antisera or highly specific monoclonal antibodies can be produced and incorporated into detection assays, such as ELISA or Western blot. Our investigations have positively identified biomarkers of exposure to endocrine-disrupting chemicals (EDCs). We intend to use this line of inquiry to study the effects of these chemicals on growth and development.

Acknowledgments

This research was supported in part by a USEPA Cooperative Agreement (CR821437) to NDD and a grant from NIEHS (P42 ES07375) to NDD.

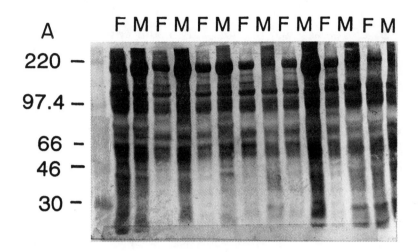

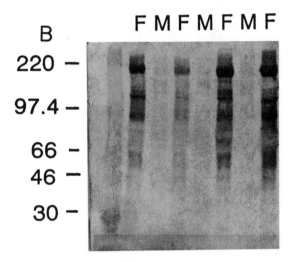

Figure 6-5 Western blot analysis of serum collected from bluegill sunfish in (A) a privately owned pond (B) nearby creek. Serum samples from individual fish were diluted and run in a gel as described in Materials and Methods. MAb 1C8 was used to disclose VTG in the samples by Western blot. F, female and M, male fish.

References

Altschul SF, Gish W, Miller W, Myers EW, Lipman DJ. 1990. Basic local alignment search tool. *J Mol Biol* 215:403–410.

Baumann PC, Smith WD, Ribick M. 1982. Hepatic tumor rates and polynuclear hydrocarbon levels in two populations of brown bullheads (*Ictalurus nebulosus*). In: Cooke M, Dennis AJ, Fisher GL, editors. Polynuclear aromatic hydrocarbons: Sixth International Symposium on Physical and Biological Chemistry. Columbus OH: Battelle Pr. p 93–102.

Baumann PC. 1992. The use of tumors in wild populations of fish to assess ecosystem health. *J Aquat Ecosyst Health* 1:135–146.

Colborn T, Clement C, editors. 1992. Chemically-induced alteration in sexual and functional development: the wildlife/human connection. Volume XXII. Princeton NJ: Princeton Sci. 403 p.

Delcuve GP, Sun JM, Davie JR. 1992. Expression of rainbow trout apolipoprotein A-I genes in liver and hepatocellular carcinoma. *J Lipid Res* 33:251–262.

Denslow ND, Nguyen H, Parten B. 1992. In-gel cleavage strategies for sequencing internal regions of proteins separated by SDS-PAGE [abstract]. San Diego CA: Sixth Symposium of the Protein Society.

Denslow ND, Chow MM, Folmar LC. 1994. Isoforms of apolipoprotein A-1 in the serum of brown bullheads (*Ameiurus nebulosus*) with liver cancer. *Canadian J Zool* 72:1522–1527.

Denslow ND, Chow MM, Folmar LC, Bonomelli SL, Heppell SA, Sullivan CV. 1997. Development of antibodies to teleost vitellogenins: potential biomarkers for environmental estrogens. In: Bengston DA, Henschel DS, editors. Volume 5, Environmental toxicology and risk assessment: biomarkers and risk assessment. Philadelphia PA: American Society for Testing and Materials (ASTM). STP 1306. p 22–36.

DeVito MJ, Thomas T, Martin E, Umbreit TH, Gallo MA. 1992. Antiestrogenic action of 2,3,7,8 tetrachlorodibenzo-p-dioxin: tissue specific regulation of estrogen receptor in CD1 mice. *Toxicol Appl Pharmacol* 113:284–292.

Folmar LC, Denslow ND, Wallace RA, LaFleur G, Gross TS, Bonomelli S, Sullivan CV. 1995. A highly conserved N-terminal sequence for teleost vitellogenin with potential value to the biochemistry, molecular biology and pathology of vitellogenesis. *J Fish Biol* 46:255–263.

Folmar LC, Denslow ND, Rao V, Chow M, Crain DA, Enblom J, Marcino J, Guillette Jr LJ. 1996. Vitellogenin induction and reduced serum testosterone concentrations in feral male carp (*Cyprinus carpio*) captured near a major metropolitan sewage treatment plant. *Environ Health Perspect* 104:1096–1101.

Jobling S, Sumpter JP. 1993. Detergent components in sewage effluent are weakly oestrogenic to fish. An in vitro study using rainbow trout (*Onchorhynchus mykiss*) hepatocytes. *Aquat Toxicol* 27:361–372.

Heppell SA, Denslow ND, Folmar LC, Sullivan CV. 1995. "Universal" assay of vitellogenin as a biomarker for environmental estrogens. *Environ Health Perspect* 103:9–15.

Lim EH, Ding JL, Lam TJ. 1991. Estradiol-induced vitellogenin gene expression in a teleost fish, *Orechromis aureus. Gen and Comparat Endocrinol* 82:206–214.

Mayer FL, Versteeg DJ, McKee MJ, Folmar LC, Graney RL, McCume DC, Rattner BA. 1992. Physiological and nonspecific biomarkers. In: Huggett RL, Kimble RA, Mehrle PM, Bergman HL, editors. Biomarkers: biochemical, physiological, and histological markers of anthropogenic stress. Boca Raton FL: Lewis. p 5–86.

McLachlan JA, Newbold RR, Teng CT, Korach KS. 1992. Environmental estrogens: orphan receptors and genetic imprinting. In: Colborne T, Clement C, editors. Chemically-induced alterations in sexual and functional development: the wildlife/human connection. Volume XXI. Princeton NJ: Princeton Sci. p 107–112.

McLachlan JA. 1993. Functional toxicology: a new approach to detect biologically active xenobiotics. *Environ Health Perspect* 101:386–387.

Pakdel F, Feon S, Le Gac F, Le Menn F, Valotaire Y. 1991. In vivo estrogen induction of hepatic estrogen receptor mRNA and correlation with vitellogenin mRNA in rainbow trout. *Molec Cellular Endocrin* 75:205–212.

Peterson RE, Theobald HM, Kimmel GL. 1993. Developmental and reproductive toxicology of dioxins and related compounds: cross species comparisons. *Crit Rev Toxicol* 23:283–335.

Safe S, Astroff B, Harris M, Zacharwski T, Dickerson R, Romkes M, Biegel L. 1991. 2,3,7,8-tetrachlorodibenzo-p-dioxin (TCDD) and related compounds as antiestrogens: characterization and mechanism of action. *Pharmacol Toxicol* 69:400–409.

Safe SH. 1994. Dietary and environmental estrogens and antiestrogens and their possible role in human disease. *Environ Sci Pollut Res* 1:29–33.

Schagger H, von Jagow G. 1987. Tricine-sodium dodecil sulfate-polyacrylamide gel electrophoresis for the separation of proteins in the range from 1 to 100 kDa. *Anal Biochem* 166:368–379.

Semple-Rowland SL, Adamus G, Cohen RJ, Ulshafer RJ. 1991. A reliable two-dimensional gel electrophoresis procedure for separating neural proteins. *Electrophoresis* 12:307–312.

Soto AM, Lin T.-M, Justica H, Silivia RM, Sonnenschein C. 1992. An "in culture" bioassay to assess the estrogenicity of xenobiotics. In: Colborne T, Clement C, editors. Chemically-induced alterations in sexual and functional development: the wildlife/human connection. Volume XXI. Princeton NJ: Princeton Sci. p 295–309.

Soto AM, Chung KL, Sonnenschein C. 1994. The pesticides endosulfan, toxaphene and dieldrin have estrogenic effects on human estrogen-sensitive cells. *Environ Health Perspect* 102:380–383.

Specker JL, Sullivan CV. 1994. Vitellogenesis in fishes: status and perspectives. In: Davey KG, Peter RE, Tobe SS, editors. Perspectives in endocrinology. Ottawa: National Research Council. p 304–315.

Sumpter JP, Jobling S. 1995. Vitellogenin as a biomarker for estrogenic contamination of the aquatic environment. *Environ Health Perspectives* 103:173–178.

Tao Y, Hara A, Hodson RG, Woods III LC, Sullivan CV. 1993. Purification, characterization and immunoassay of striped bass (*Morone saxatilis*) vitellogenin. *Fish Physiol Biochem* 12:31–46.

Wallace RA. 1985. Vitellogenesis and oocyte growth in non-mammalian vertebrates. In: Browder LW, editor. Volume 1, Developmental biology. New York NY: Plenum Pr. p 127–177.

Assessment of estrogenic activity in fish

Alison C. Nimrod, William H. Benson

Just as there is concern that exposure to environmental estrogens may result in endocrine disruption in mammalian species, there are similar concerns regarding fish and other wildlife species. In this chapter, we review the means for assessing estrogenic activity in fish; these methods exploit physiological mechanisms of hormone receptor interaction, sexual differentiation, and oviparity in fish. We describe a channel catfish (*Ictalurus punctatus*) model for vitellogenin (VTG) induction in which fish were exposed to chemicals in an acute, single injection paradigm and were monitored for VTG in the serum. To validate the model, we present data for VTG induction by several xenobiotics with known activity at the mammalian estrogen receptor and other xenobiotics identified in mammals as environmental estrogens. Results are also presented in which the model was used to demonstrate interference of the normal response to estradiol by co-administering doses of xenobiotic with estradiol. Finally, we describe a technique for assessing vitellogenesis in a small fish species, Japanese medaka (*Oryzias latipes*).

The female steroid hormone estradiol mediates effects through receptor interaction. Pharmacologists have used several estrogenic bioassays in mammals to measure the potency of drugs for possible therapeutic use. Toxicologists utilize the same bioassays to identify xenobiotics that have the potential to disrupt the endocrine system through the estrogen pathway. The basis of these bioassays are the target tissues of the hormone in mammals, i.e., the uterus, vagina, and mammary glands. The most widely accepted and "classic" assay in use is the measurement of growth in the reproductive tract of sexually immature female rodents (Galey et al. 1993). This growth can be measured most simply by weight measurements, or with greater sensitivity by histological scoring of alterations in the reproductive tract (Eroschenko 1981), or measurement of proliferation markers such as ornithine decarboxylase activity (Kupfer and Bulger 1980). Proliferation of cell lines derived from estrogen-responsive breast (Welshons et al. 1990) and endometrial cancers (Markiewicz et al. 1993) has been used as an in vitro assay to assess estrogenic activity of phytoestrogens. Estrogenic activity can also be assessed as the ability of the molecule to bind to the estrogen receptor, either as an agonist, antagonist, or partial agonist. Affinity for the receptor can be determined by radioligand competitive binding studies in tissues which have high estrogen receptor populations, the target tissues. Several researchers have used recombinant techniques to develop sensitive bioassays for estrogenic activity based on linking a transfected estrogen response element to a reporter gene. Routledge and Sumpter (1996) describe such a system in yeast and have used it to screen various environmental estrogens.

Vitellogenesis

In fish and other oviparous animals such as birds and reptiles, the process of yolk production is regulated directly by estrogen. Induction in the liver of vitellogenin (VTG), a glycophospholipoprotein, results from an estradiol-estrogen receptor inter- action followed by transcription activation (Lazier and MacKay 1993). Vitellogenin enters the bloodstream and is taken up into the oocytes where it is cleaved into the yolk proteins, phosvitin and lipovitellin. Sexually mature females produce VTG in response to signals from endogenous estrogens. Males and sexually immature females, with minimal levels of circulating estradiol, do not normally have detect- able levels of VTG in their serum. However, vitellogenesis can be induced with exogenous estradiol administration (Ng and Idler 1983). Therefore, the inducibility of VTG and the dependence of the process on estrogen receptor activation make vitellogenesis an appropriate model for assessing estrogenic activity.

Sexual Differentiation in Fish

Sex hormones, both androgens and estrogens, have been used in the aquaculture industry to control sex ratio because the sexual phenotype is not developed at hatch. While a few anomalies have been observed, such as androgens causing feminization in channel catfish (Davis et al. 1990), most species studied are femi- nized with larval estrogen treatment and masculinized by androgen treatment (Hunter and Donaldson 1983). In some species, such as the mosquitofish (*Gambusia affinis affinis*), sexual phenotypes in adults can change following steroid treatment (Howell and Denton 1989). Alteration of sexual differentiation, resulting in unex- pected population sex ratios, can be a marker of endocrine disruption that occurs in early life stages. Treatment with low levels of endocrine disrupting compounds and/or during later life stages could result in males with female characteristics and vice versa.

Identifying Estrogenic Chemicals in Fish

Thomas and Smith (1993) have proposed competitive binding of xenobiotics to estrogen receptors in fish liver, which has the greatest concentration of estrogen receptors, as a screening tool for identifying estrogenic compounds. Chlordecone was characterized as estrogenic based on its binding affinity for spotted seatrout (*Cynoscion nebulosus*) estrogen receptor (Thomas and Smith 1993). Several alkyl- phenolic compounds have affinity for the rainbow trout (RBT) hepatic estrogen receptor (White et al. 1994).

In addition to affinity of a chemical for the estrogen receptor, masculinization/ feminization and VTG induction have been utilized as indicators of estrogenic activity in fish. Such responses in fish, following exposure to environmental estro- gens, have been measured in several field and laboratory studies. Alterations in sexual differentiation such as masculinization, as determined by morphological changes in the anal fin, were observed in mosquitofish following laboratory expo- sure to stigmastanol and degradation products (Howell and Denton 1989). Sex reversal or partial masculinization/feminization in fish found in contaminated areas is reviewed by Bortone and Davis (1994). While these studies do not identify estrogenic compounds as causative agents, they do indicate the potential of sexual differentiation as an endpoint for use in estrogenic bioassays.

Vitellogenin induction has been observed in caged male RBT (*Onchorhynchus mykiss*) exposed to sewage treatment effluents (Purdom et al. 1994). Denison et al. (1981) reported that the serum of insecticide-resistant mosquitofish contained a VTG-like protein year round as opposed to only during the breeding season. Pelissero et al. demonstrated the estrogenic activity of phytoestrogens present in fish food by measuring vitellogenesis both in vivo in Siberian sturgeon (*Acipenser baeri*) (1991) and in vitro in primary cultures of RBT hepatocytes (1993). Guppies (*Poecilia reticulata*) (Wester et al. 1985) and Japanese medaka (*Oryzias latipes*) (Wester and Canton 1986), chronically exposed to β-hexachlorocyclohexane (β-HCH) produce VTG. Jobling and Sumpter (1993) used VTG induction in primary cultures of RBT hepatocytes to demonstrate the estrogenicity of alkylphenols (environmental metabolites of alkylphenol ethoxylate detergents including nonyl- and octylphenol as well as carboxylic acid derivatives).

Vitellogenesis has thus been the most utilized biomarker of estrogenic activity in fish. As with many biomarkers, one point of concern is the relevance of vitellogenesis to toxicity, i.e., whether protein induction has detrimental consequences for fish. In females, in which estradiol is responsible for the reproductive process, vitellogenesis itself can be a target of endocrine disruption. Interference with this process has the potential to compromise the development of embryos and larvae by altering nutritional stores available to them. In males and immature females, there is evidence that VTG production can lead to accumulation in and damage to the kidneys because there is no depository for VTG (Herman and Kincaid 1988; Wester and Canton 1986). The VTG response may serve as a marker of population-level effects, e.g., alteration of gamete quality and interference with sexual differentiation and development. Indeed, in male RBT exposed to ethinylestradiol (a synthetic steroidal estrogen used therapeutically) as well as alkylphenolic compounds, the concentration of VTG in blood was inversely correlated with testicular size (Jobling et al. 1996).

In our laboratory, we have been investigating estrogenic responses in fish as a means to understand the role that environmental estrogens and other endocrine disrupters may play in mediating reproductive toxicity. This has involved screening known mammalian xenoestrogens for VTG induction in a fish model, examining the effect of these compounds on the normal vitellogenic response to estradiol, and using fish as a model to assess reproductive toxicity by these compounds.

Experimental Methods and Results

Catfish model
We have utilized VTG induction in channel catfish (*Ictalurus punctatus*) as a bioassay for estrogenic compounds because this fish is an aquaculture crop in the Southeastern United States (U.S.) and, consequently, there are several sources of this fish. In the following experiments, pond-raised catfish were obtained from the

U.S.D.A. National Aquaculture Center (Stuttgart, Arkansas). There is also a monoclonal antibody (mAb) to channel catfish VTG, which has been generously provided by Dr. John Grizzle (Auburn University). The development and characterization of this antibody as well as its use in an enzyme-linked immunosorbent assay (ELISA) to measure VTG levels in pond-raised catfish has been described by Goodwin et al. (1992).

Exposure

Sexually immature catfish (65 to 95 g, both males and females) were acclimated for at least 2 weeks in a single flow-through Living Stream (Frigid Units, Inc., Toledo OH) holding tank before experimentation began. Fish were anaesthetized with MS-222 and exposed by single intraperitoneal (i.p.) injection of the test compound in an agar suspension. Following injection, fish were maintained in fasting conditions in flow-through tanks (one per treatment group). The light cycle was 16:8 hours light:dark and temperature was 22 to 24°C. Blood from the caudal vein was sampled and the serum analyzed for VTG using a competitive ELISA. Dose response and time response curves of the induction of VTG following estradiol administration were constructed. The peak of VTG appearance in the serum was 11 days, however the protein was detected by 24 hours post-injection (data not shown); in the following experiments with catfish, blood was sampled 7 days after injection. The dose required to produce half the maximal induction response at 7 days post-injection (the effective dose for 50% of test organisms [ED50]) was 0.6 mg/kg, and this dose was used as a positive control for catfish experiments (Nimrod and Benson 1996).

Validation of vitellogenesis as an estrogenic screen

Screening synthetic chemicals with known activity at the mammalian estrogen receptor served as a means to compare the estrogen-responsiveness of the catfish model with that of mammals. The estrogen receptor agonists diethylstilbestrol (DES), ethinylestradiol (EE2), and mestranol (ME2) as well as the antagonist tamoxifen (TMX) were screened in the catfish by measuring serum VTG 7 days after a single i.p. injection as described above. Doses of these compounds (0.59, 0.66, 0.68, and 0.82 mg/kg of DES, EE2, ME2, and TMX, respectively) were equimolar to 0.6 mg estradiol/kg. An additional dose of TMX (136.4 mg/kg) was included, equimolar to 100 mg estradiol/kg. Because of space constraints, the experiment was conducted as 2 exposures. Each exposure included a negative control (vehicle only) and a positive control (0.6 mg estradiol/kg). In this and the following experiments, unless otherwise indicated, all vitellogenic responses were expressed as percent of mean estradiol response for that exposure for statistical analysis. When 2 exposures were compared, the agar and estradiol percent responses were pooled and groups were compared to the appropriate control using ANOVA, followed by the multiple comparison test indicated in legends. In Figure 7-1, EE2 and ME2 exposure resulted in VTG levels significantly greater than those following estradiol treatment. In mammals, EE2 has a greater binding affinity for the mammalian estrogen receptor, 158% that of estradiol (Fritsch 1991), and ME2 is a proestrogen requiring o-demethylation to EE2. Results presented here suggest that a similar metabolic pathway occurs in catfish. While DES is known to be a potent estrogen in mammalian systems, where relative binding affinity is 141%, it was significantly less potent than estradiol in our investigations. Thomas and Smith (1993) reported DES

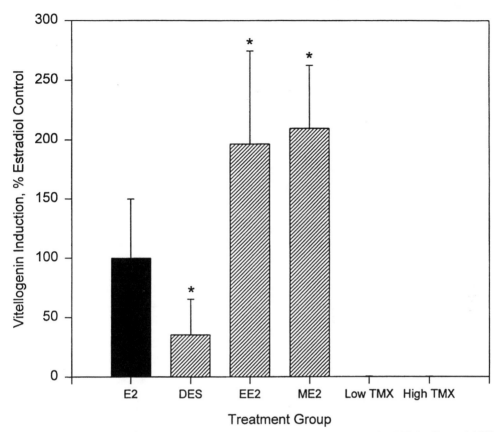

Figure 7-1 Induction of vitellogenesis in catfish by xenoestrogens. DES (n=8), EE2 (n=8), and ME2 (n=8) were compared to the estradiol (E2) control (n=16) by ANOVA followed by Dunnett's method of multiple comparisons to control group; TMX doses (n=7,8) were compared to the agar negative control (n=15) by Kruskal-Wallis ANOVA on ranks. Bars and error bars are means and standard deviations (SD), respectively.* Indicates significant difference from E2, $p<0.05$. (Adapted from Nimrod and Benson 1996).

and estradiol had similar binding affinities for the spotted seatrout liver, whereas Pelissero et al. (1993) found that DES was less effective than estradiol in stimulating RBT hepatocytes to produce VTG. Tamoxifen was not expected to have a strong estrogenic effect; TMX is classified as a partial agonist for the estrogen receptor in mammals and its action as an agonist or antagonist depends on the tissue and the presence of estradiol (Jordan 1984). Agonistic activity was not observed with TMX, even at a dose equimolar to 100 mg estradiol/kg. Therefore, known chemicals were found to have a similar order of potency in catfish as in mammals except for the activity of DES which was lower than expected based on mammalian receptor affinity data.

Screening xenobiotics for estrogenic activity
Having compared the responses to the above compounds in the catfish and mammalian models, the catfish was used to screen known or suspected environmentally relevant xenoestrogens for estrogenic activity. Preliminary exposures were used to examine each potentially estrogenic compound to determine the highest

tolerated dose as well as any indication of estrogenic activity. Compounds tested included o,p'-DDT, methoxychlor, chlordecone, lindane, β-HCH and p-nonylphenol. The pesticides and isomers were obtained from Radian International and p-nonylphenol (CAS RN 84852-15-3*) was a gift from Schenectady International. If there was no VTG induction in these preliminary exposures, the compounds were deemed void of estrogenic activity in this model. For compounds that appeared to have estrogenic activity in the preliminary exposure, a second experiment was conducted with larger sample sizes. Table 7-1 presents both the compounds that did not induce VTG and the highest nonlethal doses administered. The highest doses of lindane and chlordecone were equimolar to 100 and 50 mg estradiol/kg, respectively; doses higher than these resulted in lethality. Neither β-HCH nor o,p'-DDT induced VTG at doses equimolar to 300 mg estradiol/kg. Higher doses were impractical due to maximum volume considerations even though there was no apparent toxicity (death or morbidity). There is evidence that both β-HCH and DDT have estrogenic activity in fish as discussed previously (Denison et al. 1981; Wester et al. 1985; Wester and Canton 1986), but these were chronic exposures to low concentrations while in the present experiment maximum doses were administered. In addition, Harries et al. (1995) demonstrated VTG induction in vitro in trout hepatocytes in response to o,p'-DDT. An estrogenic response to the relatively nontoxic o,p'-DDT and β-HCH may have been noted under a chronic dosing regime if such a regime resulted in a higher concentration of these compounds at the target tissue. In addition, a chronic experiment may reveal estrogenic activity if these compounds undergo metabolic activation; there is evidence that the ortho, para prime dichlorodiphenyldichloroethylene (o,p'-DDE) metabolite of o,p'-DDT has affinity for the mammalian estrogen receptor (Nelson 1974).

The estrogenic activity of chlordecone in mammalian and avian models has been well documented (see Eroschenko 1981 for review). In fish, chlordecone has been shown to induce vitellogenesis in RBT following chronic exposure through feeding (Donohoe and Curtis 1996) and to bind to the hepatic estrogen receptor (Thomas and Smith 1993). In addition, histologically scored damage to testes and ovaries in freshwater catfish (*Heteropneustes fossilis*) has been found following exposure to chlordecone; the investigators hypothesize that toxicity may be due, in part, to estrogenic effects (Srivastava and Srivastava 1994). Vitellogenin induction in the present study following chlordecone exposure may be absent because the toxic acute dose resulted in a lower concentration at the liver than the dose required to cause estrogenic activity.

There is evidence of both estrogenic and antiestrogenic activity of lindane in rats (Raizada et al. 1980; Chadwick et al. 1988). Although there are conflicting explanations for the mechanism of action, these reports agree that lindane interferes at some point in estrogenic action. There is no evidence in the literature indicating whether these effects are similar in fish. In our study, lindane, like chlordecone, was more toxic than either o,p'-DDT or β-HCH; if lindane is estrogenic we were not able to demonstrate this in the catfish model.

Both p-nonylphenol and methoxychlor demonstrated evidence of possessing estrogenic activity (Table 7-2). While VTG levels are presented in the table as mg/mL values, statistical analysis performed on data was expressed as percent estradiol response in order to pool the controls for 2 exposures. A nonparametric ANOVA

Table 7-1 Mammalian xenoestrogens that did not induce vitellogenesis in immature channel catfish following a single i.p. injection

Compound	Highest dose administered (mg/kg)	Equimolar estradiol dose (mg/kg)
o,p'-DDT	390	300
Chlordecone	90	50
β-HCH	320	300
Lindane	107	100

was used to detect differences between groups. At both 79 and 237 mg/kg, p-nonylphenol resulted in significant VTG appearance in serum. The response was variable among individuals, with serum levels ranging from 0.6 to 9.9 mg/mL for the low dose and 0.1 to 14.7mg/mL for the higher dose. The high dose of p-nonylphenol in this experiment was 500 times more than the estradiol positive control, yet VTG levels were more than an order of magnitude less. The low potency is consistent with that seen with mammalian systems (Soto et al. 1991) as well as in vitro and in vivo fish models (Jobling and Sumpter 1993; Lech et al. 1996). When RBT hepatocytes are treated in vitro with p-nonylphenol and its related compounds (octylphenol and carboxylic acid derivatives), the potencies for VTG induction are 4 to 6 orders of magnitude less than for estradiol (Jobling and Sumpter 1993). The affinity of p-nonylphenol for the trout estrogen receptor is 1000 times less than estradiol (White et al. 1994).

Vitellogenin induction by methoxychlor was also variable; thus induction was significantly different from the agar control for only the lowest dose (127 mg/kg). The range of VTG concentrations was 0.27 to 9.99 mg/mL for the low dose and 0.03 to 13.75 mg/mL for the high dose. Methoxychlor has been shown in mammalian systems to be a proestrogen, requiring o-demethylation to possess estrogenic activity (Kupfer and Bulger 1980). If the same is true in catfish, differences in metabolizing capability may explain variability in response.

Alterations of vitellogenesis by xenoestrogens

As discussed above, one possible mechanism of toxicity of environmental estrogens is interference with the normal vitellogenic process in female fish, compromising spawning or oocyte nutritional status and thus altering development and growth of embryos and larvae. By co-administering these compounds with estradiol and measuring the vitellogenic response compared to estradiol alone, we were able to model this potential toxicity to normal vitellogenic females. Again, we started with known estrogens and antiestrogens (Figure 7-2). Ethinylestradiol, ME2, and DES (equimolar to 0.6 mg estradiol/kg) were co-administered with estradiol (0.6 mg/kg) using the same exposure and sampling conditions as in the screening experiment. The combination doses of EE2/estradiol and ME2/estradiol resulted in VTG levels greater than estradiol alone. The VTG induction with DES/estradiol was also significantly greater than estradiol alone. Because DES alone is not as potent in inducing the vitellogenic response as is estradiol, the interaction of these 2 compounds is at

Table 7-2 Vitellogenin induction following i.p. injection of p-nonylphenol and methoxychlor

Treatment	n	Dose (mg/kg)	Estradiol equimolar dose (mg/kg)	Vg[a] (mg/mL)	
Agar	15	—	—	0.2	(0.3)
Low nonylphenol	7	79	100	3.6[b]	(3.4)
High nonylphenol	6	237	300	9.5[b]	(5.7)
Low methoxychlor	8	127	100	2.5[b]	(3.3)
High methoxychlor	8	380	300	3.3	(5.1)
Estradiol	14	0.6	—	362.8	(116.2)

[a] Values are means (standard deviation).
[b] Values significantly different from agar control, $p<0.05$. Statistical analysis was conducted on vitellogenin levels expressed as % estradiol response. Nonylphenol- and methoxychlor-treated groups were compared to agar control by Kruskal-Wallis ANOVA on ranks followed by Dunn's method of multiple comparisons to a control group (adapted from Nimrod and Benson 1996).

least additive. Tamoxifen was co-administered at 2 doses, again, equimolar to 0.6 and 100 mg estradiol/kg with estradiol. At the high dose, the antiestrogen was able to inhibit the estrogenic response. Therefore, TMX would appear to have only antagonistic activity in the catfish vitellogenesis model due to absence of activity when administered alone and inhibition of response when given in combination with estradiol. The observance that an equimolar dose of TMX is ineffective in antagonizing estradiol's induction suggests that TMX, as in the mammalian system, has a weaker affinity for the receptor than estradiol.

Methoxychlor and p-nonylphenol were also tested in this paradigm of combination dosing (Figure 7-3). Both compounds were co-administered as doses equimolar to 100 and 300 mg estradiol/kg with estradiol. Despite a decreased mean of VTG with the highest nonylphenol dose, neither dose of p-nonylphenol significantly altered the normal response to estradiol. There was a reduction of VTG for both doses of methoxychlor but only the highest dose was significantly less than estradiol. The high methoxychlor/estradiol treatment group was the only one that resulted in mortality; 38% died. Therefore, it is impossible to say with any degree of certainty whether the observed decrease of serum VTG was due to an antagonism of the response directly or through general toxicity.

Detection of vitellogenin in small fish species

Utility of Japanese medaka as a reproductive toxicity model

The utility of vitellogenesis as a marker of estrogenic activity in field studies depends on the certainty to which the induction can be linked to higher level effects such as reproductive toxicity. Many laboratories are not equipped with the facilities or support needed to conduct a full life-cycle assessment of endocrine disrupting compounds on fish species such as the channel catfish or RBT. Therefore, small fish such as the Japanese medaka are useful as a model for reproductive and developmental toxicity. The small size of the medaka (2 to 4 cm) and quick maturity allow

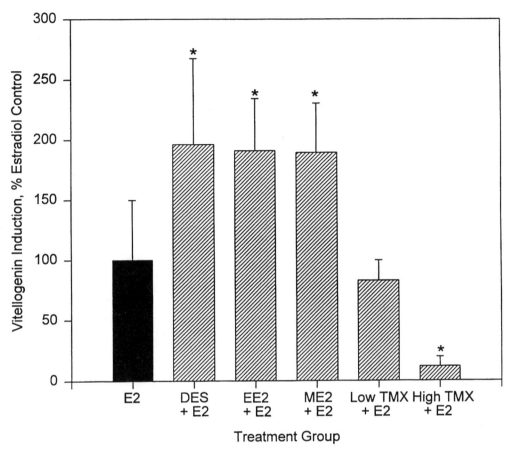

Figure 7-2 Alteration of vitellogenesis by xenoestrogens following co-administration of xenobiotic with E2. All doses (n=7 to 8) were compared to the E2 control (n=16) by Kruskal-Wallis ANOVA on ranks followed by Dunn's method of multiple comparisons to a control group. Bars and error bars represent means and SDs, respectively.* Indicates statistical difference from E2 alone, p<0.05. (Adapted from Nimrod and Benson 1996).

for large samples sizes as well as relatively short life cycle and transgenerational studies. Medaka are daily spawners during the breeding season and the eggs, which hatch in 8 to 10 days, are transparent allowing developmental observation. The time from hatching to egg production is 2 to 2.5 months. Medaka are also susceptible to sex reversal by steroid compounds (Yamamoto 1975). In our laboratory we have observed sex reversal following estradiol feeding as well as waterborne exposure (with concentrations as low as 0.1 ppb) during the first month of life (unpublished data). These factors make it ideal for studying reproductive effects observed in other models and hypothesized to occur in fish as a result of endocrine disrupter exposure. Measurable effects in the medaka include reduced egg quality from alterations in vitellogenesis and sexual differentiation changes in larvae (feminization or masculinization). In order to use the medaka in future reproductive studies with endocrine disrupters, it was necessary to confirm that the animal is susceptible to the same estrogenic effects observed with catfish. Furthermore, we would eventually like to correlate reproductive toxicity with induction or inhibition

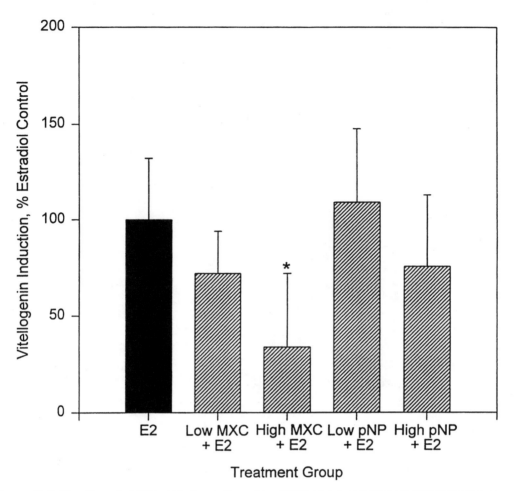

Figure 7-3 Alteration of vitellogenesis by methoxychlor (MXC) and *p*-nonylphenol (NP) following co-administration of xenobiotic with E2. Combination groups (n=5 to 8) were compared to E2 control (n=14) by ANOVA followed by Dunnett's method for multiple comparisons to a control group. Bars and error bars represent mean values and SDs, respectively. * Indicates statistical difference from E2 alone, p<0.05. (Adapted from Nimrod and Benson 1996).

in vitellogenesis. However, the small size of the medaka makes blood collection difficult. We decided to test whether the hepatic cytosolic fraction could be assayed for VTG in lieu of blood samples.

Exposure and detection of vitellogenin in serum and cytosolic fraction
Validation in catfish. A dose response study was undertaken to demonstrate the responsiveness of VTG detection in the cytosolic fraction in catfish. Juvenile catfish (males and females, 30 to 50g, four/group) were injected with 0.12, 0.6, and 3.0 mg/kg estradiol in an agar suspension once on day 1 and again on day 4. On day 7, fish were sacrificed and both blood and livers collected and frozen at −80°C until analysis. Liver tissues were homogenized in the presence of phenyl-methylsulphonylfluoride to inhibit proteases, centrifuged at 10,000 × g followed by

100,000 × g to isolate the cytosolic fraction. Vitellogenin in the cytosolic fraction was determined with a direct ELISA utilizing the previously mentioned antibody specific for channel catfish. Serum VTG was measured with an ELISA as described previously. Both serum and cytosolic VTG levels increased with increasing dose and cytosolic VTG was positively correlated with serum VTG (Pearson product moment correlation coefficient=0.647, p=0.002), see Table 7-3. As the "cytosolic fraction" referred to here was prepared from unperfused livers, it is very possible that much of the VTG detected in the cytosolic fraction is actually from the blood trapped in the liver as opposed to the cytoplasm of the hepatocytes. However, because the objective of this experiment was to determine a procedure for detecting VTG in small fish which are not easily bled, the source of VTG was not as relevant as detection.

Detection of vitellogenin in medaka. Medaka cytosol was examined for dose-response to estradiol. Adult male medaka (12 per group) were exposed through water to 0.1, 1.0, and 10.0 ppb estradiol for 6 days; exposure solution was changed daily. On day 7, fish were sacrificed, livers collected and, due to limited tissue size, pooled (3 per sample); blood was collected directly from the heart with a capillary tube and pooled (12 per sample). Hepatic cytosol was prepared as described above. A versatile mAb (HL1081-1C8) which is cross-reactive with several VTGs across several teleostean families was generously provided by Dr. Nancy Denslow (University of Florida). The development of this antibody is described by Denslow et al. (1996). This antibody was used to identify VTG in the cytosolic extracts as well as in serum by western blotting following polyacrylamide gel electrophoresis. The pooled serum samples showed a dose-response increase in VTG over the 3 doses and VTG was not detected in serum of control (ethanol-treated) fish (data not shown). The 1C8 antibody detected 2 bands in the cytosolic blots, at 200 and 120 kilodaltons (kDa). Both bands increased with increasing concentration; optical density of the bands was determined by image analysis (NIH Image, version 1.52) (Table 7-3). This suggests that the use of cytosol is a feasible alternative to assaying VTG levels in serum of small fish species. Because of dilution with other proteins, cytosol may be less sensitive than serum, but if antibody were available in sufficient quantity, an ELISA could be utilized to measure low concentrations. Work is underway to detect VTG induction in medaka following exposure to nonylphenol and methoxychlor.

Conclusions

Several means have been used to measure the activity of environmental estrogens in fish including 1) induction of vitellogenesis, 2) binding to the hepatic estrogen receptor, 3) and influence upon sexual differentiation. This chapter described the validation of VTG induction in channel catfish as a biomarker for the presence of environmental estrogens using an in vivo acute paradigm. The model was used to screen several known environmental estrogens. Of these, p-nonylphenol was able to increase VTG levels in the serum, while methoxychlor also showed some estrogenic activity. However, the present in vivo screening assay has limitations because, as indicated by chlordecone, the acute, single dose of environmental contaminants may be toxic to fish. Also, several xenobiotics that have been identified to elicit estrogenic responses in both mammals and fish were not detected in this assay,

Table 7-3 Comparison of VTG detection in serum and cytosolic fraction

	Intraperitoneal injection of catfish			Aqueous exposure of medaka	
Estradiol dose (mg/kg)	Serum Vg ELISA[a] (mg/mL)	Cytosolic Vg ELISA[a] (absorbance)	Estradiol concentration (ppb)	Cytosolic Vg Western Blot[b] 200 kDa (optical density	120kDa units)
Control	0.0 (0)	0.002 (0.001)	Control	3.1 (1.2)	2.5 (0.9)
0.12	4.1 (3.3)	0.063 (0.052)	0.1	2.6 (1.1)	10.0 (3.3)
0.6	17.0 (7.6)	0.204 (0.070)	1.0	21.8 (19.7)	88.4 (70.6)
3.0	46.4 (24.2)	0.372 (0.229)	10.0	58.3 (68.9)	119.9 (14.8)

[a] Means (SD) of 5 animals per treatment group.
[b] Means (SD) of 4 pooled samples of 3 fish each.

suggesting that a chronic, low exposure regime may be more sensitive to weak estrogenic compounds. A chronic regime would also avoid the acute toxicity that prevents sufficient concentration to accumulate at the target tissues before lethality results and may also allow for activating metabolism to occur. Vitellogenesis can also be used to examine toxic mechanisms. One mechanism, interference with vitellogenesis in mature reproducing females, was explored using p-nonylphenol and methoxychlor. Finally, the necessity to measure vitellogenesis in small fish species led to a correlation between VTG in the serum and hepatic cytosol as detected with immunoassay techniques.

Acknowledgments

Support for the research activities presented was provided in part by the Department of the Interior, U.S. Geological Survey, through the Mississippi Water Resources Research Institute, and the U.S. Environmental Protection Agency (R 823450-010).

References

Bortone SA, Davis WP. 1994. Fish intersexuality as an indicator of environmental stress. *BioScience* 44:165–172.

Chadwick RW, Cooper RL, Chang J, Rehnberg GL, McElroy WK. 1988. Possible antiestrogenic activity of lindane in female rats. *J Biochem Toxicol* 3:147–158.

Davis KB, Simco BA, Goudie CA, Parker NC, Cauldwell W, Snellgrove R. 1990. Hormonal sex manipulation and evidence for female homogamety in channel catfish. *Gen Comp Endocrinol* 78:218–223.

Denison MS, Chambers JE, Yarbrough JD. 1981. Persistent vitellogenin-like protein and binding of DDT in the serum of insecticide-resistant mosquitofish (*Gambusia affinis*). *Comp Biochem Physiol* 69C:109–112.

Denslow ND, Chow MM, Folmar LC, Bonomelli SL, Heppell SA, Sullivan CV. 1996. Development of antibodies to teleost vitellogenins: potential biomarkers for environmental estrogens. In: Bengtson

DA, Henschel DS, editors. Environmental toxicology and risk assessment: biomarkers and risk assessment. 5th volume. Philadelphia PA: American Society for Testing and Materials (ASTM). STP 1306. p 22–36.

Donohoe RM, Curtis LR. 1996. Estrogenic activity of chlordecone, o,p'-DDT and o,p'-DDE in juvenile rainbow trout: induction of vitellogenesis and interaction with hepatic estrogen binding sites. Aq Toxicol 36:31–52.

Eroschenko VP. 1981. Estrogenic activity of the insecticide chlordecone in the reproductive tract of birds and mammals. J Toxicol Environ Health 8:731–742.

Fritsch MK. 1991. Estrogens, progestins, and oral contraceptives. In: Wingard Jr LB, Brody TM, Larner J, Schwartz A, editors. Human pharmacology: molecular to clinical. St. Louis MO: Mosby Year Book. p 494–514.

Galey FD, Mendez LE, Whitehead WE, Holstege DM, Plumlee KH, Johnson B. 1993. Estrogenic activity in forages: diagnostic use of the classical mouse uterine bioassay. J Vet Diagn Invest 5:603–608.

Goodwin AE, Grizzle JM, Bradley JT, Estridge BH. 1992. Monoclonal antibody-based immunoassay of vitellogenin in the blood of male channel catfish (Ictalurus punctatus). Comp Biochem Physiol 101B:441–446.

Harries JE, Jobling S, Matthiessen P, Sheahan DA, Sumpter JP. 1995. Effects of trace organics on fish: phase 2. Report to the UK Department of the Environment. Marlow UK: Foundation for Water Research. Report # FR/D 0022.

Herman RL, Kincaid HL. 1988. Pathological effects of orally administered estradiol to rainbow trout. Aquaculture 72:165–172.

Howell WM, Denton TE. 1989. Gonopodial morphogenesis in female mosquitofish, Gambusia affinis affinis, masculinized by exposure to degradation products from plant sterols. Exp Biol Fishes 24:43–51.

Hunter GA, Donaldson EM. 1983. Hormonal sex control and its application to fish culture. In: Hoar WS, Randall DJ, Donaldson EM, editors. Volume IX, Fish physiology; Reproduction, Part B; Behavior and fertility control. Orlando FL: Academic Pr. p 223–303.

Jobling S, Sheahan D, Osborne JA, Matthiessen P, Sumpter JP. 1996. Inhibition of testicular growth in rainbow trout (Onchorhynchus mykiss) exposed to estrogenic alkylphenolic chemicals. Environ Toxicol Chem 15:194–202.

Jobling S, Sumpter JP. 1993. Detergent components in sewage effluent are weakly oestrogenic to fish: an in vitro study using rainbow trout (Onchorhynchus mykiss) hepatocytes. Aq Toxicol 27:361–372.

Jordan VC. 1984. Biochemical pharmacology of antiestrogen action. Pharmacol Rev 36:245–276.

Kupfer D, Bulger WH. 1980. Estrogenic properties of DDT and its analogs. In: McLachlan JA, editor. Estrogens in the environment. New York NY: Elsevier North Holland. p 239–263.

Lazier CB, MacKay ME. 1993. Vitellogenin gene expression in teleost fish. In: Hochachka PW, Mommsen TP, editors. Volume 2, Molecular biology frontiers; Biochemistry and molecular biology of fishes. Amsterdam: Elsevier. p 391–405.

Lech JJ, Lewis SK, Ren L. 1996. In vivo estrogenic activity of nonylphenol in rainbow trout. Fund Appl Toxicol 30:229–232.

Markiewicz L, Garey J, Adlercreutz H, Gurpide E. 1993. In vitro bioassays of non-steroidal phytoestrogens. J Steroid Biochem Molec Biol 45:399–405.

Nelson JA. 1974. Effects of dichlorodiphenyltrichloroethane (DDT) analogs and polychlorinated biphenyl (PCB) mixtures on 17 -[³H]estradiol binding to rat uterine receptor. Biochem Pharmacol 23:447–451.

Ng TB, Idler DR. 1983. Yolk formation and differentiation in teleost fishes. In: Hoar WS, Randall DJ, Donaldson EM, editors. Volume IX, Fish physiology; Reproduction Part A; Endocrine tissues and hormones. Orlando FL: Academic Pr. p 373–404.

Nimrod AC, Benson WH. 1996. Estrogenic responses to xenobiotics in channel catfish (Ictalurus punctatus). Marine Environ Res 42:155–160.

Thomas P, Smith J. 1993. Binding of xenobiotics to the estrogen receptor of spotted seatrout: a screening assay for potential estrogenic effects. Marine Environ Res 35:147–153.

Pelissero C, Le Menn F, Kaushick S. 1991. Estrogenic effect of dietary soya bean meal on vitellogenesis in cultured Siberian sturgeon Acipenser baeri. Gen Comp Endocrinol 83:447–457.

Pelissero C, Flouriot G, Foucher JL, Bennetau B, Dunogues J, Le Gac F, Sumpter JP. 1993. Vitellogenin synthesis in cultured hepatocytes; and in vitro test for the estrogenic potency of chemicals. J Steroid Biochem Molec Biol 44:263–272.

Purdom CE, Hardiman PA, Bye VJ, Eno NC, Tyler CR, Sumpter JP. 1994. Estrogenic effects of effluents from sewage treatment works. *Chem Ecol* 8:275–285.

Raizada RB, Misra P, Saxena I, Datta KK, Dikshith TSS. 1980. Weak estrogenic activity of lindane in rats. *J Toxicol Environ Health* 6:483–492.

Routledge EJ, Sumpter JP. 1996. Estrogenic activity of surfactants and some of their degradation products assessed using a recombinant yeast screen. *Environ Toxicol Chem* 15:241–248.

Soto AM, Justicia H, Wray JW, Sonnenschein C. 1991. *p*-Nonyl-phenol: An estrogenic xenobiotic released from "modified" polystyrene. *Environ Health Perspect* 92:167–173.

Srivastava AK, Srivastava AK. 1994. Effects of chlordecone on the gonads of freshwater catfish, *Heteropneustes fossilis*. *Bull Environ Contam Toxicol* 53:186–191.

Welshons WV, Rottinghaus GE, Nonneman DJ, Dolan-Timpe M, Ross PF. 1990. A sensitive bioassay for detection of dietary estrogens in animal feeds. *J Vet Diagn Invest* 2:268–273.

Wester PW, Canton JH. 1986. Histopathological study of *Oryzias latipes* (medaka) after long-term β-hexachlorocyclohexane exposure. *Aq Toxicol* 9:21–45.

Wester PW, Canton JH, Bisschop A. 1985. Histopathological study of *Poecilia reticulata* (guppy) after long-term β-hexachlorocyclohexane exposure. *Aq Toxicol* 6:271–296.

White R, Jobling S, Hoare SA, Sumpter JP, Parker MG. 1994. Environmentally persistent alkylphenolic compounds are estrogenic. *Endocrinology* 135:175–182.

Yamamoto T. 1975. Medaka (killifish): biology and strains. Tokyo, Japan: Keigaku. p 193–213.

Effect of pulp and paper mill contaminants on competence of rainbow trout macrophages

Isabelle Voccia, Jaime Sanchez-Dardon, Muriel Dunier, Stefan Chilmonczyk, Michel Fournier

In this paper, we report the effects on trout macrophage competence of 4 chemicals found in bleached pulp and paper effluents: dehydroabietic acid (DHAA), tetrachloroguaiacol (TeCG), tetrachlorocatechol (TeCC), and trichlorophenol (TCP). Each chemical was evaluated for a dose–response relationship using concentrations between 10^{-4} and 10^{-9} M. The parameters of macrophage activity studied were phagocytosis and the respiratory burst. Our results show cytotoxic properties linked to all chemicals at 10^{-5} and 10^{-4} M with the exception of TCP. For DHAA, the inhibition observed for both phagocytosis and the respiratory burst were related to the cytotoxicity. However, TeCC and TeCG demonstrated a greater suppressive effect on respiratory burst than on phagocytosis, and this effect on respiratory burst was not entirely due to cytotoxicity.

The chemical composition of bleached pulp mill effluents is complex and can vary with the pulping process (kraft or sulfite), the bleaching process (amount of chlorine used), the type of wood (hard or soft) and with time within the same process. The complexity of such discharges makes it difficult to identify the chemicals responsible for their toxicity, and measurements taken in the field fail to identify which contaminants produce toxic effects. Nonetheless, several studies have revealed that resin acids, chloroguaiacols, chlorocatechols, and chlorophenols, all found in pulping and bleaching discharges, are very persistent and bioconcentrated in the aquatic environment, as well as toxic to a wide array of aquatic organisms (Government of Canada 1992; Södergren 1993).

Dehydroabietic acid (DHAA) is the resin acid most commonly found in pulping discharges, and its cytotoxic effect has been studied on fish red blood cells and human polymorphonuclear leukocytes (Pritchard et al. 1991; Sunzel et al. 1991; Butterfield et al. 1994). Tetrachlorogaiacol (TeGC) and tetrachlorocatechol (TeCC) are amongst the most frequently found chlorinated phenols in kraft bleached pulp effluents, while trichlorophenol (TCP) is the main chlorinated phenol in sulfite bleached pulp effluents (Government of Canada 1992). Despite their occurrence in the aquatic environment, TeCG, TeCC, and TCP have not been studied individually for their effect at the cellular level.

During the last 2 decades, it has been demonstrated that several fish diseases and abnormalities occur with increased prevalence in wild fish populations in highly polluted areas (Khan and Thulin 1991). For example, the stress associated with living in water contaminated with bleached pulp discharges is known to increase the degree of parasitism and bacterial infections in fish living in these waters (Lindesjöö and Thulin 1987; Couillard et al. 1988; Rogers 1988), and this suggests a possible effect upon their immune system.

In vertebrates, the immune response is carried out on 2 levels both capable of distinguishing between "self" and "non-self": the nonspecific immune response does not require the specific recognition of an antigen while the specific immune response requires the specific recognition of an antigen and develops a memory of that antigen (Roitt et al. 1994). Polymorphonuclear leukocytes (i.e., macrophages, neutrophils) are the main effector cells of the nonspecific immune response and are involved in the engulfment (phagocytosis) and destruction (respiratory burst) of foreign matter in order to remove potential pathogens and/or to present them to the effector cells of the specific immune response. All animals are capable of recognition, processing, and elimination of non-self material by means of phagocytosis. Phylogenetically, the lower the animal, the more important is the role of its nonspecific immune response. Fish, lower vertebrates, rely heavily on phagocytosis since the nonspecific immune response is less temperature dependent than the specific immune response (Sima and Vetvicka 1990). The importance of macrophages in fish has been demonstrated by many scientists (Weeks and Warinner 1984; Thuvander 1987; Cossarini-Dunier et al. 1988; Warinner et al. 1988; Seeley and Weeks-Perkins 1991; Bowser et al. 1994; Voccia et al. 1995), and macrophages hold a lot of promise as a biomarker since research has shown that xenobiotics can often affect macrophage functions and eventually may render the fish more susceptible to pathogens. Furthermore, because fish inhabit all waters of the earth, from the continental fresh waters to all level of tropical and polar seas, they represent a good choice for the study of the effects of water pollutants.

In this study, we investigated the in vitro effects of 4 of the most persistent and abundant chemicals in bleached pulp mill discharges (DHAA, TeCG, TeCC, and TCP) on 2 parameters of the nonspecific immune response of a freshwater species, the rainbow trout (RBT) (*Onchorhynchus mykiss*). Phagocytosis and the respiratory burst of head kidney macrophages were selected and both parameters were studied by flow cytometry following exposure to various concentrations of the chemicals.

Material and Methods

Experimental animals
Juvenile RBT were purchased from the Arthabasca fish farm (Québec, Canada). Before any experiments, they were acclimated in chlorine free tap water at 15°C for 2 weeks. The fish were fed daily at 1% body weight and were kept on a photoperiod of 12-hour day/12-hour night.

Collection of samples
The fish were sacrificed, the head kidney removed using sterile conditions, and a single cell suspension was prepared with a cell strainer (Falcon) using Hank's Balanced Salt Solution (HBSS) (Gibco) supplemented with a 1% solution of penicillin and streptomycin (Gibco, Bethesda Research Laboratory [BRL]). The cell suspension was then layered over a Ficoll-Hypaque gradient (density 1.077 g/mL; Pharmacia)

and spun 30 minutes at 1000 × g to remove debris and dead cells. The cells were collected at the interphase of the medium and the Ficoll, washed twice with cold HBSS, and were adjusted to 1×10^6 cells/mL in Roswell Park Memorial Institute (RPMI) 1640 (Gibco, BRL) medium supplemented with a 1% solution of penicillin and streptomycin in sterile polysterene tube (Falcon). The cell suspensions were left on ice until use an hour later.

Chemicals

DHAA, TeCC, TeCG, and TCP were purchased at Helix Biotech Ltd. Stock solutions of DHAA, TeCC, TeCG, and TCP were prepared at 10^{-1} M by dissolving the chemicals in ethanol. Further dilutions of 10^{-2} to 10^{-6} M were made by dissolving the stock solution in ethanol.

Cytotoxicity tests

Staining of the cells with propidium iodide (PI) was used to determine the cytotoxic effect of DHAA, TeCG, TeCC, and TCP on head kidney leukocytes. Propidium iodide is an exclusion dye that binds to the nucleic acids of dead cells which then become fluorescent. To each tube either 1 µL of a 1000× solution of one of the chemicals was added (1 µL of a 10^{-1} M solution was added to make a 10^{-4} M solution, 1 µL of a 10^{-2} M solution was added to make a 10^{-5} M solution and so on up to a 10^{-9} M solution) or 1 µL of ethanol (vehicle control) or 1 µL of RPMI 1640 (negative control). Following an 18-hour incubation at 20°C, 1 µL of a 1mg/mL solution of PI was added to the tubes, and the cells analyzed by flow cytometry with a FACScan (Becton Dickinson) equipped with an argon laser emitting at 488 nm. In each experiment 10,000 cells were analyzed, and the results expressed as the percentage of dead cells.

Phagocytosis

The phagocytic activity of head kidney macrophages was determined by quantifying the number of cells that engulfed fluorescent latex microspheres (1.52 µm diameter, Polysciences) as described by Voccia et al. (1995). Negative controls were pretreated for 30 minutes with 0.2% sodium azide, and all samples were then incubated with fluorescent beads in a proportion of 1 cell:100 beads for 18 hours at 20°C. Next, the cells were centrifuged for 5 minutes at 100 × g through a gradient mixture of 3% bovine serum albumin (BSA, Sigma Chemical Co) and RPMI-1640 medium supplemented with 10% fetal calf serum (Gibco). This treatment removed unphagocytosed beads. Samples were then analyzed with a FACscan (Becton Dickinson), and 10,000 cells were analyzed. The results were expressed as the percentage of cells which phagocytosed 3 beads or more.

Respiratory burst

The production of hydrogen peroxide (H_2O_2) was measured as described by Voccia et al. (1995). Head kidney macrophages were incubated for 15 minutes with 5µM of the fluorescent probe 2',7'-dichloro-fluorescein diacetate (DCFDA) (Molecular Probes Inc). Cells were then stimulated 15 minutes with 3µg/mL of phorbol myristate acetate (PMA, Molecular Probes). The production of H_2O_2 by activated macrophages hydrolyzes the probe which then becomes fluorescent. The fluorescence was determined by flow cytometry on 10,000 cells. The results were expressed as the difference between the mean fluorescence produced by stimulated cells (PMA) and unstimulated cells.

Statistics
The data were first tested for normal distribution and homoscedasticity (homogeneity of variance) with the Bartlett's test. Then with an ANOVA one way, we determined if there was a difference between groups; if so, the Tukey test was performed. When the dataset had unequal replicates, the Bonferonni t-test was used. Significance was concluded at $p \leq 0.05$ (Zar 1984).

Results

Head kidney macrophages from RBT were exposed in vitro to increasing concentrations of DHAA, TeCG, TeCC, and TCP from 10^{-9} M to 10^{-4} M for 18 hours. Phagocytosis, evaluated by the engulfment of fluorescent latex beads, and the respiratory burst, evaluated by the production of H_2O_2, were the 2 parameters of the nonspecific immune response tested in this study. Cell viability was also measured.

Effect of DHAA on phagocytosis and the respiratory burst of head kidney macrophages
Exposure to DHAA at concentrations lower than 10^{-5} M (10^{-6} to 10^{-9}) did not affect any of the parameters tested: cell viability, phagocytosis, and respiratory burst (Figures 8-1a, 8-2a).

At 10^{-5} M, the percentage of cells that phagocytosed 3 beads or more (Figure 8-1a) and the capacity of these cells to undergo a respiratory burst (Figure 8-1b) were reduced by 35% and 38% respectively. Cells exposed to this concentration had their viability reduced by 32% indicating that the inhibitions observed were the results of a cytotoxicity rather than an effect upon a specific function of the macrophages.

The highest concentration caused complete cell death as well as a complete inhibition of both phagocytosis and the respiratory burst.

Effects of TCP on phagocytosis and respiratory burst of head kidney macrophages
Exposure to TCP did not affect the viability of head kidney macrophages at the concentrations tested (10^{-4} to 10^{-9} M) as measured with PI.

However, at 10^{-5} M, the respiratory burst (Figure 8-2b) was inhibited by 41% while the percentage of cells capable of phagocytosis (Figure 8-1b) was not affected significantly. An exposure to 10^{-4} M TCP inhibited both phagocytosis and the respiratory burst to the same extent (41% and 45%, respectively). These results indicate that at 10^{-5} M, the respiratory burst is more sensitive than phagocytosis to TCP exposure.

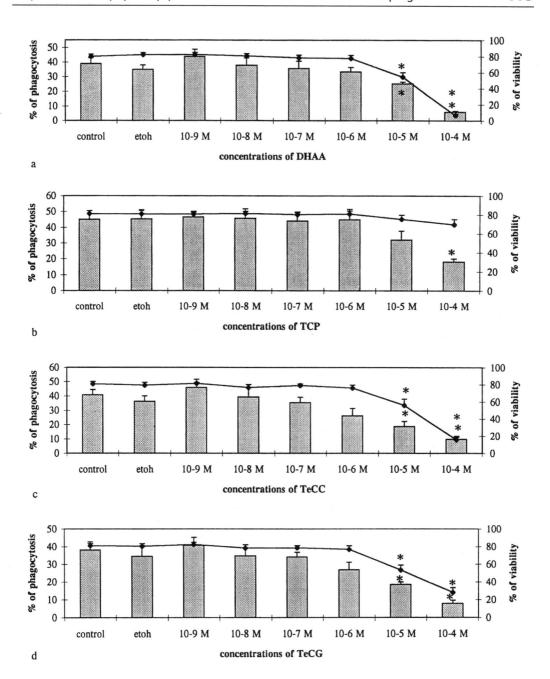

Figure 8-1 Phagocytosis of rainbow trout (RBT) (*Onchorhynchus mykiss*) head kidney macrophages exposed for 18 hours to various concentrations of Dehydroabietic acid (DHAA) (a), Trichlorophenol (TCP) (b), Tetrachlorocatechol (TeCC) (c), and Tetrachloroguaiacol (TeCG) (d). The results are expressed as mean percentage ± standard error of the mean (SEM) (bars). In parallel, the cell viability (solid lines) was measured after 18 hours, and the results are expressed as mean percent of viability ± SEM. A statistically significant difference between controls and exposed cells is indicated by asterisks (* p≤0.05).

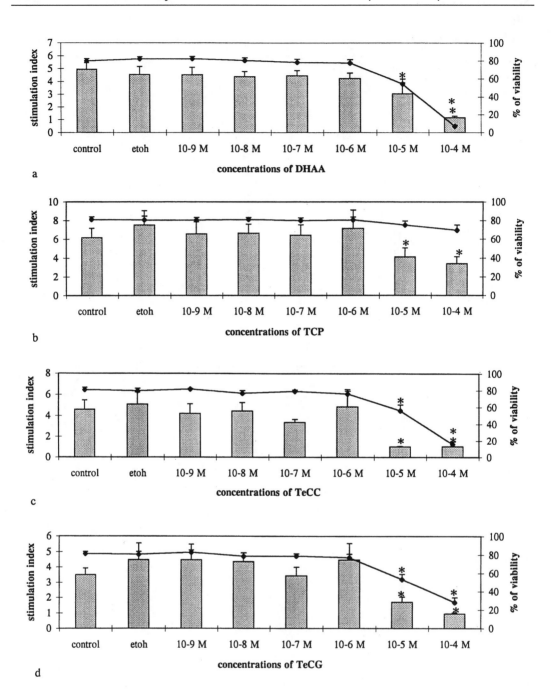

Figure 8-2 Respiratory burst response of RBT (*Onchorhynchus mykiss*) head kidney macrophages exposed for 18 hours to various concentrations of DHAA (a), TCP (b), TeCC (c), and TeCG (d). The results are expressed as mean stimulation index ± SEM (bars). In parallel, the cell viability (solid lines) was measured after 18 hours, and the results are expressed as mean percent of viability ± SEM. A statistically significant difference between controls and exposed cells is indicated by asterisks (* p≤0.05).

Effects of TeCC on phagocytosis and respiratory burst of head kidney macrophages

Exposure at concentrations equivalent to or lower than 10^{-6} M did not significantly affect the cell viability. Higher concentrations did, however, cause a reduction of 30% (10^{-5} M) and 80% (10^{-4} M) in cell viability.

At 10^{-5} M, the percentage of cells that phagocytosed 3 beads (Figure 8-1c) or more was lowered by 54%, but the ability of these cells to produce H_2O_2 (Figure 8-2c) was decreased by 77%. As with TCP, TeCC seems to affect more the ability of macrophages to produce H_2O_2 than their capacity to phagocytose.

At 10^{-4} M, both parameters of the nonspecific immune response were inhibited almost completely; phagocytosis by 76% and the respiratory burst by 78%. These inhibitions are correlated to cell death since an exposure to 10^{-4} M killed 80% of the cells.

Effects of TeCG on phagocytosis and respiratory burst of head kidney macrophages

As with the other 2 phenolic compounds tested, TeCG does not cause significant cell death at concentrations of 10^{-6} M or lower. Exposure to 10^{-5} M and 10^{-4} M killed 34% and 65% of the cells exposed, respectively.

The production of H_2O_2 was reduced by 69%, whereas phagocytosis was inhibited by 51%, and cell death represented 34%. At 10^{-4} M, viability, phagocytosis, and the respiratory burst were inhibited similarly by 65%, 79%, and 73%, respectively.

These results show that the effects of DHAA on RBT macrophages appear to be nonspecific as inhibition of functions (phagocytosis and respiratory burst) are correlated to cell death. The 3 chlorinated compounds tested (TCP, TeCC, and TeCG) affected the respiratory burst more than phagocytosis at 10^{-5} M suggesting that the respiratory burst is a more sensitive parameter of exposure to chlorophenols.

For the viability, DHAA, TeCC, and TeCG were equally cytotoxic, and TCP was the least cytotoxic.

Discussion

The aim of this study was to look at the effects, in vitro, of DHAA, TeCG, TeCC, and TCP found in bleached pulp effluents on parameters of the nonspecific immune response in fish: phagocytosis and the respiratory burst.

Small molecular weight compounds (<1000) are more likely to cross biological membranes than heavier compounds (>1000) and are considered more toxic to animals (Government of Canada 1992). Dehydroabietic acid (molecular weight [MW] 341.3), TeCC (MW 247.89), TeCG (MW 261.93), and TCP (MW 197.45) are some of the low molecular weight chemicals found in bleached pulp effluents. Nowadays, secondary treatment of effluents as well as the substitution of chlorine (Cl_2) by chlorine dioxide (ClO_2) in the bleaching process eliminate the majority of these compounds. Nonetheless, the continuous discharge over the years of these chemicals along with their persistence in the aquatic environment and their bioaccumulation in the biota make them a serious threat to aquatic life (Government of Canada 1992; Södergren 1993).

Twenty years ago, Iwama et al. (1976) observed a significant decrease in white blood cells in Coho Salmon (*Onchorhynchus kisutch*) exposed for 24 hours to DHAA. More recently, in RBT, Oikari et al. (1982) showed that DHAA accumulates principally in the plasma, liver, and the anterior kidney. The anterior kidney is the site of haematopoiesis and the main organ to develop an immune response in teleosts. Fish exposed to DHAA developed jaundice (Nikinmaa and Oikari 1982; Oikari et al. 1984; Mattsoff and Oikari 1987), and from in vitro studies it has been demonstrated that DHAA at 10^{-5} M causes haemolysis of teleost erythrocytes leading to jaundice (Bushnell et al. 1985). Butterfield et al. (1994) showed a concentration-dependent increase in membrane fluidity in red blood cells exposed to DHAA. DHAA affects both the motion and order of the lipid bilayer and the physical state of cytoskeletal proteins of red blood cell membranes.

Results from this study show that DHAA induces almost complete cell death, measured by the uptake of PI, at concentrations 10× lower (10^{-5}) than for human leukocytes, as measured by chromium 51 (Cr^{51}) release. The use of PI might be more sensitive than the use of Cr^{51} since the cells do not have to be destroyed to measure mortality. Furthermore, PI also marks apoptotic cells which are accounted for in the evaluation of cell mortality.

The level of phagocytosis and respiratory burst inhibitions observed are similar to the level of cytotoxicity which suggest that DHAA has a nonspecific cytotoxic effect on head kidney leukocytes of RBT. These results are in accordance with the detergent-like action of DHAA (Butterfield et al. 1994).

Chlorophenols are a major concern in bleached pulp effluents as Canadian pulp mills discharge more than 1,000,000 tons of organochlorine compounds in the aquatic environment (Government of Canada 1992). Chlorophenols are known as uncouplers of the oxidative phosphorylation and produce an effect proportionate to the level of chlorination (Exon 1984). Most immunotoxicological studies have focused on pentachlorophenol (PCP) which is used as a wood preservative worldwide. Pentachlorophenol was shown, in vivo, to enhance macrophage activity in rats (Exon and Koller 1983) and mice (Kerkvliet et al. 1982), however in vitro PCP exposure studies performed on fish macrophages of the Japanese medaka (*Oryzias latipes*) and mummichog (*Fundulus heteroclitus*) showed an inhibition of both the phagocytosis and the respiratory burst (Anderson and Brubacher 1992; Roszell and Anderson 1994). Since the toxicity of chlorophenols is directly related to the level of chlorination, TeCC and TeCG should be equally toxic and TCP less. Our results do confirm this statement as TeCC and TeCG induced cell death to the same level while TCP did not cause significant cell death at similar concentration. Roszell and Anderson (1994) observed that PCP produced a stronger inhibitory effect on the respiratory burst than on phagocytosis. The results obtained with TeCC and TeCG are in agreement with those found with the mummichog, as both TeCC and TeCG had a stronger inhibitory effect on the respiratory burst than on phagocytosis. Phagocytosis and the respiratory burst are functions requiring energy, and a decrease in the availability of adenosine triphosphate (ATP) would hinder both processes. However, the respiratory burst involves a series of oxidation and phosphorylation reactions which could be affected to a greater extent than phagocytosis by the uncoupling of oxidative phosphorylation caused by chlorophenolic compounds. If these effects also occur in vivo, the respiratory burst might be a more sensitive biomarker to assess the immune response to chlorophenols and pulp mill effluents than phagocytosis.

When the effects of xenobiotics in vitro are examined, one parameter can be measured but with in vivo studies, even if only one parameter is studied, the interactions between the different biological systems (e.g., endocrine, reproductive, nervous, or immune systems) cannot be neglected.

In fish, studies have shown that the production of corticosteroid (cortisol) during stress (e.g., handling and pollution) inhibits the immune response (Pickering 1984; Tripp et al. 1987; Woo et al. 1987; Maule et al. 1989). Others have reported that catecholamines (epinephrine, norepinephrine [NE]) and neurotransmitters modulate the immune response of RBT (Flory 1990; Bayne and Levy 1991; Flory and Bayne 1991), and in mammals, studies have shown that sexual hormones (e.g., oestradiol, testosterone) affect the immune response (Magusson and Einarsson 1990; Baranao et al. 1991; Magusson 1991).

Although more and more studies recognize the effects of pollutants on several biological systems, little is known about how they interact, and this emphasizes the need for further studies on the relationships between the immune system and the endocrine system, the immune system and the nervous system, or the immune system and the reproductive system.

Acknowledgments

Supported by the Canadian Network of Toxicology Centers (C.N.T.C.) and Toxicologie de L'environnement (TOXEN), Université du Québec à Montréal.

References

Anderson RS, Brubacher LL. 1992. In vitro inhibition of medaka phagocyte chemiluminescence by pentachlorophenol. *Fish Shellfish Immunol* 2:299–310.

Baranao RI, Tenenbaum A, Rumi LS. 1991. Effects of sexual steroid hormones on the functionality of murine peritoneal macrophages. *Steroids* 56(9):471–485.

Bayne CJ, Levy S. 1991. The respiratory burst of rainbow trout *Onchorhynchus mykiss* Walbaum phagocytes is modulated by sympathetic neurotransmitters and the neuropeptide ACTH. *J Fish Biol* 34(4):609–620.

Bowser DH, Frenkel K, Zelikoff JT. 1994. Effects of in vitro nickel exposure on the macrophage-mediated immune functions of rainbow trout (*Onchorhynchus mykiss*). *Bull Environ Contam Toxicol* 52:367–373.

Bushnell PG, Nikinmaa M, Oikari A. 1985. Metabolic effects of dehydroabietic acid on rainbow trout erythrocytes. *Comp Biochem Physiol* 81C(2):391–394.

Butterfield DA, Trad CH, Hall NC. 1994. Effects of dehydroabietic acid on the physical state of cytoskeletal proteins and the lipid bilayer of erythrocyte membranes. *Biochimica et Biophysica Acta* 1192:185–189.

Cossarini-Dunier M, Demael A, Lepotand D, Guerin V. 1988. Effect of manganese ions on the immune response of carp (*Cyprinus carpio*) against *Yersinia ruckeri*. *Dev Comp Immunol* 12:573–579.

Couillard CM, Berman RA, Panisset JC. 1988. Histopathology of rainbow trout exposed to a bleached kraft pulp mill effluent. *Arch Environ Contam Toxicol* 17:319–323.

Exon JH, Koller LD. 1983. Effects of chlorinated phenols on immunity in rats. *Int J Immunopharmacol* 5:131–136.

Exon JH. 1984. A review of chlorinated phenols. *Vet Hum Toxicol* 26:508–520.

Flory CM. 1990. Phylogeny of neuroimmunoregulation: effects of adrenergic and cholinergic agents on the in vitro antibody response of the rainbow trout, *Onchorhynchus mykiss*. *Dev Comp Immunol* 14:283–294.

Flory CM, Bayne CJ. 1991. The influence of adrenergic and cholinergic agents on the chemiluminescence and mitogenic response of leucocytes from the rainbow trout, *Onchorhynchus mykiss*. *Dev Comp Immunol* 15:135–141.

Government of Canada. 1992. Loi canadienne sur la protection de l'environnement. Liste des substances d'intérât prioritaire, Rapport d'évaluation n° 2: Effluents des usines pâte blanchie. Ottawa: Environnement Canada et santé et bienêtre social canada. 68 p.

Iwama GK, Greer GL, Larkin PA. 1976. Changes in some hematological characteristics of coho salmon (*Onchorhynchus kisutch*) in response to acute exposure to dehydroabietic acid (DHAA) at different exercise levels. *J Fish Res Board Can* 33:285–289.

Kerkvliet NI, Baecher-Steppan L, Claycomb AT, Craig AM, Sheggeby GG. 1982. Immunotoxicity of technical pentachlorophenol (PCP-T): depressed humoral immune responses to T-dependent and T-independent antigen stimulation in PCP-T exposed mice. *Fund Appl Toxicol* 2:90–99.

Khan RA, Thulin J. 1991. Influence of pollution on parasites of aquatic animals. *Adv in Parasitology* 30:200–237.

Lindesjöö E, Thulin J. 1987. Fin erosion of perch (*Perca fluviatilis*) in a pulp mill effluent. *Bull Eur Ass Fish Pathol* 7(1):11–14.

Magusson U. 1991. In vitro effects of prepartum concentrations of estradiol-17-beta on cell-mediated immunity and phagocytosis by porcine leukocytes. *Vet Immunol Immunopathol* 28(2):117–126.

Magusson U, Einarsson S. 1990. Effects of exogenous estradiol on the number and functional capacity of circulating mononuclear and polymorphonuclear leukocytes in the sow. *Vet Immunol Immunopathol* 25(3):235–248.

Mattsoff L, Oikari A. 1987. Acute hyperbilirubinaemia in rainbow trout (*Salmo gairdneri*) caused by resin acids. *Comp Biochem Physiol* 88C(2):263–268.

Maule AG, Tripp RA, Kaattari SL, Shreck CB. 1989. Stress alters immune function and disease resistance in chinook salmon (*Onchorhynchus tshawytscha*). *J Endocrinol* 120:135–142.

Nikinmaa M, Oikari A. 1982. Physiological changes in trout (*Salmo gairdneri*) during a short-term exposure to resin acids and during recovery. *Toxicology Letters* 14:103–110.

Oikari A, Holmbom B, Bister H. 1982. Uptake of resin acids into tissues of trout (*Salmo gairdneri* Richardson). *Ann Zool Fennici* 19:61–64.

Oikari A, Nakariand T, Holmbom B. 1984. Sublethal actions of simulated kraft pulp mill effluents (KME) in Salmo gairdneri: residues of toxicants, and effects on blood and liver. *Ann Aool Fennici* 21:45–53.

Pickering AD. 1984. Cortisol-induced lymphocytopenia in brown trout, Salmo trutta L. *Gen Comp Endocrinol* 53:252–259.

Pritchard JB, Walden R, Oikari A. 1991. Dehydroabietic acid, a major anionic contaminant of pulp mill effluent, reduces both active p-aminohippurate transport and passive membrane permeability in isolated renal membranes. *J Pharm Exp Therapeut* 259(1):156–163.

Rogers IH, Servizi JA, Levings CD. 1988. Bioconcentration of chlorophenols by juvenile chinook salmon (*Onchorhynchus tshawytscha*) overwintering in the upper fraser river: field and laboratory tests. *Water Poll Res J Canada* 32(1):100–113.

Roitt I, Brostoff J, Male D, editors. 1994. Immunologie Fondamentale et appliqué. 3rd edition. Brussels, Belgium: DeBoeck Univ.

Roszell LE, Anderson RS. 1994. Inhibition of phagocytosis and superoxide production by pentachlorophenol in two leukocytes subpopulations from *Fundulus heteroclitus*. *Mar Environ Res* 38:195–206.

Seeley KR, Weeks-Perkins BA. 1991. Altered phagocytic activity of macrophages in oyster toadfish from a highly polluted subestuary. *J Aquatic Animal Health* 3:224–227.

Sima P, Vetvicka V. 1990. Evolution of immune reactions. Boca Raton FL: CRC Press.

Södergren A, editor. 1993. Bleached pulp mill effluents. Composition, fate and effects in the Baltic Sea. Final report from environment/cellulose II project. Solna, Sweden: Swedish Environmental Protection Agency.

Sunzel B, Söderberg TA, Reuterving C.-O, Hallmans G, Holm SE, Hänström L. 1991. Neutralizing effect of zinc oxide on dehydroabietic acid-induced toxicity on human polymorphonuclear leukocytes. *Biol Trace Elem Res* 31:33–42.

Thuvander A. 1987. Cadmium exposure of rainbow trout, *Salmo gairdneri* Richardson: effects on immune functions. *J Fish Biol* 35:521–529.

Tripp RA, Maule AG, Schreck CB, Kaattari SL. 1987. Cortisol mediated suppression of salmonid lymphocyte responses in vitro. *Dev Comp Immunol* 11:565–576.

Voccia I, Sanchez-Dardon J, Dunier M, Anderson P, Fournier M, Hontela A. 1995. In vivo effects of cadmium chloride on the immune response and plasma cortisol of rainbow trout (*Onchorhynchus mykiss*). In: Chapter 47, Modulators of immune responses. Fairhaven, NJ:S.O.S. Publications. p 547–556.

Warinner JE, Mathews ES, Weeks BA. 1988. Preliminary investigations of the chemiluminescence response in normal and pollutant-exposed fish. *Mar Environ Res* 24:281–284.

Weeks BA, Warinner JE. 1984. Effects of toxic chemicals on macrophage phagocytosis in two estuarine fishes. *Mar Environ Res* 14:327–335.

Woo PTK, Leatherland JF, Lee MS. 1987. *Cryptobia salmositica*: cortisol increases the susceptibility of Salmo gairdneri Richardson to experimental cryptobiosis. *J Fish Dis* 10:75–83.

Zar JH. 1984. Biostatistical analysis. 2nd ed. Englewood Cliffs NJ: Prentice-Hall.

Reproductive and endocrine status of female kelp bass from a contaminated site in the Southern California Bight and estrogen receptor binding of DDTs

Robert B. Spies, Peter Thomas

In this study, we compared reproductive endocrine function indices in female kelp bass, collected during ovarian recrudescence at a site (PV) in the Southern California Bight contaminated with DDT, PCBs, and other anthropogenic chemicals and at a less contaminated reference site (DP). We also assessed ovarian growth, oocyte development, and liver concentrations of chlorinated hydrocarbons. We found 6-fold higher ΣDDT and 3-fold higher ΣPCB mean liver concentrations and lower mean plasma concentrations of maturational gonadotropin (GtH) in PVs females than in DP's. Further, PV fish without measurable GtH had significantly greater ΣDDT concentrations than did those with measurable GtH. Plasma concentrations of estradiol were lower in PV than in DP fish, perhaps related to lower concentrations of maturational GtH. However, in vitro testosterone production by ovaries was greater in PV than in DP fish and was positively correlated with ΣDDT and ΣPCB liver concentrations. Estradiol binding affinity to its cytosolic liver receptor was lower in PV than DP fish. An in vitro competitive binding study showed o,p'-DDT and o,p'-DDE capable of displacing estrogen from its receptor in liver preparations. These preliminary results reveal subtle differences in fish reproductive endocrine status in a heavily DDT- and PCB-contaminated marine environment. The lower maturational gonadotropin concentrations in fish from the contaminated site warrant further study of the later ovarian cycle stages to determine if contaminants delay or impair final oocyte maturation and ovulation.

Past discharges of sewage in the Southern California Bight near Los Angeles have included large amounts of 2 classes of chlorinated hydrocarbons — the dichloro-diphenyltrichloroethanes (DDT and its metabolites dichlorodiphenyldichloroethylene [DDE], dichlorodiphenyldichloroethane [DDD], and dichlorodiphenylchloroethane [DDMU]) and the polychlorinated biphenyls (PCBs). Both of these classes of chlorinated aromatic hydrocarbons are highly lipid-soluble, and consequently have accumulated to concentrations in the parts-per-million (ppm) range in local marine life (Gossett et al. 1983; Mearns and Young 1980; Mearns et al. 1991; Pollack et al. 1991; Spies et al. 1989). For example, several species of fish living on the Palos Verdes Shelf, where large amounts of DDTs have been deposited from discharges through the Los Angeles County sewage outfall, have accumulated concentrations of ΣDDT (total measured DDT, DDE, and DDD) to over 100 μg/g wet weight in liver (McDermott and Heesen 1975; Gossett et al. 1982). Likewise, fish in the ocean adjacent to Los Angeles have also accumulated high concentrations of ΣPCB (total measured PCBs) (Mearns et al. 1991).

Both classes of chlorinated hydrocarbons include compounds that are deleterious to animals (Bitman et al. 1968; Hart et al. 1971; Carlson et al. 1973; Kimbrough 1974; Silkworth and Grabstein 1982; Brouwer et al. 1989; Heath et al. 1969) and have been specifically shown to affect fish (Hansen et al. 1974; Freeman et al. 1982; Bengtsson and Larsson 1981). These compounds are noted especially for their reproductive toxicity (Helle et al. 1976; Jensen et al. 1977; Bulger and Kupfer 1985; Reijnders 1986; Golub et al. 1991 and references therein; Monosson, Chapter 13), which appears to result at least in part from the steric similarity of estrogen and chlorinated aromatic hydrocarbons having halide or alkyl groups in the *p-p'* positions in the biphenyl group (Bitman and Cecil 1970). It is clear that some DDTs and PCBs bind to estrogen receptors in the higher vertebrates and may alter the normal course of reproduction (e.g., Nelson 1974). Binding of coplanar PCBs to the Ah receptor, which in turn activates a variety of isozymes of the mixed-function oxidase systems, probably plays a large part in PCB toxicity as well (e.g., Silkworth and Grabstein 1982; Sutter et al. 1991).

Both DDTs and PCBs have been associated with disruption of reproductive endocrine function in fish. Female Atlantic croaker fed 3 to 5 mg/kg body weight/day of Aroclor 1254 for 2 to 4 weeks exhibited decreases in in vitro gonadotropin release, plasma estradiol and testosterone concentrations, ovarian steroid synthesis, estrogen receptor concentration, plasma vitellogenin (VTG) concentrations and ovarian growth (Thomas 1988, 1989). A loss in the gonadotropin response to stimulation by luteinizing hormone-releasing hormone (LHRH) (which was, in turn, associated with a decline in hypothalamic serotonin concentrations) was observed in male croaker fed 1 mg Aroclor 1254/kg body weight/day for 1 month (Khan and Thomas 1996). Male cod given food contaminated with Aroclor 1254 (approximate doses of 0.02 to 1 mg/kg body weight/day) for 5.5 months exhibited altered patterns of steroid biosynthesis (Freeman et al. 1982). There was stimulation of steroid biosynthesis with increases of testosterone and 11-ketotestosterone (11-KT) in fish fed approximately 0.1 mg PCB/kg body weight/day and apparent inhibition of these hormones at higher doses (Freeman et al. 1982). Brook trout fed 1 mg DDT/kg/week for 5 months showed enhanced numbers of eggs produced while those in the 2 mg/kg/week dose group for 5 months produced fewer eggs than the controls (Macek 1968).

In southern California, previous work with 2 species of common nearshore fishes, the kelp bass *(Paralabrax clathratus)* and the white croaker *(Genyonemus lineatus)*, indicated that fish collected on the Palos Verdes Shelf had significantly poorer reproductive potential than those collected in less contaminated nearshore environments further south in the Southern California Bight near Dana Point in Orange County (Cross and Hose 1988; Hose et al. 1989). A greater proportion of white croaker from the contaminated site had only non-vitellogenic eggs. Fewer of the more contaminated croaker could be artificially spawned, oocyte atresia was higher, and fecundity and egg fertility were lower. The ovarian concentrations of both ΣPCB and ΣDDT were within a factor of 2 of the liver concentrations for this species. The authors proposed that inhibition of spawning was associated with an ovarian ΣDDT concentration of 4 µg/g and higher. For the kelp bass from the contaminated site (Palos Verdes), there was a larger proportion of females that did not spawn after treatment with LHRHa in the laboratory, and the females that produced hydrated eggs (fish were stripped manually) had poorer fertilization success. Mean hepatic ΣDDT concentration was 8.3 µg/g and ΣPCB was 2.6 µg/g in the kelp bass from Palos Verdes.

In this study we investigated possible reproductive impairment in more detail by comparing endocrinological measures in sexually mature female kelp bass to see if they differed between more and less contaminated sites and whether they varied with tissue concentrations of chlorinated hydrocarbons. In addition, we determined if DDTs and PCBs could displace estradiol from its receptor in liver tissue.

Methods

Field studies

Kelp bass, which are summer spawners (Smith and Young 1966; Quast 1968), were collected from a contaminated site, the Palos Verdes Peninsula, and Dana Point, a less contaminated comparison site, in June 1992. The Palos Verdes Peninsula and Dana Point are rocky headlands in the Southern California Bight, and the near-shore areas have reefs supporting a variety of marine life — the preferred habitat of kelp bass (Figure 9-1). The Palos Verdes area was contaminated with DDTs, and to some extent PCBs, through discharges from the Los Angeles County Sanitary District outfall located at a depth of 60 m on the Palos Verdes Shelf.

The collections, using the R/V *Vantuna*, occurred on 8–11 June 1992 (early) with additional collections on 18 June and 22–25 June 1992 (late), with the collecting effort balanced between the 2 sites within each block of time (Table 9-1). The numbers of fish analyzed were based on an analysis of statistical power taking into consideration the variation in reproductive measures seen in the 1986 studies of Cross and Hose. Based on this analysis, a sampling goal of 40 mature female fish/ site during June was established.

Kelp bass were collected individually by hook and line. Fish with a minimum size of 250 mm standard length (SL) were sampled (sexually mature females capable of spawning that year [J.E. Hose personal communication]). Blood samples were taken from the caudal vein within 5 minutes of capture, centrifuged on board at 1000 × g, and the plasma was stored on dry ice for subsequent hormone analyses. Fish were Floy-tagged and transported to Occidental College's Redondo Beach Laboratory, where they were held in temperature-controlled (set to field conditions), flow-through seawater tanks.

Laboratory dissections were done the morning following collection. Fish were anesthetized with ice-cold sea water or MS-222, sacrificed, and liver and gonadal tissues removed for morphological, endocrinological and chemical analyses. Sections of gonads were removed and placed in physiological media for the endocrinological assays. A 2- to 3-g section of the liver was removed with solvent-cleaned instruments and stored at −20°C for chemical analysis. Gonad tissue (0.5 g) was fixed in 10% buffered formalin and prepared for histological examination of oocyte maturity stages. A 1- to 10-g sample of the liver was also frozen in liquid nitrogen for estradiol binding assays. Otoliths were also taken from some fish for age determination.

Measurement of reproductive indices, gonad histology, and age

The gonadosomatic index (GSI) was calculated as the proportion: GSI=wet weight of the gonad/wet weight of the fish.

Each fish was scored for percentages of oocytes in various stages of development and degree of oocyte atresia using mounted and stained tissue sections of ovaries. The following stages were recognized: perinucleolar nucleoli, cortical alveoli, partly yolked, and fully yolked. One or two slides of ovary were prepared for each fish using standard methods for paraffin sections. Three different areas on a slide were

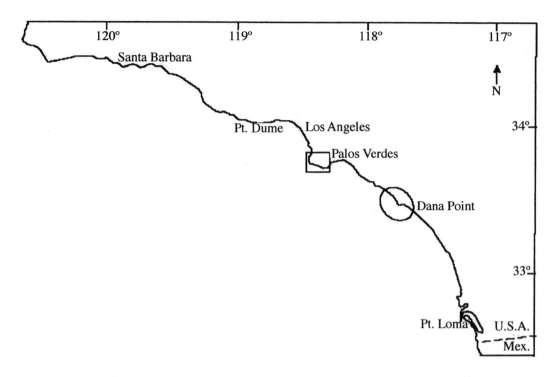

Figure 9-1 Location of fish collection sites in the Southern California Bight. Fish collection areas are boxed (contaminated) or circled (less contaminated).

selected at random by the reader, and a total count of oocytes in each of the above categories was made for that area. Between 75 and 125 oocytes were counted in each of the 3 areas on one slide. There were usually about 300 oocytes evaluated in each individual for calculating the proportion of each stage present.

Each ovary was also scored (0 to 3) for the degree of oocyte atresia apparent in tissue sections. The scores were based on the following criteria: 0, lack of atresia; 1, atresia present but mild; 2, moderate amounts and degree of atresia present; and 3, extensive and advanced atresia present. Early stages of atresia were characterized by initial breaks in the chorion and disruption of the nuclear membrane. More advanced stages of atresia were characterized by complete fragmentation of the chorion, degeneration of lipid vacuoles and yolk protein droplets, increased cytoplasmic eosinophilia, and complete dissolution of the nucleus. The final stages of oocyte atresia were characterized by complete fragmentation of the chorion and nucleus, replacement of the cytoplasm by granular, eosinophilic-necrotic material, and variable infiltration by macrophages.

Age was determined by counting rings in thin sections of otoliths generally following the methods of Secor (1991). Two readers were used to come to a common agreement on age of each individual fish.

Table 9-1 Summary of field-collected kelp bass in June 1992

Location	Date	Number of females retained
Palos Verdes	June 8	15
Palos Verdes	June 9	8
Dana Point	June 10	9
Dana Point	June 11	8
Dana Point	June 18	6
Palos Verdes	June 22	22
Dana Point	June 23	9
Dana Point	June 24	7

Endocrinological methods

Chemicals. Estradiol [2,4,6,7–^{3}H(N)] was obtained from Amersham and testosterone [1,2,6,7–^{3}H(N)] from New England Nuclear. The radiolabeled steroids 17,20ß-dihydroxy-4-pregnen-3-one (17α,20ß-P) and 17,20ß,21-trihydroxy-4-pregnen-3-one (20ßS) were prepared from radiolabeled 11-deoxycortisol and from 17α–hydroxyprogesterone, respectively, by enzymatic conversion according to the procedure of Scott et al. (1982).

Estrogen receptor assay and competition assay. The organochlorines tested in the liver estrogen receptor competition assays (*o,p'*- DDD; *p,p'*- DDD; *o,p'*- DDE; *p,p'* - DDE; *p,p'*- DDT; and *o,p'*- DDT) were obtained from Aldrich Chemical or Chem Service Inc.

Tissue incubations. Ovarian tissues were incubated in a Dubnoff shaker under oxygen at room temperature (25°C) in Dulbecco's modified Eagle's medium (DMEM, Sigma) buffered with 1.2 g L^{-1} sodium bicarbonate and supplemented with penicillin-G (60 mg L^{-1}) and streptomycin sulfate (100 mg L^{-1}), pH 7.6. Ovarian tissues were incubated for 17 to 20 hours, and the incubation times were consistent within each set (date) of assays. Ovarian tissues (50 to 150 mg well^{-1}) were pre-incubated in DMEM in 24-well incubation plates for at least 1 hour. Ovarian incubations were performed in duplicate.

Analyses of estradiol, testosterone, and progestins. Estradiol, testosterone and the progestins were measured by RIA techniques as described in Singh et al. (1988) and Trant and Thomas (1989). Plasma incubation media (50 to 150 µL, 2 replicates) were extracted with 2 mL hexane/ethyl acetate (70/30) prior to the assay. Dextran-coated charcoal was used to separate bound from free steroid. Coefficient of interassay variance was determined to be between 11 and 14.6% for estradiol media and plasma assays and 9.4 and 10.2% for testosterone assays. Mean spike recoveries were 88.6%.

Analyses of gonadotropin. Gonadotropin (GtH II) was measured by a modification of the heterologous RIA for sciaenid fishes (Copeland and Thomas 1992), which uses iodinated spotted seatrout gonadotropin and Atlantic croaker gonadotropin standards and antiserum. The RIA was validated for measurement of GtH in kelp bass by establishing that plasma and pituitary extracts from this species diluted parallel to the Atlantic croaker standard. Each sample was measured in duplicate. Blood plasma GtH II results were based solely on the croaker standard dilution curve [pg GtH II/mL].

Liver estrogen receptor assay. The liver estrogen cytosolic and nuclear receptor assays were performed on liver samples according to the method described in Smith and Thomas (1990). Prior to the assays, the liver samples were stored in a − 80°C freezer. Nuclear fractions were prepared by extraction of the nuclear pellet from low speed centrifugation (1000 × g) with a high salt (0.6 M KCl) buffer. Prior to assay samples were incubated with Dextran-coated charcoal to remove any steroids present.

Cytosolic and nuclear fractions were incubated with a range of ^{3}H-estradiol concentrations, 40 nM to 0.3125 nM final concentration, in the absence (for total binding) or presence (for nonspecific binding) of 100-fold excess cold estradiol, concentration for 18 to 20 hours at 4°C. Dextran-coated charcoal was used to separate receptor-bound from free steroid. Receptor abundance (B_{max}) and dissociation constants (K_d) were calculated by Scatchard analysis. Data for samples which had high nonspecific binding were not included in the subsequent statistical analyses. Data from samples with high nonspecific binding were not reported. Metabolism of ^{3}H-estradiol in the radioreceptor assay was not investigated because an earlier study with spotted seatrout liver extracts had shown insignificant conversion of ^{3}H-estradiol under these assay conditions (Smith and Thomas 1991).

Protein-bound phosphorus (vitellogenin). Protein-bound (alkali-labile) phosphorus was measured in plasma as an assessment of VTG concentrations according to the spectrophotometric procedure of Craik and Harvey (1984) and modified to measure small plasma volumes (0.05 mL plasma). Standard curves were obtained from serial dilutions (1:2) from a stock solution of 400 mg/L obtained by adding 878 mg KH_2PO_4 to Milli-Q water. Interassay variance was 9.1%, and intraassay variance was < 6%.

Chemical methods
Liver samples were analyzed for DDTs and PCBs by Arthur D. Little Co. using a gas chromatograph with electron capture detection and fitted with a 30-meter, DB-5 column and a DB-17 or equivalent column. The lower of the 2 values obtained using these columns is the concentration reported. Approximately 10% of the samples were also analyzed by mass spectroscopy in the single-ion-monitoring mode in order to confirm the identity of the compounds. More than 90% of the data had accuracy and precision better than ±30 to 35%.

Reported values were corrected for the recovery of spikes added to the samples prior to extraction. The total PCB concentration was calculated by summing the concentrations of PCB congeners 8, 18, 28, 44, 52, 66, 101, 105, 118, 128, 138,

153, 170, 180, 187, 195, 296, and 209 and multiplying by 2 (NOAA 1989). The total DDT concentration is calculated by summing o,p'-DDE, p,p'-DDE, o,p'-DDD, p,p'-DDD, o,p'-DDT, p,p'-DDT, and DDMU. For both calculations, a value of one-half the detection limit was used in the summation if the analyte was reported as not detected. Chemical concentrations are expressed on a wet weight basis.

Binding of xenobiotic compounds to the estrogen receptor
Binding of representative organochlorine compounds to the kelp bass hepatic cytosolic estrogen receptor was investigated by in vitro competition assays following the procedures described in Smith and Thomas (1990) and Thomas and Smith (1993). The ability of the organochlorine compounds to displace $[H^3]$-estradiol from its receptor was tested over a range of concentrations (10^{-9} and 10^{-8} to 10^{-3}M). The organochlorines were added to the assay system dissolved in an organic carrier (ethanol, final concentration 0.1%), which did not interfere with receptor binding.

Statistical methods
Parametric analyses were carried out, mainly by ANOVAs and analysis of covariance (ANCOVA) using STATVIEW (v. 4.0, Abacus Concepts, Berkeley CA) or SuperANOVA (v. 1.11 Abacus Concepts, Berkeley CA) for the Macintosh. All parametric tests were performed with log-transformed data. When cofactors were not an issue, nonparametric tests were carried out: Mann-Whitney U-test for 2-group unpaired analyses, Spearman rank correlation for correlations, and Kruskall Wallis for the equivalent of 1-way analyses of variance. Mean values of measures are reported with standard deviations (SD).

Results

Field-exposed kelp bass

Morphometrics and age
The average weight of captured fish was 695 ($\pm$534) g at Palos Verdes and 895 ($\pm$470) g at Dana Point, a significant difference (p=0.007). The relationship between body weight and SL was very similar, and location was not a significant source of covariation (p=0.15) in the log-log regression of weight on length (not shown). We conclude that although weight differences occurred between sites, the weight-length relationships were similar, i.e., "the condition," or shape, of the fish at each site was similar.

Analysis of otoliths from 22 Palos Verdes fish and 25 Dana Point fish revealed ages of 4 to 15 years. There was no significant difference in mean ages of the fish from the 2 locations (PV=8.7 $\pm$ 2.4 years, DP=7.8 $\pm$ 2.6 years; p=0.72, Mann-Whitney U test).

Tissue contaminant concentrations
A 6-fold difference between sites was found in the concentrations of ΣDDT (total DDT, the sum of all isomers of DDT, DDE, DDD, and DDMU) in the livers of female

kelp bass collected in June 1992 (Figure 9-2a). Mean values were 3429 (±4468) ng/g in Palos Verdes fish and 524 (±419) ng/g in Dana Point fish. This difference was significant at p=0.0001 on a wet-weight basis, as well as on a lipid-weight basis (Mann Whitney U test). The *p,p'*-DDE form constituted greater than 97% of ΣDDT. The hepatic concentrations of *o,p'*-DDE showed large differences between the 2 sites (no figure, p=0.001, Mann Whitney U); mean wet weight concentrations were 10.03 (±5.49) ng/g for Dana Point fish and 36.4 (±49.6) ng/g for Palos Verdes fish. The site differences in *o,p'*-DDE were also significant at p=0.001 on a lipid-weight basis (Mann Whitney U, data not shown).

The differences in concentrations of ΣPCB in liver were not as great, only about 3-fold on a wet weight basis (911 ± 934 ng/g for Palos Verdes fish and 315 ± 259 ng/g for Dana Point fish (Figure 9-2b). These differences were highly significant on either a wet-weight (p=0.0001, Mann Whitney U) or lipid-weight basis (p=0.013, Mann Whitney U, data not shown). No significant relationships were found between wet weight of the fish and liver ΣDDT concentrations (Spearman's r=0.02, p=0.86) or ΣPCB concentrations (Spearman's r=0.045, p=0.86).

The liver lipid content of Palos Verdes fish (12.2 ± 6.6%) was greater than that of Dana Point fish (8.2 ± 5.2%) (no figure, p=0.0009, Mann Whitney U), and the wet weight of the fish was not a significant source of variation (p=0.36).

Lipid content of liver was correlated with ΣDDT concentration in Palos Verdes fish (Spearman's r=0.47, p=0.0016) and also in fish from both sites combined (Spearman's r=0.50 p<0.0001).

Gonad size, presence of yolky oocytes, and oocyte atresia
All females collected and meeting the size criteria had large, well-developed ovaries containing yolky oocytes. The one exception was an intersex fish collected from Palos Verdes on 9 June 1993, which had small oocytes without yolk (up to cortical alveoli stage) and a cord of testicular material as well. This fish was excluded from all of the analyses of reproductive parameters. All other fish had small perinucleolar oocytes, slightly larger cortical alveoli oocytes, and partially yolked oocytes in their gonads, as would be expected in a multiple spawning fish during the spawning season. In addition, most fish had fully yolked oocytes 40/41 (97.6%) from Palos Verdes and 33/35 (94.3%) from Dana Point, which is not a significant difference (Mann-Whitney U, p=0.23).

The ratio of the gonad weight to the body weight (gonadosomatic index) was not different between the 2 sites, 0.040 ± 0.013 at Dana Point and 0.043 ± 0.019 at Palos Verdes (Figure 9-4a, p=0.14).

The degree of atresia in yolked oocytes, which can be a general indication of lack of spawning followed by resorption of unspawned eggs, was not significantly different for fish collections from the 2 areas (p=0.78) (Table 9-2). Atretic immature oocytes were rarely seen, and it appears that resorption of immature oocytes was not a significant process in fish from either site.

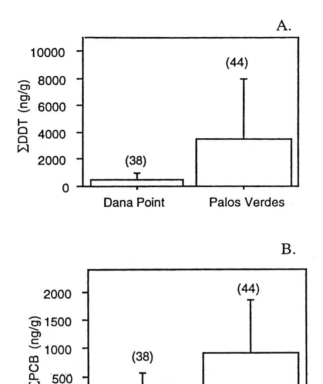

Figure 9-2 Concentrations of contaminants in livers of kelp bass (wet weight basis) (±SD) A. ΣDDT, B. ΣPCB. The numbers of fish analyzed are in parentheses.

Endocrine status

Plasma gonadotropin. The mean concentrations of plasma gonadotropin were greater in fish from Dana Point (317.8 ± 257.8 pg/mL) than from Palos Verdes (217.2 ± 275.4 pg/mL) (significantly different by ANOVA, $p=0.048$; and approaching significance, $p=0.085$, by Mann-Whitney U) (Figure 9-3a). A significant number of fish had concentrations below the detection limit (50.0 pg/mL), so we also compared the number of fish from each site that had measurable gonadotropin. There was a trend toward fewer fish from the contaminated site with maturational gonadotropin present in plasma for all dates: 51% (18/35) in Palos Verdes fish and 74% (23/31) in Dana Point fish. These data are further segregated by early and late June dates in Figure 9-3b. In early June nearly twice the proportion of fish from Dana Point had measurable gonadotropin in their blood than those from Palos Verdes. These differences narrowed late in June, but the proportions with measurable gonadotropin were still greater in fish from Dana Point.

The actual concentrations of plasma gonadotropin for fish that had measurable amounts were very similar: Palos Verdes, 424 ± 234 pg/mL, and Dana Point, 428 ± 203 pg/mL ($p=0.69$) (no figure).

Table 9-2 Percentages of fish from each collection site with ovaries in various stages of atresia.

Location	0 (no atresia)	Mild	Moderate	Severe
Dana Point (n=36)	30.6	38.9	25	5.6
Palos Verdes (n=43)	25.6	39.5	23.3	11.6

Recent studies by Oda et al. (1993) reveal a diel pattern of oocyte maturation in southern California kelp bass, with oocytes starting final maturation in the morning and spawning occurring in the late afternoon and evening. Therefore, time of day is an important cofactor in analyses of endocrinological differences between sites. So, when comparing concentrations of ΣDDT in fish that did and did not have measurable amounts of gonadotropin in their blood, we make the comparison between fish caught in the morning and those caught in the afternoon. To avoid the potentially confounding effect of site, the data on ΣDDT concentrations from the Palos Verdes fish only are presented in Figure 9-3c. The analysis of the Palos Verdes fish collected in the morning indicates that ΣDDT concentrations in liver were significantly greater in fish that did not have gonadotropin in their blood (mean 5900 ng/g) than those that did (1900 ng/g) (p=0.03). The possible effects of ΣPCB were also examined in a similar analysis using fish from both sites, but the analysis of variance (ANOVA) indicated that the differences between concentrations were not significant (p=0.29).

Estradiol and testosterone in blood. The overall mean plasma concentrations of testosterone were not different between sites (1.56 ± 1.35 ng/mL for Palos Verdes and 1.98 ± 1.44 ng/mL for Dana Point) (Figure 9-4c, p=0.14), but estradiol concentrations were significantly lower in Palos Verdes fish (4.17 ± 2.87 ng/mL, n=44) than in Dana Point fish (5.84 ± 3.9 ng/mL, n=38) (Figure 9-4d, p=0.048). However, the plasma concentrations of testosterone and estradiol can vary in fishes by time of day, time of month, and season, and both steroids generally had lower plasma concentrations early in the month, in the afternoon, and at Palos Verdes. An ANOVA of log-transformed testosterone concentrations with the appropriate cofactors included showed the following factors to be significant or nearly significant: location (p=0.06), capture time (p=0.0001), and capture date (p=0.005). Liver concentrations of ΣDDT were not a significant source of variation (p=0.22). For estradiol, the corresponding analysis showed: location (p=0.02), capture time (p=0.0001), and capture date (p=0.04) as significant sources of variation. Liver concentrations of ΣDDT were again not a significant (p=0.40) source of variation, nor were ΣPCB concentrations (p=0.33).

The variation in the concentrations of testosterone and estradiol due to location, however, could be partially explained by the presence of gonadotropin in the blood. If the sex steroid data are analyzed with the presence of measurable gonadotropin as a cofactor, then the following results are obtained. For testosterone the significant sources of variation included: capture time (p=0.004) and presence of gonadotropin (p=0.006). Date (early or late in June) was marginally significant

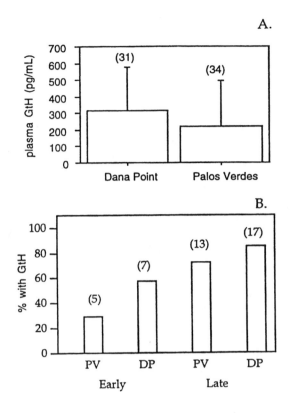

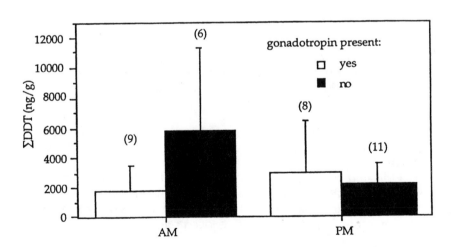

Figure 9-3 Plasma gonadotropin (II) concentrations (±SD) in fish from Palos Verdes and Dana Point. A. Plasma concentrations, B. Percentage of fish from each site with detectable gonadotropin (early=8–11 June; late=18–24 June), and C. Liver ΣDDT concentrations of fish captured in morning and afternoon according to whether measurable amounts of maturational gonadotropin were present in the blood plasma (Palos Verdes only).

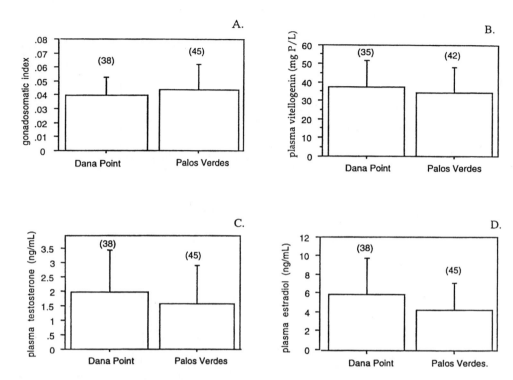

Figure 9-4 Vitellogenic growth measures in fish from Palos Verdes and Dana Point female kelp bass (±SD). A. Gonadosomatic index, B. Protein phosphorus (VTG), C. Plasma testosterone, D. Plasma estradiol.

(p=0.08); location (p=0.68) and liver ΣDDT concentration (p=0.22) were not. For estradiol, an ANOVA indicated that time of capture (p=0.0006) and presence of gonadotropin (p=0.007) were significant sources of variation. Date (early or late) (p=0.11), location (p=0.33), and liver ΣDDT concentration (p=0.95) were not significant.

Vitellogenin in blood. Concentrations of plasma protein phosphorus, a measure of the yolk precursor protein VTG, were not significantly different between sites: Palos Verdes, 34.2 ± 14.2 mg P/L; Dana Point, 37.6 ± 14.1 mg P/L (Figure 9-4b). An ANCOVA indicated that plasma concentrations of VTG varied significantly as a function of plasma estradiol concentrations (p=0.02) and the presence of measurable amounts of gonadotropin (p=0.05) but did not vary significantly for location (p=0.94), date of capture (p=0.66), ΣDDT concentration (p=0.54), or ΣPCB concentration (p=0.71).

Estradiol and testosterone production by ovaries (in vitro). In vitro ovarian estradiol production is shown in Figure 9-5a for fish from the 2 sites according to whether measurable gonadotropin was present in the blood (yes, no). An ANOVA on log-transformed basal estradiol production indicated that location was not a significant (p=0.78) source of variation, nor was the presence of gonadotropin at the time of capture (p=0.20), hepatic ΣDDT (p=0.15), or ΣPCB (p=0.12) concentra-

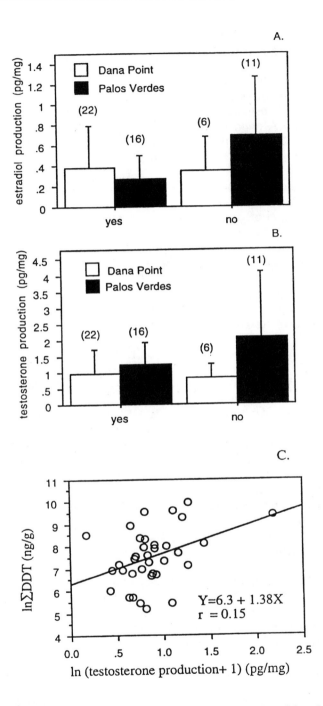

Figure 9-5 In vitro steroid production (pg steroid/mg tissue) by ovaries of female kelp bass (±SD) according to whether measurable plasma gonadotropin (II) was detected (yes) or not (no). A. Estradiol production, B. Testosterone production. C. Liver ΣDDT concentrations and in vitro testosterone production rates by ovaries. Data from Palos Verdes fish only.

tions. Date of capture was a significant source of variation (p=0.001), with production values early in June being higher.

Basal testosterone production was approximately 2- to 4-fold greater than that of estradiol from ovaries (compare Figure 9-5a and Figure 9-5b, noting the difference in scales). Production of testosterone was greatest for Palos Verdes fish and for fish early in June. An ANOVA of in vitro basal testosterone production indicated the following: location (p=0.0004) and date (p=0.0002) were significant sources of variation, but capture time was not (p=0.25).

We analyzed the relationships between the liver concentrations of the contaminants and testosterone production for each site separately. For Dana Point there was not a significant relationship between ΣDDT concentration in liver and testosterone release (Spearman's r=0.015, p=0.93), nor between ΣPCB concentration in liver and testosterone release (Spearman's r=0.011, p=0.95). For Palos Verdes there were significant relationships between ΣDDT concentration in liver and unstimulated testosterone release (Spearman's r=-0.34, p=0.047) (Figure 9-5c) and ΣPCB concentration in liver and testosterone production (Spearman's r=-0.36, p=0.038). The strongest relationships were therefore between the liver concentrations of either of the 2 contaminants and testosterone production from gonads of Palos Verdes fish.

We considered the possibility that estradiol or testosterone production might exhibit a different pattern if production were expressed for the whole gonad and normalized to body size. Analyzing the data in this way produced patterns very similar to the unnormalized data (no figure).

Progestins in plasma. In teleost fish one or more progestins are produced prior to spawning, and these progestins induce final oocyte maturation. We suspected that the maturation inducing steroid was either 17α,20ß,21-trihydroxy-4 pregnen-3-one (20ß-S) or 17α,20ß,-dihydroxy-4-pregnen-3-one (17α,20ß-P), and we measured both. Site differences in 20ß-S were not significant (Palos Verdes, 0.25 ± 0.23 ng/mL p=0.36). However, plasma concentrations of 20ß-S were higher in late June than early June (p=0.0001), and they are higher in the morning than the afternoon (p=0.001). The highest concentrations occurred in fish caught early in the morning and late in the month that had gonadotropin present in the blood.

Concentrations of 17α,20ß-P were marginally significantly higher in Palos Verdes females (1.7 ± 0.75 ng/mL versus 1.4 ± 0.63 ng/mL) (p=0.058), higher in the morning (p=0.001), and higher in fish with gonadotropin present (p=0.027) (no figure). The time of month did not significantly affect the concentrations of 17α,20ß-P (p=0.41).

Estradiol receptors. We attempted to measure estradiol receptor concentrations and their dissociation constants in livers of fish from both sites. The number of fish from Palos Verdes from which we were able to obtain reliable data was limited due to a problem of unknown origin in some of their livers. This was manifested in high nonspecific binding in the nuclear receptor assays. Therefore, the nuclear receptor assays were somewhat problematical and these data should be considered preliminary. In fish with valid measurements, there was a significantly larger cytosolic binding coefficient (Kd) in Palos Verdes fish than Dana Point fish (Figure 9-6)

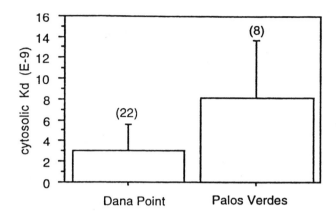

Figure 9-6 Cytosolic equilibrium dissociation constant of the hepatic estrogen receptor in fish from the 2 sites

(p=0.002). There was no correlation of cytosolic Kd with liver ΣDDT concentrations (r=0.14, p-0.70) nor with ΣPCB concentrations (r=0.11, p=0.75) in Palos Verdes fish. There were no significant site differences in the abundance of cytosolic estradiol receptors (Palos Verdes, 5.4 ± 5.1 E-11 M/g; Dana Point 3.6 ± 2.0 E-11 M/g), nuclear estrogen receptors (Palos Verdes, 0.30 ± 0.19 E-12 M/g; Dana Point 0.38 ± 0.49 E-12 M/g), nor nuclear Kd (Palos Verdes, 5.6 ± 3.34 E-9; Dana Point 11.0 ± 17.9 E-9).

Competition for the estrogen receptor by chlorinated hydrocarbons
The results of the experiments to determine if DDT and its derivatives interfere with binding of estrogen to its receptor in the liver are shown in Figure 9-7. As can be seen, o,p'-DDE and o,p'-DDT showed consistent interference with binding of estradiol to its receptor at concentrations of 10^{-4} to 10^{-7}M. In comparison to estradiol, which was tested as an unlabeled compound, these 2 compounds were approximately 100 and 1000 ×, respectively, less potent. In contrast, p,p'-DDE, o,p'-DDD, p,p'-DDD, p,p'-DDT showed little or no interference with binding at the concentrations tested. Aroclor 1254 also showed negligible binding to the estrogen receptor (data not shown).

Discussion

As with previous studies, we compared reproductive and endocrine measures at 2 sites. We realize that differences in water temperatures or other factors during gametogenesis could result in subtle differences between sites in these parameters. We have, therefore, placed the greatest emphasis on reproductive measures that differed between sites and also showed some relationship to tissue concentrations of contaminants in Palos Verdes fish.

Studies of kelp bass and white croaker collected in the same areas in the mid 1980s indicated a number of differences in the reproductive status of mature

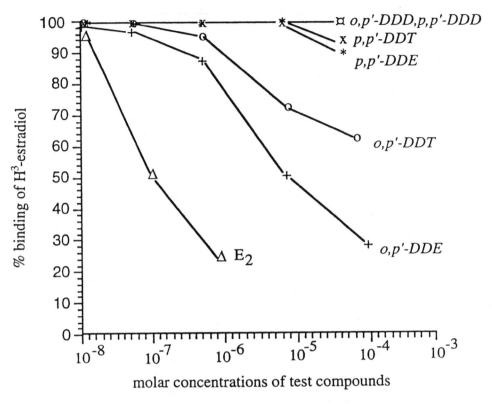

Figure 9-7 Competition by estrogen and DDT compounds for the estrogen receptor in kelp bass liver. Percent binding of H^3-estradiol in the presence of DDTs and estrogen.

females (Cross and Hose 1988, 1989; Hose et al. 1989). Of particular note was the lack of yolky oocytes observed in mature kelp bass collected from around the Palos Verdes Peninsula (Cross and Hose 1988). This phenomenon was not observed in kelp bass during this study, as all females over 250 cm SL had yolky oocytes in their ovaries. In fact, concentrations of protein-bound phosphorus (VTG) and the rate of estradiol production were not different between fish from the 2 sites, although the estradiol concentrations were lower in Palos Verdes fish. Therefore, we found no abnormalities in oocyte growth through vitellogenesis in sexually mature female kelp bass collected around the Palos Verdes Peninsula in 1992. It should be noted that ΣDDT in kelp bass tissues had steadily decreased from a peak in the early 1970s through the late 1980s (Mearns et al. 1991).

Cross and Hose (1989) collected kelp bass from both sites and subjected them to spawning trials. A smaller portion of those collected near the Palos Verdes Peninsula responded to hormone treatment with LHRHa; they also had poorer spawning success. In the normal cascade of events leading to spawning in female fish, stimulation of the brain by environmental cues results in secretion of a neurohormone (GnRH, homologous to mammalian LHRH) that stimulates the pituitary to release maturational gonadotropin into the blood stream, which in turn leads to

maturational changes in the ovary. Our finding of significantly higher concentrations of ΣDDT in fish caught in the morning without measurable plasma gonadotropin (II), as compared to those that did have measurable quantities of
gonadotropin (Figure 9-3c), may support these earlier observations of poor spawning success.

The results of a study of European flounder (*Platichthys flesus*) suggest that DDT in
the brain of fish can alter diurnal behavior. Although the number of fish studies
was small, fish receiving a high DDT dose (their brains contained 3.5 to 34.4 μg/g)
increased their day-time swimming, an alteration of their normal diel activity
pattern (Bengtsson and Larsson 1981). In another study bluegill sunfish (*Lepomis
macrochirus*) showed hyperactivity shortly after exposure to DDT (Ellgaard et al.
1977). The present results demonstrate that certain DDT metabolites can bind to
estrogen receptors in fish tissues. Hydroxylated metabolites of PCBs can also bind
to hepatic estrogen receptors (Thomas, unpublished). The brains and pituitaries of
fish have been shown to contain estrogen and androgen receptors (ARs) (e.g., Kim
et al. 1978), and it is likely that certain PCBs and DDT or its derivatives (e.g., *o,p'*-
DDE) and PCB metabolites can bind to brain estrogen receptors. Further, experimental work has shown that steroids can exert both a negative and positive
feedback on gonadotropin release both at the brain and pituitary (Billard 1978;
Trudeau et al. 1991). Therefore, the impairment of neuroendocrine function suggested by our data may be related to binding of the contaminants to estrogen
receptors in the brain. Alterations in hypothalamic concentrations of serotonin, a
neurotransmitter which regulates gonadotropin secretion in teleosts (Kahn and
Thomas 1994), have recently been demonstrated in Atlantic croaker treated with
Aroclor 1254 (Khan and Thomas 1996). These results suggest that alterations in
neurotransmitter function may be the proximate mechanism by which PCBs and
possibly other organochlorines alter gonadotropin secretion. Although the large
differences in ΣDDT concentrations of fish with and without measurable plasma
GtH suggest that this class of compounds is responsible for the differences observed in this study, other contaminants such as heavy metals can act directly on
the pituitary gland as well, affecting the release rate of gonadotropin (Cooper et al.
1987; Thomas 1993), and we cannot exclude a role for these compounds as well.

Estradiol concentrations were lower in the blood of Palos Verdes females relative to
those of Dana Point (p=0.048), and testosterone showed a trend (not significant)
toward lower concentrations in the blood in Palos Verdes fish. These differences
were especially apparent in the morning and early in June. The analyses of covariance suggested that the blood concentrations of these steroids fluctuated with
gonadotropin blood concentrations, which would suggest that these effects may be
due to alterations of hormone secretion at higher levels of the reproductive endocrine axis (in the brain and in the pituitary). However, there was also a strong
positive correlation of in vitro testosterone production by ovaries with hepatic
ΣDDT concentrations. These results indicate that there may be a direct stimulatory
effect of DDT compounds on ovarian production of steroids as well as effects
mediated from higher levels of the reproductive endocrine axis. While the mechanism underlying increased testosterone production with ΣDDT exposure is not
known, previous studies have demonstrated direct effects of chemicals on steroidogenesis (Singh 1989; Thomas 1990; Thomas and Khan, Chapter 3).

There is also evidence that PCBs can alter steroid synthesis. Male cod given food contaminated with Aroclor 1254 (1, 5, 10, 25, and 50 μg/g) for 5.5 months exhibited altered patterns of steroid biosynthesis (Freeman et al. 1982). At a food concentration of 5 μg/g, there was stimulation of biosynthesis with increases of testosterone and 11-KT and an inhibition of synthesis at higher concentrations. However, in the present study there was a discrepancy between increased testosterone production in vitro from ovaries of Palos Verdes fish and lower concentrations of testosterone in the blood. One mechanism that might reconcile these findings is that environmental exposure to DDTs and PCBs increases steroid metabolism resulting in a decline of plasma concentrations (Sivarajah et al. 1978; Nowicki and Norman 1972). Kelp bass in southern California would be an interesting model in which to investigate this potential mechanism of endocrine disruption by organochlorines in a natural environment.

The 2 progestins measured in this study showed differing patterns with respect to site. Blood plasma concentrations of 20ß-S did not differ between sites, while those of 17α,20ß-P were marginally significantly higher in Palos Verdes. Since the relative importance of these 2 progestins in final oocyte maturation is undefined in this species, the significance of these findings is not known.

The cytosolic equilibrium dissociation coefficient (Kd) of the estrogen receptor in the liver was found to be more than twice as large in Palos Verdes fish than for Dana Point fish (8.1×10^{-9}, compared to 3.1×10^{-9}, see Figure 9-6). Although the Kd could only be determined in 8 fish from the former and 22 fish from the latter site, the difference was significant. This suggests that binding affinity of estrogen to its receptor was lower in Palos Verdes fish than in Dana Point fish. The high degree of nonspecific binding of estradiol to unknown liver components in Palos Verdes fish, but not Dana Point fish, indicates some additional biochemical difference in these fish, possibly alterations in lipid metabolism. We found higher concentrations of lipid in the livers of Palos Verdes fish; moreover lipoproteins have been shown to bind both steroids and organochlorines (Ungerer and Thomas 1996).

Besides the apparent effects of ΣDDT on the hormonal cascade from the brain-pituitary axis discussed above, there are other subtle endocrine effects observed. First, testosterone production was greatly enhanced in fish from the contaminated site and is apparently closely linked to ΣDDT concentrations. Second, the binding affinity of estradiol to its cytosolic receptor in the liver is lower in fish from the contaminated site. The possible consequences of these phenomena on the reproductive cycle of these fish is not known and also warrants further study.

The results of the separate experiment to measure competitive binding of estradiol to its liver receptor indicated that both o,p´-DDE and o,p´-DDT were weak competitors, displacing labeled estrogen from its receptor at about 100 to 1000 $\times$, respectively, less effectively than unlabeled estrogen. Our results corroborate earlier studies with mammals in which only their ortho, para derivatives of DDE and DDT were capable of binding to the estrogen receptor and have the potential to exert estrogenic effects (Nelson 1974; Bulger and Kupfer 1985). This provides a molecular mechanism for the interference of these chlorinated compounds with hormone-mediated processes in fish.

It is worth noting that the size and age of collected fish indicate that Palos Verdes fish are significantly smaller than those at Dana Point while there were no differences in mean age.

In summary, the results of the present field study show differences in several reproductive endocrine indices in female kelp bass captured from a heavily contaminated and a less contaminated site in the Southern California Bight. Moreover, some of these endocrine alterations were associated with increased hepatic burdens of ΣDDTs and PCBs. However, the reproductive consequences of these endocrine changes are unclear and require further study, especially during the later stages of the reproductive cycle.

Acknowledgments

Dr. Andrew Gunther, Mr. Jordan Gold, and Mr. David Bell of Applied Marine Sciences were key to the success of this study. We gratefully acknowledge Margaret Matsui and other staff and students of Occidental College and the crew of the R/V *Vantuna* for catching the fish. Ms. Mary Beth Hawkins and Ms. Diane Breckenridge-Miller carried out the endocrinological measures. We thank Dr. John Stegeman, Dr. Michael Martin, Dr. John Hunter, Dr. Jo Ellen Hose, Dr. Jeff Cross, Dr. Robert Dexter, Mr. Harrison Stubbs, and Dr. Penny Swanson for comments on this study. We are thankful to Mr. Michael Salazaar, Dr. John Cubit, and Dr. William Conner of NOAA for their support while this study was in progress. Support for this project was provided by NOAA contract No. 50-DGNC-1-00007.

References

Bengtsson B-E, Larson Å. 1981. Hyperactivity and changed diurnal activity in flounders, *Platichthys flesus*, exposed to DDT. *Mar Pol Bull* 12:100–102.

Billard R. 1978. Testicular feedback on the hypothalamo-pituitary axis in rainbow trout *Salmo giairdneri*. *R Ann Biol Anim Biochem Biophys* 18:813–818.

Bitman J, Cecil HC. 1970. Estrogenic activity of DDT analogs and polychlorinated biphenyls. *J Agr Food Chem* 18:1108–1112.

Bitman J, Cecil HC, Harris HJ, Fries GF. 1968. Estrogenic activity of *o,p'*- DDT in the mammalian uterus and avian oviduct. *Science* 162:371–372.

Brouwer A, Reinjders PJH, Koeman JH. 1989. Polychlorinated biphenyl (PCB)-contaminated food induces vitamin A and thyroid hormone deficiency in the common seal *Phoca vitulina*. *Aquatic Toxicol* 15:99–106.

Bulger WH, Kupfer D. 1985. Estrogenic activity of pesticides and other xenobiotics on the uterus and male reproductive tract. In: Thomas JA, Korach KS, McLachlan JA, editors. Endocrine toxicity. New York NY: Raven Pr. p 1–24.

Carlson RW, Duby RT. 1973. Embryotoxic effects of three PCBs in the chicken. *Bull Environ Contam Toxicol* 9:261–266.

Cooper RL, Goldman JM, Rehnberg GL, McElroy WK, Hein JF. 1987. Effects of metal ions on pituitary hormone secretion in vitro. *J Biochem Toxicol* 2:241–249.

Copeland PA, Thomas P. 1992. Isolation of maturational gonadotropin subunits from spotted seatrout *Cynoscion nebulosus* and development of a ß-subunit-directed radioimmunoassay for gonadotropin measurement in sciaenid fishes. *Gen Comp Endocrinol* 88:100–110.

Craik JCA, Harvey SM. 1984. A biochemical method for distinguishing between the sexes of fishes by the presence of yolk protein in the blood. *J Fish Biol* 25:293–303.

Cross JN, Hose JE. 1988. Evidence for impaired reproduction in white croaker *Genyonemus lineatus* from contaminated areas off southern California. *Mar Environ Res* 24: 185–188.

Cross JN, Hose JE. 1989. Reproductive impairment in two species of fish from contaminated areas off southern California. Proceedings, Oceans '89. Washington DC: Marine Technology Society. p 382–384.

Ellgaard EG, Ochsner JC, Cox JK. 1977. Locomotion hyperactivity induced in the bluegill sunfish, *Lepomis macrochirus*, by sublethal concentrations of DDT. *Can J Zool* 55:1077–1081.

Freeman HC, Sangalang G, Flemming B. 1982. The sublethal effects of a polychlorinated biphenyl (Aroclor 1254) diet on the Atlantic cod, *Gadus morhua*. *Sci Total Environ* 24:1–11.

Golub MC, Donald JM, Reyes JA. 1991. Reproductive toxicity of commercial PCB mixtures: LOAELs and NOAELs from animal studies. *Environ Health Perspect* 94:245–253.

Gossett RW, Brown DA, Young DR. 1982. Predicting the bioaccumulation and toxicity of organic compounds. Long Beach CA: Southern California Coastal Water Research Project Annual Report. p 149–156.

Gossett R, Puffer HW, Arthur RH, Young DR. 1983. DDT, PCB, and benzo(a)pyrene levels in white croaker, *Genyonemus lineatus*, from southern California. *Mar Poll Bull* 14:60–65.

Hansen DJ, Parrish PR, Forester J. 1974. Aroclor 1016: Toxicity to and uptake by estuarine animals. *Environ Res* 7:363–373.

Hart MM, Adamson RH, Fabro S. 1971. Prematurity and intrauterine growth retardation induced by DDT in rabbit. *Archives Internat Pharmacodyn Therapie* 192:286–290.

Heath RG, Spann JW, Kreitzer JF. 1969. Marked DDE impairment of mallard reproduction in controlled studies. *Nature* 224:47–48.

Helle E, Olsson M, Jensen S. 1976. PCB levels correlated with pathological changes in seal uteri. *Ambio* 5:261–263.

Hose JE, Cross JN, Smith SG, Diehl D. 1989. Reproductive impairment in fish inhabiting a contaminated coastal environment off southern California. *Environ Poll* 57:139–148.

Jensen S, Khilstrom JE, Olsson M, Lundberg C, Orgerg J. 1977. Effects of PCB and DDT on mink, *Mustela vison*, during the reproductive season. *Ambio* 6:239.

Khan IA, Thomas P. 1996. Disruption of neuroendocrine function in Atlantic croaker exposed to Aroclor 1254. *Mar Environ Res* 42, 145–149.

Kim YS, Stumpf WE, Sar M, Martinez-Vegas MC. 1978. Estrogen and androgen target cells in the brain of fishes, reptiles, and birds: phylogency and ontogeny. *Amer Zool* 18:425–433.

Kimbrough RD. 1974. The toxicity of polychlorinated compounds and related chemicals. *CRC Review in Toxicol* 445–497.

Macek KJ. 1968. Reproduction in Brook trout *(Salvelinus fontinalis)* fed sublethal concentrations of DDT. *J Fish Res Bd Canada* 25, 1787–1796.

McDermott DJ, Heesen TC. 1975. DDT and PCB in Dover sole around outfalls. Long Beach CA: Southern California Coastal Water Research Project Annual Report. p 117–121.

Mearns AJ, Young DR. 1980. Trophic structure and pollutant flow in a harbor ecosystem. In: Bascom W, editor. Biennial report for the years 1979–1980. Long Beach CA: Southern California Coastal Water Research Project. p 289–308.

Mearns AJ, Matta M, Shigenaka G, Mac Donald D, Buchman M, Harris H, Golas J, Lauenstein G. 1991. Contaminant trends in the Southern California Bight: inventory and Assessment. Seattle WA: National Oceanic and Atmospheric Administration (NOAA)/NOS. NOAA Tech. Mem. NOS ORCA 62.

Nelson JA. 1974. Effects of dichlorodiphenyltrichloroethane (DDT) analogs and polychlorinated biphenyl (PCB) mixtures on 17ß-[³H] estradiol binding to rat uterine receptor. *Biochem Pharmacol* 23:447–450.

[NOAA] National Oceanic and Atmospheric Administration. 1989. National Status and Trends Program: A summary of data on tissue contamination from the first three years (1986–1988) of the Mussel Watch Project. NOAA Technical Memorandum NOS OMA 49. NOAA NOS Office of Oceanography and Marine Assessment, Rockville, Maryland.

Nowicki HG, Norman W. 1972. Enhanced hepatic metabolism of testosterone, 4-androstene-3, 17-dione, and estradiol-17ß in chickens pretreated with DDT or PCB. *Steroids* 19:85–97.

Oda DL, Lavenberg RJ, Rounds JM. 1993. Reproductive biology of three California species of *Paralabrax* (Pisces: Serranidae). *CalCOFI Rep* 34:122–132.

Pollack GA, Uhaa IJ, Fan AM, Wisniewski JA, Witherell I. 1991. A study of chemical contamination of fish from southern California. II. Comprehensive study. Sacramento CA: Office of Environmental Health Assessment, California Environmental Protection Agency.

Quast JC. 1968. Observations on the food and biology of the kelp bass, *Paralabrax clathratus*, with notes on its sport fishery at San Diego, California. *Calif Fish Game Fish Bull* 139:81–108.

Reijnders PJH. 1986. Reproductive failure in common seals feeding on fish from polluted coastal waters. *Nature, London* 324:456–457.

Scott AP, Sheldrick EL, Flint APF. 1982. Measurement of 17α, 20ß-dihydroxy 4-pregnen-3-one in plasma of trout, *Salmo giardneri*. Richardson: Seasonal changes and responses to salmon pituitary extract. *Gen Comp Endocrinol* 46:441–451.

Secor DH. 1991. Manual for otolith removal and preparation for micro structural examination. Palo Alto CA: Electric Power Research Institute. Project #1991-01.

Silkworth JB, Grabstein EM. 1982. Polychlorinated biphenyl immunotoxicity: dependence on isomer planarity and Ah gene complex. *Toxicol Appl Pharmacol* 65:109–115.

Singh H, Griffith RW, Takahashi A, Kawauchi H, Thomas P, Stegeman JJ. 1988. Regulation of gonadal steroidogenesis in *Fundulus heteroclitus* by recombinant salmon growth hormone and purified salmon prolactin. *Gen Comp Endocrinol* 72:144–153.

Singh H. 1989. Interaction of xenobiotics with reproductive endocrine functions in a protogynous teleost, *Monopterus albus*. *Mar Environ Res* 28:285–289.

Sivarajah K, Franklin CS, Williams WP. 1978. The effects of polychlorinated biphenyls on plasma steroid levels and hepatic microsomal enzymes in fish. *J Fish Biol* 13:401–409.

Smith CL, Young PH. 1966. Gonad structure and the reproductive cycle of the kelp bass *Paralabrax clathratus* (Girard) with comments on the relationships of the serranus genus *Paralabrax*. *Calif Fish Game* 52:283–292.

Smith JS, Thomas P. 1990. Binding characteristics of the hepatic estrogen receptor of the spotted sea trout, *Cynoscion nebulosus*. *Gen Comp Endocrin* 77:29–42.

Spies RB, Kruger H, Ireland R, Rice Jr. DW. 1989. Stable isotope ratios and contaminant concentrations in a sewage-distorted food web. *Mar Ecol Progr Ser* 54:157–170.

Sutter TR, Guzman K, Dold KM, Greenlee WF. 1991. Targets for dioxin: genes for the plasminogen activator Inhibitor-2 and interleukin-1ß. *Science* 254:415–418.

Thomas P. 1988. Reproductive endocrine function in female Atlantic Croaker exposed to pollutants. *Mar Env Res* 24:179–183.

Thomas P. 1989. Effects of Aroclor 1254 and cadmium on reproductive endocrine function and ovarian growth in Atlantic Croaker. *Mar Env Sci* 28:499–503.

Thomas P. 1990. Teleost model for studying the effects of chemicals on female reproductive endocrine function. *J Exp Zool Suppl* 4:126–128.

Thomas P. 1993. Effects of cadmium on gonadotropin secretion from Atlantic Croaker pituitaries in vitro. *Mar Env Res* 35:141–145.

Thomas P, Smith JS. 1993. Binding of xenobiotics to the estrogen receptor of spotted seatrout: A screening assay for possible estrogenic effects. *Mar Env Res* 35:147–151.

Trant JM, Thomas P. 1989. Isolation of a novel maturation-inducing steroid produced in vitro by ovaries of Atlantic Croaker. *Gen Comp Endocrinol* 75:397–404.

Trudeau VL, Sloley BD, Wong AOL, Peter RE. 1991. Mechanisms of sex steroid negative and positive feedback control of gonadotropin (GTH) secretion in teleosts, pp. 224–226, In: Scott AP, Sumpter JP, Kime DE, Rolge MS, editors. Reproductive physiology of fish. Norwich UK: Fish Symposium 91.

Ungerer J, Thomas P. 1996. Transport and accumulation of organochlorines in the ovaries of Atlantic Croaker (*Micropogonias undulatus*). *Mar Environ Res* 47:167–171.

Early mortality syndrome in salmonid fishes from the Great Lakes

Susan V. Marcquenski, Scott B. Brown

From 1968 to 1996, early life-stage mortalities occurred in coho and chinook salmon, lake trout and brown trout and steelhead from the Great Lakes; however, their causes were not conclusively determined. "Early Mortality Syndrome" (EMS) describes several of these syndromes affect sac fry, swim-up fry, and feeding fry. Clinical signs include loss of equilibrium, swimming in a spiral pattern, lethargy, hyperexcitability, hemorrhage, and death. Within a species, mortality rates vary among fry from different female parents. Annual EMS mortality ranged from 10 to 30% until January 1993 when 60 to 90% of coho in Wisconsin, Illinois, Indiana, and Michigan hatcheries died from the late eyed-egg stage through the feeding fry stage. These catastrophic losses prompted the Fish Health Committee and the Board of Technical Experts of the Great Lakes Fishery Commission to invite experts to address these possible causes: hatchery cultural techniques, broodstock management, genetics, pathogens, nutrition, ecosystem changes, and known contaminants such as polychlorinated biphenyls (PCBs). Early Mortality Syndrome can be prevented or reversed when eggs or fry are exposed to thiamine. Whether EMS results from a simple dietary deficiency or is due to interactions between thiamine and other environmental factors is unknown. Cayuga Syndrome and M74 are 2 other early life-stage mortality syndromes in which eggs contain very low levels of thiamine and affected fry respond to thiamine treatments. Cayuga Syndrome affects Atlantic salmon in New York Finger Lakes, and M74 affects Atlantic salmon from the Baltic Sea.

From 1968 to the present, early life-stage mortality has been documented in salmonids from Lakes Ontario, Michigan, and to a lesser extent, Lakes Huron and Erie. Species exhibiting mortality include lake trout (*Salvelinus namaycush*), chinook salmon (*Onchorhynchus tshawytscha*), coho salmon (*Onchorhynchus kisutch*), steelhead (*Onchorhynchus mykiss*), and brown trout (*Salmo trutta*). Mortality was first observed by hatchery personnel responsible for rearing progeny from feral broodstocks that mature in these Great Lakes. Hatcheries in the province of Ontario and in the United States (U.S.) states bordering the Great Lakes depend on these feral broodstocks for eggs to sustain a multimillion dollar sport fishery. Although this mortality has only been observed in fish culture situations, it likely contributes to the lack of natural lake trout reproduction in Lake Michigan and Lake Ontario.

Early life-stage mortality was variable from 1968 through 1992 and tended not to exceed 20 to 30% for any species. Hatcheries compensated by simply increasing the number of eggs collected during spawning. However, in January 1993, coho mortality dramatically increased to 60 to 90% in Wisconsin, Illinois, Indiana, and Michigan hatcheries. Mortality in other Lake Michigan salmonids also increased but did not reach these extreme levels. Hatcheries could no longer compensate for these catastrophic losses by collecting more eggs. Eggs from the Pacific Coast could not be imported into the Great Lakes Basin due to concerns about nonindigenous pathogens such as Infectious hematopoietic necrosis virus and viral hemorrhagic septicemia virus (VHSV). This prompted the Great Lakes Fishery Commission to sponsor 2 workshops to facilitate renewed and more extensive investigations into the causes of these early life-stage mortalities.

The term Early Mortality Syndrome (EMS) was developed at the first workshop and by definition includes present and historic early life-stage mortalities that share common features and affect salmonids in the Great Lakes. As a result of the 2 workshops, thiamine (Vitamin B1) deficiency was implicated as a possible cause of EMS. Low levels of thiamine have also been associated with 2 other early life-stage mortality syndromes affecting Atlantic salmon (*Salmo salar*) in New York Finger Lakes (Cayuga Syndrome) and in the Baltic Sea (M74). This chapter will describe the historic occurrence of early life-stage mortalities in Great Lakes salmonids, discuss the possible causes of EMS, briefly compare EMS with Cayuga Syndrome and M74, and report the focus of current research.

Definition of Terms

For the purposes of this chapter, an "eyed egg" is the embryonic stage at which the eye pigment is visible in the unhatched egg. The "sac-fry" stage begins when the egg hatches and persists until the yolk sac is reduced and the viscera are internalized. The "swim-up" stage begins when fry become more active and swim-up to the water surface to begin exogenous feeding. "Feeding fry" describes fry that have been feeding exogenously for some time. Although salmonid fry pass through all of these stages, there are species specific differences in the amount of time a fry remains at a particular developmental stage.

Historic Occurrences of Early Life-stage Mortality in the Great Lakes

In 1964 and 1965, the Michigan Department of Natural Resources imported coho salmon eggs from the Pacific Coast. Fisheries biologists viewed this as an opportunity to utilize the abundant alewife populations in Lake Michigan as forage for salmon. The coho were reared in hatcheries and stocked in the Lake. Mature coho returned to spawn in Michigan tributaries in Fall 1967 and 1968. Eggs were collected from the fish and incubated in state hatcheries. Mortality (11 to 39%) was observed at the swim-up and feeding fry stages. From 1968 to 1972, coho fry deaths in Michigan hatcheries were thought to be associated with high egg concentrations of DDT and its metabolites, but no statistically significant relationships were found (Johnson and Pecor 1969; Pecor 1972). During the same years, Wisconsin hatcheries also reported variable mortality due to a "nervous syndrome" in coho fry from Lake Michigan broodstocks (Degurse et al. 1973). Mortality was not related to concentrations of polychlorinated biphenyls (PCBs), DDT, or its metabolites in the eggs. These authors suggested that investigations into the vitamin, enzyme-hormone conditions of the coho (broodstock and their progeny) might be more productive than repeated analyses of known hydrocarbon residues.

In the late 1970s and early 1980s, Mac et al. (1985, 1993) addressed the lack of successful lake trout reproduction in Lake Michigan by studying a swim-up fry mortality in progeny from feral broodstock. They could not link the observed fry mortality with PCB concentrations in the eggs; however, there was a significant relationship between total PCB concentration in the eggs and mortality that occurred before hatching.

In 1982, Giesy et al. (1986) attempted to correlate swim-up mortality in Lake Michigan chinook salmon with concentrations of chlorinated hydrocarbons. The authors did not observe consistent trends between concentrations of individual chlorinated hydrocarbons in eggs and percent survival to the swim-up stage; however, when the residues were classified into 4 principal components, 2 of the principal components containing primarily toxaphene and PCB residues were negatively correlated to fry survival.

Frimeth (1990) reported a swim-up fry mortality affecting the progeny of coho salmon from the Credit River, a tributary of Lake Ontario. During 1977 to 1988, mortality ranged from 20 to 30% and occurred during the swim-up stage. However, in 1989, mortality occurred earlier, just after the embryos reached the eyed-egg stage and was characterized by premature hatch. Based on observations of pre-hatch in coho by Halter and Johnson (1974), Frimeth hypothesized that contaminants might have been responsible for this condition. While most mortality occurred at the eyed-egg stage, death still occurred in a percentage of the fry that reached the swim-up stage.

From 1979 to 1984, Symula et al. (1990) studied a sac-fry mortality affecting the Seneca Lake strain of lake trout from Lake Ontario. The predominant clinical sign was yolk-sac edema, termed "blue sac." Fry reared at lower water temperatures had a lower prevalence of blue sac than fry reared at higher temperatures. For this reason, the authors hypothesized that the edema did not result from a simple chemical toxicity as was shown to occur for DDT (Burdick et al. 1964) and for 2,3,7,8-tetrachlorodibenzo-p-dioxin (TCDD) (Walker et al. 1991). Understanding the etiology of blue sac was further complicated when 2 bacteria, *Cytophaga psychrophila* and a cold water strain of *Aeromonas salmonicida* were cultured from the fry. The underlying cause of blue sac was never resolved.

Skea et al. (1985) investigated a feeding-fry mortality in Lake Ontario steelhead and Lake Michigan chinook from 1981 to 83. This mortality, called "syndrome", could not be correlated to a specific contaminant in eggs or fry, although mortality was highest in steelhead progeny from females with the highest total contaminant burdens. The onset of this mortality occurred over a 4-week period after the fry began exogenous feeding. Fry that starved died at a later developmental stage, clearly separating starvation from losses due to the syndrome. The authors suggested that this syndrome may have resulted from pesticides or nutritional deficiencies during oogenesis and/or vitellogenesis.

In 1990, Smith et al. (1994) described egg mortality in coho and chinook salmon from Lake Ontario. Variable mortality was observed among progeny from different females and was unrelated to 2,3,7,8-TCDD equivalent concentration (toxicity equivalence concentration [TEC]) in the eggs. Most chinook mortality occurred prior to the eyed-egg stage. Most coho mortality occurred during the eyed-egg stage just before hatch, although some mortality occurred even earlier.

In 1990 and 1991, Fitzsimons et al. (1995) studied a swim-up fry syndrome in progeny from Lake Ontario lake trout. Affected fry were anorexic, hyperexcitable, and could not maintain equilibrium in the water column (Fitzsimons 1995). Mortality could not be correlated to rearing temperature, feeding practices, or contaminant burdens in eggs (PCBs, pesticides, dioxins, furans, polycyclic aromatic hydrocarbons [PAHs], and trace metals). Fitzsimons (1995) discovered that injecting sac fry with thiamine or immersing affected fry in a thiamine solution increased survival. Injecting fry with other B vitamins (nicotinic acid, riboflavin, folic acid, or pyridoxine hydrochloride) did not improve survival. Much of the subsequent research on EMS, Cayuga Syndrome, and M74 has been based on these initial experiments showing a link between thiamine and fry mortality.

Clinical Signs of EMS

Clinical signs of EMS are similar among species and over time, but differ from blue sac and dioxin toxicity based on descriptions from earlier published studies and present observations (Table 10-1). Table 10-1 was constructed from clinical signs described in the referenced literature; a blank box indicates the clinical sign was not mentioned in the cited publication. A blank box may be more indicative of the level of detail the authors used to describe affected fish than an indication that the clinical sign was truly absent. Signs of EMS include loss of equilibrium, swimming in a spiral or corkscrew pattern, lethargy, dark pigmentation, hyperexcitability when touched, failure to feed, tetany, hemorrhages in various locations, hydrocephalus, and death (Johnson and Pecor 1969; Pecor 1972; Degurse et al. 1973; Frimeth 1990; Wisconsin Department of Natural Resources and Michigan Department of Natural Resources, unpublished data; Great Lakes Fishery Commission 1994; Mac et al. 1985; Mac 1988; Mac et al. 1993; Fitzsimons et al. 1995; Fitzsimons 1995; Skea et al. 1995).

Within a species, progeny from different females have variable mortality rates (5 to 100%), suggesting there is a female-dependent "factor" involved in the syndrome. The intestine of most dead fry is empty, however death due to EMS occurs before death due to starvation (Skea et al. 1985). It appears that fry with EMS do not completely utilize the yolk because they have larger amounts of residual yolk than healthy fry of the same age (Great Lakes Fishery Commission 1994).

Before January 1993, the onset of EMS in coho and other salmonids from Lake Michigan was predictable and occurred at the swim-up stage, continuing into the feeding fry stage. Death occurred over 10 to 14 days (Table 10-2) and mortality rates ranged from 10 to 20% (Figure 10-1). However, from January 1993 to 1996, mortality occurred at the sac-fry stage in coho and chinook salmon, brown trout, and steelhead progeny from Lake Michigan broodstocks. Mortality was also observed in coho embryos during the late eyed-egg stage. An increased prevalence of premature hatching, termed "half-hatch", occurred up to a week before the expected hatching date. Coho and other salmonid fry mortality occurred over a longer period (Table 10-2) and the number of fry that died was 3 × greater than fry that died in 1986 and 1987 (Figure 10-1).

Table 10-1 A comparison of clinical signs among salmonids exhibiting mortality at an early life stage. All species are progeny from Lake Michigan or Lake Ontario broodstocks, except for the lake trout studied by Walker et al. which were obtained from Lake Superior and injected with 2,3,7,8-TCDD.

Clinical sign	Coho					Lake trout				Steelhead		Chinook	
	Johnson, Pecor 1969; Pecor 1972	Degurse et al. 1973	Frimeth 1990	WI DNR MI DNR unpub. data	Smith et al. 1994	Mac et al. 1985, 1993; Mac 1988	Symula et al. 1990	Walker et al. 1991	Fitzsimons et al. 1995; Fitzsimons 1995	Skea et al. 1985	Skea et al. 1985	Mac 1988	Smith et al. 1994
Death before eye-up					X	X							X
Eyed-egg death/half-hatch	X	X	X	X	X	X		X					
Microphthalmia				X	X								
Yolk sac edema and death				X[1]			X	X					
Residual yolk at death				X		X			X				
Empty intestine	X	X		X		X			X				
Female dependent factor	X	X	X	X		X			X	X	X		
Loss of equilibrium	X	X		X		X			X	X	X		
Spiral swimming	X	X		X		X				X	X	X	
Lethargy/fry lay on tank bottom on their sides	X	X		X		X			X				
Dark pigment				X						X	X		
Hyper-excitable	X	X		X					X	X	X		
Tetany	X	X		X		X				X	X		
Hemorrhage				X									
Hydrocephalus								X					
Death at swim-up and after	X	X	X	X		X			X	X	X	X	

[1] A slight amount of yolk-sac edema was observed occasionally in coho salmon exhibiting EMS.

Table 10-2 Changes in the onset and duration of EMS in coho and chinook salmon and steelhead trout based on Temperature Units °C[1]. Mean ± SD (range) (Lasee 1994).

Species Years Lake	EMS begins	EMS peaks	EMS ends	Duration of EMS (end minus onset)
Coho 1986 and 1987 Lake Michigan N=4 hatcheries	684 ± 6 (680–693)	722 ± 49 (680–770)	799 ± 8 (680–924)	116 ± 133 (0–231)
Coho 1993 and 1994 Lake Michigan N=7 hatcheries	561 ± 111 (429–729)	712 ± 102 (600–880)	868 ± 100 (713–979)	306 ± 129 (181–506)
Chinook 1986 and 1987 Lake Michigan N=4 hatcheries	655 ± 145 (506–793)	735 ± 196 (539–909)	870 ± 86 (770–944)	213 ± 61 (146–264)
Chinook 1993 and 1994 Lake Michigan N=8 hatcheries	721 ± 209 (363–902)	801 ± 245 (369–1015)	987 ± 73 (896–1097)	266 ± 180 (128–550)
Steelhead trout 1986 and 1987 Lake Michigan N=4 hatcheries	533 ± 72 (473–616)	610 ± 28 (578–638)	716 ± 59 (651–781)	182 ± 19 (165–210)
Steelhead trout 1993 and 1994 Lake Michigan N=7 hatcheries	477 ± 28 (420–500)	592 ± 80 (524–700)	789 ± 221 (633–1200)	312 ± 207 (146–700)

[1] A temperature unit is the product of water temperature °C and number of days the eggs or fry were reared at that temperature, e.g., eggs incubated for 15 days at 10°C accrue 150 temperature units.

Early Mortality Syndrome versus Premature Hatch versus Blue-sac Disease versus Swim-up Syndrome versus Drop-out Syndrome versus Feeding-fry Syndrome

There has been some discussion regarding whether the swim-up fry mortality occurring before 1993 in Lake Michigan and Lake Ontario was of the same origin as the sac-fry mortality described for Lake Michigan salmonids from 1993 to 1996. The following statements support the idea that the sac-fry mortality exhibited by salmonids in 1993 was a manifestation of the same syndrome observed in salmonids from 1968 to 1992: 1) There was a continuum of observations of salmonid fry mortalities for the same species from the late 1960s to the early 1990s in Lake Michigan and Lake Ontario; 2) Similar clinical signs were described for affected fry during that period: death at the eyed-egg stage, lethargy, loss of equilibrium,

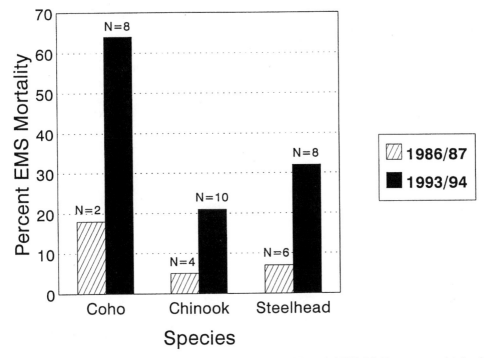

Figure 10-1 A comparison of EMS mortality between 1986-87 and 1993-94. Data were obtained from hatchery questionnaires and compiled by Becky Lasee, LaCrosse Fish Health Center, LaCrosse WI (Lasee 1994). Data were requested for fry dying from EMS in January 1986 and 1987, and for fry dying from EMS in January 1993 and 1994. Percent EMS mortality was averaged among hatcheries where EMS occurred. N is the number of hatcheries from which data were obtained for each period.

swimming in a spiral pattern, differential mortality among family groups, and death at the swim-up fry and feeding fry stages (Table 10-1); 3) Although the onset of mortality occurred a week to 10 days before swim-up from 1993 to 1996, the period of mortality was longer (30 days) and continued through the swim-up fry and feeding fry stages. Based on these points, EMS should be considered synonymous with "swim-up syndrome", "drop-out syndrome", and "feeding fry syndrome" which were terms used by hatchery personnel to describe this unusual mortality. It is unclear at this time whether the egg mortality described for coho from Lake Michigan (Great Lakes Fishery Commission 1994), coho from Lake Ontario (Frimeth 1990), and chinook and coho salmon from Lake Ontario (Smith et al. 1994) are a manifestation of EMS at an even earlier developmental stage. Early Mortality Syndrome is distinctly different from blue-sac disease (Symula et al. 1990) and dioxin toxicity (Walker et al. 1991).

Possible Causes of Early Mortality Syndrome

The catastrophic increase in coho fry mortality in 1993 prompted the Fish Health Committee and the Board of Technical Experts of the Great Lakes Fishery Commission to sponsor 2 EMS workshops (12–14 July 1994 in Ann Arbor MI and 2–3 February 1995 in Romulus MI). Hypotheses regarding possible causes of EMS were solicited from experts and presented at the first workshop. Topics included hatchery cultural techniques, broodstock management, genetics (inbreeding), pathogens, nutrition, ecosystem changes, and known contaminants such as PCBs. Invited experts presented evidence that supported or refuted these hypotheses as likely causes of EMS based on epidemiological criteria (Fox 1991). Full summaries of these presentations can be found in the Proceedings of a Workshop on EMS-Early Mortality Syndrome 1994; copies may be obtained from the Great Lakes Fishery Commission, Ann Arbor MI. The following is a synopsis of the highlights of the workshops.

Fish culture

Questionnaires were sent to hatcheries that had experienced EMS epizootics. Hatchery personnel responded to questions pertaining to cultural techniques (water temperature, dissolved oxygen, alkalinity, type of incubator, type of feed). Responses indicated that these factors were variable among the hatcheries and thus no cultural factor or set of factors was common to all hatcheries where EMS occurred.

Broodstock management and genetics

Feral salmonid broodstocks support state and provincial stocking programs in Lake Michigan and Lake Ontario. Spawning practices have remained basically the same for the past 30 years. There has not been an "infusion" of new genetic material into the Great Lakes since the early 1970s, which may have resulted in a tendency toward inbreeding. However, inbreeding by itself does not appear to cause EMS. There is anecdotal evidence that chinook eggs obtained from Lake Michigan and transferred to Minnesota hatcheries developed EMS as expected. Surviving fish were stocked into Lake Superior. When the fish matured, eggs were collected, reared in hatcheries, and EMS did not occur (Darryl Bathel, Minnesota Department of Natural Resources, personal communication). Similarly, EMS does not occur in Seeforellen brown trout maintained as a captive broodstock by the state of Michigan, however progeny from Seeforellen brown trout that mature in Lake Michigan do experience EMS (Steve Fajfer, Wisconsin Department of Natural Resources, personal communication). It is unlikely that EMS results from inbreeding. Early Mortality Syndrome is only expressed in progeny from salmonids that mature under environmental conditions present in Lakes Michigan and Ontario, and to a lesser extent, Lakes Huron and Erie, from which we are just now obtaining information.

Pathogens

Since 1989, fry with EMS were screened for pathogens using standard cultural techniques, histopathology, and electron microscopy. Aside from opportunistic infections of bacterial gill disease, pathogens were not detected in the fry. The intensity of infection of an acanthocephalan parasite (*Echinorhynchus salmonis*) has increased in Lake Michigan salmonids since the mid 1970s and presently causes severe hemorrhaging in the intestine. It is unknown whether this has an effect on egg quality and fry survival.

Ecosystem change

Significant changes in the abundance of Lake Michigan forage fish occurred in the mid to late 1980s and concomitant introductions of exotic species such as the spiny water flea (*Bythotrephes cedarstroemi*) and zebra mussels (*Dreissena polymorpha*) were also observed. Monitoring the sport harvest in Wisconsin waters has shown that Lake Michigan salmonids have not changed their dietary preference for alewife (*Alosa pseudoharengus*) (Paul Peeters, Wisconsin Department of Natural Resources, personal communication). Primary productivity has decreased in Lake Ontario over the past 15 years (Johengen et al. 1994). The biomass of alewife and rainbow smelt (*Osmerus mordax*) declined over the same period due to a combination of decreased lake productivity and increased predation pressure by salmonines (Rand et al. 1994). Food web interactions are complex, and further study is needed to clarify the relationship between ecosystem changes and EMS prevalence in Lake Michigan and Lake Ontario.

Contaminants

A direct link between contaminants and EMS has not been established despite many attempts (Pecor 1972; Degurse et al. 1973; Skea et al. 1985; Mac et al. 1993; Fitzsimons et al. 1995). While recognizing this lack of evidence, workshop participants felt that contaminants might be important in the etiology of EMS because concentrations are highest in the lakes where EMS mortality is greatest (Lake Michigan and Lake Ontario).

Nutrition

Compelling evidence supporting a nutrition based hypothesis was presented by John Fitzsimons, Department of Fisheries and Oceans, Burlington, Ontario. His initial experiments showed that EMS could be prevented or ameliorated by injecting lake trout fry with thiamine, Vitamin B_1 (Fitzsimons 1995). This surprising observation provided a stepping stone for others working on EMS and related early life-stage mortalities. Those attending the workshop agreed that further work was needed to clarify the relationship between thiamine and EMS, and whether other factors such as contaminants are also important in its etiology.

Definition of Early Mortality Syndrome

The following is a working definition of EMS that was developed at the workshop. It is based on information available at that time. Early Mortality Syndrome is

> Excess mortality (beyond expected losses) occurring from the eyed-egg stage through the period of first feeding which cannot be explained by rearing environment, husbandry, or infectious diseases. The primary indicators are above-normal loss of eyed eggs, loss of fry at hatch, and loss of fry from hatch to feeding. Clinical signs may include hyperexcitability, anemia, spiral swimming, dark coloration, lethargy (laying on the bottom or the surface), emaciation, feeding difficulties, and deformities.

Additional information is now available regarding the onset of EMS, thiamine levels in eggs, and response of affected fry to thiamine treatments, and more descriptive observations of clinical signs have been made. For the purpose of this chapter, a modified definition of EMS is as follows:

> Early Mortality Syndrome affects the progeny of salmonids that reach sexual maturity in the environmental conditions present in Lakes Michigan, Ontario, and to a lesser extent, Lakes Huron and Erie. Mortality may begin as early as the late eyed-egg stage and continue through the period of first feeding. Mortality is variable among progeny from different female parents. Clinical signs include extreme lethargy, hyperexcitability when touched, empty intestine, greater amounts of residual yolk remaining at death compared to healthy fry of the same age, swimming in a spiral pattern, loss of equilibrium, hemorrhage, slight yolk sac edema, microphthalmia, dark skin pigmentation, and death. Thiamine levels in eggs are low compared to eggs from reference sites. Survival of affected fry is greatly improved if they are exposed to waterborne concentrations of thiamine ranging from 500 to 1000 ppm.

Related Syndromes

Researchers investigating early life-stage mortalities of Atlantic salmon presented information on "Cayuga Syndrome" and "M74" at the Second EMS Workshop in Romulus, Michigan. In a reciprocal exchange, several North American researchers studying EMS presented their findings at the Second Workshop on Reproduction Disturbances in Fish, held 20–23 November 1995 in Stockholm, Sweden. The American Fisheries Society and the Great Lakes Fishery Commission sponsored a symposium entitled "Early Mortality Syndrome: Reproductive Disruptions in Fish from the Great Lakes, New York Finger Lakes, and the Baltic Region" on 28 August 1996 in Dearborn, Michigan. The extent of current knowledge regarding EMS, M74, and Cayuga Syndrome is due to the great level of cooperation among scientists from North America and Europe. The following are brief synopses of Cayuga Syndrome and M74.

Cayuga Syndrome

Cayuga syndrome is a sac-fry mortality syndrome affecting progeny of Atlantic salmon that mature in Cayuga Lake, Keuka Lake, and Seneca Lake (all New York Finger Lakes). This syndrome was first observed in 1974 at the New York State Department of Environmental Conservation hatchery in Rome NY (Fisher, Spitsbergen, Getchell et al. 1995). Fisher, Spitsbergen, Lamonte et al. (1995) have suggested that Cayuga Syndrome is caused by a naturally occurring thiamine deficiency. Low thiamine levels in eggs may result from broodstocks feeding extensively on alewife which contain thiaminase, an enzyme that destroys thiamine (Greig and Gnaedinger 1971). Clinical signs of this syndrome include yolk-sac opacities, subcutaneous, pericardial and retrobulbar edemas, vitelline congestion or hemorrhage, branchial congestion, foreshortened maxillae, hydrocephalus, and death. Mortality occurs during the sac-fry stage and affects 100% of the fry from an individual female (Fisher, Spitsbergen, Cretchell et al. 1995). The syndrome can be reversed by injecting the yolk-sac with 40 µg/g thiamine hydrochloride or by a single immersion of the affected sac fry in a 1% thiamine solution for one hour (Fisher et al. 1996). Thiamine levels in fry exhibiting the syndrome were just at or slightly above 0.33 nmol/g which was the detection limit of the assay. Fry from a reference site contained 1.82 nmol/g thiamine (Fisher et al. 1996). No relation between pathogens and/or contaminants and sac-fry mortality was found (Fisher, Spitsbergen, Cretchell et al. 1995).

M74

M74 is a sac-fry mortality syndrome affecting progeny from Atlantic salmon that mature in the Baltic Sea (Norrgren et al. 1993; Bengtsson et al. 1994; Karlsson et al. 1996; Börjeson and Norrgren, Chapter 11) and progeny from seatrout (*Salmo trutta*) in Swedish and Finnish waters of the Baltic Sea (Soivio 1996). M74 was first described in 1974. From 1974 to 1991, mortality was generally less than 30%. In 1992 mortality increased, reaching 80 to 90% in 1993 and declining to about 55% in 1995 (Börjeson 1996). As is the case with Cayuga Syndrome, M74 affects 100% of the fry from a specific female, suggesting a female-dependent factor is involved. Clinical signs include initial hyperactivity, lack of coordination, hyper-pigmentation, yolk-sac precipitate, lethargy with sudden outbursts of swimming, and exophthalmia. Brain lesions i.e. pyknotic and karyorrhectic nuclei in the telen-cephalon, diencephalon, mesencephalon, and cerebellum; vacuolation and occa-sional disruption of the ependymal lining and a hydropic degeneration of the periventricular areas were also observed histologically (Lundström et al. 1996). Mortality can occur at the early, intermediate or late sac-fry stage. Fry may show signs of M74 throughout the sac-fry stage, however individuals generally die within 3 to 5 days after clinical signs appear (Lundström et al. 1996). The time from the onset of clinical signs to death is longer for fry that develop M74 at the late sac-fry stage.

Egg color is variable among Atlantic salmon from the Baltic Sea due to the amount of astaxanthin (a carotenoid) in the egg. Lignell (1994) has shown a relationship between the occurrence of M74 and yellow eggs (eggs with low astaxanthin levels). Low levels of antioxidants such as astaxanthin may put the fry at risk for oxidative stresses such as lipid peroxidation (Pettersson and Lignell 1996).

Based on the therapeutic effect of thiamine to reduce EMS mortality in lake trout (Fitzsimons 1995), similar treatments were administered to Atlantic salmon exhibiting M74. Survival was higher in treated fry compared to untreated controls (Bylund and Lerche 1995). Amcoff et al. (1996) measured lower levels of thiamine in newly fertilized Atlantic salmon eggs (0.19 nmol/g) and fry (0.09 nmol/g) that exhibited M74 compared to those that did not (eggs, 1.70 nmol/g; fry 1.27 nmol/g). These authors also prevented mortality due to M74 by immersing fry in 500 ppm thia-mine-enriched water for 1 hour every fifth day from hatching to first feeding. There may be a thiamine threshold that determines whether or not fry develop M74. Of 44 family groups for which egg concentrations of thiamine were below 0.33 nmol/g, 43 developed M74.

Table 10-3 Mean total thiamine concentrations (nmol/g) in salmonid eggs that develop EMS versus concentrations in eggs from reference sites. N is the number of females from which eggs were obtained for thiamine analyses.

Species	Lake Superior	Lake Michigan*	Lake Huron*	Lake Erie*	Lake Ontario*	Hatchery	Pacific Coast
Lake trout	21.8[a] (N=17)	3.9[a] (N=30)	4.6[a] (N=17)	2.8[b] (N=5)	2.3[a] (N=30)	36.3[c] (N=6)	
Coho salmon	65.8[d] (N=5)	1.3[e] (N=17)	4.3[e] (N=12)				6.8[g] (N=20)
Chinook salmon		2.0[e] (N=10)	3.1[f] (N=6)		1.3[h] (N=12)	18.2[h] (N=8)	6.1[g] (N=10)
Steelhead trout	12.9[e] (N=10)	2.2[e] (N=34)				22.3[e] (N=10)	
Brown trout		1.2[e] (N=11)					

* EMS has been documented in at least one species from this Great Lake.
[a] Fitzsimons and Brown 1996.
[b] Fisher et al. 1996.
[c] Dale Honeyfield, Biological Resource Division, U.S. Geological Survey, Wellsboro PA, personal communication.
[d] John Hnath, Michigan Department of Natural Resources, Mattawan MI and Dale Honeyfield, National Biological Service, Wellsboro, PA, personal communication.
[e] Susan Marcquenski, Wisconsin Department of Natural Resources, Madison WI and Scott Brown, Environment Canada, Burlington, Ontario, unpublished data.
[f] J. Hnath, Michigan Department of Natural Resources, Mattawan MI and Scott Brown, Environment Canada, Burlington, Ontario, personal communication.
[g] Rich Holt, Oregon State University, Corvalis OR, and Scott Brown, Environment Canada, Burlington, Ontario, personal communication.
[h] John Fitzsimons, Department of Fisheries and Oceans, Burlington, Ontario, personal communication.

Significant ecosystem changes have occurred in the Baltic Sea over the past 20 years. Infrequent infusions of salt water from the Atlantic Ocean have decreased salinity in the Main Basin. This has decreased the recruitment of Baltic cod which is the primary piscivore in the Baltic Sea. The decline of Baltic cod decreased predation on Baltic herring (Clupea harengus) and sprat (Clupea sprattus), causing a dramatic increase in the biomass of the clupeid populations. Both species contain thiaminase and are also utilized as forage by Atlantic salmon (see Börjeson and Norrgren, Chapter 11).

Focus of Current EMS Research

Relationship between EMS and thiamine

Thiamine levels in salmonid eggs from Lake Michigan and Lake Ontario are very low compared to levels in eggs of the same species from reference sites, e.g., Lake Superior, hatcheries, inland lakes, or the Pacific Coast (Table 10-3). Although EMS has been observed in chinook and coho from Lake Huron, mortality has been very low compared to progeny from Lake Michigan. To date, the only salmonid in Lake Erie that exhibits EMS is the lake trout.

To best compare egg levels of thiamine among species, the concentration should be calculated on a "per egg" basis. Egg size is variable among and within species from different geographic areas. Theoretically, a large and small egg may contain the same level of thiamine on a "per gram" basis, but will differ greatly if measured on a "per egg" basis. This concept becomes important if the idea of a thiamine threshold is used as part of the definition of EMS, M74, or Cayuga Syndrome. Table 10-3 reports thiamine concentrations as nmol/g because data were not available for all species to make the mathematic conversion to nmol/egg.

Most clinical signs of EMS are consistent with signs of thiamine deficiency: loss of equilibrium, hemorrhage, and ataxia (Halver 1989). Fitzsimons (1995) and Hornung et al. (1996) have improved fry survival in "at risk" populations by administering thiamine to freshly fertilized eggs, sac fry, or combinations of the two. Mortality due to EMS was almost completely prevented by immersing newly fertilized coho eggs in 480 or 960 ppm thiamine HCl during water hardening; untreated controls exhibited 29% mortality (Hornung et al. 1996). Hornung et al. (1996) also showed that water hardening steelhead eggs in 480 ppm thiamine HCl and immersing the resultant fry 3 weeks after hatch in 480 ppm thiamine HCl for 1 hour decreased EMS mortality from 72% to 27%. Similar treatments are now used on a production scale by hatcheries in Wisconsin, Illinois, Indiana, and Michigan to increase survival of coho, chinook, steelhead, and brown trout that develop EMS.

Relationship between EMS and diet

It has been established that eggs containing low levels of thiamine are likely to develop EMS when they reach the sac-fry or swim-up fry stage. At present, attempts are being made to reproduce EMS by feeding captive lake trout and Atlantic salmon a diet containing amprolium, a thiamine antagonist (Honeyfield et al. 1996). If clinical signs consistent with EMS are observed and egg thiamine concentrations similar to those from Lake Ontario or the New York Finger Lakes are achieved, it will support the hypothesis that EMS is caused by a simple thiamine deficiency.

Studies have also been initiated to determine the thiamine content of several species in the Lake Ontario food web (Fitzsimons et al. 1996). Adelman and Ji (1996) have shown alewife and smelt from Lake Michigan contain thiaminase, although there may be some seasonal differences in activity of the enzyme. Alewife is the primary forage species for lake trout and the Pacific salmon in Lake Ontario and Lake Michigan. One hypothesis is that feeding extensively on fish that contain thiaminase may cause a thiamine deficiency in developing eggs which is later expressed as EMS.

Relationship between EMS, thiamine, and contaminants

To date, no direct correlation has been observed between EMS and concentrations of PCBs, DDT and its metabolites, or dieldrin in salmonids from Lake Michigan and Lake Ontario (Wisconsin Department of Natural Resources, Madison WI, unpublished data; Michigan Department of Natural Resources, Mattawan MI, unpublished data;

Giesy 1986; Skea et al. 1985; Mac et al. 1993; Fitzsimons et al. 1995). However, recent work has shown that there may be interactions between thiamine and contaminants such as 2,3,7,8-TCDD. Eggs injected with 2,3,7,8,-TCDD and immersed in thiamine solutions during egg and fry development had higher survival and fewer signs of TCDD toxicity (yolk-sac edema, cranio-facial deformities, etc.) than injected eggs that were incubated without thiamine treatments (Tillitt et al. 1996). The role of contaminants in the expression of EMS is unclear at this time.

Relationship between EMS and oxidative stress

Developing salmonid eggs require protection from oxidative stress because they contain large amounts of unsaturated fatty acids. Additionally, increased aerobic metabolism may generate oxidative radicals during embryonic development (Cowey et al. 1985). Endogenous stores of antioxidant vitamins are also essential for normal embryonic growth and development of fish (Cowey et al. 1985; Blom and Dabrowski 1995).

Pettersson and Lignell (1996) and Börjeson et al. (1996) have shown that concentrations of antioxidants (carotenoids and vitamin E) are lower in sac fry that develop M74 compared to healthy sac fry. Both females and their offspring with M74 have elevated levels of hepatic mixed-function oxidase suggesting the involvement of dioxin-like contaminants (Norrgren et al. 1993). Using the same indicators of oxidative stress, Palace (1996) showed that adult female lake trout from Lake Ontario had higher mixed-function oxidase enzyme activities and elevated levels of lipid hydroperoxides, indicating more oxidative stress, compared to lake trout from Lake Manitou, Ontario (where EMS does not occur). However, the greater oxidative stress was unrelated to the presence of EMS in their progeny. Mixed-function oxidase activity in lake trout fry at the swim-up stage was similar among progeny from Lake Ontario (both with and without EMS) and the reference site. Early Mortality Syndrome could not be predicted based on the amount of antioxidant vitamins and carotenoids (A, C, E, and astaxanthin) in the eggs. These vitamins declined in lake trout embryos in a similar manner throughout their development regardless of whether the fry later developed EMS.

The lack of consistent relationships between indices of oxidative stress and EMS in lake trout embryos (Palace 1996) differs from observations of Atlantic salmon with M74 (Börjeson et al. 1996), but is similar to initial findings in other salmonids from the Great Lakes region. Injecting newly fertilized eggs with beta-carotene or astaxanthin did not prevent EMS in steelhead from Lake Michigan (Hornung et al. 1996); injecting sac fry with antioxidant vitamins A, C, or E did not prevent Cayuga Syndrome in Atlantic salmon from Cayuga Lake (Fisher et al. 1996).

Based on these studies, there does not appear to be a relationship between EMS and oxidative stress. The strongest causal relationship to date is the link between low levels of thiamine in fish eggs and the therapeutic effect of thiamine to reverse or prevent EMS. There is a need to 1) clarify why thiamine levels are so low in eggs from salmonids that mature in Lake Michigan and Lake Ontario; 2) reveal the biochemical basis for EMS (e.g., What role do low levels of thiamine play in the etiology of EMS); and 3) resolve the possible relationships among thiamine metabolism, contaminants, and oxidative stress.

Conclusions

At present, the etiologies of EMS, Cayuga Syndrome, and M74 are not completely understood. Current information supports the hypothesis that Cayuga Syndrome is the consequence of a thiamine deficiency based on the extensive consumption of forage containing thiaminase. All 3 syndromes affect top salmonid predators in ecosystems with simple food webs. Several forage species in these food webs contain thiaminase. The Great Lakes and the Baltic Sea ecosystems have undergone dramatic changes over the past 20 years, e.g., shifts in forage abundance, introductions of exotic species at multiple trophic levels, and changes in the biomass of top piscivores. These 2 ecosystems have been exposed to various levels of xenobiotic compounds during the past 50 years which differentiates them from the New York Finger Lakes. Early Mortality Syndrome, M74, and Cayuga Syndrome can be prevented by exposing eggs and/or fry to thiamine solutions. Thiamine levels in eggs from family groups that go on to develop EMS, Cayuga Syndrome, or M74 are low compared to levels in eggs from reference sites. This does not necessarily mean that fish from the Baltic Sea, Finger Lakes, and the Great Lakes become thiamine deficient as a result of the same processes. In the Baltic region, carotenoids like astaxanthin appear important in the etiology of M74, but a similar relationship has yet to be demonstrated for the Great Lakes. The temporal coincidence of dramatic increases in M74 mortality (peaking in 1993) and EMS mortality (peaking in 1993) suggests factors that may act on a global scale. Although there are still many unknowns regarding the etiology of EMS, M74, and Cayuga Syndrome, substantial progress has been made in a relatively short time. This level of achievement is due to interagency partnerships and professional cooperation among scientists studying these syndromes in North America and the Baltic region.

Acknowledgments

We are indebted to North American and Baltic region scientists for freely sharing their data, ideas, and good will. Work on this manuscript was made possible by support from the Wisconsin Department of Natural Resources' Bureau of Fisheries Management and Habitat Protection, Federal Aid in Sport Fish Restoration, and Environment Canada's GL2000 Program.

References

Adelman IR, Ji YQ. 1996. Thiaminase levels in alewife and smelt from Lakes Superior, Michigan and Huron. American Fisheries Society Symposium on Early Mortality Syndrome: Reproductive Disruptions in Fish of the Great Lakes, New York Finger Lakes, and the Baltic Region; 1996 Aug 28; Dearborn MI.

Amcoff P, Norrgren L, Börjeson H, Lindeberg J. 1996. Lowered concentrations of thiamine (vitamin B$_1$) in M74-affected feral Baltic salmon (*Salmo salar*). Report from the Second Workshop on Reproduction Disturbances in Fish; 1995 Nov 20–23; Stockholm, Sweden. Swedish Environmental Protection Agency Report 4534. p 38–39.

Bengtsson B-E, Bergman A, Brandt I, Hill C, Johansson N, S dergren A, Thulin J. 1994. Reproductive disturbances in Baltic fish. Stockholm: Swedish Environmental Protection Agency Report 4319.

Blom JH, Dabrowski K. 1995. Reproductive success of female rainbow trout (*Onchorhynchus mykiss*) in response to graded dietary ascorbyl monophosphate levels. *Biol Reprod* 52:1073–1080.

Börjeson H. 1996. Report of the Second Workshop on Reproduction Disturbances in Fish; 1995 Nov 20–23 1995; Stockholm, Sweden. Swedish Environmental Protection Agency Report No. 4534.

Börjeson H, Förlin L, Norrgren L. 1996. Investigation of antioxidants and prooxidants in salmon affected by the M74 Syndrome. Report of the Second Workshop on Reproduction Disturbances in Fish; 1995 Nov 20–23; Stockholm, Sweden. Swedish Environmental Protection Agency Report 4534. p 95–96.

Burdick GE, Harris EJ, Dean HJ, Walker TM, Skea J, Colby D. 1964. The accumulation of DDT in lake trout and the effect on reproduction. Trans Am Fish Soc 93:127–136.

Bylund G, Lerche O. 1995. Thiamine therapy of M74 affected fry of Atlantic Salmon Salmo salar. Bull. Eur. Ass. Fish Pathol. 15:93–97.

Cowey CB, Bell JG, Knox D, Fraser A, Youngson A. 1985. Lipids and antioxidant systems in developing eggs of salmon (Salmo salar). Lipids 20:567–572.

Degurse PE, Crochett D, Nielsen HR. 1973. Observations on Lake Michigan coho salmon (Onchorhynchus kisutch) propagation mortality in Wisconsin with an evaluation of the pesticide relationship. Madison WI: Wisconsin Department of Natural Resources Fish Management Report No. 62. 11 p.

Fisher JP, Spitsbergen JM, Getchell R, Symula J, Skea J, Babenzein M, Chiotti T. 1995. Reproductive failure of landlocked Atlantic salmon from New York's Finger Lakes: investigations into the etiology and epidemiology of the "Cayuga Syndrome". J Aquat Anim Health 7:81–94.

Fisher JP, Spitsbergen JM, Lamonte T, Little EE, DeLonay A. 1995. Pathological and behavioral manifestations of the "Cayuga Syndrome," a thiamine deficiency in larval landlocked Atlantic salmon. J Aquat Anim Health 7:269–283.

Fisher JP, Fitzsimons JD, Combs Jr. GF, Spitsbergen JM. 1996. Naturally occurring thiamine deficiency causing reproductive failure in Finger Lakes Atlantic salmon and Great Lakes lake trout. Trans Am Fish Soc 125(2):167–178.

Fitzsimons JD. 1995. The effect of B-vitamins on swim-up syndrome in Lake Ontario lake trout. J Great Lakes Res 21 (Supplement 1):286–289.

Fitzsimons JD, Huestis S, Williston B. 1995. Occurrence of a swim-up syndrome in Lake Ontario lake trout in relation to contaminants and cultural practices. J Great Lakes Res 21 (Supplement 1):277–285.

Fitzsimons JD, Brown S. 1996. Effect of diet on thiamine levels in Great Lakes lake trout and relationship with early mortality syndrome. Report of the Second Workshop on Reproduction Disturbances in Fish; 1995 Nov 20–23; Stockholm Sweden. Swedish Environmental Protection Agency Report 4534. p 76–78.

Fitzsimons JD, Brown S, Niimi AJ. 1996. Thiamine levels in the food chains of the Great Lakes. American Fisheries Society. 1994. Symposium on Early Mortality Syndrome: Reproductive Disruptions in Fish of the Great Lakes, New York Finger Lakes, and the Baltic region; 1996 Aug 28; Dearborn MI.

Fox GA. 1991. Practical causal inference for ecoepidemiologists. J Tox Env Health 33:359–373.

Frimeth J. 1990. Lake Ontario coho salmon. In: Mac MJ, Gilbertson M, editors. Proceedings of the Roundtable on Contaminant-Caused Reproductive Problems in Salmonids; 1990 Sep 24–25; Windsor, Ontario. Windsor, Ontario: International Joint Commission.

Giesy JP, Newsted J, Garling DL. 1986. Relationship between chlorinated hydrocarbon concentrations and rearing mortality of chinook salmon (Onchorhynchus tshawytscha) eggs from Lake Michigan. J Great Lakes Res 12(1):82–98.

Great Lakes Fishery Commission. Proceedings of a Workshop on EMS-Early Mortality Syndrome; 1994 Jul 12–14; Ann Arbor MI. Ann Arbor MI: Great Lakes Fishery Commission Fish Health Committee.

Greig RA, Gnaedinger RH. 1971. Occurrence of thiaminase in some common aquatic animals of the United States and Canada. Seattle WA: U.S. Department of Commerce Special Scientific Report-Fisheries No. 631. 7 p.

Halter MT, Johnson HE. 1974. Acute toxicities of a polychlorinated biphenyl (PCB) and DDT alone and in combination to early life stages of coho salmon (Onchorhynchus kisutch). J Fish Res Board Can 31:1543–1547.

Halver JE, editor. 1989. Fish nutrition. New York NY: Academic Pr.

Honeyfield DC, Brown S, Fitzsimons J, Fynn-Aikins K. 1996. Analysis of thiamine by HPLC and progress in reproducing early mortality syndrome under laboratory conditions. Report of the Second Workshop on Reproduction Disturbances in Fish; 1995 Nov 20–23; Stockholm Sweden. Swedish Environmental Protection Agency Report 4534. p 86.

Hornung MW, Miller L, Peterson RE, Marcquenski S, Brown S. 1996. Evaluation of nutritional and pathogenic factors in early mortality syndrome in Lake Michigan salmonids. Report of the Second Workshop on Reproduction Disturbances in Fish; 1995 Nov 20–23; Stockholm Sweden. Swedish Environmental Protection Agency Report 4534. p 82–83.

Johengen TH, Johannsson OE, Pernie GL, Millard ES. 1994. Temporal and seasonal trends in nutrient dynamics and biomass measures in Lakes Michigan and Ontario in response to phosphorus control. Can J Fish Aquatic Sci 51(11):2570–2578.

Johnson HE, Pecor C. 1969. Coho salmon mortality and DDT in Lake Michigan. Transactions of the 34th North American Wildlife Natural Resources Conference; 1969 Mar 2–5; Washington DC. Washington DC: Wildlife Management Institute. p 159–166.

Karlsson L, Pettersson E, Hedenskog M, Börjeson H, Eriksson R. 1996. Biological factors affecting the incidence of M74. Report of the Second Workshop on Reproduction Disturbances in Fish; 1995 Nov 20–23; Stockholm Sweden. Swedish Environmental Protection Agency Report 4534. p 25.

Lasee B. 1994. Compilation of hatchery questionnaires for the Proceedings of a Workshop on EMS-Early Mortality Syndrome, Great Lakes Fishery Commission Fish Health Committee; 12–14 July 1994; Ann Arbor MI.

Lignell Å. 1994. Astaxanthin in yolk-sac fry from feral Baltic salmon. Swedish Environmental Protection Agency Report 4346 p 94–96.

Lundström J, Norrgren L, Börjeson H. 1996. Clinical and morphological studies of Baltic salmon yolk-sac fry suffering from the M74 syndrome. Report of the Second Workshop on Reproduction Disturbances in Fish; 1995 Nov 20–23; Stockholm Sweden. Swedish Environmental Protection Agency Report 4534. p 26–27.

Mac MJ, Edsall CC, Seelye JG. 1985. Survival of lake trout eggs and fry reared in water from the upper Great Lakes. J Great Lakes Res 11(4):520–529.

Mac MJ. 1988. Toxic substances and survival of Lake Michigan salmonids: field and laboratory approaches. In: Evans MS, editor. Toxic contaminants and ecosystem health: a Great Lakes focus. New York NY: J Wiley. p 389–401.

Mac MJ, Schwartz TR, Edsall CC, Frank AM. 1993. Polychlorinated biphenyls in Great Lakes lake trout and their eggs: relations to survival and congener composition 1979–1988. J Great Lakes Res 19(4):752–765.

Norrgren L, Andersson T, Bergqvist P-Å, Björklund I. 1993. Chemical, physiological, and morphological studies of feral Baltic salmon (Salmo salar) suffering from abnormal fry mortality. Environ Toxicol Chem 12:2065–2075.

Palace VP. 1996. Oxidative stress in lake trout (Salvelinus namayacush) exposed to organochlorine contaminants that induce phase I biotransformation enzyme systems [doctoral dissertation]. Winnipeg, Manitoba: Univ of Manitoba.

Pecor, C. 1972. Pesticide residues in coho salmon eggs and their relationship to fry mortality [master's thesis]. East Lansing MI: Michigan State Univ.

Pettersson A, Lignell A. 1996. Decreased astaxanthin levels in the Baltic salmon and the M74 syndrome. Report of the Second Workshop on Reproduction Disturbances in Fish; 1995 Nov 20–23; Stockholm Sweden. Swedish Environmental Protection Agency Report 4534. p 28–29.

Rand PS, Lantry BF, O'Gorman R, Owens RW, Stewart DJ. 1994. Energy density and size of pelagic prey fishes in Lake Ontario, 1978–1990: implications for salmonine energetics. Trans Amer Fish Soc 123:519–534.

Skea JC, Symula J, Miccoli J. 1985. Separating starvation losses from other early feeding fry mortality in steelhead trout (Salmo gairdneri), Chinook salmon (Onchorhynchus tshawytscha), and lake trout (Salvelinus namaycush). Bull Environ Contam Toxicol 35:82–91.

Smith IR, Marchant B, van den Heuvel MR, Clemons JH, Frimeth J. 1994. Embryonic mortality, bioassay derived 2,3,7,8-tetrachlorodibenzo-p-dioxin equivalents, and organochlorine contaminants in Pacific salmon from Lake Ontario. J Great Lakes Res 20(3):497–509.

Soivio A. 1996. M74 in Finland. Report of the Second Workshop on Reproduction Disturbances in Fish; 1995 Nov 20–23; Stockholm Sweden. Swedish Environmental Protection Agency Report 4534. p 42–43.

Symula J, Meade J, Skea JC, Cummings L, Colquhoun JR, Dean HJ, Miccoli J. 1990. Blue-sac disease in Lake Ontario lake trout. J Great Lakes Res 16(1):41–52.

Tillitt DE, Wright PJ, Cantrell SM, Hannik M. 1996. The role of dioxin-like chemicals in early mortality syndrome of Great Lakes salmonids: mechanism, affected tissues, and implications for nutritional interactions. American Fisheries Society Symposium on Early Mortality Syndrome: Reproductive

Disruptions in Fish of the Great Lakes, New York Finger Lakes, and the Baltic region; 1996 Aug 28; Dearborn MI.

Walker MK, Spitsbergen JM, Olson JR, Peterson RE. 1991. 2,3,7,8-tetrachlorodibenzo-p-dioxin (TCDD) toxicity during early life stage development of lake trout (*Salvelinus namaycush*). *Can J Fish Aquat Sci* 48:875–883.

M74 syndrome: a review of potential etiological factors

Hans Börjeson, Leif Norrgren

The Baltic salmon (*Salmo salar*) is confined to the Baltic Sea, and since 1974, it has been threatened by an alevin mortality syndrome termed M74. The syndrome, which affects all alevins in a family group, is initially expressed as an abnormal neuromuscular swimming behavior. Alevins suffering from M74 are characterized by low levels of antioxidants and thiamine. An elevated activity of cytochrome P450 enzymes indicates a high burden of xenobiotics in Baltic salmon. The incidence of M74 is influenced by the stocks of cod, herring, and sprat in the Baltic. A high biomass of cod reduces the incidence of M74, whereas high biomasses of herring and sprat increase the rate. In the early 1990s, high incidences of M74 occurred, and wiggling behavior was observed among ascending broodfish. This behavior was treatable with 1 intraperitoneal injection of thiamine. Similarities with reproduction disturbances found among salmonids from the North American Great Lakes region include thiamine deficiency and successful therapy with thiamine.

In 1974, a previously unknown alevin mortality was observed in Swedish compensation hatcheries rearing salmon smolt from spawners ascending from the Baltic Sea. Smolt are reared to compensate for interference with natural smolt reproduction in the rivers of the Baltic Sea resulting from hydroelectric activities. The number of rivers with naturally spawning salmon has been reduced to about 20 from 60 historically by human activities (Ackefors et al. 1991). The mortality syndrome was called "M74", and since 1974 its incidence has fluctuated, as has its influence on the recruitment of Baltic salmon. M74 is characterized by an abnormal neuromuscular swimming behavior and general lethargy. Preliminary observations indicate that the etiology of the syndrome is highly complex and a multifactorial background appears probable. These factors include meteorological and oceanographic components as well as anthropogenically induced changes such as eutrophication and emission of pollutants. In situations when all factors are favorable for the development of M74, the effects of, e.g., pollutants may be a disaster for the Baltic salmon, although the effect of the pollutant burden alone may be tolerated by the salmon. In this article, we review current information on the M74 mortality of the alevins of Baltic salmon and discuss different factors observed in association with the syndrome.

M74 Syndrome

General characteristics of M74

The M74 syndrome develops during the yolk-sac resorption period. Clinical signs characterizing M74, which normally are displayed when two-thirds of the yolk-sac has been resorbed, are largely behavioral and indicate a polyneuropathy including an initial hyperactivity, followed by lack of coordination, loss of negative phototaxis, erratic swimming, rapid exhaustion, and lethargy. Other clinical signs are hyperpigmentation, yolk-sac precipitate, and exophthalmia. As affected alevins approach death, their color becomes greyish, which is similar to the effect of anoxia. The syndrome normally affects all alevins of a family group, and mortality as high as 100% occurs over a period of a few days. The mortality rate after the first clinical sign is variable and seems to be temperature dependent; at lower temperatures mortality occurs for a couple of weeks, whereas high temperatures shorten the death period.

In the early 1990s, a wiggling behavior was observed among ascending adults of both sexes. In 1992, 144 female used as broodfish from 7 different populations, representing 13 % of the total broodstock used, showed wiggling behavior. The offspring of these females was followed to the swim-up stage, and the progeny of 143 of these females succumbed to M74. The total M74 mortality for the offspring of the 1110 females used was 73 percent. So while wiggling behavior among females is a good indicator of M74 mortality in their offspring, the behavior cannot discriminate all females giving M74 spawn.

Historical review

The Baltic salmon constitute geographically separated populations of Atlantic salmon (*Salmo salar* L.) which are genetically distinct from other Atlantic salmon populations (Ståhl 1987; Davidson et al. 1989). The Baltic salmon has been confined to the Baltic drainage area (Figure 11-1) as a result of events following the last glacial period.

The compensatory smolt rearing program was developed in the early 1950s as a result of interference of hydroelectric exploitation with natural smolt reproduction. The smolt rearing program was based upon adult salmon returning from the Baltic proper to spawn in their native river. At ripeness, spawning salmon were stripped and the progeny were reared to 2-year-old smolt which were released back into the river. The success of the compensatory program has been followed since its inception.

Mortality during the alevin stage was low until 1974, when some family groups of sac fry displayed 100% mortality following a few days of abnormal neuromuscular swimming behavior and lethargy, behaviors not seen before. Since then, alevins originating from feral spawners in the Baltic Sea have been observed for the M74 syndrome in the compensatory hatcheries. The M is taken from the Swedish word for environment, *miljö*, and the 74 from the year in which it was first observed. Since 1974, the occurrence of M74 has fluctuated between years (Figure 11-2) and river populations (Figure 11-3). Figure 11-2 shows a summary of M74 in the Baltic salmon from 3 different river populations (the location of the river is indicated by arrows in Figure 11-1). Two distinct peaks in M74 mortality occurred in 1979 and 1993 with an intervening period in the early 1980s when the M74 syndrome was not observed at all. The last peak in M74 mortality, in 1993, followed the longest period without any inflow events during this century (see below, Matthäus 1993).

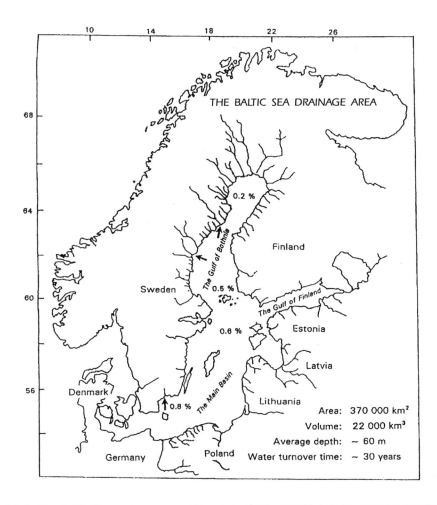

Figure 11-1 *The Baltic Sea drainage area. The percentages refer to salinity, and the arrows indicate the location of the rivers summarized in Figure 11-2.*

Biochemical changes

Carotenoids

When M74 mortality was observed in 1974, it was noticed that M74 occurred at a higher rate in alevins developing from pale roe than those from dark-colored roe. Well-pigmented roe always developed into healthy alevins. Figure 11-4 illustrates the difference in coloration of roe from Baltic salmon of the River Lule lven stock; the pale roe developed into M74 sac fry whereas the dark-colored roe produced healthy alevins. This obvious difference in coloration led the manager of the hatchery at River Luleälven to classify the salmon roe into 4 color groups (yellow, yellow orange, orange, and dark orange) with the aid of a color fan and to register the M74 incidence. In 1976/77, roe of 164 females of the River Luleälven stock were classified, and the result is shown in Figure 11-4a. Figure 11-4b shows the result from the same stock for the year class 1992/93 when 348 females were

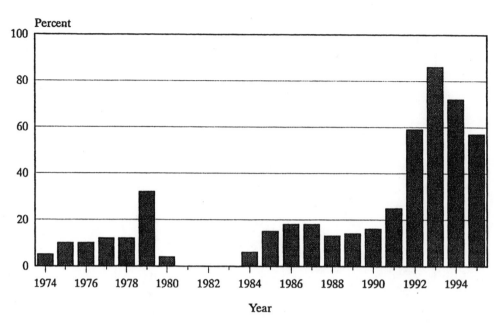

Figure 11-2 M74 mortality rate in Baltic salmon by year (1974–1995). The data were compiled from spawning salmon from 3 river populations (indicated by arrows on the map in Figure 11-1).

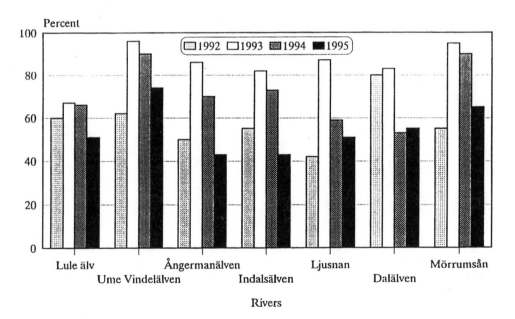

Figure 11-3 Mortality rate from M74 by river population for the year classes 1992 to 1995. Data from 7 major Swedish salmon rivers emptying into the Baltic Sea.

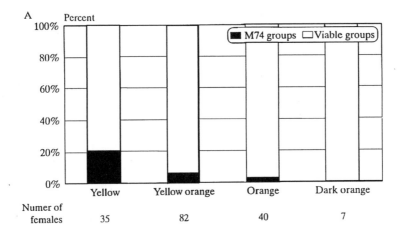

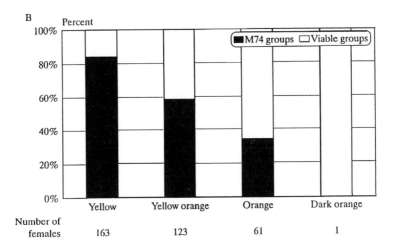

Figure 11-4 Percentage of families from the River Luleälven salmon population that died from M74, grouped according to roe color for hatching years 1977 (A) and 1993 (B). A) Hatching year 1977. 164 females were stripped, weights from 1.9 kg to 14.0 kg, mean 5.8 kg. Total M74 in the population, 20%. B) Hatching year 1993. 348 females were stripped, weights from 2.9 kg to 18.6 kg, mean 8.8 kg. Total M74 in the population, 84%.

stripped. In 1977, 20% of the family groups with yellow roe developed into alevins dying of M74. In 1993, the corresponding figure was 84%. Twenty-one percent of the stripped females gave yellow roe in 1976, whereas 47% of the roe was classified as yellow in 1992. M74 was not evident among the dark orange roe. This situation is common to all Swedish salmon populations in the Baltic region.

Roe coloration is dependent on the amount of carotenoids, especially astaxanthin, which is known to be an effective antioxidant in biological systems (Krinsky 1989; Christiansen et al. 1995). Measurements of concentrations of astaxanthin and total carotenoids in roe are shown in Table 11-1. The total concentration of carotenoids in yellow roe was 2.0 ± 0.94 mg/kg with an astaxanthin/carotenoids ratio (ACR) of

Table 11-1 The coloration of Baltic salmon roe classified by eye with aid of a color fan, and the measured levels of total carotenoids, astaxanthin, and the astaxanthin/carotenoid ratio (ACR). Year of hatching is 1995. The results are the mean ± SD. The statistical test was conducted between 1 roe color group and the next color group by using Student's *t*-test.

	Yellow roe mean ± SD	Yellow orange roe mean ± SD	Orange roe mean ± SD	Dark orange roe mean ± SD
Family groups (N)	6	25	26	8
Carotenoids (mg/kg)	2.0 ± 0.9	3.6 ± 1.3**	5.3 ± 1.7***	10.3 ± 2.9***
Astaxanthin (mg/kg)	0.9 ± 1.3	3.0 ± 1.0***	4.8 ± 1.8***	9.9 ± 3.1***
ACR	0.36 ± 0.35	0.83 ± 0.11***	0.90 ± 0.10*	0.96 ± 0.05 [NS]

   * significance level of P≤0.05
  ** significance level of P≤0.01
 *** significance level of P≤0.001
NS not significant.

0.36, whereas the corresponding figures for dark orange roe were 10.3 ± 2.9 mg/kg and a ratio of 0.96. In yellow roe that developed into viable alevins the ACR was very close to 1, which may indicate that astaxanthin, the most effective antioxidant of the carotenoids (Krinsky 1989), was not involved in protection against any free radicals, suggesting that yellow roe giving healthy alevins was low in burdens producing free radicals. Thus ACR can be used as a predictor of M74 but may also be valuable as a measure of the oxidative stress of the roe. However, in Table 11-1, carotenoids were measured in newly fertilized eggs with low or no metabolic activity, and therefore the ACR reflects the oxidative stress in the adult female during gonadal development rather than in the roe.

Efforts to supply astaxanthin to females 1 month before stripping, to eggs at fertilization or to alevins at hatching have not been successful so far, probably because of difficulties in getting the highly lipophilic substance accessible to the developing embryo.

Assessment of roe coloration in Baltic salmon is an easy and effective way to predict roe at high risk for developing M74.

α–Tocopherol and ubiquinone levels
Other parameters used to evaluate the level of oxidative stress in alevins are measurements of the membrane-bound antioxidants α-tocopherol (E) and ubiquinone (Q) in their livers. At the first sign of M74 there seems to be a higher oxidative stress in the liver of the groups suffering from M74 than in the viable groups, as is shown in Table 11-2. However, the α-tocopherol levels seem to be low also in the viable group. The quotient of E/Q indicates a disturbed reduction/oxidation condition in both viable and M74 affected groups. In a preliminary analysis of 15 alevins from a family group of farmed broodfish, the E/Q quotient was 11±4.6 which is almost 2 × higher than a quotient of 6.1 calculated for viable alevins of feral broodfish. In M74 alevins, the E/Q quotient is lowered to 3.8,

Table 11-2 Concentrations of vitamin E and ubiquinone (Q) in livers from alevins with M74 and from viable alevins. Three analyses per family group in 11 M74 groups and 8 viable groups of alevins were performed. Year of hatching is 1995. The results are the mean ± SD, P-value from ANOVA.

	Viable alevins mean ± SD	M74 alevins mean ± SD	P-value from ANOVA
Family groups (N)	8	11	
α–tocophorol (E) (mg/kg)	0.244 ± 0.098	0.118 ± 0.054	< 0.0001
Ubiquinone (Q) (mg/kg)	0.041 ± 0.008	0.031 ± 0.013	< 0.0002
α–tocophorol/ubiquinone	6.1 ± 2.66	3.8 ± 1.25	< 0.0001

mainly caused by reduced α-tocopherol levels (Table 11-2). The disparity between the E/Q quotient in offspring from farmed and feral broodfish may be of dietary origin. The E/Q disparity between normal and M74 alevins of feral Baltic broodfish however, most likely depends on other factors involved in the etiology of M74 because the salmon are feeding in the same area of the Baltic.

Reduced ubiquinone (QH_2) has been shown to regenerate oxidized α–tocopherol (Mukai et al. 1990) and Beyer (1990) reported that QH_2 protected the mitochondrial membrane against free radicals. Thus, α–tocopherol and ubiquinone act as a reduction/oxidation pair to a certain extent, and a reduced level of ubiquinone may interfere with electron transport in the respiratory chain. The resulting impairment in energy turnover may result in lethargy, one of the main characteristics of M74 alevins.

Cytochrome P450 induction

The observations of disturbances in carotenoids, tocopherol, and ubiquinone levels may indicate oxidative stress in M74-affected alevins. This is supported by observations of broodfish and their offspring suffering from M74. Norrgren, Andersson et al. (1993) showed that feral females producing normal or M74 affected offspring were characterized by significantly different hepatic cytochrome P450 activity levels; females with viable offspring showed less than half the levels of hepatic cytochrome P450 activity compared with those giving M74 offspring. In addition, the hepatic cytochrome P450 activity, measured by 7-ethoxyresorufin-O-deethylase activity (EROD), of yolk-sac fry originating from farmed Baltic salmon was less than 15% of the EROD activity of viable alevins of feral Baltic salmon, whereas M74 sac fry had almost twice the EROD activity compared with viable feral alevins. These results indicate that feral salmon of the Baltic stock were being affected by cytochrome P450-inducing compounds. The presence of P450-inducing substances in roe that subsequently developed M74 as alevins has been confirmed. Extract of roe predicted to develop M74 alevins was prepared in a column with acetone/hexane and hexane/diethylether followed by dialysis to separate high molecular lipids from xenobiotics at 600 to 800 dalton. This extract was injected into newly hatched yolk-sac fry of farmed origin and resulted in a dose-dependent hepatic cytochrome

P450 induction as measured by EROD activity (Norrgren, Lundstrom et al. 1993). However, no M74-like clinical signs were observed, which most probably depends on the presence of high levels of thiamine, which is present in alevins of farmed origin (see below). High activity of cytochrome P450 enzymes has been shown to generate oxidative stress (Gonzalez and Nebert 1990; Nebert et al. 1990; Wheeler and Guenther 1991; Palace et al. 1996). The antioxidants α–tocopherol and astaxanthin act to quench free radicals (Miki 1991). The reduction in α–tocopherol and astaxanthin in individuals suffering from M74 may consequently reflect enhanced oxidative stress.

Thiamine levels
Norrgren, Andersson et al. (1993) observed lowered glycogen content in yolk-sac fry suffering from M74, possibly indicating that oxidative metabolism was disturbed, potentially resulting from low thiamine concentrations. This finding prompted a preliminary study of thiamine status in alevins hatched in spring 1994. Three groups of sac fry, sampled shortly before swim-up stage, were analyzed. These groups originated from feral and farmed broodfish, and the relative amounts of thiamine found in feral M74, feral viable, and farmed viable alevins, respectively, were 1:35:40. The M74 group of sac fry had 0.04 mg/kg of total thiamine, measured as whole body content. This indicates a similarity to the Early Mortality Syndrome (EMS) of lake trout (*Salvelinus namaycush*) in the Great Lakes (Fisher et al. 1996) and the Cayuga Syndrome in Atlantic salmon from the New York Finger Lakes (Fisher et al. 1994). Regarding the finding that the syndromes in the Great Lakes area respond to thiamine treatment (Fisher 1995; Fitzsimons 1995), this also applies to the M74 syndrome in Baltic salmon (Amcoff et al. 1995; Bylund and Lerche 1995). The total incidence of M74 in the Swedish salmon populations in the Baltic in 1995 amounted to 55%, and 350 family groups of alevins (> 2 million) were successfully treated with thiamine. The treatment, however, had to be repeated in order to be successful, and it was temperature dependent. In the temperature range 8 to 16°C, immersion in 500 ppm buffered thiamine solution for 1 hour had to be repeated from less than once per week to every third day to successfully treat all groups.

Analysis of the thiamine status of eggs and alevins has shown a wide variation between thiamine levels and development of M74. The M74 syndrome occurs below a threshold of 0.1 mg/kg in eyed eggs, while the mean thiamine concentration in eyed eggs of feral broodfish developing into viable alevins of 0.8 mg/kg (maximum of 2.67 mg/kg) was still only one-eighth of the mean value in eyed eggs of farmed broodfish of 6.7 mg/kg (Amcoff et al. 1995)

The great variability in thiamine concentration in roe from one salmon population in the same year strengthens the hypothesis of multiple causes. Genetic factors influencing the capacity of maternal assimilation, storage, and transfer of thiamine into roe must be considered. It is striking to note that when survivors from the year class of 1974 returned as spawners in the early 1980s, the problem with M74 seemed to disappear (Figure 11-2). As shown above, there is a great difference in the activity of the drug metabolizing cytochrome P450-enzyme systems in different groups of yolk-sac fry, which indicates different body burdens of P450-inducing agents. The interrelation between thiamine status and P450-induction has not, to our knowledge, been studied in fish. However, in feeding experiments with rats, high doses of polychlorinated biphenyls (PCBs) and DDT have led to development of thiamine deficiency (Yagi et al. 1979; Pelissier et al. 1992). A similar explanation can not be excluded in salmonids.

The wiggling behavior of broodfish, mentioned above, appears to be associated with thiamine as wiggling is eliminated within 1 day of intraperitoneal (i.p.) injection of thiamine (100 mg/kg body weight thiamine dissolved in physiological saline).

Reconditioning of broodfish

One important factor behind the acute cause of alevin mortality from M74 is lack of thiamine. It has been shown that M74 threatening the Baltic salmon and the reproduction disturbances of salmonids in the Great Lakes area can be treated by administration of thiamine (Amcoff et al. 1995; Bylund and Lerche 1995; Fisher 1995; Fitzsimons 1995). However, the cause of the shortage of thiamine is still unknown and most probably has multiple causes. The agents causing M74 are probably found in the food. In order to test this hypothesis, a reconditioning study of feral female spawners started in 1993 after stripping in November 1992. The fish were fed a commercial broodfish diet and 5 of these females spawned in autumn 1993. The results of the first year of reconditioning are shown in Table 11-3. These results are in agreement with our observation on the reversibility of the syndrome in alevins since 2 of the females (1 and 2) spawned M74-affected offspring as feral ascending spawners but gave viable offspring 1 year later after reconditioning. Two other females (3 and 4) gave viable offspring both as feral and reconditioned spawners, whereas one female (5) had M74-affected progeny in both years. This female, showing a negative weight gain, and hence had not taken food, does not contradict the hypothesis of food as a vector for the agents causing M74. However, commercial broodfish feeds are well supplied with thiamine and other essential nutrients, and the level of contaminants is low, illustrating that food quality is essential and that M74 is a reversible syndrome.

Ecological Factors

The Baltic Sea

The Baltic is one of the largest brackish-water seas in the world, with a low and rather constant salinity of 0.6 to 0.8% in the surface water of the main basin (Figure 11-1). The drainage area is about 1.65 million km^2 and is inhabited by around 140 million people. The area is heavily exploited due to industrialization, agriculture, and forestry. As a result of the exploitation, the Baltic Sea is eutrophicated (Rosenberg et al. 1990) and contaminated with various xenobiotics, e.g., PCBs and DDT (Jensen et al. 1969). Water exchange between the Baltic and the North Sea is a natural process governed by meteorological and oceanographic factors but is severely restricted by the shallow Kattegat and the narrow straits between the 2 seas. Great influxes of highly saline and oxygenated water — termed "major Baltic inflows" — are typical but relatively rare and unpredictable phenomena in the Baltic Sea.

Table 11-3 Reconditioning of 5 ascending spawners of the River Dalälven stock caught and stripped of roe in 1992 and M74 mortality in their progeny. Hatching success in June 1993 and weights. The outcome of repeated stripping in autumn 1993 and hatching success in June 1994. The reconditioning was performed in a coastal net pen with commercial broodfish feed. M74 indicates alevins dying from M74, OK indicates viable alevins.

Spawning females	1	2	3	4	5
Weight at spawning, Nov 1992 (kg)	10.1	5.1	5.7	11.4	7.4
Weight at reconditioning start, May 1993	6.6	3.6	3.6	7.3	5.0
Fate of progeny, June 1993	M74[a]	M74[a]	OK[b]	OK[b]	M74[a]
Weight at stripping, Nov 1993	7.8	7.8	3.7	8.2	4.0
Fate of progeny, June 1994	OK[b]	OK[b]	OK[b]	OK[b]	M74[a]

[a] alevins dying from M74
[b] viable alevins

The number of species in the brackish Baltic Sea is relatively low, although both freshwater and marine species live together in the same areas. The intermittent saltwater inflow to the Baltic (Matthäus 1993) makes the ecosystem prone to changes in the biotic and abiotic conditions, which may be reflected in fluctuations in the recruitment and biomass of marine species such as sprat (*Sprattus sprattus* L.), herring (*Clupea harengus* L.) (Parmanne et al. 1994; Sparholt 1994), and cod (*Gadus morhua* L.) (Bagge et al. 1994). These 3 species constitute about 80% of the fish biomass of the Baltic Sea (Rudstam et al. 1994). The cod is by far the most important predator of these clupeids (Bagge et al. 1994). Sprat and herring are the main food items for the anadromous Baltic salmon, constituting about 90% of its diet (Christensen and Larsson 1979). Stickleback (*Gasterosteus aculeatus* L.) constitute a few percent of the diet, and in the southernmost part of the Baltic, sand eels (*Ammodytes lanceolatus* and *A. lancea*) can be important prey for the salmon (Christensen and Larsson 1979)

Vertebrates from higher trophic levels have suffered from various types of environmentally induced diseases. The numbers of grey seal (*Halichoerus grypus*) and ringed seal (*Phoca hispida*) decreased during the 1960s (Helle et al. 1976), and white-tailed sea eagles (*Haliaëtus albicilla*) were experiencing reproductive dysfunction (Helander et al. 1982). Reproductive failure in both seals and eagles has been correlated to high burdens of chlorinated hydrocarbons, including PCBs and DDT (Jensen et al. 1969). In recent years, improved reproduction in both seal and eagle populations has been recorded. During this period, however, lower vertebrates, i.e., many species of fish, have been shown to suffer from various types of environmental distress, including reproductive disturbances (Norrgren et al. 1996).

Water inflow events
The incidence of M74 peaked in 1993 and has since then decreased by 10% annually (Figure 11-2). This last peak of M74 mortality followed the longest period, lasting from 1983 to 1992, without any inflow events during this century and

coincided with the 1993 inflow of saline and oxygenated water into the deep basins of the Baltic. This event, classified as moderate by Matthäus (1993), was estimated to be in the order of one-third of the intensity of the inflow events in 1976. Since World War II, major inflows have occurred in 1952, 1969, and 1976, intermingled with weak and medium inflow events (Matthäus 1993; Matthäus and Lass 1995). Inflow events are important for the ecological conditions necessary to support marine life in the basins of the main Baltic, which is the main feeding area for the Baltic salmon populations, where they feed primarily on sprat and herring (Christensen 1961; Thurow 1966)

Influence of cod stocks
The most important predator of sprat and herring in the main basin of the Baltic Sea is cod (Bagge et al. 1994; Sparholt 1994). Under normal conditions in the Baltic the relationship between the biomass of salmon and cod is of the order 1:100 (Anon 1995a; Bagge et al. 1994), which means that cod is the only predator of importance, man included, in regulating the stocks of sprat and herring. Recruitment of cod in the Baltic is highly dependent on adequate oxygen and salinity levels in the water of the deep basins, their primary spawning areas, and these conditions require regular inflow events of saline and oxygenated water to the Baltic (Bagge et al. 1994; Wieland et al. 1994). Since 1974, there has been an inverse association between biomass of cod (Anon 1995b) and the occurrence of M74 in Baltic salmon ($R = -0.75$; $R^2 = 0.56$) which indicates that 56% of the variation in M74 is inversely proportional to fluctuations in the biomass of cod. When the stock of cod in the Baltic is low due to reproduction failure, there is a loss of regulation of the clupeid stocks, which then increase in age and biomass and become less suitable as feed for salmon as organochlorine concentrations in Baltic herring increase significantly with age (Perttil et al. 1982).

As shown by Norrgren, Andersson et al. (1993), both females and their alevins of feral origin in the Baltic display an elevated body burden of inducers of the cytochrome P450-dependent enzymes, which are probably organochlorine compounds, some of which (hexachlorobenzene, 1,2,3,7,8-pentachlorodibenzofuran, 2,3,4,7,8-pentachlorodibenzofuran, 3,3',4,4',5-pentachlorophenyl), at least during the period 1988 to 1992, showed an increasing trend in Baltic salmon (Paasivirta et al. 1995). As mentioned above, Yagi et al. (1979) and Pelissier et al. (1992) have demonstrated experimentally that high levels of certain organochlorine compounds induce thiamine deficiency in rats, and this might also be possible in fish. An increased demand for thiamine due to elevated EROD activity that coincides with low thiamine content in salmon because of food web dynamics may imply disaster for the Baltic salmon.

M74 versus Early Mortality Syndrome: a Comparison

Both M74 and Early Mortality Syndrome (EMS) are characterized by low levels of thiamine and in both roe and alevins these mortality syndromes can be treated with thiamine. In contrast to EMS, the adults of some progeny that display M74 may also display abnormal behavior such as wiggling and lethargy. These behaviors are reversible with thiamine. The abnormal neuromuscular swimming behavior in alevins is very similar in EMS and M74, as are the increased incidences of yolk-sac precipitates and pericardial hemorrhages. The association between low levels of astaxanthin in the roe of Baltic salmon and high incidences of M74 has, to our knowledge, not been observed in the salmonids of the Great Lakes area producing EMS-affected alevins. The evident variation in pigmentation of roe from Baltic salmon (Figure 11-4) is unique. Also, there is a role for anti-oxidant vitamins such as tocopherol in protection against free radicals in M74-affected alevins. Ecological disturbances seem to be an important factor for both syndromes, even if the disturbances are of different types. In the Great Lakes region, a nonindigenous fish species, the alewife (*Alosa pseudoharengus*), with high thiaminase activity, is associated with EMS (Fisher et al. 1996). In the Baltic Sea, the disturbances are caused by an imbalance of the main fish species, sprat, herring, and cod, thus making the clupeids less suitable as food for the salmon. So far, there are no indications that high thiaminase activity is responsible for the low thiamine content in Baltic salmon suffering from M74.

Conclusions

The acute putative cause of the M74 syndrome is a lack of thiamine, although the causes of the thiamine deficiency are not understood. Several factors may be involved, including changes in the ecosystem of the Baltic caused by irregular inflow events of oxygenated and high-saline water, changing the foodweb dynamics, and, potentially, increased requirements for thiamine due to metabolism of anthropogenic xenobiotics.

Prospective research includes the study of carotenoids in the foodweb and salmon and will also attempt to explain why roe pigmentation is a good marker for M74. Also, thiamine production and turnover in the biota of the Baltic and uptake and turnover of thiamine in the salmon will be studied, together with interactions of thiamine, carotenoids, and xenobiotics in the salmon.

Acknowledgments

Investigations summarized in this article were financed by grants from the Swedish National Board of Fisheries, the Swedish Environmental Protection Agency, and the Swedish Council for Forestry and Agricultural Research. We would also like to thank Roland Eriksson, Manager of the Salmon Hatchery at River Luleälven, for data on roe color.

References

Ackefors H, Johansson N, Wahlberg B. 1991. The Swedish compensatory programme for salmon in the Baltic: an action plan with biological and economical implications. *Proceedings, ICES Marine Science Symposium* 192:109–119.

Amcoff P, Norrgren L, Börjeson H, Lindeberg J. 1995. Lowered concentrations of thiamine (Vitamin B_1) in M74-affected feral Baltic salmon (*Salmo salar*). Second Workshop on Reproduction Disturbances in Fish; 1995 Nov 20–23; Stockholm, Sweden. Swedish Environmental Protection Agency Report 4534.

Anon. 1995a. Report of the Baltic salmon and trout assessment working group. *ICES C. M. 1995, Assess.*16.

Anon. 1995b. Report of the working group on the assessment on demersal and pelagic stocks in the Baltic. *ICES C. M. 1995, Assess.*18.

Bagge O, Thurow F, Steffensen E, Bay J. 1994. The Baltic cod. *Dana* 10:1–28.

Beyer RE. 1990. The participation of coenzyme Q in free radical production and antioxidation. *Free Radical Biology and Medicine* 8:545–565.

Bylund G, Lerche O. 1995. Thiamine therapy of M74 affected fry of Atlantic salmon *Salmo salar. Bull Eur Ass Fish Pathol* 15(3):93–97.

Christensen O. 1961. Preliminary Results of an Investigation on Food of Baltic Salmon. *ICES C. M.* No 93.

Christensen O, Larsson P-O. 1979. Review of Baltic salmon research: a synopsis compiled by the Baltic Salmon Working Group. Christensen O, Larsson P-O, editors. Charlottenlund, Denmark: International Council for the Exploration of the Sea (ICES). Cooperative Research Report No 89.

Davidson WS, Birt TP, Green JM. 1989. A review of genetic variation in Atlantic salmon, *Salmo salar* L., and its importance for stock identification, enhancement programmes and aquaculture. *J Fish Biol* 34:547–560.

Fisher JP, Spitsbergen JM, Combs GG. 1994. Reproductive failure in wild-caught Atlantic salmon from New York's finger lakes: epizootiology of the Cayuga syndrome. Abstract from International Symposium on Aquatic Animal Health; 1994 Sep 4–8; Seattle WA. American Fisheries Society. p w20.2.

Fisher JP. 1995. Continued investigations into the role of thiamine and thiaminease-rich forage in the Cayuga syndrome of New York's landlocked Atlantic salmon Second Workshop on Reproduction Disturbances in Fish; 1995 Nov 20–23; Stockholm, Sweden. Swedish Environmental Protection Agency Report 4534.

Fisher JP, Fitzsimons JD, Combs GF, Spitsbergen JM. 1996. Naturally occurring thiamine deficiency causing reproductive failure in Finger Lakes Atlantic salmon and Great Lakes lake trout. *Trans Am Fish Soc* 125(2):167–178.

Fitzsimons JD. 1995. The effect of B-vitamins on a swim-up syndrome in Lake Ontario lake trout. *J Great Lakes Res* 21(1):286–289.

Gonzalez FJ, Nebert DW. 1990. Evolution of the P450 gene superfamily: animal - plant "warfare" molecular drive, and human genetic differences in drug oxidation. *Trends Genet* 6:186–212.

Helander B, Olsson M, Jensen S. 1982. Residue levels of organochlorine and mercury compounds in unhatched eggs and the relationships to breeding success in white-tailed sea eagles *Haliaëtus albicilla* in Sweden. *Holoarct Ecol* 5:349–366

Helle E, Olsson M, Jensen S. 1976. PCB levels correlated with pathological changes in seal uteri. *Ambio* 5:261–263.

Jensen S, Johnels AG, Olsson M, Otterlind G. 1969. DDT and PCB in marine animals from Swedish waters. *Nature* 224:247–250.

Krinsky NI. 1989. Antioxidant functions of carotenoids. *Free Radical Biology and Medicine*, 7:617–635.

Matthäus W. 1993. Major inflows of highly saline water into the Baltic Sea: a review. *ICES C.M. 1993/ C:52.*

Matthäus W, Lass HU. 1995. The recent salt inflow into the Baltic Sea. *J Physic Oceanog* 25:280–286.

Miki W. 1991. Biological functions and activities of animal carotenoids. *Pure Appl Chem* 63:141–146.

Mukai K, Kikuchi S, Urano S. 1990. Stopped-flow kinetic study of the regeneration of tocopheroxyl radical by reduced ubiquinone-10 in solution. *Biochim Biophys Acta* 1035(1):77–82.

Nebert DW, Petersen DD, Fornace AJ. 1990. Cellular responses to oxidative stress: the (Ah) gene battery as a paradigm. *Environ Health Persp* 88:13–25.

Norrgren L, Andersson T, Bergqvist P-A, Björklund I. 1993. Chemical, physiological and morphological studies of feral Baltic salmon (*Salmo salar*) suffering from abnormal fry mortality. *Environ Toxicol Chem* 12:2065–2075.

Norrgren L, Lundström J, Andersson T, Börjeson H, Bergqvist P-A. 1993. Microinjection of different lipid soluble compounds in salmonid embryos. Swedish Environmental Protection Agency *Report* 4346:82–86.

Norrgren L, Amcoff P, Börjeson H, Larson P-O. 1996. Reproduction disturbances in Baltic fish: a review. American Fisheries Society; 1996 Aug 26–29; Dearborn MI. In preparation.

Paasivirta J, Vuorinen PJ, Vuorinen M, Koistinen J, Rantio T, Hyötyiäinen T, Welling L. 1995. TCDD-toxicity and M74 syndrome of Baltic salmon (*Salmo salar* L.). *Organohalogen Compounds* 25:355–359.

Palace VP, Klaverkamp JF, Lockhart WL, Metner DA, Muir DCG, Brown SB. 1996. Mixed-function oxidase enzyme activity and oxidative stress in lake trout (*Salvelinus namaycush*) exposed to 3,3',4,4',5-pentachlorobiphenyl (PCB 126). *Environ Toxicol Chem* 15:955–960.

Parmanne R, Rechlin O, Sjöstrand B. 1994. Status and future of herring and sprat stocks in the Baltic Sea. *Dana* 10:29–59.

Pelissier MA, Siess MH, Lhuissier M, Grolier P, Suchetet M, Narbonne JF, Albrecht R, Robertson LW. 1992. Effect of prototypic polychlorinated biphenyls on hepatic and renal vitamin contents and on drug-metabolizing enzymes in rats fed diets containing low or high levels of retinyl palmitate. *Fd Chem Toxic* 30(8):723–729.

Perttil M, Tervo V, Parmanne R. 1982. Age dependence of the concentrations of harmful substances in Baltic herring (*Clupea harengus*). *Chemosphere* 11(10):1019–1026.

Rosenberg R, Elmgren R, Fleischer S, Jonsson P, Persson G, Dahlin H. 1990. Marine eutrophication case studies in Sweden. *Ambio* 19(3):102–108.

Rudstam LG, Aneer G, Hildén M. 1994. Top-down control in the pelagic Baltic ecosystem. *Dana* 10:105–129.

Sparholt H. 1994. Fish species interactions in the Baltic Sea. *Dana* 10:131–162.

Ståhl G. 1987. Genetic population structure of Atlantic salmon. In: Ryman N, Utter F, editors. Population genetics and fishery management. Seattle WA: Univ of Washington Pr. p 121–140.

Thurow F. 1966. Beiträge zur Biologie und Bestandskunde des Atlantischen Lachses (*Salmo salar* L.) in der Ostsee *Ber Dt Wiss Komm Meeresforsch XVIII*, H 3/4:223–379.

Wheeler CW, Guenther TM. 1991. Cytochrome P-450-dependent metabolism of xenobiotics in human lung. *J Biochem Toxicology* 6:163–169.

Wieland K, Waller U, Schnack D. 1994. Development of Baltic cod eggs at different levels of temperature and oxygen content. *Dana* 10:163–177.

Yagi N, Kamohara K, Itokawa Y. 1979. Thiamine deficiency induced by polychlorinated biphenyls (PCB) and dichlorodiphenyltrichloroethane (DDT) administration to rats. *J Environ Pathol Toxicol* 2:1119–1125.

Laboratory and field observations of sublethal damage in marine fish larvae: lessons from the *Exxon Valdez* oil spill

Richard M. Kocan, Jo Ellen Hose

The effects of oil exposure have been extensively studied in Pacific herring (*Clupea pallasi*) larvae from Prince William Sound (PWS) since the *Exxon Valdez* oil spill (EVOS) of 1989. Laboratory and field investigations performed by our group showed identical adverse effects in newly hatched herring larvae. These included precocious hatch, chromosome damage, increases in the incidence and severity of anatomical malformations, and reduced growth in the 1989 year class. The extent of chromosome damage and malformations were positively correlated with oil concentrations both in the laboratory and in the field.

Although the consequences of the observed sublethal damage cannot be predicted with any certainty, it appears likely that larval survival would be reduced. Field measurements showed that larval mortality was higher at oiled areas. This finding is intriguing in light of subsequent changes in the PWS herring fishery. In 1993, when the 1989 year class recruited into the spawning population, over two-thirds of the adult population died. The cause was presumably a viral epizootic. Since similar disease epizootics and mass mortalities have not been observed in other Alaskan herring populations, speculation has centered upon the role of previous oil exposure in initiating the viral disease. Available techniques could not have predicted this epizootic, but current studies are underway to determine links between oil exposure, disease prevalence, reproductive capacity, and mortality.

The *Exxon Valdez* oil spill (EVOS) of 1989 presented scientists with an unprecedented opportunity to study the effects of a massive oil spill on a complex and productive ecosystem for which decades of fisheries data existed on several economically important fishes such as Pacific herring (*Clupea pallasi*). Definitive data have been slow to emerge because of a lack of consensus between Natural Resource Damage Assessment (NRDA) and Exxon-funded scientists over even the most basic information such as the exact trajectory of the *Exxon Valdez* oil (EVO) and methods to reliably measure Prudhoe Bay crude oil in sediments and marine organisms. The extent of exposure to marine fishes, particularly herring, is still being debated since Exxon scientists found EVO in only 1 of 175 samples taken in 1989–1990 (herring eggs from a heavily contaminated beach 1 month after the spill) (Bence and Burns 1995), whereas NRDA scientists did not collect sufficient tissue for determination of EVO at parts-per-billion (ppb) concentrations. Levels of dissolved EVO in water were believed to be at low- to sub-ppb levels throughout the spring following the spill, although a significant quantity of EVO was dispersed throughout the water column to a depth of at least 25 m and was detected throughout summer 1989 (Short and Harris 1996a). Such dispersed oil probably would also be bioavailable to water column organisms such as herring larvae or prey items.

The EVOS coincided with the annual migration of herring to their spawning sites within Prince William Sound (PWS), and fish spawned 2 to 4 weeks after the spill. Since roughly half of the herring eggs were deposited within the oil trajectory (Brown, Baker et al. 1996), effects of EVO on development could be investigated both in situ and under controlled laboratory conditions. The results of many NRDA in situ studies in 1989 were inconclusive due to physical and environmental differences between oiled and unoiled sites. However, 1 of the 1989 laboratory experiments demonstrated damage in newly hatched larvae from oiled areas (Hose et al. 1996), results which conflict with those reported in a similar Exxon-funded study (Pearson et al. 1995). Although the study of Hose et al. (1996) has been criticized because of the poor condition of the 1989 samples and the lack of corresponding EVO measurements in eggs, NRDA studies have yielded a fairly consistent picture of damage to the embryolarval stages of the 1989 year class (Brown, Norcross, Short 1996). A critical evaluation of both the NRDA and Exxon herring studies is presented elsewhere (Brown, Norcross, Short 1996).

These herring data are perhaps best analyzed using a weight-of-evidence approach employing the ecoepidemiological criteria for causality described by Fox (1991). Evidence that damage to the sensitive embryolarval stages in 1989 was caused by EVO exposure is consistent with 6 of 7 essential criteria: probability, time order, strength of association, specificity, consistency on replication, and biological coherence (the seventh criterion, predictive performance, was not examined) (Brown, Norcross, Short 1996). Two criteria, consistency of the association and statistical coherence in the form of a monotonic dose-response relationship, strongly affirm causality (Fox 1991). This paper will focus on data that support these 2 key criteria, emphasizing the consistency between sublethal damage to embryolarval stages measured in the field in 1989 (Brown, Baker et al. 1996) and in related laboratory experiments (Kocan et al. 1996).

The very low abundance of the 1989 year class and the concurrent collapse of the PWS herring fishery in 1993-1994 intensify the importance of damage measured in 1989 larvae (Brown, Norcross, Short 1996). Over two-thirds of the adult population disappeared and are presumed to have died in 1993, and spawning among the survivors was severely reduced. The PWS fishery has remained closed since 1993. Mass mortalities in the spawning population were suspected to be caused in part by an epizootic of viral hemorrhagic septicemia virus (VHSV) (Meyers et al. 1994). Since the collapse occurred when the 1989 year class was fully recruited into the spawning population, one of the causal hypotheses is that previous exposure to EVO was involved in initiating the VHSV epizootic (Brown, Norcross, Short 1996). The causes of the population decline may never be definitively proven, but data relating to each causal factor, including EVO exposure, were examined by Brown, Norcross, and Short (1996). Studies currently underway to define the effects of oil exposure during development may eventually provide evidence for a possible link between exposure, subsequent disease, and mortality.

Methods

Methods used in the field studies have been previously described (Brown, Baker et al. 1996). Briefly, eggs were collected from 3 sites at each of 2 oiled areas (Naked Island and Rocky Bay on Montague Island) and from an unoiled area (Fairmont Bay in north PWS) and incubated in the laboratory until hatching (Hose et al. 1996). Adjacent mussels were also collected and analyzed for a suite of polycyclic aromatic hydrocarbons [PAHs] characteristic of EVO (EVO-PAH) (Short and Harris 1996b). Although patchy at both areas, oiling was generally greater at Naked

Island (2,377 ± 1128 ppb, mean ± SE) than at Rocky Bay (2,103 ± 1257 ppb). Only trace amounts of EVO-PAH were found at the unoiled Fairmont Bay (29 ± 5 ppb).

Laboratory experiments were conducted in 1991 with herring embryos continuously exposed to oil–water dispersions (OWD) of Prudhoe Bay crude oil. High molecular weight (HMW) components (diesel range, C12 to C28) ranged from nominal concentrations of 0.01 mg*L^{-1} to 9.67 mg*L^{-1} (Kocan et al. 1996). This experiment was not intended to simulate exposure conditions during the EVOS but rather provided information on the types of effects to be expected in the field, a ranking of the sensitivity of these effects, and whether those effects formed a dose-response pattern using a graded series of EVO exposures. Similarly, the level of analytical chemistry used in this experiment was sufficient to document the stability of the OWD during the experimental period but not to define concentrations of individual PAHs present.

Herring spawning sites that were oiled and unoiled in 1989 were used as in situ exposure sites in 1991, even though some oiled areas had been abandoned as spawning sites following the EVOS (Kocan et al. 1996). Embryos were allowed to incubate in situ for 8 to 12 days, then returned to the laboratory for hatching. Dry weights were measured in a subsample of larvae from each treatment.

A suite of sublethal endpoints identical to those used in 1989 field studies was evaluated in larvae, consisting of hatch timing, morphological defects, chromosome damage, and weight. Hatch timing was determined by recording the proportions of larvae hatching on successive days, and the peak hatch date was determined graphically. Morphological defects were scored according to severity using graded indices (GSI scores) (Hose et al. 1996; Kocan et al. 1996). Scores between 0 and 3 were assigned for each of 3 categories (skeletal defects, craniofacial abnormalities, and finfold reductions) and were summed for the total GSI score. Chromosome damage was assessed by measuring the percentage of aberrant anaphase-telophase mitotic configurations in cells from larval pectoral fins.

GSI scores and the percentage of chromosome damage were compared using analysis of variance (ANOVA) followed by pairwise tests. Larval weights were analyzed using t tests. The criterion for statistical significance was set at p≤ 0.05.

Results

There was close correspondence of all sublethal responses between laboratory and field experiments. Experimental exposures of herring embryos to an OWD of EVO produced premature hatching with the oiled larvae hatching between 2 and 5 days earlier than controls (Kocan et al. 1996). Peak hatch was several days earlier at oiled PWS sites (particularly at Rocky Bay on Montague Island) relative to the unoiled sites (Brown, Baker et al. 1996).

Similar larval malformations were observed following exposure to EVO in both the laboratory and in PWS (Figure 12-1). GSI scores for every individual category and the total were significantly elevated (p≤ 0.01) at oiled sites around PWS in 1989

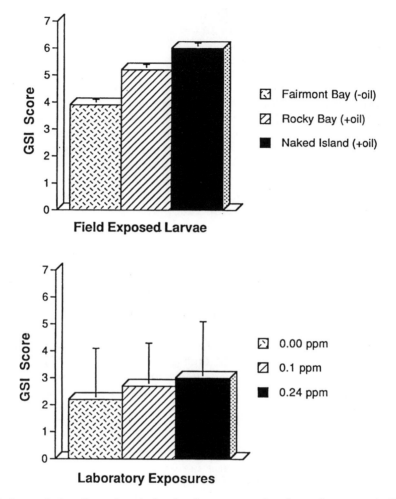

Figure 12-1 Anatomical malformations in herring larvae exposed to increasing concentrations of an oil–water dispersion (OWD) of Prudhoe Bay crude oil in the laboratory (bottom) and in herring larvae exposed in situ at oiled and unoiled sites in Prince William Sound in 1989 (top). The severity of malformations is quantified using a graduated severity index (GSI score). Similar differences between exposed and unexposed embryos are observed in both instances.

(relative to the unoiled Fairmont Bay) but not in subsequent years (Hose et al. 1996). In 1989, every category of GSI scores was significantly correlated (0.01 < p < 0.05) with the concentrations of total EVO-PAH or individual PAH components in adjacent mussels. For the laboratory exposure, all GSI scores were significantly different (p≤ 0.05) from the control at nominal OWD concentrations of ≥ 0.24 mg*L^{-1} HMW components. GSI scores for the 0.01 ppm OWD group were similar to those of controls. The GSI score was directly correlated with increasing OWD dose (r^2 = 0.75, p < 0.01).

In the 1989 field study, total GSI scores at both oiled sites were significantly elevated (p < 0.05) over the score for the unoiled site. The larval GSI score was highest at the site with the highest mean EVO-PAH concentrations (Naked Island, 2377 ppb) but not significantly greater than that of the other oiled site (Rocky Bay, 2103 ppb).

The types of defects observed were identical in field- and laboratory-exposed larvae, consisting of skeletal curvatures (scoliosis or lordosis), stunting, optic malformations, reductions or absence of the jaws or otic capsules, and reduction of the finfold width. Significantly higher frequencies of yolk sac or pericardial edema were observed in laboratory-exposed larvae and in larvae collected near oiled beaches of PWS in 1989 (Marty et al. in press). Edema of the yolk sac and pericardium could not be consistently evaluated in newly hatched 1989 larvae because of variable deterioration of the yolk sac (Hose et al. 1996), although Pearson et al. (1995) did not find elevated frequencies of pericardial edema in larvae from oiled areas.

Chromosome damage as measured by the anaphase aberration rate was also elevated in oil-exposed larvae from the laboratory and the field in 1989 (Figure 12-2). Laboratory exposures yielded a statistically significant increase (p < 0.05) in anaphase aberration rates at nominal OWD $\geq$ 0.1 mg*L^{-1} and a nonsignificant doubling of the AAT rate at 0.01 mg*L^{-1} (p=0.07) (Kocan et al. 1996). There was a significant (r^2 = 0.89, p < 0.01), direct correlation between the anaphase aberration rate and the OWD dose. In 1989, chromosome damage in naturally spawned larvae was significantly elevated at all oiled sites in PWS (0.01 < p < 0.05) (Hose et al. 1996). Rankings were similar for both GSI scores and chromosome damage: Fairmont Bay (oiled) < Rocky Bay (oiled) < Naked Island (oiled). Anaphase aberration rates were also significantly correlated with the concentrations of total EVO-PAH (r^2 = 0.88, p < 0.01) and every mutagenic individual PAH measured in adjacent mussels.

Larval weights of EVO-exposed larvae were reduced in both laboratory and field studies (0.01 < p < 0.05) (Figure 12-3). Larvae exposed to EVO in the laboratory weighed about 40% less than controls (Kocan et al. 1996). After corrections for age differences, larvae from oiled areas in 1989 weighed significantly less than those from unoiled areas (Brown, Baker et al. 1996). The difference between weights at unoiled and oiled PWS sites was about 20%.

Discussion

The effects of embryonic oil exposure in Pacific herring observed both in the field and in the laboratory are consistent with toxicity primarily evident at hatching and in the early larval period. During the embryonic period, significant mortality was infrequently observed in PWS (Brown, Baker et al. 1996), and embryonic malformations are generally difficult to detect until hatching. Manifestations of oil exposure at hatching include alterations in hatching dynamics, primarily precocious hatching, and weight reductions, increased malformations, and genetic damage in newly hatched larvae (Kocan et al. 1996). These adverse effects were observed throughout the larval period within the EVO trajectory (Brown, Baker et al. 1996). Although seldom a component of oil spill investigations, genetic effects were

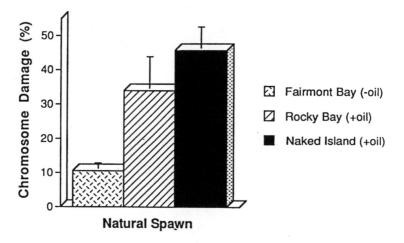

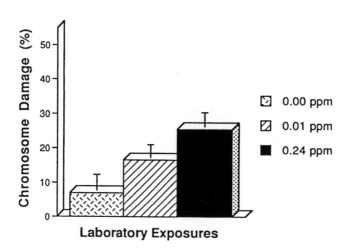

Figure 12-2 Chromosome damage in herring larvae exposed to increasing concentrations of an OWD of Prudhoe Bay crude oil in the laboratory (bottom) and in herring larvae exposed in situ at oiled and unoiled sites in PWS in 1989 (top). Chromosome damage is measured using the anaphase aberration rate in pectoral fin cells. Similar differences between exposed and unexposed embryos are observed in both instances.

measured repeatedly in several different NRDA collections of larval herring during spring 1989 (Brown, Norcross, Short 1996) and following the earlier *Argo Merchant* spill (Longwell 1977). As herring larvae grew throughout spring 1989, increased rates of malformations and anaphase aberrations persisted within the oil trajectory although their magnitude diminished with time and with distance from oiled beaches (Brown, Baker et al. 1996). In contrast, weight reductions and increased malformation rates were not observed in newly hatched larvae from oiled areas in the Exxon-funded study (Pearson et al. 1995).

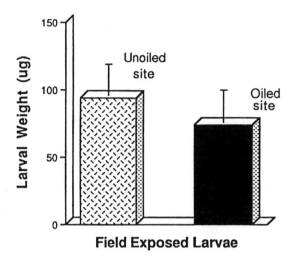

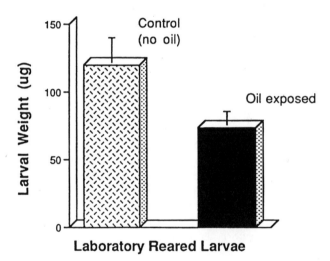

Figure 12-3 Dry weights of herring larvae exposed to an OWD of Prudhoe Bay crude oil in the laboratory (bottom) and weights of larvae exposed in situ at oiled and unoiled sites in PWS in 1991 (top). Similar differences between exposed and unexposed larvae are observed in both instances.

In both the laboratory and PWS in 1989, monotonic dose-response relationships were statistically significant ($p<0.05$) between 2 biological effects (malformation scores and anaphase aberration rates) and measures of ambient EVO-PAH concentrations (Hose et al. 1996; Kocan et al. 1996). Definitive effects thresholds could not be calculated, although published literature suggests that they might be in the low ppb range (Black et al. 1983; Hose et al. 1983; 1984). The effect threshold for malformations was reported by Pearson et al. (1985) to be influenced by the amount of oil droplets adhering to the eggs; however, oil droplets were never observed in Kocan et al.'s laboratory study (Kocan et al. 1996). This experiment is being repeated with low EVO-PAH concentrations and detailed supportive chemistry. Preliminary results suggest that malformations and chromosome damage in larval herring can be induced by exposure to EVO-PAH in the low ppb range (Hose, unpublished). It is hoped that these experiments will provide information useful in modelling the effects of the EVOS in which maximum levels of EVO-PAH in herring eggs were 300 to 1000 ppb (Pearson et al. 1995; Brown, Baker et al. 1996). A recent study using Pacific herring and silversides (*Menidia beryllina*) has also documented that malformations result from exposure to concentrations $\geq$ 75 ppb (the lowest concentration tested) of the water soluble fraction (WSF) of a biodegraded Alaska North Slope crude oil (Middaugh et al. 1997).

Viable hatch (the percentage of normal live larvae) was reduced following exposure to oil in the laboratory (Kocan et al. 1996) . Although malformed larvae weighed less than control larvae, normal-appearing, oil-exposed larvae were also about 30% lighter and within the weight range of abnormal, unexposed larvae. These results suggesting that oil exposure reduces growth in viable larvae are supported by two 1989 studies of larval herring growth rates in PWS (Brown, Baker et al. 1996; Norcross et al. 1996). Growth rates of nearshore larvae were lower in oiled areas although observed differences were consistent with temperature variations (Brown, Baker et al. 1996). Norcross et al. (1996) measured an unusually low growth rate of 0.15 mm*d^{-1} throughout the oil trajectory; growth rates previously reported for Alaska herring range from around 0.3 to 1.5 mm*d^{-1} (Wespestad and Moksness 1990; McGurk et al. 1993). Fish from the 1989 year class were small at ages 3 and 4 but not outside the historical range observed in PWS (Brown, Norcross, Short 1996). However, adults from the 1988 year class were also small in 1992 and 1993, presumably due to the poor productivity in PWS from 1990 to 1994.

Sublethal effects such as those we observed are thought to result in enhanced mortality. Following the EVOS, egg to larval mortality rates and instantaneous larval mortality rates were elevated within oiled areas, and the differences could not be attributed to temperature (McGurk and Brown 1996). Site-specific egg deposition measurements, abnormality estimates, and instantaneous mortality rates were combined to estimate larval production (Brown, Baker et al. 1996). Roughly equal numbers of eggs were deposited at oiled and unoiled areas, but 100 to 200 × more viable larvae were produced at unoiled areas. Returns of the 1989 year class have been the lowest in over 20 years although substantial numbers of eggs were laid (Brown, Norcross, Short 1996). From 8 to 9% extra biomass was added in 1989 because of the PWS fishery closure (Pearson et al. 1995), resulting in record biomass measurements from 1989 to 1992 (Brown, Norcross, Short 1996). The fishery collapse in PWS occurred over the next 2 years. In 1995 and 1996, the percentages of VHSV-infected herring have declined although the population abundance has been low since 1993. However, in Sitka Sound, Alaska, which has identical productivity conditions, the herring population has remained at historically high abundances without exhibiting a population collapse or significant VHSV infections. Population level changes have seldom been demonstrated in fish following oil spills, although the 1978 year class of 2 flatfish disappeared following the *Amoco Cadiz* spill, and reproductive indices and growth were altered at contaminated areas (Davis et al. 1984).

Other consequences of precocious hatching, low growth, malformations, and genetic damage are poorly understood but might include reduced fitness, higher susceptibility to predation, reproductive impairment, and increased susceptibility to disease (Kurelec 1993). Developmental changes, particularly of the immune and reproductive systems, might irreversibly reduce fish survival and reproductive capacity. Biomarkers for reproductive impairment (Monosson et al. 1994; Ghosh and Thomas 1995) and reduced immunity (Arkoosh et al. 1996; Rozell and Anderson 1996) exist for adult fish but not for larval fishes. Larval survival remains one of the most sensitive measurements (Monosson et al. 1994) with some relation to subsequent population abundance. Studies such as those conducted in PWS following the oil spill provide an excellent opportunity to correlate effects between the laboratory and the field. The lingering uncertainty regarding the relationship between the observed oil toxicity in larvae and the subsequent population collapse in PWS herring underscores the need for long-term monitoring of all life stages of a key fish species.

References

Arkoosh MR, Clemons E, Huffman P, Sanborn HR, Casillas E, Stein JE. 1996. Evaluation of the leukoproliferative response of English sole (*Pleuronectes vetulus*) as a biomarker for immune dysfunction. *Arch Environ Contam Toxicol* 42:181–186.

Bence AE, Burns WA. 1995. Fingerprinting hydrocarbons in the biological resources of the *Exxon Valdez* spill area. In: Wells PG, Butler JN, Hughes JS, editors. *Exxon Valdez* oil spill: fate and effects in Alaska waters. Philadelphia PA: American Society for Testing and Materials (ASTM). ASTM STP 1219. p 84–140.

Black JA, Birge WJ, Westerman AG, Francis PC. 1983. Comparative toxicology of aromatic hydrocarbons. *Fund Appl Toxicol* 3:353–358.

Brown ED, Baker TT, Funk F, Hose JE, Kocan RM, Marty GD, McGurk MD, Norcross BL, Short J. 1996. Studies on Pacific herring in Prince William Sound following the *Exxon Valdez* oil spill. In: Rice SD, Spies RB, Wolfe DA, Wright BA, editors. *Exxon Valdez* Oil Spill Symposium Proceedings. Bethesda MD: American Fisheries Society Symposium Number 18. p 448–462.

Brown ED, Norcross BL, Short JW. 1996. An introduction to studies on the effects of the *Exxon Valdez* oil spill on early life history stages of Pacific herring, *Clupea pallasi*, in Prince William Sound, Alaska. *Can J Fish Aquat Sci* 53:2337–2342.

Davis WP, Hoss DE, Scott GI, Sheridan PF. 1984. Fishery resource impacts from spills of oil or hazardous substances. In: Cairns J, Buikema A, editors. Restoration of habitats impacted by oil spills. Stoneham MA: Butterworth. p 157–172.

Fox G. 1991. Practical causal inference for ecoepidemiologists. *J Toxicol Environ Health* 33:359–373.

Ghosh S, Thomas P. 1995. Antagonistic effects of xenobiotics on steroid-induced final maturation of Atlantic croaker oocytes in vitro. *Mar Environ Res* 39:159–163.

Hose JE, Hannah JB, Puffer HW, Landolt ML. 1984. Histological and skeletal abnormalities in benzo(a)pyrene-treated rainbow trout alevins. *Arch Environ Contam Toxicol* 13:675–684.

Hose JE, McGurk MD, Marty GD, Hinton DE, Brown ED, Baker TT. 1996. Sublethal effects of the *Exxon Valdez* oil spill on herring embryos and larvae: morphologic, cytogenetic, and histopathological assessments, 1989–1991. *Can J Fish Aquat Sci* 53:2355–2365.

Hose JE, Puffer HW, Oshida PS, Bay SM. 1983. Developmental and cytogenetic abnormalities induced in the purple sea urchin by benzo(a)pyrene. *Arch Environ Contam Toxicol* 12:319–325.

Kocan RM, Hose JE, Brown ED, Baker TT. 1996. Pacific herring (*Clupea pallasi*) embryo sensitivity to Prudhoe Bay petroleum hydrocarbons. Laboratory evaluation and in situ exposure at oiled and unoiled sites in Prince William Sound. *Can J Fish Aquat Sci* 53:2366–2375.

Kurelec B. 1993. The genotoxic disease syndrome. *Mar Environ Res* 35:341–348.

Longwell AC. 1977. A genetic look at fish eggs and oil. *Oceanus* 20:46–58.

Marty GD, Hose JE, McGurk MD, Brown ED, Hinton DE. Histopathology and cytogenetic evaluation of Pacific herring larvae exposed to petroleum hydrocarbons in the laboratory or in Prince William Sound, Alaska, after the *Exxon Valdez* oil spill. *Can J Fish Aquat Sci.* In press.

McGurk MD, Brown E. 1996. Egg-larval mortality of Pacific herring in Prince William Sound, Alaska, after the *Exxon Valdez* oil spill. *Can J Fish Aquat Sci* 53:2343–2354.

McGurk MD, Paul AJ, Coyle KO, Ziemann DA, Haldorson LJ. 1993. Relationship between prey concentration and growth, condition, and mortality of Pacific herring, *Clupea pallasi,* larvae in an Alaska subarctic embayment. *Can J Fish Aquat Sci* 50:163–180.

Meyers TR, Short S, Lipson K, Batts WN, Winton JR, Wilcock J, Brown E. 1994. Association of viral hemorrhagic septicemia virus with epizootic hemorrhages of the skin in Pacific herring *Clupea harengus pallasi* from Prince William Sound and Kodiak Island, Alaska, USA. *Dis Aquat Org* 19:27–37.

Middaugh DP, Chapman PJ, Shelton ME. 1997. Responses of embryonic and larval inland silversides, *Menidia beryllina,* to a water-soluble fraction formed during biodegradation of artificially weathered Alaska North Slope crude oil. *Arch Environ Contam Toxicol* 32:410–419.

Monosson E, Fleming WJ, Sullivan CV. 1994. Effects of the planar PCB 3,3'4,4'- tetrachlorobiphenyl (TCB) on ovarian development, plasma levels of sex steroidhormones and vitellogenin, and progeny survival in the white perch (*Morone americana*). *Aquat Toxicol* 29:1–19.

Norcross BL, Frandsen M, Hose JE, Marty GD, Brown E. 1996. Larval herring distribution, abundance, and sublethal assessment in Prince William Sound during 1989. *Can J Fish Aquat Sci* 53:2376–2386.

Pearson WH, Moksness E, Skalski JR. 1995. A field and laboratory assessment of oil spill effects on survival and reproduction of Pacific herring following the *Exxon Valdez* spill. In: Wells PG, Butler JN, Hughes JS, editors. *Exxon Valdez* oil spill: fate and effects in Alaska waters. Philadelphia PA: American Society for Testing and Materials (ASTM). ASTM STP 1219. p 84–140.

Pearson WH, Woddruff DL, Kiesser SL, Fellingham GW, Elston RA. 1985. Oil effects on spawning behavior and reproduction in Pacific herring (*Clupea harengus pallasi*). Washington DC: American Petroleum Institute (API). The Am. Petroleum Inst. Pub. No. 4412. 105 p.

Short JF, Harris PM. 1996a. Chemical sampling and analysis of petroleum hydrocarbons in the near-surface seawater of Prince William Sound, Alaska, after the *Exxon Valdez* oil spill. In: Rice SD, Spies RB, Wolfe DA, Wright BA, editors. *Exxon Valdez* Oil Spill Symposium Proceedings. American Fisheries Society (AFS) Symposium Number 18, Anchorage, Alaska. Bethesda MD: AFS. p 17–28.

Short JF, Harris PM. 1996b. Petroleum hydrocarbons in caged mussels deployed in Prince William Sound, Alaska, after the *Exxon Valdez* oil spill. In: Rice SD, Spies RB, Wolfe DA, Wright BA, editors. *Exxon Valdez* Oil Spill Symposium Proceedings. American Fisheries Society (AFS) Symposium Number 18, Anchorage, Alaska. Bethesda MD: AFS. p 29–39.

Wespestad VG, Moksness E. 1990. Observations on growth and survival during the early life history of Pacific herring *Clupea pallasi* from Bristol Bay, Alaska, in a marine mesocosm. *Fish Bull US* 88:191–200.

Reproductive and developmental effects of contaminants in fish populations: establishing cause and effect

Emily Monosson

There is little question that reproduction and development have been disrupted or disturbed in some wild fish populations as a result of environmental contaminants. However, determination of cause-effect linkages between exposure to contaminants and reproductive and developmental effects has been difficult. The goal of this paper was to identify the qualities that were common to published studies considered successful in terms of linking exposure to contaminants with reproductive and developmental problems in fish. This was done by sorting field and laboratory studies into 1 of 3 tables based on the degree of confidence that the studies were able to demonstrate a cause-and-effect relationship. These tables are based upon similar tables constructed by participants at this workshop titled "Chemically induced alterations in functional development and reproduction of fishes," held at the Wingspread Conference Center in Racine WI. An examination of the studies included in these tables suggests that although very few studies have linked contaminants to changes in population size or structure, contaminants can be linked to reproductive and developmental effects in fish through a combination of detailed field and laboratory research.

Twenty years ago, when discussing the sublethal effects of pollutants on fish populations, Rosenthal and Alderdice (1976) stated, "Frequently at the population level either the potential cause is known and the probable effect is inferred, or the effect is observed and the probable cause is unknown or implied." How far has environmental toxicology come in 20 years? How good are we at making inferences from laboratory studies? Are we any better able to identify the effects of environmental contaminants on fish populations in the field? Establishing cause and effect is a central problem in wildlife toxicology.

In July 1995, a workshop was held at the Wingspread Conference Center in Racine WI, where participants focused on the effects of contaminants on reproduction and development in fishes. The participants were divided into workgroups and asked to respond to the following question: "To what extent are environmental contaminants contributing to fish population declines or impeding recovery of depleted stocks?" (Wingspread Consensus Statement, Chapter 1) There are 2 main parts to this question: 1) are there cases in which cause (chemical contamination) and effect (reproduction and development) in wild fish populations have been linked? and 2) have any contaminants been linked to altered population dynamics in these populations? In response, the workgroups constructed tables that, in the opinion of the participants, contained some of the best known examples of field research on reproductive and developmental effects of contaminants on fish populations as well as some of the laboratory studies that were crucial in confirming any cause–effect relationships.

There are many comprehensive reviews available that include details of the effects of environmental contaminants on reproduction and development in fish (von Westernhagen 1988; Sinderman 1994; Kime 1995). There is even literature available that synthesizes much of the work done at specific sites (e.g., Johnson et al. 1995; Cook et al. Chapter 2; McMaster et al. 1996). That is not the goal here. This paper focuses on the placement of the selected studies within 3 tables (Tables 13-1 to 13-3) based on the tables developed at the Wingspread meeting. The tables in this paper were designed with the intent of organizing selected field and laboratory studies based on the degree of certainty by Wingspread participants that the studies (or combination of studies) demonstrated a cause-and-effect relationship. The goal of this paper is to use these tables to help identify useful and perhaps necessary qualities for linking cause and effect.

Because this is one of the first attempts to organize the available data in such a manner, there is likely to be much disagreement over the content and/or format of these tables. The intent here was to begin a discussion on how we might be able to address the question of the effects of contaminants on fish populations. By providing these tables as one possible approach, it is hoped that other more effective approaches will follow.

Methods

The studies included in this paper are divided into 3 tables. Table 13-1 contains studies in which there is a high degree of certainty (by Wingspread participants) that developmental and reproductive changes observed in the field are the result of contaminant exposure. Table 13-2 contains studies in which effects have only been correlated or associated with contaminant exposure, and Table 13-3 includes only a few of the studies and sites where the importance of contaminants in contributing to population declines or changes is unknown (but suspected).

Table 13-1

The categories in Table 13-1 are: location or site of study, effects observed in wild populations of fish (limited to reproductive and developmental endpoints including early life-stage mortality), suspected contaminants, species, related laboratory studies, and degree of confidence that the population size has been adversely affected by suspected contaminants. It should be noted that this last category stresses population size rather than "effects at the population level." Observations such as reduced gonadosomatic index (GSI), altered sex steroid hormone concentrations, or vitellogenesis in male fish can affect fish populations, but to date it is unclear how these changes affect recruitment or population size. In cases where similar cause–effect situations have occurred in many different locations, only 1 set of studies was included as an example. Three criteria required for inclusion in Table 13-1 are 1) observations in the field that were clearly related to the presence of contaminants either in the water, in sediments, or in fish tissues; 2) replication of field observations in the laboratory; and 3) a high degree of confidence, by Wingspread participants, that these studies demonstrate a cause-and-effect relationship. In general, laboratory studies in Table 13-1 were designed primarily to support the field studies. When studies conducted completely under laboratory conditions could not be located, other studies (which include collecting samples of eggs from

Table 13-1 Reproductive and developmental effects in wild populations of fish that are probably caused by contaminants

Site	Observation	Contaminant	Species	Laboratory confirmation	Contaminant-related population decline?	References
Lake Ontario	blue-sac disease, ↑larval mortality	TCDD and related AhR[a] compounds	Lake trout (Salvelinus namaycush)	Lake trout (Salvelinus namaycush)	Probable[b]	Walker and Peterson 1994; Cook et al. 1996; Zabel et al. 1995; Guiney et al. 1996
Puget Sound	↓plasma estradiol ↓larval survival ↓maturation	PAH-contaminated sediment	English sole (Parophrys vetulus)	English sole (Parophrys vetulus)	Possible[c]	Johnson et al. 1988, 1995; Casillas et al. 1991; Stein et al. 1991; Landahl et al. 1997
Prince William Sound AK	↑embryo mortality ↓larval survival	Petroleum hydrocarbons	Pacific herring (Clupea pallasi) Pink salmon (Oncorhynchus gorbuscha)	Pacific herring (Clupea pallasi) Pink salmon (Oncorhynchus gorbuscha)	Possible Possible[d]	Moles et al. 1987; Bue et al. 1996; Sharr et al. 1994; Brown et al. 1996; Hose et al. 1996; Kocan, Hose et al. 1996; Kocan, Marty et al. 1996; Kocan and Hose, Chapter 12
England	↑vitellogenesis in male fish	Sewage effluent	Rainbow trout (Oncorhynchus mykiss) Carp (Cyprinus carpio)	Rainbow trout (Oncorhynchus mykiss) Carp (Cyprinus carpio)	Unknown Unknown	Jobling, Sumpter 1993; Purdom et al. 1994; White et al. 1994; Jobling et al. 1996
Lake Superior Jackfish Bay	↓sex steroids ↓gonad size	BKME[e] phytosterols	White sucker (Catostomus commersoni) Lake whitefish (Coregonus clupeaformis)	Goldfish	Unknown	MacLatchy, Van Der Kraak 1995; van den Heuvel et al. 1995; McMaster et al. 1996
Houston Ship Channel	delayed puberty, impaired recrudescence	PAH	Atlantic croaker (Micropogonias undulatus)	Atlantic croaker (Micropogonias undulatus)	Unknown	Thomas personal communication; Thomas, Budiantara 1995
Eden Water, Scotland	vertebral dysplasia	Trifluralin	Brown trout (Salmo trutta)	Salmon parr (Salmo salar L.)	Unknown	Couch et al. 1979; Wells, Cowan 1982
Eleven Mile Creek FL	masculinization, precocious puberty	KME[f] phytosterols	Mosquitofish (Gambusia affinis) American eel (Anguilla rostrata)	Mosquitofish (Gambusia affinis)	Unknown	Howell et al. 1980; Denton et al. 1985; Caruso, Suttkus 1988; Howell, Denton 1989; Davis, Bortone 1992; Bortone, Davis 1994

a Chemicals that are (AhR) agonists
b Lake trout were considered extinct in Great Lakes. Lake trout are currently stocked, and although fertilized eggs have been produced by stocked fish, there is no recruitment (Cook et al. Chapter 2).
c Incorporation of field data into Leslie Matrix model predicts that effects of contaminants may exacerbate effects of fishing pressure (Landahl and Johnson 1993; Johnson et al 1995; Landahl et al 1997).
d Population size has been affected in these populations, however, role of contaminants is unclear (Biggs and Baker 1993; Funk et al. 1993).
e Bleached kraft mill effluent (BKME)
f Kraft mill effluent (KME)

contaminated sites and then rearing under laboratory conditions) were included. Replication of effects observed in the field under laboratory conditions is critical to understanding cause and effect. Thus, a brief summary of laboratory studies included as examples in Table 13-1 are provided below.

Summary of Table 13-1
In Lake Ontario, blue-sac disease and larval mortality in Lake trout (*Salvelinus namaycush*) have been associated with 2,3,7,8-tetrachlorodibenzo-*p*-dioxin (TCDD) and/or related AhR-active compounds (Guiney et al. 1996; Cook et al. Chapter 2). In the laboratory, embryos were either injected or exposed via the water with TCDD or related AhR-active compounds (reviewed in Walker and Peterson 1994). For TCDD injected into the eggs, concentrations ranged from 0.024 to 0.058 µg/kg of TCDD; for static water exposures concentrations in exposed eggs ranged from <0.015 to 0.400 µg/kg TCDD. Larvae developed blue-sac disease and were prone to early mortality under these conditions. Similar effects were observed in egg injection studies using higher doses of related compounds.

In Puget Sound, observations of reduced plasma estradiol concentrations and impaired ovarian development in English sole (*Parophyrs vetulus*) have been associated with polycyclic aromatic hydrocarbon (PAH) exposure (Johnson et al. 1988; Casillas et al. 1991). Laboratory studies using injections of Duwamish Waterway sediment extracts (DWSE) (containing mixtures of organic pollutants) resulted in reduced plasma estradiol concentrations in adult female and juvenile English sole (Stein et al. 1991).

In Prince William Sound (PWS), increased embryo mortality of pink salmon (*Oncho-rhynchus gorbuscha*) and increased larval mortality in Pacific herring (*Clupea pallasi*) were observed following exposure to petroleum hydrocarbons from the *Exxon Valdez* oil spill (EVOS) (Sharr et al. 1994; Brown et al. 1996; Hose et al. 1996). Strip-spawned pink salmon eggs and herring embryos were collected from field sites with a known history of oil contamination and were incubated in the laboratory. Reduced survival was observed in salmon offspring from females that were likely exposed as embryos to petroleum hydrocarbons (reviewed in Sharr et al. 1994). Larval malformations and cytogenetic effects were increased in herring larvae hatched from eggs collected from oiled sites (Brown et al. 1996). In addition, increased morphological defects and reduced hatching were observed in eggs spawned from adults returning to a previously oiled site 3 years after the spill (Kocan, Marty et al. 1996). Laboratory studies in which herring eggs were exposed to Prudhoe Bay crude oil (ranging from 0.01 mg/L to 9.67 mg/L) reproduced many of the effects observed in the field (i.e., morphological defects, increased chromosomal damage, and reduced growth) (Kocan, Hose et al. 1996; Kocan and Hose, Chapter 12).

Vitellogenin production in male rainbow trout (RBT) (*Onchorhynchus mykiss*) and carp (*Cyprinus carpio*) has been observed at various sites in England, known to be contaminated with sewage effluent (Purdom et al. 1994; Harries et al. 1996). In the laboratory, Jobling et al. (1996) identified several different organic chemicals present in sewage effluent that were capable of displacing the estrogen receptor isolated from RBT livers. In addition, in vitro studies using RBT hepatocyte cultures indicate that several different alkylphenol-polyethoxylate breakdown products (concentrations ranged from 1 to 100 µM for 4 days of exposure) are capable of inducing vitellogenesis (Jobling and Sumpter 1993). Nominal concentrations of 30 µg/L of 4 different alkylphenols found in sewage effluents induced vitellogenin (VTG) production and inhibited testes growth in adult male RBT (Jobling et al. 1996).

In Jackfish Bay, Lake Superior, a reduction of sex steroids and gonad size were observed in white sucker (*Catostomus commersoni*) and lake whitefish (*Coregonus clupeaformis*) exposed to bleached kraft mill effluent (BKME) containing phytohormones (McMaster et al. 1996). In the laboratory, goldfish injected i.p. with either β-sitosterol (a plant sterol) or oxidized β-sitosterol (10 to 100 µg/g) also exhibited reduced plasma concentrations of T and 11-KT (in male fish) and reduced plasma concentrations of E and T (in female fish) (MacLatchy and Van Der Kraak 1995).

In the Houston ship channel, delayed puberty and impaired recrudescence in Atlantic croaker (*Micropogonias undulatus*) have also been associated with PAHs (Peter Thomas, University of Texas, Austin, personal communication). Female Atlantic croaker exposed to 2.5 and 5% water soluble fraction (WSF) of diesel oil for 8 weeks in the laboratory demonstrated disrupted ovarian growth and oocyte development and a failure or delay of sexual maturation (Thomas and Budiantara 1995; Peter Thomas, personal communication).

Several years following a chemical spill containing trifluralin, vertebral dysplasia was observed in brown trout (*Salmo trutta*) from Eden Water, Scotland (Wells and Cowen 1982). In the laboratory, sheepshead minnows (*Cyprinodon variegatus*) and salmon parr (*Salmo salar* L.) exposed to trifluralin also developed vertebral dysplasia. Sheepshead were dosed with 5.5 to 30 µg/L of trifluralin in the water from zygote through 28 days of life (Couch et al. 1979). Salmon parr were exposed to 0.5mg/L of trifluralin for 11 hours and then subsampled over a 12-month period (Wells and Cowan 1982).

In Eleven Mile Creek, Florida, masculinization of mosquitofish (*Gambusia affinis*) (Howell et al. 1980) and precocious puberty in the American eel (*Anguilla rostrata*) (Caruso and Suttkiss 1988) were associated with KME containing phytosterols. Female mosquitofish exposed in the laboratory to a mixture of stigmastanol (a plant sterol) and *Mycobacterium smegmatis* (a bacteria which can degrade plant sterols into steroid hormones) for 30 days developed male-like gonopodia similar to those observed in the field (Davis and Bortone 1992; Bortone and Davis 1994).

Table 13-2

The categories in Table 13-2 are location or site of study; effects observed in wild populations of fish (limited to reproductive and developmental endpoints including early life-stage mortality); suspected contaminants; concentrations associated with observations (or when no attempt was made to calculate "effect level," concentration ranges are provided); species; related laboratory studies; and degree of confidence that population size has been adversely affected by suspected contaminants. The criteria for inclusion in this table are 1) observations in the field that are associated (or correlated) with contaminants in fish tissues and 2) some evidence of

Table 13-2 Selected studies in which reproductive and developmental effects in fish have been associated with contaminant exposure in the field

Site	Observation	Contaminant	Conc range[a] ppm wet wt	Species	Related laboratory studies	References
Palos Verdes CA	↓fecundity ↓maturation ↓induced spawn	DDT	3.8(O)	White croaker (Genyonemus lineatus)		Hose et al. 1989
	↓induced spawn ↓maturational gonadotropin ↓estradiol			Kelp bass (Paralabrax clathratus)	Kelp bass (Paralabrax clathratus)	Cross and Hose 1989; Spies and Thomas, Chapter 9
Baltic Sea	↓viable hatch ↓larval survival	PCB DDE PAH	0.24(O) 0.02(O)	Baltic herring (Clupea harengus)	Lake trout (Salvelinus namaycush), Brook trout (Salvelinus fontinalis), Sheepshead minnows (Cyprinodon variegatus), White perch (Morone americana), Minnows (Phoxinus phoxinus)	Freeman, Idler 1975; Hansen et al. 1975; Bengtsson 1980; Hansen et al. 1985; von Westernhagen 1988; Monosson et al. 1994; Walker, Peterson 1994; Kocan et al. 1987
Baltic Sea	↓embryo survival ↓larval survival	PCB	0.12(O)	Baltic flounder (Platichthys flesus)	Lake trout (Salvelinus namaycush), Brook trout (Salvelinus fontinalis), Sheepshead minnows (Cyprinodon variegatus), White perch (Morone americana), Minnows (Phoxinus phoxinus)	Freeman, Idler 1975; Hansen et al. 1975; Bengtsson 1980; von Westernhagen et al. 1981; von Westernhagen 1988; Monosson et al. 1994; Walker and Peterson 1994
Lake Michigan	↓embryo survival	PCB	0.25–7.76(E) 4.19–13.88(T)	Lake trout (Salvelinus namaycush)	Lake trout (Salvelinus namaycush), Brook trout (Salvelinus fontinalis), Sheepshead minnows (Cyprinodon variegatus), White perch (Morone americana), Minnows (Phoxinus phoxinus)	Freeman, Idler 1975; Hansen et al. 1975; Bengtsson 1980; Mac et al. 1993
Lake Geneva	↑embryo mortality ↓fertility[b]	PCB DDT	0.10–0.31(E) 0.04–0.17(E)	Arctic charr (Salvelinus alpinus L.)	Lake trout (Salvelinus namaycush), Brook trout (Salvelinus fontinalis), Sheepshead minnows (Cyprinodon variegatus), White perch (Morone americana), Minnows (Phoxinus phoxinus)	Freeman and Idler 1975; Hansen et al. 1975; Bengtsson 1980; Monod 1985
Martin Lake TX, Hyco Reservoir NC	↓larval survival ↑ovarian histopathology	selenium	4.8–12.8(H) 4.3(O)	Bluegill sunfish (Lepomis macrochirus) Red-ear sunfish (Lepomis microlophus)	Bluegill sunfish (Lepomis macrochirus)	Baumann and Gillespie 1986; Gillespie and Baumann 1986; Sorensen 1986; Gillespie et al. 1988; Sorensen and Thomas 1988

a Concentrations associated with observation, concentration ranges, or means are provided when no attempt was made to calculate an effect level. O=ovaries, H=liver, E=eggs, T=adult tissues.

b Fertility based on percentage of eggs with embryos (Walker et al. 1996) similar observations from laboratory studies. As with Table 13-1, when studies conducted completely under laboratory conditions could not be located, other studies (which include collecting fish from contaminated sites and then spawning in the laboratory, measuring steroid production, or steroid receptor binding in vitro) were included. In general, laboratory studies designed to specifically answer questions raised by the studies in Table 13-2 (i.e., using same or similar species and environmentally relevant doses, chemical mixtures and/or routes of exposure) either were not conducted or could not be found. The result in almost all cases was a lack of confirmation of effects in a specific species at environmentally relevant concentrations of the suspect contaminants. The studies listed in Table 13-2 are summarized below.

Summary of Table 13-2
In San Pedro Bay, California, reduced fecundity, fertility, and ability to induce spawning in white croaker (*Genyonemus lineatus*) were associated with concentrations of DDT greater than 3.8 ppm in the ovaries (Hose et al. 1989). The ability to induce spawning was also reduced in kelp bass *(Paralabrax clanthratus)* collected from the same site (Cross and Hose 1989). Reduced plasma concentrations of both maturational gonadotropin and estradiol were found in a subsequent study with kelp bass (collected from the same area) by Spies and Thomas (Chapter 9). In vitro studies demonstrated increased testosterone production in ovaries of kelp bass that were more highly contaminated with DDT (Spies and Thomas, Chapter 9). Preliminary in vitro studies also indicated reduced binding affinity of estradiol to the cytosolic estradiol receptor in the liver in fish contaminated with DDT.

Reduced embryo and larval survival, hatching rate, and fertility have been associated with polychlorinated biphenyls (PCBs) alone or in combination with dichlorodiphenyltrichloroethane (DDT), dichlorodiphenyldichloroethylene (DDE), or polycyclic aromatic hydrocarbons (PAHs) in several different locations around the world and in several different species of fish including Baltic herring (*Clupea harengus*) (Hansen et al. 1985), Baltic flounder (*Platichthys flesus*) (von Westernhagen et al. 1981), lake trout (*Salvelinus namaycush*) (Mac et al. 1993), and Arctic charr (*Salvelinus alpinus* L.) (Monod 1985). The concentrations of organochlorines associated with these effects are listed in Table 13-2. Laboratory exposures to PCB mixtures and or individual PCB congeners have resulted in similar effects in several different species of fish. For all of the laboratory studies selected for citation in Table 13-2 (and summarized below), PCB treatment was applied to adults so that eggs and offspring were exposed via transfer from the female. In minnows (*Phoxinus phoxinus*), oral exposure resulted in concentrations of Clophen A50 ranging from approximately 1 to 200 ppm wet weight in the adult fish (whole fish) (Bengtsson 1980). The highest concentrations caused delayed spawning and reduced hatching in the offspring. In sheepshead minnows (*Cyprinodon variegatus*), exposure to Arochlor 1254 via water resulted in concentrations ranging from 0.9 to 170 ppm wet weight in spawned eggs (Hansen et al. 1973). Fry survival was reduced when egg concentrations averaged 5 ppm, while hatching was not affected until egg concentrations reached 170 ppm. In brook trout (*Salvelinus fontinalus*), an Arochlor 1254 concentration of 78 ppm in the eggs (adults were exposed via the water) reduced hatching success (Freeman and Idler 1975). In white perch (*Morone americana*) exposed via intraperitoneal (i.p.) injections, ovarian concentrations of PCB congener 33'44'-tetrachlorobiphenyl (TCB) ranged from approximately 2 to 40 ppm dry weight (Monosson et al. 1994). Increased larval mortality was observed in offspring from females with the highest concentrations of TCB. Petroleum hydrocarbons extracted from Baltic Sea sea-surface microlayer samples exhibited an increased incidence of abnormal larvae and reduced hatching success in both Atlantic cod (*Gadus morhua*) and Baltic herring (*Clupea harengus*) at the highest concentrations tested (between 180 and > 200 μg/L) (Kocan et al. 1987). It is notable that the concentrations of test chemicals found to be effective in some of these studies were often much higher than concentrations measured in the field.

Population declines in many different species of fish have been observed at several different sites where tissue concentrations of selenium were known to be increasing (reviewed in Sorensen 1986). At many of these sites selenium was considered to be the major contaminant. Abnormal larval development leading to reduced larval survival has been observed in offspring from selenium contaminated female bluegill sunfish (*Lepomis macrochirus*) (Gillespie and Baumann 1986) collected from the field. In addition, field studies indicate that accumulation of selenium is greater in the ovaries than in whole body (Baumann and Gillespie 1986; Gillespie and Baumann 1986). Together these studies suggest that larval survival may be affected by maternally transferred selenium. Although a laboratory study failed to show a great degree of toxicity in embryonic or larval RBT (Hodson et al. 1980), this study utilized a waterborne exposure beginning just after fertilization, rather than a maternal exposure. In addition to effects on larvae, selenium has been associated with oocyte atresia, abnormally shaped follicles and a reduction in developing oocytes in red-ear sunfish (*Lepomis microlophus*) collected from a selenium contaminated lake (Sorensen and Thomas 1988).

Table 13-3

Table 13-3 was included in this paper to provide some perspective on what we do not know. This third table contains only a small selection of situations in which contaminants may be important factors in population declines. In many locations where fish populations are either extinct or reduced in size, contaminants are known to be present; however, the research to identify or eliminate the role that contaminants play has not yet been conducted. Further, in all or most of these cases there are many confounding factors such as overfishing and habitat degradation. Understanding the potential interaction between the effects of contaminants and these confounding factors has not yet been addressed.

The categories in Table 13-3 are location or site of study, effects observed in wild populations of fish (limited to reproductive and developmental endpoints including early life-stage mortality), and species. The criteria for inclusion in this table are 1) observations of population declines, or changes observed in a large number of individuals that may adversely affect populations and 2) the presence of contaminants in water, sediments, or fish tissues at a particular site.

Table 13-3 summary

In the Baltic Sea, observations of high mortality in yolk-sac fry of the Baltic salmon (*Salmo salar*) (M74 syndrome) were hypothesized to be associated with organic

Table 13-3 Selected studies reporting effects in wild populations of fish in which some component may involve contaminant exposure

Site	Observation	Species	References
Baltic Sea	M74 (Early mortality syndrome)	Baltic salmon (*Salmo salar*)	Norrgren et al. 1993; Borjeson, Norrgren Chapter 11
Lake Michigan	Swim-up mortality	Lake trout (*Salvelinus namaycush*)	Mac, Edsall 1991; Mac, Schwartz 1992
Lake Huron	Population decline	Lake herring (*Coregonus artedii*), Walleye (*Stizostedium vitreum vitreum*)	Hartman 1988
Lake Michigan	Population decline	Lake herring (*Coregonus artedii*)	Hartman 1988
Lake Michigan	Altered sex ratios	Bloater (*Coregonus hoyi*)	Monosson et al. Chapter 4
Connecticut River	Population decline	Shortnose sturgeon (*Acipenser brevirostrum*)	Kynard 1997; Kocan, Matta, Salazar 1996
Hudson River	Population decline	Striped bass (*Morone saxatilis*)	Rago et al. 1988; Sinderman 1994; Buckley et al. 1985; Westin et al. 1985
Chesapeake Bay	Population decline	Striped bass (*Morone saxatilis*)	Rago et al. 1988; Buckler et al. 1987; Mehrle et al. 1987; Hall et al. 1989
East Coast, US	Low larval survival Reproductive impairment	Winter flounder (*Pleuronectes americanus*)	Nelson et al. 1991; Perry et al. 1991; Black et al. 1988
North Sea	Altered sex ratios	Common dab (*Limanda limanda*)	Lang et al. 1995
Bothnian Bay	Sterility	Burbot (*Lota lota*)	Pulliainen et al. 1991

chemicals including dioxins and related compounds (Norrgren et al. 1993). Subsequent studies have linked M74 with a thiamine deficiency, and treatment of hatchery-reared salmon fry reduces the incidence of M74 (see Report of the Second Workshop on Reproduction Disturbances in Fish, 1995). However, the cause of this deficiency is unclear and may involve exposure to environmental contaminants including organochlorines or the interaction of contaminant exposure with other more "naturally" occurring events.

In Lake Michigan, reduced hatching success in lake trout has been associated with maternally transferred PCBs. However, lake trout survival is also affected by a post swim-up severe mortality syndrome (Mac and Schwartz 1992). The cause of this syndrome is unknown and does not appear to be associated with PCB contamination. In the late 1960s and early 1970s observations of swim-up mortality in salmonids both in Lake Michigan and other sites were attributed to DDT contamination (reviewed in Mac and Edsall 1991); however, concentrations of DDT have since declined to below those associated with swim-up mortality. Thus, the authors suggest that this mortality may involve exposure to compounds with activity similar to DDT.

Population declines observed in the 1940s and 1950s in both lake herring (*Coregonus artedii*) and walleye (*Stizostedium vitreum vitreum*) in Lake Huron are thought to be the result of a decline in water quality, eutrophication, and chemical contamination in Saginaw Bay (reviewed in Hartman 1988). Similarly, it is possible that one component contributing to the decline of Lake Michigan lake herring population was a decline in water quality in Green Bay, an important spawning ground for herring (reviewed in Hartman 1988). In all of these examples it is important to note that these populations were also subject to fishing pressure in addition to changes in predator or competitor populations, and it is unknown how contaminant exposure may interact with these other components.

In the late 1960s, the Lake Michigan bloater (*Coregonus hoyi*) population ratio was skewed towards an almost completely female population (Brown et al. 1987). This coincided with high tissue concentrations of DDT and DDE (Hesselberg et al. 1990). As tissue concentrations of DDT and DDE decreased over the years, there was a trend toward equal numbers of male and female bloaters. In mammalian systems, o,p'-DDT is estrogenic. Recent studies indicate that p,p'-DDE is antiandrogenic in mammals (Kelce et al. 1995; Gray et al. 1996). The effects of developmental exposure to o,p'-DDT and p,p'-DDE in fish are currently unknown. However, if these compounds are active in fish, it is possible that they may affect sexual differentiation or maturation (reviewed in Monosson et al. Chapter 4) resulting in altered population ratios.

Shortnose sturgeon (*Acipenser brevirostrum*) populations have declined at several sites including the Connecticut River. Many of these sites have been impacted by the location of hydroelectric dams in addition to other factors including chemical contamination (reviewed in Kynard 1996). Both of these factors may contribute alone or in combination to observed population declines. In the Connecticut River, it has been hypothesized that either inadequate spawning substrate (as a result of hydroelectric dams), alone or in combination with the presence of coal tar deposits in the vicinity of the spawning substrate, may contribute to the population decline. Laboratory studies demonstrated reduced embryo and larval survival in shortnose sturgeon embryos exposed to coal tar-contaminated sediment (Kocan, Matta, Salazar 1996).

The decline of striped bass (*Morone saxatilis*) populations along the east coast in the late 1970s has been attributed to several factors including overexploitation, degradation of nursery areas, and chemical contaminants (reviewed in Sinderman 1994 and in Rago et al. 1988). There is some evidence that contaminants may have contributed to these declines in both the Hudson River (Buckley et al. 1985; Westin et al. 1985) and contaminants in combination with other environmental factors (e.g., pH, temperature changes, salinity) in the Chesapeake Bay population (Buckler et al. 1987; Mehrle et al. 1987; Hall et al. 1989). However, because of the large commercial and sport interest in striped bass, it is difficult to assess the importance of contaminants in the observed population declines. Population recoveries, have, in large part been attributed to better management of stocks, although it is notable that contaminants in some populations have declined as well (e.g., PCBs in the Hudson River population, [Sloan et al. 1988, 1991]).

Many field studies along the Northeast coast of the United States (U.S.) have associated reduced larval growth and survival in winter flounder (*Pleuronectes americanus*) with poor water quality and contaminant exposure (Nelson et al. 1991; Perry et al. 1991; Black et al. 1988). In the late 1960s and early 1970s high mortality in flounder larvae was attributed to DDT and DDE contamination (reviewed in Sinderman 1994). The more recent observations have been attributed to mixtures of several different contaminants that are often present at highly contaminated field sites including polyaromatic hydrocarbons, organochlorines, and heavy metals. The importance of these observations in combination with other pressures such as habitat degradation and fishing pressure on winter flounder populations is unclear.

Analysis of a long-term data set (from 1981 to 1995) revealed slight (approximately 5%) changes in the sex ratios of the common dab (*Limanda limanda*) in the North Sea (Lang et al. 1995). Proportions of male dab increased in the central and northwestern locations of the North Sea, while the opposite occurred in the southeastern locations. Although these changes were statistically significant, the biological significance is unknown. The authors discuss the possibility that these changes may be linked to chemical exposure (particularly to endocrine disrupting contaminants such as p,p'-DDE and some PCBs), although they note that other factors such as fishing practices may also contribute to altered sex ratios.

Reduced sexual maturation was observed in burbot (*Lota lota*) along the North coast of the Bothnian Bay (Pulliainen et al. 1991). Closest to the Tornio River, a large percent of the population was found to be sterile (from 87 to 98%). Sterile burbot were also collected at other sites along the Northern coast (29 to 55% sterile) (Pulliainen et al. 1991). The authors suggest that compared to previous studies of burbot populations, these numbers are high and may be related to the presence of chemical contamination. They also mention that there are many unknowns, including changes in environmental factors or diseases that may also cause sterility. In addition it is unclear how these factors may interact with exposure to chemical contaminants.

Discussion

Since the 1970s, there has been a great effort to understand the sublethal effects of environmental contaminants on wildlife populations. One goal of this Wingspread meeting was to address the question: "To what extent are environmental contaminants contributing to fish population declines or impeding recovery of depleted stocks?" Addressing this issue required participants to ask several questions, including 1) are there cases which have linked environmental contaminants with altered reproduction or development in fish; 2) why were we more confident that some studies made these linkages and others did not; and 3) did any of these studies link reproductive or developmental effects to effects on population dynamics (decline, recovery, demographics)? The 3 tables presented in this paper were an attempt to organize past and current research in order to answer these questions.

1) Cases that have successfully linked cause and effect. There were only 8 cases for which Wingspread participants felt confident that chemical contaminants could be linked with reproductive and/or developmental effects in wild fish populations (Table 13-1). A recent comprehensive review by Kime (1995) listed over 200 studies in which at least 60 different environmental contaminants were shown to affect reproduction in adults and embryo and larval growth and survival in dozens of species of fish. Either only a fraction of these chemicals are available or active in the field, or we have not been very successful in identifying those that are active in the field. Further examination of the studies reviewed by Kime (1995) suggests the latter; of the approximately 200 studies reviewed, only 10% were field studies. Laboratory studies have contributed greatly to our understanding of how chemicals can affect reproduction and development in fish. Laboratory studies are important for several reasons including the identification of mechanisms of action, the development of biological indicators of contaminant exposure, and screening for potentially hazardous chemicals. However, the critical first step in identifying the effects of chemical contaminants on wild fish populations (or linking cause and effect in the field) depends on observations made in the field.

    The imbalance between the past emphasis on laboratory studies, versus field studies, as discussed by Gilbertson and Schneider (1991) has "left regulatory officials concerned with "potential effects", with few case studies of actual "damage." How do we move from a discussion of "potential effects" to identification of actual cause-and-effect linkages?

2) Confidence in cause-and-effect linkages. There is little question that reproduction and development have been disrupted or disturbed in some wild fish populations as a result of environmental contaminants (Consensus Statement, Chapter 1). In some cases, we are confident of the cause-and-effect relationship (Table 13-1); in other cases, there is only an association or correlation between cause and effect (Table 13-2); and in the majority of cases, there is only some suspicion that contaminants may be involved (Table 13-3). What contributes to our confidence in these linkages? Several qualities considered to be important for "improving our predictive capability" were listed in the Wingspread Consensus Statement (Chapter 1). Some of those qualities are reflected in the studies listed in Table 13-1. The qualities common to Table 13-1 studies include knowledge of current and/or historical reproductive health (or dysfunction), observations of adverse effects on reproduction or embryo and larval development and survival, knowledge of exposure to toxicants or toxicant mixtures, and laboratory replication of

observed effects using environmentally relevant doses, routes of exposure and species.

3) Linkage of reproductive or developmental effects to population dynamics. It is clear from the content of these tables that we have not addressed this problem sufficiently. Because of the logistical difficulties of conducting population assessments in fish, changes in the size or structure of fish populations are often difficult to detect and may not be noticeable until the changes are dramatic. This may be particularly true for fish populations that are not of commercial or sport interest, and so they are not assessed routinely. Thus, one important question is: are there "indicators" or observations that can be made in individual fish (e.g., reduced GSI, altered steroid hormone concentrations, reduced embryo or larval survival or growth) that are predictive of changes in population size or structure? There has been a great emphasis on development of these potential indicators of population-level effects. In fact, many of the laboratory studies were designed for this purpose. However, the relationship between many contaminant-induced endpoints in individuals and population size or recruitment is unclear. Some attempts have been made to quantify the effects of both natural and anthropogenic stresses on fish populations using ecological modeling techniques (Vaughn et al. 1984; Schaaf et al. 1987; Sinderman 1994; Landahl et al. 1997). However, field observations must be quantified in terms of life-history variables such as age-specific fecundity or reproductive output before they can be incorporated into mathematical models.

One example of how field data may be used to estimate population-level effects of environmental contaminants is provided by Landahl et al. (1997). Reproductive endpoints (e.g., fertility, spawnability, and larval development) measured in English sole (*Parophrys vetulus*) from reference and contaminated sites were used in a Leslie matrix model developed to evaluate the effect of pollutant-induced changes in each endpoint on population size. The scientists predicted that given equal fishing pressure, populations in contaminated sites may decline at a faster rate than the population from the reference site as a result of pollutant-induced declines in fecundity, which may in turn decrease population growth rate (assuming there is no density-dependent compensation) (Johnson et al. 1995; Landahl et al. 1997). Population models could be very useful for assessing the effects chemical contaminants have on population size or structure. However, the ability to make linkages between commonly measured endpoints often affected by contaminants such as reduced GSI, altered steroid hormone or VTG concentrations, and the life history variables needed for modeling, (fecundity, reproductive output and/or age-specific survival) are crucial if these observations are to be useful in predicting the effects of environmental contaminants on population size.

The difficulty in linking cause and effect at either the population level (or in some cases at the level of the individual), may in part stem from the lack of current understanding of many important interactions. These include interactions between the effects of specific contaminants and the effects of 1) mixtures of environmental contaminants (at both the physical and biological level); 2) overfishing on populations; 3) habitat loss or change, particularly habitats that include important spawning grounds (Sinderman 1994); and 4) many factors involved in determining survival including predation, food availability, and water temperature. To date these interactions are often noted as being important, but the amount of research designed to further our understanding of these interactions is sparse.

Conclusion

This paper has addressed some of the issues raised by the question "To what extent are environmental contaminants contributing to fish population declines or impeding recovery of depleted stocks." It is clear from the studies included in this paper that few studies have either attempted linking or have been successful in linking chemical contaminants to population-level changes in fish (e.g., population declines or recoveries). However, as demonstrated by the studies contained in Table 13-1, chemical contaminants can be linked to reproductive and developmental effects in individual fish. In general, these studies involved a combination of detailed field and laboratory work. In addition, many of the laboratory studies were designed to test a hypothesis generated by the field studies, often resulting in environmentally relevant laboratory studies. Cause-and-effect linkages can be determined at the individual level; the next step is to understand the effects of reproductive or developmental changes in individuals on whole populations.

Acknowledgments

I am greatly indebted to all the participants of the Wingspread Conference, especially Dr. Rosalind Rolland, and to Dr. Benjamin Letcher (NBS Conte Anadromous Fish Laboratory) and an anonymous reviewer for their comments and careful review of this paper.

References

Baumann PC, Gillespie RB. 1986. Selenium bioaccumulation in gonads of largemouth bass and bluegill from three power plant cooling reservoirs. *Env Toxicol Chem* 5:695–701.

Bengtsson B. 1980. Long-term effects of PCB (Clophen A50) on growth, reproduction and swimming performance in the minnow, *Phoxinus phoxinus*. *Water Res* 14:681–687.

Biggs ED, Baker T. 1993. Summary of known effects of the *Exxon Valdez* oil spill on herring in Prince William Sound, and recommendations for future inquiries. *Exxon Valdez* Oil Spill Symposium Abstracts. Anchorage AK: Oil Spill Public Information Center. p. 264–267.

Black DE, Phelps DK, Lapan RL. 1988. The effect of inherited contamination on egg and larval winter flounder, *Pseudopleuronectes americanus*. *Mar Env Res* 25:45–62.

Bortone SA, Davis WP. 1994. Fish intersexuality as indicator of environmental stress. *Bioscience* 44:165–172.

Brown EH, Argyl RL, Payne NR, Holey ME. 1987. Yield and dynamics of destabilized chub (*Coregonus spp.*) populations in Lakes Michigan and Huron, 1950–1984. *Can J Fish Aquat Sci* 44(Supl 2):371–383.

Brown ED, Baker PT, Hose JE, Kocan RN, Marty GD, McGurk MD, Norcross BC, Short JF. 1996. Injury to the early life history stages of Pacific herring in Prince William Sound after the *Exxon Valdez* oil spill. In: Rice SD, Spies RB, Wolfe DA, Wright BA, editors. *Exxon Valdez* Oil Spill Symposium Proceedings. American Fisheries Society (AFS) Symposium No. 18, Anchorage AK. Bethesda MD: AFS. p 448–462.

Buckler DR, Mehrle PM, Cleveland L, Dwyer FJ. 1987. Influence of pH on the toxicity of aluminum and other inorganic contaminants to East Coast striped bass. *Water, Air, Soil Pollution* 35:97–106.

Buckley LJ, Halavik TA, Laurence GC, Hamilton SJ, Yevich P. 1985. Comparative swimming stamina, biochemical composition, backbone mechanical properties, and histopathology of juvenile striped bass from rivers and hatcheries of the Eastern United States. *Trans Am Fish Soc* 114:114–124.

Bue B, Sharr S, Moffitt SD, Craig AK. 1996. Effects of the *Exxon Valdez* oil spill on pink salmon embryos and preemergent fry. In: Rice SD, Spies RB, Wolfe DA, Wright BA, editors. *Exxon Valdez Oil Spill Symposium Proceedings*. American Fisheries Society (AFS) Symposium No. 18, Anchorage AK. Bethesda MD: AFS. p 618–627.

Caruso JH, Suttkus RD. 1988. Abnormal expression of secondary sex characteristics in a populations of *Anguilla rostata* (Pieces: *anguillidae*) from a dark colored Florida stream. *Copeia* 1988:1077–1079.

Casillas E, Misitano D, Johnson LL, Rhodes LD, Collier TK, Stein JE, McCain BB, Varanasi U. 1991. Inducibility of spawning and reproductive success of female English sole (*Parophrys vetulus*) from urban and nonurban areas of Puget Sound, Washington. *Mar Env Res* 31:99–122.

Couch J, Winstead JT, Hanson DJ, Goodman LR. 1979. Vertebral dysplasia in young fish exposed to the herbicide trifluralin. *J Fish Dis* 2:35–42.

Cross JN, Hose JE. 1989. Reproductive impairment in two species of fish from contaminated areas off southern California. Proceedings, Oceans '89; New York NY. Volume II, Ocean pollution. Washington DC: Marine Technology Society. p 382–384.

Davis WP, Bortone SA. 1992. Effects of kraft mill effluent on the sexuality of fishes: An environmental early warning? In: Colborn T, Clement C, editors. Chemically induced alterations in sexual and functional development: the wildlife/human connection. Princeton NJ: Princeton Scientific. p 113–126.

Denton DE, Howell WM, Allison JJ, McCollum J, Marks B. 1985. Masculinization of female mosquitofish by exposure to plant sterols and *Mycobacterium smegmatis*. *Bull Env Cont Tox* 35:627–632.

Freeman HC, Idler DR. 1975. The effect of polychlorinated biphenyl on steroidogenesis and reproduction in the Brook Trout (*Salvelinus fontinalis*). *Can J Biochem* 53:666–670.

Funk FC, Carlile DW, Baker T. 1993. The Prince William Sound herring recruitment failure of 1989: oil spill or natural causes? *Exxon Valdez* Oil Spill Symposium Abstracts. Anchorage AK: Oil Spill Public Information Center. p. 258–261.

Gilbertson M, Schneider RS. 1991. International Joint Commission workshop on cause-effect linkages: preface. *J Tox Env Health* 33:359–373.

Gillespie RB, Baumann PC. 1986. Effects of high tissue concentrations of selenium on reproduction by bluegills. *Trans Am Fish Soc* 115:208–213.

Gillespie RB, Baumann PC, Singley CT. 1988. Dietary exposure of bluegills (*Lepomis macrochirus*) to (75) Se: uptake and distribution in organs and tissues. *Bull Env Cont Tox* 40:771–778.

Gray LE, Monosson E, Kelce WR. 1996. Emerging issues: the effects of endocrine disrupters on reproductive development. In: DiGiulio RT, Monosson E, editors. Interconnections between human and ecosystem health. London UK: Chapman and Hall. p 46–74.

Guiney PD, Cook PM, Casselman JM, Fitzsimmons JD, Simonin HA, Zabel EW, Peterson RE. 1996. Assessment of 2,3,7,8-tetrachlorodibenzo-p-dioxin-induced sac fry mortality in lake trout (*Salvelinus namaycush*) from different regions of the Great Lakes. *Can J Fish Aquat Sci* 53:2080–2092.

Hall Jr LW, Ziegenfuss MC, Bushong SJ, Unger MA, Herman RL. 1989. Studies of contaminant and water quality effects on striped bass prolarvae and yearlings in the Potomac River and Upper Chesapeake Bay in 1988. *Trans Am Fish Soc* 118:619–629.

Hansen DJ, Schimmel SC, Forester J. 1973. Aroclor 1254 in eggs of sheepshead minnows: Effect on fertilization success and survival of embryos and fry. Proceedings of the 27th Annual Conference of the Southeastern Association of Game and Fish Commissioners; 1973. p 420–423.

Hansen DJ, Schimmel SC, Forester J. 1975. Effects of Aroclor 1016 on embryos, fry, juveniles, and adults of sheepshead minnows (*Cyprinodon variegatus*). *Trans Am Fish Soc* 104:583–588.

Hansen PD, von Westernhagen H, Rosenthal H. 1985. Chlorinated hydrocarbons and hatching success in Baltic herring spring spawners. *Mar Env Res* 15:59–76.

Harries JE, Sheahan DA, Jobling S, Matthiessen P, Neall P, Routledge EJ, Rycroft R, Sumpter JP, Tylor T. 1996. A survey of estrogenic activity in United Kingdom inland waters. *Env Tox Chem* 15:1993–2002.

Hartman WL. 1988. Historical changes in the major fish resources of the Great Lakes. In: Evans MS. Toxic contaminants and ecosystem health: a Great Lakes focus. New York NY: J Wiley. p 103–131.

Hesselberg RJ, Hickey JP, Nortrup DA, Willford WA. 1990. Contaminant residues in the bloater (*Coregonus hoyi*) of Lake Michigan (1969–1986). *J Great Lakes Res* 16:121–129.

Hodson PV, Spry DJ, Blunt BR. 1980. Effects on rainbow trout (*Salmo gairdneri*) of a chronic exposure to waterborne selenium. *Can J Fish Aquat Sci* 37:233–240.

Hose JE, Cross JN, Smith SG, Diehl D. 1989. Reproductive impairment in a fish inhabiting a contaminated coastal environment off southern California. *Mar Poll* 57:139–148.

Hose JE, McGurk MD, Marty GD, Biggs ED, Baker TT. 1996. Sublethal effects of the *Exxon Valdez* oil spill on herring larvae: morphologic, cytogenic, and histopathological assessments, 1989–1991. *Can J Fish Aquat Sci* 53:2355–2365.

Howell WM, Denton TE. 1989. Gonopodial morphogenesis in female mosquitofish, *Gumbusia affinis affinis*, masculinized by exposure to degradation products form plant sterols. *Env Biol Fish* 24:43–51.

Howell WM, Black DA, Bortone SA. 1980. Abnormal expression of secondary sex characters in a population of mosquitofish: evidence for environmentally induced masculinization. *Copeia* 1980:676–681.

Jobling S, Sumpter JP. 1993. Detergent components in sewage effluent are weakly oestrogenic to fish: An in vitro study using rainbow trout (*Onchorhynchus mykiss*) hepatocytes. *Aquat Tox* 27:361–372.

Jobling S, Sheahan D, Osborne JA, Matthiessen P, Sumpter JP. 1996. Inhibition of testicular growth in rainbow trout (*Onchorhynchus mykiss*) exposed to estrogenic alkylphenolic chemicals. *Env Tox Chem* 15:194–202.

Johnson LL, Casillas E, Collier TK, McCain BB, Varanasi U. 1988. Contaminant effects on ovarian development in English sole (*Parophrys vetulus*) from Puget Sound, Washington. *Can J Fish Aquat Sci* 45:2133–2146.

Johnson LL, Landahl JT, Kardong K, Horness BH. 1995. Chemical contaminants, fishing pressure, and population growth of Puget Sound English sole (*Pleuronectes vetulus*). Puget Sound Research '95 Proceedings. Olympia WA: Puget Sound Water Quality Authority, PO Box 40900, Olympia WA. p 686–689.

Kelce WR, Stone CR, Laws SC, Gray LE, Kemppainen JA, Wilson EM. 1995. Persistent DDT metabolite p,p'-DDE is a potent androgen receptor antagonist. *Nature* 375:581–585.

Kime, D.E. 1995. Effects of pollution on fish reproduction. *Reviews in fish biology and fisheries* 5:52–96.

Kocan RM, Von Westernhagen H, Landolt ML, Furstenberg G. 1987. Toxicity of sea-surface microlayer: effects of hexane extract on Baltic herring (*Clupea harengus*) and Atlantic cod (*Gadus morhua*) embryos. *Mar Env Res* 23:291–305.

Kocan RM, Hose JE, Brown ED, Baker TT. 1996. Pacific herring (*Clupea pallasi*) embryo sensitivity to Prudhoe Bay petroleum hydrocarbons: laboratory evaluation and in situ exposure at oiled and unoiled sites in Prince William Sound. *Can J Fish Aquat Sci* 53:2366–2375.

Kocan RM, Marty GD, Okihiro MS, Brown ED, Baker TT. 1996. Reproductive success and histopathology of individual Prince William Sound herring three years after the *Exxon Valdez* oil spill. *Can J Fish Aquat Sci* 53:2388–2393.

Kocan RM, Matta M, Salazar SM. 1996. Toxicity of weathered coal tar for shortnose sturgeon (*Acipenser brevirostrum*) embryos and larvae. *Archives of Environmental Contamination and Toxicology* 31:161–165.

Kynard B. 1997. Life history, latitudinal patterns, and status of shortnose sturgeon, *Acipenser brevirostrum*. *Env Biol Fish*. In press.

Landahl J, Johnson L. 1993. Contaminant exposure and population growth of English sole in Puget Sound: The need for better early life-history data. *Am Fish Soc Symposium* 14:117–123.

Landahl JT, Johnson LL, Collier TK, Stein JE, Varanasi U. 1997. Marine pollution and fish population parameters: English sole (*Pleuronectes vetulus*) in Puget Sound, WA. *Trans Am Fish Soc*. In press.

Lang T, Damm U, Dethlefsen V. 1995. Changes in the sex ratio of north sea dab (*Limanda limanda*) in the period 1981–1995. Endocrinically active chemicals in the environment. Fraunhofer-Institit fur umweltchemie und okotoxikologie Abt. Biochemische okotoxikologie; 1995 Mar; Berlin. p 95–100.

Mac MJ, Edsall CC. 1991. Environmental contaminants and the reproductive success of lake trout in the Great Lakes: An epidemiological approach. *J Tox Env Health* 33:375–394.

Mac MJ, Schwartz TR. 1992. Investigations into the effects of PCB congeners on reproduction in Lake Trout from the Great Lakes. *Chemosphere* 25:189–192.

Mac MJ, Schwartz TR, Edsall CC, Frank AM. 1993. Polychlorinated biphenyls in Great Lakes Lake Trout and their eggs: Relations to survival and congener composition 1979–1988. *J Great Lakes Res* 19:752–765.

MacLatchy DL, Van Der Kraak GJ. 1995. The phytoestrogen β-sitostoerol alters the reproductive endocrine status of goldfish. *Tox Appl Pharm* 134:305–312.

McMaster ME, Van Der Kraak GJ, Munkittrick KR. 1996. An epidemiological evaluation of the biochemical basis for steroid hormonal depressions in fish exposed to industrial wastes. *J Great Lakes Res* 22(2):153–171.

Mehrle PM, Cleveland L, Buckler DR. 1987. Chronic toxicity of an environmental contaminant mixture to young (or larval) striped bass. *Water, Air, Soil Pollution* 35:107–118.

Moles A, Babcock MM, Rice SD. 1987. Effects of oil exposure on pink salmon, *O. gorbuscha*, alevins in a simulated Intertidal environment. *Mar Env Res* 21:49–58.

Monod G. 1985. Egg mortality of Lake Geneva Charr (*Salvelinus alpinus* L.) contaminated by PCB and DDT derivatives. *Bull Env Cont Tox* 35:531–536.

Monosson E, Fleming WJ, Sullivan CV. 1994. Effects of the planar PCB 3,3',4,4'-tetrachlorobiphenyl (TCB) on ovarian development, plasma levels of sex steroid hormones and vitellogenin, and progeny survival in the white perch (*Morone americana*). *Aquat Tox* 29:1–19.

Nelson DA, Miller JE, Rusanowsky D, Greig RA, Sennefelder GR, Mercaldo-Allen R, Gould E, Thurburg FP, Calabrese A. 1991. Comparative reproductive success of winter flounder in Long Island Sound: a 3-year study (biology, biochemistry, chemistry). *Estuaries* 14:318–331.

Norrgren L, Andersson T, Bergqvist PA, Bjorklund I. 1993. Chemical, physiological and morphological studies of feral Baltic salmon (*Salmo salar*) suffering from abnormal fry mortality. *Env Tox Chem* 12:2065–2075.

Perry DM, Hughes JB, Hebert AT. 1991. Sublethal abnormalities in embryos of winter flounder from Long Island Sound. *Estuaries* 14:2–15.

Pulliainen E, Korhonen K, Kankaaranta L, Maki K. 1991. Non-spawning burbot on the northern coast of the Bothinian Bay. *Ambio* 21:170–175.

Purdom CE, Hardiman PA, Bye VJ, Eno NC, Tyler CR, Sumpter JP. 1994. Estrogenic effects of effluents from sewage treatment works. *Chem Ecol* 8:275–285.

Rago PJ, Richards RA, Deuel DG. 1988. Emergency striped bass research study, report to Congress 1988. U.S. Fish and Wildlife Service and National Marine Fisheries Service. p 1–55.

Report of the second workshop on reproduction disturbances in fish - Abstracts. 1995. Swedish Environmental Protection Agency; 1995 Nov 20–23; Stockholm, Sweden. Swedish Environmental Protection Agency Report 4534.

Rosenthal H, Alderice DF. 1976. Sublethal effects of environmental stressors, natural and pollutional, on marine fish eggs and larvae. *J Fish Res Board Can* 33:2047–2065.

Schaaf WE, Peters DS, Vaughan DS, Coston-Clements L, Krouse CW. 1987. Fish population responses to chronic and acute pollution: the influence of life history strategies. *Estuaries* 3:267–275.

Sharr S, Seeb JE, Bue BG, Craig A, Miller GD. 1994. Injury to salmon eggs and preemergent fry in Prince William Sound - restoration study number 93003. Anchorage AK: Alaska Department of Fish and Game, Division of Commercial Fisheries Management and Development, 333 Raspberry Road, Anchorage AK. p 1–28.

Sinderman CJ. 1994. Quantitative effects of pollution on marine and anadromous fish populations. Woods Hole MA: Northeast Fisheries Science Center, National Oceanic and Atmospheric Administration (NOAA). NOAA Technical Memorandum NMFS-F/NEC-104. p 1–22.

Sloan R, Young B, Vecchio V, McKown K, O'Connell E. 1988. PCB concentrations in the striped bass from the marine district of New York State. Albany NY: New York State Department of Environmental Conservation. Technical Report 88-1 (BEP). p 1–79.

Sloan R, Young B, McKown K, Veccio V. 1991. PCB in striped bass from New York marine waters. Albany NY: New York State Department of Environmental Conservation. Technical Report 91-1 (BEP). p 1–61.

Sorensen EB. 1986. The effects of selenium on freshwater teleosts. In: Hodgson E, editor. Reviews in environmental toxicology. Amsterdam: Elsevier Science. p 59–116.

Sorensen E, Thomas P. 1988. Selenium accumulation, reproductive status, and histopathological changes in environmentally exposed redear sunfish. *Arch Tox* 61:324–329.

Stein JE, Hom T, Sanborn HR, Varanasi U. 1991. Effects of exposure to a contaminated-sediment extract on the metabolism and disposition of 17β-estradiol in English sole (*Parophyrs vetulus*). *Comp Biochem Phys* 99C:231–240.

Thomas P, Budiantara L. 1995. Reproductive life history stages sensitive to oil and naphthalene in Atlantic croaker. *Mar Env Res* 39:147–150.

Van den Heuvel MR, Munkittrick KR, Van Der Kraak GJ, Servos MR, Dixon DG. 1995. Hepatic 7-ethoxyresorufin-o-deethylase activity, plasma steroid hormone concentrations, and liver bioassay-derived 2,3,7,8-TCDD toxic equivalent concentrations in wild white sucker (*Catostomus commersoni*) caged in bleached kraft pulp mill effluent. *Can J Fish Aquat Sci* 52:1339–1350.

Vaughn SD, Yoshiyama RM, Breck JE, DeAngelis DL. 1984. Modeling approaches for assessing the effects of stress on fish populations. In: Cairns VW, Hodson PV, Nriagu JO, editors. Contaminant effects on fisheries. New York NY: J Wiley. p 260–277.

von Westernhagen H, Rosenthal H, Dethlefsen V, Ernst W, Harms U, Hansen PD. 1981. Bioaccumulating substances and reproductive success in Baltic flounder, *Platichthys flesus. Aquat Tox* 1:85–99.

von Westernhagen W. 1988. Sublethal effects of pollutants on fish eggs and larvae. In: Hoar WS, Randall DJ, editors. Fish physiology. New York NY: Academic Pr. p 253–346.

Walker MK, Peterson RE. 1994. Aquatic toxicity of dioxins and related chemicals. In: Schecter A. Dioxins and health. New York NY: Plenum Pr. p 347–387.

Walker MK, Cook PM, Butterworth BC, Zabel EW, Peterson RE. 1996. Potency of a complex mixture of polychlorinated dibenzo-p-dioxin, dibenzofuran, and biphenyl congeners compared to 2,3,7,8-tetrachlorodibenzo-p-dioxin for causing fish early life stage mortality. *Fund Appl Tox* 30:178–186.

Wells DE, Cowan AA. 1982. Vertebral dysplasia in salmonids caused by the herbicide trifluralin. *Environ Pollut* 29:249–260.

Westin DT, Olney CE, Rogers BA. 1985. Effects of parental and dietary organochlorines on survival and body burdens of striped bass larvae. *Trans Am Fish Soc* 114:125–136.

White R, Jobling S, Hoare SA, Sumpter JP, Parker MG. 1994. Environmentally persistent alkylphenolic compounds are estrogenic. *Endocrinol* 135:171–181.

Zabel EW, Walker MK, Hornung MW, Clayton MK, Peterson RE. 1995. Interactions of polychlorinated dibenzo-p-dioxins, dibenzofuran, and biphenyl congeners for producing rainbow trout early life stage mortality. *Tox Appl Pharm* 134:204–213.

SETAC

A Professional Society for Environmental Scientists and Engineers and Related Disciplines Concerned with Environmental Quality

The Society of Environmental Toxicology and Chemistry (SETAC), with offices in North America and Europe, is a nonprofit, professional society that provides a forum for individuals and institutions engaged in the study of environmental problems, management and regulation of natural resources, education, research and development, and manufacturing and distribution.

Goals

- Promote research, education, and training in the environmental sciences
- Promote systematic application of all relevant scientific disciplines to the evaluation of chemical hazards
- Participate in scientific interpretation of issues concerned with hazard assessment and risk analysis
- Support development of ecologically acceptable practices and principles
- Provide a forum for communication among professionals in government, business, academia, and other segments of society involved in the use, protection, and management of our environment

Activities

- Annual meetings with study and workshop sessions, platform and poster papers, and achievement and merit awards
- Monthly scientific journal, *Environmental Toxicology and Chemistry*, SETAC newsletter, and special technical publications
- Funds for education and training through the SETAC Scholarship/Fellowship Program
- Chapter forums for the presentation of scientific data and for the interchange and study of information about local concerns
- Advice and counsel to technical and nontechnical persons through a number of standing and *ad hoc* committees

Membership

SETAC's growing membership includes more than 5,000 individuals from government, academia, business, and public-interest groups with technical backgrounds in chemistry, toxicology, biology, ecology, atmospheric sciences, health sciences, earth sciences, and engineering.

If you have training in these or related disciplines and are engaged in the study, use, or management of environmental resources, SETAC can fulfill your professional affiliation needs. Membership categories include Associate, Student, Senior Active, and Emeritus.

For more information, contact SETAC, 1010 North 12th Avenue, Pensacola, Florida, USA 32501-3370; T 850 469 1500; F 850 469 9778; E setac@setac.org; http://www.setac.org.